DATE DUE

SEP 1 5 2011	

DEMCO, INC. 38-2931

MY BROTHER, MY ENEMY

PHILIP SMUCKER

MY BROTHER, MY ENEMY

America and the
Battle of Ideas across
the Islamic World

Prometheus Books

59 John Glenn Drive
Amherst, New York 14228–2119

Published 2010 by Prometheus Books

Inquiries should be addressed to
Prometheus Books
59 John Glenn Drive
Amherst, New York 14228–2119
VOICE: 716–691–0133
FAX: 716–691–0137
WWW.PROMETHEUSBOOKS.COM

14 13 12 11 10   5 4 3 2 1

Library of Congress Cataloging-in-Publication Data

Smucker, Philip.
    My brother, my enemy : America and the battle of ideas across the Islamic world /
by Philip Smucker.
        p. cm.
    Includes bibliographical references and index.
    ISBN 978–1–61614–184–4 (cloth. : alk. paper)
    1. Islamic countries—Relations—United States. 2. United States—Relations—
Islamic countries. 3. United States—Foreign public opinion, Muslim.
4. Anti-Americanism—Islamic countries. 5. Smucker, Philip—Travel—Middle East.
I. Title.

DS35 .74.U6S64 2010
303.48'27301767—dc22

                                                                          2010013080

Printed in the United States of America on acid-free paper

For my Virginia forefathers
who articulated the rights of men
and abhorred the scourge of war

"The most certain way to make a man your enemy
is to tell him you esteem him such."

—George Washington

CONTENTS

FOREWORD

It was August, 2006, in Baghdad, and waiting for a Blackhawk "taxi" from the military airport was a man whose business card described him as a "strategic message adviser" to the Coalition. "Casey won't get out in front and sell this war," he told me. "He doesn't want to go down in history as another as Westmoreland." He was accusing General George Casey, the head of the multinational forces in Iraq, of losing the American people, just as the ill-fated commander in Vietnam, William Westmoreland, had "lost" the war at home.

It had certainly been a dreadful summer in Iraq. Three thousand bodies a month were being dumped on the streets of the capital. Many had been shot in the back of the head and bore signs of torture, such as holes drilled through kneecaps. The city seemed to be in the grip of madness. A 155 mm shell was buried under a football pitch and wired to explode as children were playing. (It did, killing twelve.) A car bomb, a rocket attack, and a suicide bombing all took place on a single morning, all visible from the roof of the BBC bureau, such was the concentration of violence.

But it was the Iraqi people, not Americans, who needed selling on the war. That was why the occupation's marketing man—or strategic message adviser—was forced to wait for a helicopter, sweating in a flak jacket over his blue blazer and buttoned-down shirt despite the unbearable heat and humidity of an Iraqi summer. The city was just too dangerous, too hostile, for him to make the short drive from the airport to the Green Zone. How had things gone so badly wrong? US forces had, after all, removed one of the twenty-first century's most brutal dictatorships. American troops, even allowing for the need to say the right thing in front of a reporter, were almost uniformly idealistic about the mission. They had good intentions and were puzzled, even hurt, by the idea that Iraqis were trying to kill them at every turn.

You can count on the fingers of one hand the number of Western journalists with firsthand experience of the Sunni insurgency in Iraq—and Philip Smucker is one of them. He stayed with a family whose sons were active in the "resistance" and got to know some senior jihadists (at some risk since he was posing, rather improbably, as a Bosnian Muslim). Smucker charts Iraq's unraveling from its earliest days in *My Brother, My Enemy*. The cause was not the "thousands of tactical errors" Condoleezza Rice attributed to the US forces, although there were many errors. This was a tragedy whose author was in the Oval Office, a president who famously did not "do nuance," who didn't know the difference between Shias and Sunnis (perhaps apocryphally, perhaps not).

Above all, the Iraq war was fought because President Bush was in the grip of an abstract idea about imposing democracy on the Middle East. He had not thought much about how the Iraqis themselves would react. They were always going to see a foreign, "Christian" army as occupiers. On the day the Americans triumphantly rolled into Baghdad, and Saddam's statue came down amid a welter of shoes, I spoke to one man, a Sunni, and another, a Shia, on the streets of the capital. They both said, in very similar terms, that they were grateful to the Americans for removing Saddam, but if the US forces stayed too long, blood would flow.

The Bush administration was deaf to this. The result was that American forces made the crucial error of failing to understand their enemy, whether the enemy was the Iraqi "resistance" or al Qaeda internationally. Smucker argues that Iraq was the trap al Qaeda hoped the West would walk into. Osama bin Laden planned the 9/11 attacks "to lure the tiger from its lair." It worked. Or as Henry Kissinger put it, "Afghanistan wasn't enough. And we need to humiliate them." So President Bush went abroad "in search of monsters to destroy," a pursuit his predecessor John Quincy Adams had warned against.[1] Iraq followed. Smucker calls it a "meaningless war": one that was not fought for reasons of self-defense and that actually increased the threat to Americans at home and overseas. Iraq, Smucker writes, persuaded Muslims that "the United States is a superpower without morality." It "created the impression that the United States is at war with Islam."

President Obama has broken with that past, at least rhetorically. Gone is the idea that democracy can be imposed on the region at the point of a gun. To redefine America's relationship with the Muslim world, President Obama went to Cairo to speak of "mutual interest and mutual respect … based upon the truth that America and Islam are not exclusive, and need not be in competition."[2] Obama does nuance. He is a realist, taking the world as he finds it. This means lowering his sights and defining victory less ambitiously, as in Afghanistan, which Obama has made "his war" and which may yet come to overshadow his presidency. In Afghanistan, Obama has been left with few good or easy choices, as elsewhere around the globe.

The latest focus of what the United States no longer calls "the global war on terror" is Yemen. The Salafi fighters that Smucker got to know in Iraq spoke the same language of international jihad that he had heard earlier in the northern reaches of Yemen at the Dar al-Hadith madrassa. Very few Western journalists have made it to this part of Yemen, as it is at the center of a civil war and the government bans travel there. Students and teachers from Somalia, Britain, and the United States were at Dar al-Hadith. The Yemeni government now restricts visas precisely because of fears that Americans and others are traveling to Yemen for training and indoctrination before returning to their home countries to carry out terrorist acts.

In the Yemeni capital, Sana'a, you can find one of Osama bin Laden's former bodyguards, Nasser al-Bahri. Now a businessman with a pricey leather jacket and fashionable gold watch, he is hoping to cash in on his al Qaeda past with a book deal. Osama bin Laden was "a true humanitarian, tender-hearted, with a good sense of humour," al-Bahri reminisced in a departure from the usual view of the al Qaeda founder.[3] In contrast to Washington's growing fears, al Qaeda members in Yemen are not seen by the government there as either numerous or terribly threatening. But there are tens of thousands of Yemeni tribesmen whose jihadist ideology is not so very far from al Qaeda's. Again, Obama's choices are limited. "US intervention would make the whole people one with al Qaeda," warned al-Bahri.[4] He was repeating only what was the conventional wisdom in Yemen, voiced by everyone from tribal sheikhs to government ministers.

Obama gets this, though. Fearful of multiplying support for al Qaeda in Yemen many times over, the president has not decided to send troops. With the neocons out of power in Washington, al Qaeda is also facing troubles of its own. Its leaders have lost their opposing ideologues in this unfortunate clash of civilizations. (The term "clash of civilizations" was popularized by the Harvard political scientist Samuel Huntington, who argued that cultural and religious conflict would replace the Cold War. It was a theory that fitted the worldview of both the neocon outriders of the Bush White House and the jihadists.)

So it seems that Obama is not going to give al Qaeda the war it seeks in Yemen. That means relying on the Yemenis and on a government that has been accused of doing deals with al Qaeda in the past. President Ali Abdullah Saleh is said to have tolerated al Qaeda in Yemen as long as it exported its violence and was not active in his backyard. President Saleh is also believed to have used Sunni al

Qaeda fighters against the Shia rebels in the north, who were always seen by his government as its main threat. Subsequently, a new generation of al Qaeda leaders in Yemen announced that they will target Yemeni politicians, too. President Saleh, in the interest of self-preservation, has come around to the idea of doing what Washington requires of him.

As elsewhere in the Islamic realm, a proxy war has its drawbacks. The Yemeni government will take Washington's money and probably do some unpalatable things with it: bomb villages, arrest opponents, and skim off a generous amount that will go into officials' pockets. Short of invading Yemen, the United States has little choice but to acquiesce in this. Yemen is a lesson in the limits of Western power (although a lesson learned early and therefore less expensively than Iraq or Afghanistan). This is the pattern across the Middle East, where our allies are not the ones we'd want, just the ones we have. The Obama administration has accepted that. In any case, as Smucker writes from raw experience: "Americans are not good neocolonial rulers capable of bestowing democracy on the masses." He argues that American ideals and blood do not always have to be sacrificed on the battlefield in order to win this long war of attrition.

But is Obama's pragmatism the old policy of supporting dictators and oppressive regimes in the Arab world? It often looks to be. The Bush administration, it is true, was not doing much for democracy during the last years of its life. That means there is more continuity in the substance of US policy than might be supposed. Under President Obama, however, rhetoric has been brought back in line with action. America no longer looks so hypocritical for cozying up to the military dictatorships, feudal monarchies, and authoritarian regimes of the Middle East. That may be realistic, but it isn't much to celebrate. Western-leaning Arab intellectuals—our friends—still feel abandoned and betrayed. Smucker argues that many Muslims around the world do understand and fervently wish for democracy—often despite the self-interest of their autocratic rulers. The trick is to support this without getting embroiled in unwinnable wars. The effort is necessary from a self-interested, albeit pragmatic American point of view. The Bush administration was not wrong to think that terrorism is partly a response to US support for authoritarian regimes. To al Qaeda, these regimes are the "near enemy" and the United States, for maintaining them, is the "far enemy."

Still, there is another dynamic at work that is often overlooked. Unpopular governments, from Rabat to Riyadh, use the Israeli-Palestinian conflict as a means of deflecting anger that might threaten them. These regimes' backing of the Palestinian cause may be a matter of tactics, but Smucker believes that al Qaeda's is not, contrary to much of what is written. Al Qaeda's belief in Palestine is part of its core ideology, he says. One of bin Laden's spiritual mentors was Abdul Azzam, who wrote an influential fatwa that declared: "Every Muslim on Earth should unsheathe his sword to liberate Palestine." This is a cry that resonates because Jerusalem is valued at least as much by Muslims as it is by Jews.

My Brother, My Enemy points out that the Palestinian issue has "infected all others" because "the Israeli occupation is seen as an American one," sustained by US dollars, weapons, and diplomatic support. To Arab audiences, images of Israeli tanks in Gaza merge with those of American tanks in Iraq and Afghanistan. So President Obama quickly made Middle East peace one of the objectives of his presidency, declaring that "the situation for the Palestinian people is intolerable. America will not turn our backs on the legitimate Palestinian aspiration for dignity, opportunity, and a state of their own."[5] But the stratospheric hopes inspired by such rhetoric have already been dashed against the walls that surround Jerusalem's old city. Obama picked a fight with the Israeli government on settlements only to be forced into what appears at the time of writing to be a humiliating retreat.

Authors like Michael Scheuer, the former head of the CIA's bin Laden desk, question the value of the US-Israeli alliance. Israel has no oil but antagonizes the countries that do and that the West needs. Israel is America's closest ally in the region, but the United States would not have so many enemies in the Middle East if it did not support the Jewish state. Should the United States abandon Israel? Smucker strongly disagrees with the Israel bashers but wants more pressure for the two-state solution (Israel and an independent Palestine). Such pressure has never really been applied in a serious fashion, neither by Europe, which is a market for most of what Israel sells, nor the United States, which underwrites Israel's security.

Even if Israel were forced by concerted international pressure to leave the West Bank, what chance would there be of an eventual Middle East peace, given the absolutist aims of the Palestinian militant groups? *My Brother, My Enemy* quotes my interview with an eighteen-year-old woman in Gaza who had volunteered to be a suicide bomber. Umm Anas (her nom de guerre) was a member of Islamic Jihad and a graduate of its martyrdom summer school, which had turned out a number of similarly committed young women. The suicide belt, actually a sturdy pair of wool knickers with pouches for explosives, lay on the table between us as she spoke. "This is a gift from God," she said, full of calm but implacable hatred as she talked about the opportunity to kill herself and as many Israelis as possible. "We were created to become martyrs."

It would have been easy to see her merely as a cipher, manipulated by the Islamic Jihad minders who fussed around arranging a pair of Kalashnikovs in a picturesque manner for our camera. But she seemed far more intelligent and articulate than these older men who were prepared to send her to her death. It would have been easy, too, to dwell on her religious fanaticism, her absolute belief in the afterlife and her coming reward in it, all so foreign to the secular, Western mind. But on the way out, our Gaza producer, a Palestinian resident of the territory, cautioned me not to forget her own central explanation of her motives: the occupation. "I will fight for my land. I am sure of this," she had said. Umm Anas's definition of occupied land included, however, not only the West Bank but Haifa, Ashdod, and Tel Aviv. That is a point of view that would make any peace agreement with Israel impossible, as it is a call for Israel's destruction.

Would-be martyrs, in any case, are not leading the Palestinians. In Damascus, Smucker secured a rare interview with Khalid Meshal, political leader of the main militant group, Hamas. Although the group's founding charter commits itself to the destruction of Israel, Meshal told him that Meshal's organization is ready to accept a Palestinian state based on the 1967 borders with Israel. (At least, that is what he said.) Similarly, even such an architect of the settlement project as Ariel Sharon came to believe that one day Israel had to vacate the West Bank, which was captured by Israel in the 1967 war. After more than four decades of occupation, Israel would face a growing international campaign to grant full political rights to the Palestinians, he feared. If Israel made its occupation permanent, it would have to choose between being a democracy and being a Jewish state. Giving Palestinians voting rights would mean, in a generation, an Arab majority in the West Bank and Israel. "We Jews have bad memories of being a minority in someone else's state," Sharon's successor, Ehud Olmert, told me when he was prime minister, carrying on Sharon's policies.

The outlines of a peace settlement are plain. The problem has always been how to get there. After months of trying, President Obama has achieved little and there seems to be no prospect of a breakthrough. Nevertheless, this is the prize his administration is still pursuing. Smucker believes it is an urgent necessity. He says: "A two-state peace deal for Israel and Palestine remains the one straw that can break al Qaeda's proverbial camel's back. It would help to foster peace not just in the Middle East but across the Islamic realm, whose inhabitants represent about 20 percent of the world's population."

If this small miracle happened, al Qaeda would still remain a threat. The Nigerian "underpants" bomber's attempt to bring down Flight 253 on Christmas Day was a plot supposedly organized by al Qaeda in Yemen. Al Qaeda promised to place even more bombs on planes. "While you support your leaders in killing our women and children, understand that we have come to you with slaughter, and prepared men who love death as much as you love life," the al

Qaeda statement said. "You will be killed as you kill, and tomorrow is not far away."

President Obama has decided not to overreact to this by invading any new countries, but his response to al Qaeda is still heavily weighted toward military action. Tens of thousands of new US troops have been sent to Afghanistan. It is perhaps surprising that Obama's administration now boasts that it is actually killing more al Qaeda suspects than President Bush's did in his last year of office. "When it comes to counterterrorism, this administration has taken out more al Qaeda high-level operatives, has been more aggressive in pinning them down…than a lot of what's taken place previously," Obama told *Time* magazine, in a line crafted to bolster his martial credentials.

If al Qaeda is evicted from Pakistan's Waziristan, or Afghanistan or Yemen, it will find sanctuary elsewhere. Yet the larger question remains, as Smucker writes, "Will this lethal virus find endless sustenance?" There is no shortage of failed or failing states around the world. Smucker says that Sahelian Africa could be—if we mishandle it—the "next terrorist safe haven." So al Qaeda "terrorism" will probably be with us for decades. Obama has understood that the way to beat terrorism is not just to kill more terrorists, but to stop more from being created. "We must recognize," he says, "that America's strength comes not just from the might of our arms or the scale of our wealth but from our enduring values."[6] The slow and subtle application of US power will not be so wasteful of lives. But it also promises no final moment of "victory" and carries with it many compromises with unpleasant and sometimes brutal regimes. US policy still seems trapped between bellicose simplicity (Bush) and moral ambivalence (Obama). *My Brother, My Enemy* is Philip Smucker's response to that dilemma.

Paul Wood, BBC Middle East correspondent

Sana'a/Jerusalem
January 2010

Chapter 1
MARK OF THE BEAST

One of the more amusing "debates" I've seen on the subject of terrorism was an exchange between Fox News host Sean Hannity and documentarian Michael Moore. It went like this:

MOORE: You're afraid of a few hundred guys on monkey bars?
HANNITY: No, millions.
MOORE: Millions?
HANNITY: Millions that buy into Islamic fanaticism.
MOORE: Millions who are going to attack us?
HANNITY: I believe there's millions of people that believe there's virgins in heaven if they commit a suicide bombing.[1]

Recent polling data have shown that nearly half of all Americans believe that Muslims are prone to violence. Many openly doubt the loyalty of Muslim Americans.[2] This is a worrisome trend in a country that was founded on an ideal of religious tolerance. Maybe it should not surprise us, however, that our citizens remain a bit terrified of the "other." Many terrorism "experts" and television commentators make a living by arguing that fears of Islam are real, and they need to be faced up to and dealt with by sound and logical security measures. If you believe, like Hannity, that there are millions of Islamic terrorists anxious to take their place in heaven by attacking us, you are probably the exception, not the rule.

Nevertheless, as the old expression from the 1960s goes, "Just because you are paranoid doesn't mean someone is not out to get you!" International terrorist organizations are, indeed, out to get us. They have more than jungle gyms to train on. Yet it has been a gross error for the US government to focus on "Islamic terrorism" as an existential threat to the US homeland at the expense of a sound foreign policy that can engage and pacify the Islamic world.

Walid Phares is a respected scholar of Islam, and he is of Lebanese-Christian descent; he writes extensively about what he says are the goals of international jihadism. He points out that on one side of the equation there are the Samuel Huntingtons, who warn the world about a coming "clash of civilizations,"[3] and on the other side there are the jihadists, who not only "believe in the clash of civilizations, but are consciously practicing it."[4] He argues that the enemy we face is represented by jihadism, "an ideology trying to destroy the current order and replace it with another world order altogether."[5]

It is true that there are some elements within modern Islam, including persons within al Qaeda's leadership, that see the struggle in Palestine as the same as the fight in Chechnya, Iraq, Afghanistan, and Somalia. In the broader view, they see these fights as part of a "defensive" jihad against Western aggression. But intellectuals and ideologues who stir up fears that these same fringe extremists are about to seize control of 1.2 billion Muslims and turn them—en masse—against us by sending legions of suicide bombers toward America by land, sea, and air are simply wrong.

In the successful documentary film on the subject of the rising tide of Islamic extremism, *Obsession: Radical Islam's War against the West*, Americans have been warned that an enemy out there somewhere wants to destroy our way of life.[6] A promotional blurb on the inside sleeve of the DVD states that "the film traces the parallels between the Nazi movement of World War II, the Radicals of today, and the Western world's response to the threats." Examined in detail, however, it becomes clear why some rational, decent Muslims might believe that the bizarre views put forth in the movie have long since entered the mainstream of the American media. In fact, the movie, promoted on CNN, on Fox News, and as a "free" DVD inserted into selected copies of the *New York Times*, is the journalistic equivalent of asking, "Why haven't the Muslims stopped beating their wives yet?"

On December 10, 2006, CNN's attractive, young anchor Kyra Philips promoted the movie in no uncertain terms, calling it a "fascinating and chilling look at the parallels between Nazism and modern terrorism." In an unusually lengthy cable news segment lasting ten minutes, she interviewed the film's producer, Raphael Shore, in Jerusalem, where he was allowed to put forward, unquestioned, the bold assertion that "Arabs grew up with Nazis and continued the battle against the West."

Philips did not stop plugging the film after her initial introduction, gushing, "I encourage everyone to see this film but also to look into this relationship between Adolf Hitler and Amin al-Husani... and how he came together with Hitler and talked about the extermination of the Jews." As if that was not enough promotion, Philips then said, "the movie left many of us speechless," adding, "we appreciate what you have done."[7]

The film is highly misleading. To discuss the 1941 meeting of al-Husani, grand mufti of Jerusalem, with Hitler and to hype it as the centerpiece of a broader "Islamo-fascist" Muslim conspiracy that was set on dethroning Western civilization is similar to tarring and feathering all the Italians for Benito Mussolini's extensive ties to the same Jew hater. It also completely ignores the essential creed of Nazism: Aryan supremacy, which reduced all Semites and "swarthy-skinned" persons—not just the Jews—to the level of dogs and rats. A witness in the movie *Obsession* asserts that influential Muslims indeed aided and abetted Hitler's efforts to exterminate the Jews. Alfons Heck, a self-described "Hitler Youth officer," states that the mufti went on to help raise an SS division of Muslims—mostly Bosnians—to aid the German war effort.[8]

These wild allegations and innuendos discredit and dishonor hundreds of thousands of Muslims who fought and died in defense of Europe and the United States during World War II. Indeed, while the mufti was co-opted by promises from the powerful Third Reich (as were French officials and thousands of other Christians) and spent a portion of the war in Berlin, Hitler's views did not and still do not in any way represent the views of Muslims as a whole.

In cherry-picking evidence to build a convincing screed, the film chooses not to point out that several Palestinian brigades and thousands of Palestinians fought with the British to save Britain and put an end to the spread of fascism. Such a revelation might have impaired the film's propaganda value as a tool to persuade Americans and other Westerners of what they should fear. The so-called fascist jihad uniting Hitler and Arabs, whom Hitler actually despised, never approached fruition. Indeed, it was a nonstarter. In the end, hundreds of thousands of African Muslims helped in the liberation of France. Nearly half of the French forces landing in France in 1944 were Africans, almost all of them Muslims. In Africa itself, King Muhammad V of Morocco helped save Moroccan Jews from extermination, another astounding truth ignored by the movie's propagandists.[9] In South Asia, Pakistan's founder, Muhammad Ali Jinnah, a proponent of secular rule, ferociously denounced Hitler and helped rally Muslim troops to go to the front. Who would know from the film *Obsession* that the Paris Mosque was a refuge for Jewish children?[10]

The movie, which features a number of influential US ideologues, goes on to provide the viewer with its own creative definition of the Arabic word "jihad," which means both war and personal struggle. One so-called former and now-reformed terrorist says, "Yes. It means 'the struggle within,' but *Mein Kampf* means 'my struggle.'"[11]

Video footage of screaming, sword-wielding imams is flashed on the screen and the jihadists are accused of demonizing poor Ariel Sharon as a blood-sucking vampire—no less.

Obsession, which was promoted by leading right-wing and right-leaning Jewish groups in the United States, attempts vigorously to refute the argument that US foreign policy has had anything to do with the emergence of a global jihad. (Not surprisingly, the distributors sent millions of copies of the DVD to "battleground" states in advance of the 2008 election.)

In the film, an analyst suggests there is too much self-flagellation going on: "People...started asking 'What could Americans have done?' They were blaming themselves." As this point is made, the title of the *Christian Science Monitor*'s series "Why Do They Hate Us?" and a headline reading "To Prevent Terrorism, US Foreign Policy Must Change" flash across the screen to represent the supposedly nonsensical argument that foolish Americans are tempted to believe. The film strongly implies that Americans are naïve even to consider their own nation's role in the rise of Islamic extremism. The real message is: "There is nothing Americans could have possibly done to inspire such barbaric and anti-American animosity. We are right, they are wrong. We need to kill them before they kill us."

These folks also want to tell us, "Watch out, you are being bamboozled!" Steven Emerson, often featured on Rupert Murdoch's Fox Network as an expert on the threat of terrorism inside North America, lashes out at the Palestinians for being "liars and deceivers," as if Israeli politicians—or for that matter, all politicians—have never practiced deceit for their own political gain. There is plenty of guilt to go around for the sorry state of world affairs; it is just that Emerson and his anti-Muslim associates make no effort to distribute it fairly.

Emerson, like Glenn Beck and Rush Limbaugh, is a foe of moderation, once even denouncing President Obama for daring to suggest that the United States was *not* at war with Islam. He wrote: "The only problem with that statement is that it implies somehow that we in the US are responsible for creating that impression" that the United States is at war with Islam.[12] Another of the film's notable analysts, Caroline Glick, a Jewish American senior editor at the *Jerusalem Post*, took a similar tack when in 2008, she told the *National Review* that Obama was "blaming the US for its enemies' hatred and malicious designs."[13] She might as well have called him the flagellator-in-chief.

Still, the anti-Muslim opinions expressed in the movie should not be seen as those of mere fringe elements. After all, they have been embraced by "credible" American news organizations, particularly the mainstream cable stations. They have the power to persuade.

Nevertheless, the *Obsession* propaganda screed reveals the often intolerant beliefs of some of the so-called experts on the subject of radical Islam. One such "expert" is Brigitte Gabriel, a Lebanese-Christian anti-Muslim activist and author of the book titled *Because They Hate*.[14] Together with other statements, she is on record as saying that the "degraded state of Arab societies is caused by Islam," and that "Muslim people have less to contribute than their counter-parts in civilized nations." More disturbing for dedicated non-governmental and US government groups working to encourage the growth of civil society and democracy within Islamic countries, she bluntly states in an interview with the *New York Times Magazine* that "moderate Muslims at this point are truly irrelevant."[15] In other words, the only ones we should concern ourselves with are the extremists. Gabriel is no minor character. A lobbyist, she is president and founder of the American Congress for Truth, whose "board of advisers" includes Dr. Walid Phares and James Woolsey, a former Central Intelligence Agency (CIA) director.

Not surprisingly, almost everyone involved in the making and production of *Obsession* openly supported the US invasion of Iraq as a means of cracking down on so-called radical extremism. Many of these people are on record as making statements supporting the dis-credited "connection" between al Qaeda and Saddam Hussein. These "experts" were part of a more powerful clique of aggressive militarists who drove the United States into that meaningless war, a war that—in the end—wasted some one trillion US tax dollars."[16] Can they be trusted now to help us understand radical Islam? Apparently the daytime producers in our major cable networks thought so.

✷✷✷

As Neil MacFarquhar writes in his balanced book *The Media Relations Department of Hizbollah Wishes You a Happy Birthday* about his years spent reporting for the *New York Times* in the Middle East, "It is the powerful who developed the argument that Western freedoms are a cultural phenomenon foreign to Arab and Islamic values."[17] This same powerful elite also often promotes an understanding of history incorrectly asserting that Islam has always been far more radical and intolerant than Christianity. Walid Phares tells us what we should supposedly fear, when he writes, "The world's democracies are coming to realize, not without pain, that the new enemies of international law have a vision of the future that is literally a restoration of the distant past."[18]

Yet Islam is a religious creed, not a coherent ideology as its harshest critics would have us believe. Nor is it inherently militant. In different passages in the same verse, the Koran says, "Slay them wherever you find them. Drive them out of the places from which they drove you. Fight against them until idolatry is no more and Allah's religion reigns supreme." Taken alone without the Prophet's admonitions on humility and tolerance, this passage would be cause for alarm. Closely following this passage, however, the Koran plainly states, in an apparent contradiction, "There shall be no compulsion in religion."[19]

Anyone who reads the Bible will also find numerous instances of contradiction, which, in truth, represent a grappling with the paradoxes of human nature.

In *God's Crucible: Islam and the Making of Europe, 570–1215,* Pulitzer Prize–winning historian David Levering Lewis examines in detail the varied interpretations of Islam's expansion put forward by the religion's earliest leaders or caliphs. (Until the collapse of the Ottoman Empire in 1924, the Muslim world was ruled—though sometimes only nominally—by one supreme leader, the caliph.) Lewis argues that early Islamic history puts on display varied interpretations of the same holy texts. He points out correctly that Mohammed himself never proclaimed Islam to be a campaigning faith that should be forced upon the unwilling.

Lewis's balanced look at the origins of Islam does not overlook the killing and slaughtering of innocents in the name of religion that took place on all sides. Lewis cites the slaughter of Qurayza Jews at the "Battle of the Trench," when "headless bodies were tossed into the trench in a gruesome butchery of some seven hundred, lasting from sun up to dusk," as a cause of some of the earliest and greatest Muslim-Jewish enmity.[20] Yet other episodes in Islam's long history tell another story. When Caliph Umar, along with his best generals, conquered Christian-ruled Jerusalem in 638 CE, "Hebrews on whom Heraclius had declared a virtual open hunting season eight years earlier" fought with the invaders as allied militias, the Hebrews following in Umar's wake to take their rightful place back in their holiest city. Umar proceeded almost immediately to put into writing a decree that there "shall be no compulsion" to convert to Islam, setting the tone for an expanding Muslim empire that would provide far more leeway to competing religions than would Christianity.

On several other levels, ancient Islam outpaced Christianity, including intellectually in the fields of mathematics, science, and writing. Though Islam would eventually falter by comparison with Christianity in terms of women's rights, early Muslim regimes provided a role for women that was "the most enlightened among the revealed creeds," as Lewis points out.[21] The first caliphates in Damascus and Cordoba also presided over a flourishing free trade zone that suggested, in no uncertain terms, that the business of Islam was business, not war.

Lewis shines a magnifying glass on the sharp contrast between the enlightened views of Andalusian Muslim rulers on the Iberian peninsula and the course set earlier by the Christian Visigoths, whose councils had decreed that "the king will tolerate no one in his kingdom who is not Catholic." The conquest of Spain by Moorish, Arab, and Berber Muslims crossing from North Africa brought great prosperity and advanced development not only to what today is Spain but also—eventually—to all of Europe. Even the Andalusian Jews, inhabitants of the Iberian peninsula since well before the time of Christ, welcomed the conquerors and prospered in the early years of the conquest. Spain's new rulers allowed a broad spectrum of mores and beliefs as they fostered a civil society and pluralism that had had no equal in the West since Augustan Rome.[22]

The true flowering and expansion of the Andalusian Islamic experiment in Europe took place during the rule of Cordoban Caliph Abd al-Rahman. The blond-haired, blue-eyed son of Prince Mohammad and a Frankish slave ascended the throne at the age of twenty-two in 912 CE and ruled for half a century marked by religious freedom and prosperity. Lewis points out that the tolerance Abd al-Rahman promoted was based "more on condescension than generosity" and on a pragmatic recognition that "it made good sense to let infidel conversions proceed, as it were, naturally," and notes that, at least under Abd al-Rahman, "forced conversion was alien to Islam in al-Andalus, as it was elsewhere in the Ummah," the Islamic hierarchy and realm of the day.[23]

For a few hundred years, most Jews and Christians on the Iberian peninsula enjoyed opportunities unavailable to anyone else on Earth. In a statement that could just as easily describe modern America, Lewis points out that the Andalusian rulers found "Jews to be indispensable as scribes, clerks, physicians, and court officials."[24] Nor was there such a thing as strict "prohibition" (of alcohol) for non-Muslims. Although the Prophet specifically forbade alcoholic consumption, Christians on the peninsula grew rich from vineyards, even selling their produce clandestinely to cosmopolitan Muslims, who partook of the best wines in Europe.

By comparison, Charlemagne's European experiment was a bleak failure, driven mainly by greed and warmongering crusaders. Common folk were forced to accept exploitation by a regal-military class and its clerical advisers. The high morals of Christianity were simply lost in a feudal system in which peasants and beasts of burden were treated with equal disdain. These were, after all, the Dark Ages, and Lewis points out that the greed of the church ravaged the rural economy.

A lasting legacy of Andalusia's golden age, however, stemmed from Islam's view that all workers were capable and should be given an opportunity to succeed. It was the egalitarian spirit that, in another age, would be termed "to each according to his ability." In this regard, Andalusian caliphs set an example that was hundreds of years ahead of Europe's Renaissance. Modern historians of all religions and creeds still marvel at the emphasis placed by the caliphate and its governors on the need for public education. Cordoba's seventy libraries had no match in size or value in the Western world. The main library alone had some four hundred thousand (original or hand-copied) volumes, which would be the envy of many modern American colleges. By comparison, a leading abbey in Switzerland, which boasted one of the most literate communities of monks in Europe, had a mere six hundred books.[25] Only hundreds of years later, when Europe finally broke free of its constant warfare, would its rulers and citizens embrace the standards set forth from Baghdad and Damascus to Cordoba and Timbuktu. (Yes. Even Timbuktu had more books than Switzerland.) All things considered, the early history of Islam is an embarrassingly poor advertisement for the fearmongers who fret at the return of a caliphate that in any case isn't in the making either in modern Europe or in the Middle East. Fears that today's fundamentalist ideologues want to return the world to the Dark Ages, or even the Middle Ages, are laced with irony and hyperbole.

My point is not to deny that there is an ideological, political, and social conflict still brewing between Islam and the West. Political vanities and militant legacies aside, religious ideology still plays an ungainly and inordinate role in today's troubled world. As famed

Middle Eastern scholar Bernard Lewis points out: "Christians and Muslims share a common triumphalism. In contrast to the other religions, including Judaism, they believe that they alone are the fortunate recipients and custodians of God's final message to humanity."[26] Just as many young Christians are under false impressions about the benevolent and dominant role of their own religion in history, young Muslims are similarly schooled in a biased manner to believe that their own religion is glorious and superior to other creeds.

There are also ongoing struggles within Islam: a wrestling match between the "good angels" and "bad angels," the militants and the peacemakers. The militant angels can only proceed, however, if the broader Islamic world believes that the faith is under threat from the West—that is, the militants require the complicity of the broader Islamic world just as our own misguided politicians require the complicity of our own anxious minions. As Bernard Lewis also points out, "The two phases of the Prophet's career, the one of resistance, the other of rule, are both reflected in the Qur'an where in different chapters, the believers are to obey God's representatives and to disobey the Pharoah."[27] The "Pharoah" remains a paradigm for everything from pro-Western Islamic leaders to perceptions of American imperialist designs. Mohammed did not demand that his people rise up and slaughter their enemies. Bernard Lewis points out that—in some cases—he is on record as advising his lieutenants to treat prisoners well, also insisting that Allah forbids the killing of women and children.[28]

It is my purpose in *My Brother, My Enemy* to shed some light on the Islamic realm but also to dispel myths and anxieties that foster hatred and prevent friendship. For when the West looks toward the horizon and envisions an Islamo-fascist movement attempting to spread its tentacles across the globe, it is looking only at a mirage, a false specter created out of our own fears. Worse, when we pay lip service to such talk, we are essentially elevating the fringe element within Islam to an undeserved level of international prominence. When we go hunting for that false specter, we also violate our basic principle of good security. It was John Quincy Adams who cogently warned the country on July 4, 1821, to listen to its own better angels, stating that the United States "goes not abroad in search of monsters to destroy, she is the well-wisher to the freedom and independence of all."[29]

As most Americans realized in the aftermath of the US military's massive invasion of Iraq, it was a ginned up terrorist-hunting expedition in search of "monsters." Moreover, it only played into the broader schemes of the extremist element that seeks to draw young Muslims into the fray against an "infidel" superpower.

How much more pleasant it is to let our enemies self-destruct on their own bluster than to listen to our own leaders digging themselves into a hole with false declarations of "victory." After Barack Obama's election as president in November 2008, al Qaeda's number two, Dr. Ayman al-Zawahiri, made his disappointment at losing American bogeyman George W. Bush more than apparent. He was left searching for the proper metaphor for a new American commander in chief who had called the Iraq invasion a "stupid war."[30]

Al-Zawahiri dismissed the new African American president as "a house negro," meaning a black man who gets to live in the "big house" because he kowtows to the interests of the slave master. This "Uncle Tom" accusation did not quite qualify as a racial epithet, since the Egyptian pediatrician added that Obama was "the direct opposite of honorable black Americans" like Malcolm X. Al Qaeda appeared worried about the growing wellspring of Muslim public support for Obama's efforts that resounded even on Web sites run by allies of al Qaeda. A publication known as *Al-Samoud*, linked to the Taliban in Afghanistan, viewed Obama's election as a welcome sign that Americans did not want to prolong a conflict "ignited by Bush's insanity and his satanic policy."[31]

Osama bin Laden had burnished his own reputation as an ideological godfather of holy war on the back of American blunders for far too long. Bin Laden's poetry, laced with ancient Arabic cadences, often highlighted the need to continue the jihad and fight back against American aggression. The following is a typical passage:

"These Crusader hosts…have spread…like locusts, crowding its soil, eating its fruits and destroying its verdure; and this is a time when nations contend against Muslims like diners jostling around in a bowl of fruit."[32] Bin Laden's poetic diatribes might have been relegated to the dustbin of literary history if the United States had made the right overtures before or after 9/11. Our ignorance of the impact of conflicts across the Islamic realm—beginning with the Afghan struggle to throw off the yoke of Soviet oppression—eventually gave rise to a "perfect storm" of resentment toward the United States in the Muslim world that may only now have begun to dissipate ever so slightly. The growing number of terrorists still waiting in the wings to capitalize on American inaction or further blunders, however, remains unmeasured and possibly still growing. Their vows are not to be taken lightly.

As citizens of a nation renewing its own sense of tolerance and peacemaking potential, however, we need to remain wary of those in the higher ranks of the American government who have bought the pessimistic spin put forth by many on the extreme right. These people in the American government and the extreme Right will tell you that America has always been doing everything it can to foster peace in the Middle East against unassailable odds and that the extremists will never be satisfied. They want to overlook any American culpability in—as it were—stirring up the terrorists' hornet's nest and providing recruiting fodder for our enemies. Even the suggestion that the United States has some ultimate responsibility for the fix we are in across the globe provokes them to denounce their opponents as unpatriotic. This ignores the fact that in the wake of the invasion of Iraq, terrorist attacks around the world rose by a factor of 600 percent.[33]

Our blunders in Iraq—which included the well-publicized use of torture—combined with an abject failure to address the crisis in Israel and Palestine left American prestige in tatters even among people in countries that were long-time American allies. That is a great deal to reverse with one presidential election.

Is it really so idealistic and naïve in the wake of the blows to American credibility abroad to ask, as Australian David Kilcullen does in *The Accidental Guerrilla*, that American power be matched by American virtue?[34]

My account of my journey into the Islamic realm is not chronological. I begin with a recent visit to Jerusalem's Old City, which at times in history has been a lightning rod for extremists and yet has also been a shining example of religious tolerance. It sets the mood for a measured refutation of those who believe that a two-state solution for Israel and Palestine is not a step toward letting the air out of the extremist propaganda bubble and calming the broader Islamic realm. Naysayers, who want Americans to buckle down and prepare for the coming war with Islam, criticize President Obama for trying to sell a two-state solution in Palestine and Israel. Steven Emerson, for example, derides Obama: "The president seems to believe that a two-state solution in Israel is the panacea for stopping the spread of radical Islam. How tragically and dangerously wrong that is. A two-state solution—assuming for the moment that it [Palestine] is not armed to the teeth with missiles that could down every plane at Ben Gurion Airport—will never satisfy the Islamist groups."[35]

But who said anything about a panacea or about trying to appease Islamist groups? Living by our ideals is a noble enough end in itself. The efforts to re-create Jerusalem as an open and international city and to help Israel and Palestine settle into a two-state solution are commonsense approaches that also promote the American ideals of freedom of religion, freedom of speech, and the right to live in peace with one's neighbors. These approaches will also put us back on track toward regaining the kind of international respect America enjoyed after World War II when we helped set up the state of Israel.

My take on this conundrum is not revolutionary. Juan Cole, chair of Arabic Studies at the University of Michigan, says, "resolving the conflict in a way acceptable to all the major parties involved should be the highest priority of the [Obama] Administration. This step would resolve 90 percent of America's problems with the Muslim world and would potentially lead to improved relations with states such as Syria and Iran."[36] Richard Clarke, former director of National Security in the US government, concurs: "If we could achieve a Middle East peace, much of the support for al Qaeda would evaporate overnight."[37]

Hamas as an organization might well begin to lose its own raison d'être and ability to recruit among the long-embittered Palestinian youth. Hamas is, after all, a political party, a paramilitary group, and a humanitarian organization all wrapped up in one. It could—if we are lucky—morph into something far more peaceful in the future.

For now, the push for peace has only just begun anew. The new administration is still trying—with great futility—to force Israel to end the occupation of the West Bank and discontinue its policy of turning a blind eye to the building of new homes inside and outside existing Israeli settlements there. At the same time, the administration is also trying—its officials insist—to sideline the growing support for Hamas by improving the economy and security in the West Bank and Gaza. Yet without using the leverage of billions of US dollars to level the playing field, that effort does not look promising.

Israel's blindside bombing of Gaza, which occurred on the eve of Obama's inauguration, threatened, early on, to ruin the honeymoon in the Muslim world of a man with the middle name of Hussein. Predictably, al Qaeda lashed out: "This is Obama, whom the American machine of lies tried to portray as the rescuer who will change the policy of America." Al Qaeda denounced the Israeli air strikes on Gaza as "Obama's gift to you before he takes office."[38]

A former chief of the CIA's bin Laden division, Michael Scheuer, in *Marching toward Hell*, calls on Washington to simply abandon its Jewish allies in the Middle East.[39] In an iconoclastic rant, Scheuer argues that Israel's survival is not essential to US security. He says that US support for Israel should be weighed against the "threat America faces from Islamist militancy," which he argues "is huge and growing and motivated by a faith that perceives itself under attack by US foreign policy, part of which is seen as US subservience to Israel."[40]

This is not the argument I will put forward. Israel might not be essential to US security, but neither were the six million Jews killed in the Holocaust. The few million that we saved—value added for the US experiment—were also a great sign of hope for the future of humanity and a boost to the world's perception of the United States as a humane nation.

In my view, it is not desirable, nor humane, nor realistic, as Scheuer suggests, to turn back the hands of time and abandon the Israelis. On the other hand, it is entirely possible, while defending Israel's right to exist, to address in addition the legitimate concerns of the Palestinians. Indeed, as the United States is the chief sponsor and advocate of the Israeli experiment, there are no other nations in a position to do this. And while efforts to address the rights of both parties to the conflict appear—on the surface—to be fraught with dangers and obstacles, there is an imperative beyond even doing the right thing. Simply doing nothing will most certainly increase al Qaeda's recruiting pool and increase the chances that a decade or two or three in the future, Hamas, Hizbollah, or another like-minded group will obtain a nuclear weapon and dash any hopes for international stability.

As the respected *Ha'aretz* newspaper columnist Akiva Eldar, who is often accused by Binjamin Netanyahu's allies of being a "self-hating Jew," explained to me in Tel Aviv, "there is a red line to democracy on the green line." He continued, "Actually, Israel's policies in the West Bank and Gaza amount to apartheid."[41] These are his words, not mine. He had not taken that assessment from Jimmy Carter and, indeed, it was a recognition he came to as a journalist familiar with South Africa's Bantustans decades earlier. As long as the outrages taking place in the West Bank and Gaza—he argues along with other voices in Israel today—are unopposed in the United States, we will continue to hand our most vocal and adept opponents grist for their propaganda mill.

President Obama's initial efforts in the Islamic realm have been rhetorically bold, but they amount to baby steps against a backdrop of three decades of dubious US foreign policy choices. Change in this part of the world will not come in days, weeks, or months. Beyond addressing Israel and Palestine, there is much more work to be done to turn the tide against terrorism and mind-numbing autocratic rule. For too long, the Islamic world, partially but not entirely due to its inordinate oil wealth, has been treated according to a double standard. Whereas Washington has helped nurture the growth of democracy in most of Asia, in South America, and in parts of Africa, the Islamic world has been treated differently. Many in the Middle East have long since concluded that their despised authoritarian governments are rewarded for cooperating with and looking after Washington's self-serving interests. They've concluded this against a backdrop of Washingtonian bluster about US support for "democratic institutions."

It is not too late to better steer the ship of state amid changing winds. Real support for democratic openness and civil society in the Islamic world can help alter an anti-American dynamic that was exacerbated by past policies. Moreover, support for autocrats, including those sacred cows in Saudi Arabia and Egypt, will have to end if the United States is to be taken at its word. Metaphorically, if America goes hunting down monsters from Casablanca to Jakarta, it is likely to end up entangled in new webs of terror. On the other hand, if it treads lightly, employs the intelligence networks of its allies, and addresses the roots of terrorism, it can hope for a better world—one that reflects universal and American ideals. No doubt, pushing for democracy is likely to be a messy business. It might well produce governments with which we do not agree. However, over the course of several decades, these efforts are far more likely to provide stability than our support for the current status quo of dictators and oppression. There are great risks, but the long-term rewards outweigh those of the old ways.

In Egypt, that largest of Arab nations, President Mubarak, whose regime's human rights violations and undemocratic ways are well documented, has always duped American diplomats with the basic idea of après-moi le déluge. Mubarak has been a master in convincing American leaders that, should we abandon his leadership, we should expect an Islamist takeover. There is no evidence, however, to support his claim, a claim that senior Egyptian officials have tried all too often to sell me as well. Running counter to such arguments, national polls in Egypt have suggested that some four out of five Egyptians believe that democracy is a very good system of government. Whereas the war in Iraq soured many citizens toward America's professed ideals, citizens of countries like Egypt and Indonesia do not see democracy as the private domain of the US government. America may have an unbroken record of over two hundred years of democratic rule at home, but it has no monopoly on democratic thinking, particularly abroad. Washington—as late as 2010—was still paying the Egyptian government two billion plus annually for security that serves to strengthen the regime's ability to torture and abuse its own citizenry.[42]

Despite the United States' history of confusing the average Muslim as to our ideals and intentions, my travels for this book in the last four years from Jerusalem to Casablanca to Timbuktu to Kabul and on to Jakarta have made it clear to me that there is also a wellspring of goodwill toward the United States. This is in spite of the misconceptions among many Americans, who may not have had the chance or may not have bothered to befriend young Muslims. These Americans suffer from the distinct disadvantage of having a slew of "experts" and "analysts" defining for them just who the followers of Islam are. In most cases the analysis is tainted by an obsession with trumped-up fears.

There is no doubt that in Pakistan and Afghanistan, the invasion of Iraq has had a profoundly negative impact on our ability to persuade these populations of our goodwill and decent intentions. Not only did the war in Iraq siphon off resources amid a whirlwind of intelligence errors and military showdowns, but also it gave credence to conspiracy theorists who contended that the United States really was never bent on capturing or killing the perpetrators of the 9/11 attacks, or Osama bin Laden in particular. After Iraq became such an obvious debacle—along with the public relations disasters of Abu Ghraib and Guantanamo—Pakistanis, for example, threw up their hands in disgust and did little to address the rising tide of extremism in their own country. As Ahmed Rashid, the most astute voice on South Asia stated in *Descent into Chaos*, it was not "possible to convince people that the struggle against extremism was not just America's war but equally Pakistan's."[43] Most Pakistanis—from those in largely secular, big cities to those in devout and poverty-stricken villages—simply felt that if America was going to fight its "war on terror" in South Asia, it should be left to fight it on its own. Pakistan's government did little to address the inflamed jihadi literature. As Rashid also points out, in the wake of the US invasion of Afghanistan, "some forty publications with circulations of over one million were published by extremist groups," not to mention the mushrooming of videotaped propaganda unleashed on the general public.[44] Only after waves of suicide bombings forced the government into action did the Pakistanis attempt to crack down on the Frankenstein they had helped bring to life, starting in the 1970s. At the time of writing, it remains unclear whether Pakistan can put the lid back on Pandora's box even with public support for its own renewed war on radicals.

What has become clear to me, however, in my travels is that—beyond the issue of Israel and Palestine—which, if unaddressed, is likely to wreak havoc in the future—America can rest assured that there are, despite the chattering nabobs of negativism, a number of positive signs on the horizon with regard to its relations with the Islamic realm. I hope to make clear over the course of this text what some of the good omens suggest.

Change, while it may be inspired from without, is more likely to come from within. Iran, in particular, while probably not on the verge of revolutionary change, has shown the rest of the Islamic world that the general public does not have to sit down and take it when a host of angry mullahs attempts to impose restrictions on their lives. When dozens of American journalists found themselves expelled from Iran in the course of a crackdown on dissent, I was dispatched from Kabul by my McClatchy editor Roy Gutman to the dusty perimeter, namely Herat, a lovely, ancient city that sits at the edge of eastern Iran and provides one of the better positions from which to observe the internal struggles within modern Persia.

After a flight into Herat on a Russian Antonov and a short motor-cycle ride to a truckers' stop, I found myself in the midst of an exciting debate. Amid the tire irons and crowbars in a disabled Russian armored personnel-carrier-turned-teahouse, several Iranian truckers were debating allegations that their government had stolen Iran's June 12 presidential elections. Jaffar, fifty-nine, a driver from Mashad, argued that his government would never cheat his country-men out of an election.

But as he spoke, Maruche, twenty-nine, a Sunni Muslim truck driver from near Torbat e-Jam in eastern Iran, asked the older driver: "How can you say there was no cheating?" He was angry that a fellow Iranian would lie to an American reporter—even if he didn't care much for Americans. Maruche stormed out of the teahouse. He would not talk to me in the midst of his fellow truck drivers, but he invited me to sit with him in the cab of his truck. He was angry about what he said had happened in his village on election day.

"The election center was controlled by the government," he said. "We saw that with our own eyes. I know about the ballot stuffing because my uncle is a police officer and was a supervisor in the polling station. He saw one man in the polling station put a hundred ballots into a box. No one can dare protest this in our village or they will simply disappear."

Maruche's allegations came as the Iranian government admitted that in fifty cities there were more votes than there were registered voters. For several hours, I listened as Iranian truck drivers in Herat told similar tales of voting irregularities. It was the government crackdown, its heavy-handed brutality, however, that sparked the most debate. Some drivers defended the government, calling the demonstrators "hooligans and criminals" who deserved punishment, while others defended them. Several drivers blamed their nation's unrest on foreign powers, singling out the United States as a key meddler in Iranian affairs. Those who spoke in dissenting voices did so with real fear that government spies were watching.

Covered in grease, Mehdi, a truck driver and father, took a break from working on his broken axle. "Why shouldn't we be outraged?" he said. "I drove through Tehran and saw government thugs breaking into university dormitories, dragging out our best students, even PhD candidates, and beating them. I have two sons in that uni versity demonstrating, and I've worked all my life so they can live in freedom. We all deserve a voice, and those of us who dare to speak out should be prepared to die!" he said. As he spoke, another Iranian driver, a lanky, gray-bearded man carrying a new soccer ball for his son, sat down and offered everyone a cigarette. "You shouldn't talk to this man," he told Mehdi. "Don't you know that our intelligence officers are everywhere? They even murder opponents of the regime in Europe."

"Nonsense!" insisted Mehdi. "I am just an ordinary truck driver, but in Tehran they will hear my voice. I drove right past the demonstrations when they were beating people and I took pictures with my mobile phone. When I left the city, I stopped into a coffee shop and heard that in the city of Shahrood, yet another man had been killed for protesting. People care about their votes, the millions that have been stolen," he said. "The people who stole those votes don't love our nation."

What was unfolding before me was a thing of beauty; precisely the kind of debate that the Bush administration had claimed it wanted to foster, but one that could not possibly have taken place on that administration's watch. Few spoke of the usual bogeyman, America. Iranians were talking about what was good for Iran—which coincidentally was also what was good for America. It was almost too good to be true, and there was no sense in spoiling the party with dumbed-down political cant. Though the Iranian crackdown on pro-democracy forces was brutal and relentless, the US president had been wise to avoid Republican urgings—particularly from John McCain, who had supported a militaristic policy toward Iraq—to take a moral stand and insert America into the Iranian struggle. When the brutality reached its height, Obama did speak up, but by and large, and for our own good, he held his tongue. The silence spoke volumes.

The legacy of the Bush administration has left the United States with severe limits on its international political capital. President Obama has begun the long slog to restore the nation's lost credibility, but it will not happen overnight, and it is wise to tread lightly in some countries while pushing for peace in others. Taken on the surface, the crackdown on dissent in Iran can be viewed as a negative development that displays the intransigent and dictatorial nature of a ruling theocracy. On another level, however, it also highlights the likelihood of and long-term hope for positive change across the Islamic realm. Just as many Muslims were under the false impression that most Americans approved of and supported the policies of the Bush administration, many Americans have been led to believe that Iran remains a theocracy due to the compliance and complicity of the broader population. But Tehran's mostly liberated younger generation and democracy advocates have already given the lie to this false impression through hours and hours of exported mobile telephone uploads and smuggled news clips. Their courage should make any American with a heart proud of them as our brothers in arms—or maybe more appropriately brothers in tongue.

In the wake of 9/11, fast-fingered and light-footed jihadists seized upon the revolutionary license provided through the US-made Internet in a rush to spin events in their favor. Almost a decade after the attacks, the hate speech and angry anti-American tirades are not as popular as they once were with the younger generation of Muslims, particularly with the American military lowering its own profile. As a new age dawns, a young generation of Muslims is as interested or even more interested in precisely the same uses of the cell phone and Internet as are the youth of Europe and America. For the oppressed, the technology offers special opportunities.

One of the most enlightening chats I had in Afghanistan didn't come in discussions with American soldiers or Afghan governors. It came when I met Mohammad Faqiri, the spokesman for Herat University's New Generation Club, a small university group. Faqiri was a young intellectual who dressed fashionably and had little interest in religion. He called himself a "secularist." His group was in disfavor with the government and so it had not even managed to obtain an official license, which was required at Herat University for any youth group.

Faqiri spoke with me at length in a fried-chicken shop and then brought his club members over to meet me at the modern Iranian-built hotel that I was staying in—one that ominously, I noted, had talking elevators with cameras inside them. Members of Faqiri's club—only ten of them, including an equal number of males and females—had spent their childhood growing up as refugees in Iran, and so they had a unique perspective on the changes taking place in that country. Despite the rule of the mullahs, but because of the long-running wars in Afghanistan, Iran was several decades ahead of Afghanistan in terms of gender rights and education. There were all kinds of things to admire in Iran that Afghanistan still lacked.

We sat in a private conference room, drinking tea and soda. Faqiri warned me that his group had "some pretty advanced views for young people in a traditional Muslim nation," but he added that he was sure that his group was in agreement about the need for secular rule in Iran. "The Iranian government has finally exposed itself as a theocratic, totalitarian regime," Faqiri said. "Iranian leaders are trying to hang on to power by killing people and destroying their free media."

That was a shift in sentiment, if one considers the role Iran had played in Afghanistan in recent years as a cultured, wise, and stable big brother. In Afghanistan, the Taliban could intimidate, but the basic desires for freedom and democratic change—almost despite the troubled US invasion—were already at work. Whether they would prevail was another matter entirely.

Everything I heard during that long afternoon from the Afghan university students left me with the immediate impression that—as a longtime war correspondent focused on conflict—I was missing the most satisfying story of all. The young women in the New Generation Club were particularly impressive. "We have a free government and a repressed society, Iran has an open society and a repressive government," said Shabnam Simia, who had lived in Iran as a refugee for sixteen years. Simia's head was covered with a scarf, but her jeans and flashy belt made her appear ultramodern. Simia insisted that Iran's civil society—the very society that was now rising up against the mullahs—was far more developed than her own. She provided the example of women who were unable to go out at night or go to cafés or picnics together on the edge of town because of Afghanistan's stringent moral police.

She said she longed for the social rights that modern Iranian women enjoy, but detested a government that beats women protesting for democracy. "We see on the television now that the Iranian people are asking for help and they are hopeless, so we must do what we can with our moral support to help them prevail." Well, indeed, I thought. She was expressing the sentiment that ran like a thread through Europe and the United States as well. Faqiri, a history student at the university, said that the group admired what he called the "humanist" views of American politicians, including Abraham Lincoln. "The leaders in Iran can't even deal with history," he insisted. "Look at President Ahmadinejad—he can't even accept the Holocaust as a real event in the twentieth century."

Whatever you think about the Taliban's chances of making a political comeback in Afghanistan, it is worth recalling these signs that a young generation is bearing witness to the beginnings of a new society; one that has already given birth to the vibrant Afghan news media. And the competition is flagging. Iran, which had relished its own regional clout and global influence as it challenged the policies of George W. Bush, is bursting with dissent and relying on state-backed militiamen to keep order.

At the same time, Afghanistan, while roiled by anti-American and anti-Afghan insurgents, was slowly, beneath the surface, developing into a more modern nation with millions of new cell-phone users, a vast array of cable TV choices, and easy Internet access for a young generation of Afghans, at least in its cities. The Twitter and Facebook revolution had Afghan youth abuzz with stories of Iranian brutality as well as Karzai's corruption.

It is far easier to despair about the threat from Islamo-fascism than it is to see the writing on the wall in a new era, one in which the United States is still the last superpower standing. Let's hope we don't miss the wave. While it has diminished influence in a new multipolar world, the United States still can and should hope to reap the whirlwind of its own goodwill, decency, and innovative spirit. After all, the business of America is business—not politics.

It would be easy to stand aside and let the world return to a tense status quo after a decade of increased turbulence, but time and global demands will not wait. There are real dangers out there and new threats developing on the horizon. America must seize the initiative as hopeful eyes turn to her. For as Adams also said on that hot July day in 1821, "Her march is the march of the mind. She has a spear and a shield: but the motto upon her shield is, Freedom, Independence, Peace."[45]

When I began this book several years ago, I did not have a precise title in mind, but I wanted to write a book that would shed light on the false arguments and conjured-up differences that make many in both the Islamic world and the West—the United States and Europe—believe that we are at war with one another. If there is one shining light—a small personal insight—that I have gained through the reporting and writing I have done since then, I suspect it is the recognition that Islam and the West are not on course for a clash of civilizations. Indeed, my work on *My Brother, My Enemy* has reaffirmed a basic principle I always knew to be true: "Love your enemies, and do good, and lend, expecting nothing in return; and your reward will be great and you will be sons of the most high."[46]

Chapter 2
THIS LAND IS MY LAND

Moving past the two immense watchtowers of the Damascus Gate, I wound my way through the back alleys and amused tour groups to the heart of the old Jewish quarter. There, on a balcony overlooking a stone courtyard, I came upon a Jewish gentleman dressed in a flowing, white gown and playing softly on a harp. It might have been a scene out of Monty Python, a few decades ago. Appropriately, this would be my first encounter with "Obamamania" in the Holy Land, only days after Obama's election. As I watched, an idealistic young American approached with a blue and white Obama button and offered it to the harpist as a kind of "olive branch" from one stranger to another. A young student in a skull cap, who happened to be passing by, stopped suddenly. Offended by the overture, he rudely interrupted, snapping, "Don't do it!"

"What?" replied the bearded Jew in flowing robes.

"Don't do it!" repeated the student, as though it would betray the state of Israel for all eternity.

It is worth adding here that only three countries in the world—

in a standard straw poll—would have voted for McCain over Obama in the last election. One of them would have been Israel, assuming that the Palestinians in the West Bank and Gaza were not allowed to vote. In contrast, a *Jerusalem Post* exit poll suggested that some 78 percent of American Jews voted for, not against, Obama.[1]

"Don't do it!" repeated the kid in the skull cap.

The harpist, who as it turned out was a music student with a rather pragmatic-sounding business on the side, selling Biblical-era outfits to theater students, was having none of it.

"What?" he snapped back, staring down the intruder. "No." He took the button defiantly and patted it down proudly against his chest. "Obama is for Israel and I offer my blessings to him for success. He can stop the starvation in Africa and bring peace to the Middle East. He is—after all—the president—the number one!"

From a young man who looked prophetic himself, such a commendation was surely a good omen for the start of a new quest in the Holy Land. Everyone I met that day had some amusing point to make about the new American president and the prospects for peace presented by his election. It was certainly a bright, colorful morning in Jerusalem.

In the first few months after the election of Barack Obama as the forty-fifth president of the United States of America, the entire Middle East was abuzz with the possibilities that this sweeping change in America might present to the Holy Land. If you stood in front of Jerusalem's Damascus Gate, as I did, watching hundreds of merchants, scholars, and visitors—Arabs, Jews, Christians, and not a few atheists—pass under the majestic arches, you could not help but wonder if perceptions of the United States as a regional player—even as a potential peacemaker—had been altered by the political earthquake that had hit the United States in November 2008. What did it mean that the son of an immigrant, half-African, half-Caucasian, had suddenly been handed the title "leader of the free world"? In a land where progress is measured in decades and centuries and not in the months that Americans prefer, I knew that

it was foolish to expect too much, too soon from a new US administration. Nevertheless, what I would hear over the next few weeks
on the streets of Jerusalem, Beirut, and Damascus moved me—
personally—away from my acquired and cultivated journalistic
cynicism and toward a new, if cautious, optimism about the possibilities of peace in the Middle East.

Jerusalem's old city is an astonishing place. As an outsider
walking the streets—currently a kind of international zone that
would continue as such under the most logical of peace plans—one
is hard-pressed not to be taken aback by the melding of divergent
cultures and religions, all within the radius of just one-third of a
square mile. Contained within the walls, most of them built by
Suleiman the Magnificent, is enough historical and spiritual treasure
to spark holy wars well into the next millennium. For Jews there is
the Temple Mount, for Christians the Church of the Holy Sepul-
cher, and for Muslims the al-Aqsa Mosque and the golden Dome of
the Rock.

The city reminds me of a hands-on museum, in which all the
people appear anxious to express themselves in public and for the
whole world to see. Degrees of devotion are relative, but each religion does its level best to look as fervent as or more devout than the
others. Five times a day, Arab shop owners unfurl their personal rugs
and tapestries to pray in the alleyways facing Mecca. Christian pilgrims, huffing and perspiring fanatically with wooden crosses across
their backs, walk in the footsteps of Jesus, carefully genuflecting at
each station. At the Wailing Wall, Hasidic Jews bob up and down in
reverence and wedge their carefully folded prayers between well-
worn crevices.

If there were ever a venue where the right to worship openly was
paramount, it would be in Jerusalem. It is something that maybe all
of us should pray for—at least once—no matter what our faith, or
simply hope for if we have no faith. In his seminal speech on relations between the United States and the Islamic world in Cairo,
Barack Obama spoke wistfully of a "day when the mothers of

Israelis and Palestinians can see their children grow up without fear; when the Holy Land of three great faiths is the place of peace that God intended it to be; when Jerusalem is a secure and lasting home for Jews and Christians and Muslims, and a place for all of the children of Abraham to mingle peacefully together."[2]

Jerusalem's Jewish quarter seemed the appropriate place to begin my postelection quest. Israelis are believed to have occupied the quarter since the eighth century BCE. In 1948, they were forced to flee. In 1967, however, during the Six-Day War, Israeli paratroopers retook the Jewish quarter, which has been held, excavated, and inhabited by about two thousand Jews ever since.

Outside the gates of a yeshiva, a Jewish school, two bongo drummers, one with dreadlocks, the other with a very long beard, beat their drums and sang along to popular music. An old Jewish gentleman in a skull cap strolled past. He started laughing when I asked him what the election of Obama meant for Israel. "I think the next president will be a Jew!" he wailed in a twisted French accent amid peals of his own laughter. "He opened the door to black people. And so, you understand, *le changement, le changement*. I'm sure the next president will be a Jew!"

It was interesting that he took the election of Obama as a sign that opportunities for Jews might be expanding in America. As far as I knew, Jews in America were already doing fairly well, even in national politics, but he had a twinkle in his eye and I did not begrudge him the hope of even better days.

"But do you think that Jews and Palestinians can live together?" I asked him.

"Together?"

"Yes. Together."

"They have a lot of land in the world. Why do they want this piece of land? Why?"

"I would think the Arabs would also ask you that question."

"The same question?" He looked startled that I had even asked.

One of the two drummers had his own view: "Obama will be

good because he does not come to us from on high," he said tossing his hand in the air and lowering it to his feet. "He has risen up from the ground, you see, so he knows ree-aal-ity."

He no doubt preferred the kind of prophet that arose from the masses and not those the Almighty might dispatch from loftier heights in a flash of fire and smoke. Certainly, it could be argued, America's next prospective peacemaker, Barack Obama, had humbler roots than his immediate predecessor. What leverage that would give him in the Holy Land was a different question entirely.

Continuing through the Jewish quarter, I crossed a parking lot and came to the gates of the Sephardic Education Center. As a reporter I had fond memories of the Sephardic Jews in Europe. Maybe it was something to do with their having suffered two holocausts, not just one, that made them so sympathetic to their fellow human beings. They also had a sagacity beyond their years. In Sarajevo, at the height of the Serbian shelling of the Muslims in Sarajevo, I had befriended a kind, old rabbi, Jacob Finci, who ran La Benevolencia Foundation, a Sephardic group that managed several soup kitchens and did wondrous things for the city's embattled Muslims. I had always found it ironic that the Jews had banded together with the Muslims in Sarajevo in order to survive efforts by Orthodox Christian Serbs to murder nearly everyone in the city. And I still thought of Sarajevo as an appropriate starting point for all the naysayers who still insist that peace is not in the cards for Jerusalem.

At the Sephardic Center, the school's director, Rabbi Yosef Benarroch, invited me into his office for a chat. As it turned out, he was living in a Jewish "settlement" well within the boundaries of the West Bank, most of which has been under Jewish occupation since 1967. When I asked the rabbi if he had bothered to make the acquaintance of his Palestinian neighbors, he looked at me as if I were crazy. "It isn't safe these days, you know," he said. He said that he had not met any of his neighbors, but that other leaders in his community had made what he called "some peaceful overtures."

He had expectations for the new American president, however.

"I think a lot of people realize that a lot of bridges have been burnt and that he is going to try to bridge differences," he said. "I think that the people of Israel know that, with the Obama administration, there is going to be a strong, strong push to try to resolve the conflict over here."

In the immediate wake of Obama's election, hopes were high and none more so than the hopes of those in the small clique of Jewish Americans working for peace in Israel. That same day, I met up with a Jewish human rights activist, Tania Hary, who was in charge of international relations with "Gisha," the Israeli Center for Freedom of Movement, whose work was focused on helping to relieve the problems of Palestinians living in Gaza. Hary was an American citizen and also a recent university graduate. She explained that many in Israel's older generations remained extremely wary of the changes taking place in the United States. They were asking, she said, what would the election of Barack Obama mean for the security of their young nation? How would they live with Arabs after all the violence of the past decades?

Even her most beloved kinfolk were terrified of the prospects. "My grandmother has some of the ugliest views I've ever heard, but I love her anyway," said Hary, reminding me of my own affection for several now deceased, staunchly conservative relatives. "She calls left-wingers all kinds of names from the book and I just say, 'Well, grandma, I voted for Obama too!' and she has nothing to say, nothing at all." She laughed heartily at the thought, adding, "well, right, you see, so it goes both ways." By that, I think she meant love and tolerance.

I've been to some contentious places in my years as a foreign reporter, including other fought-over "holy lands," but Israel and Palestine rank among the most violently and intellectually disputed lands I've come across.

Much of what is called "religious strife" in Israel and Palestine is a mirage, however. Surveys have shown that Israelis are less, not more, religious than their relatives in the diaspora, and a vast swath of Palestinians are similarly areligious in many respects. What

passes for a modern religious standoff is far more of a highly politi-
cized, often militarized land dispute than anything else—albeit with
tens of thousands of religious fanatics on either side encouraging
the animosity and keeping tensions at a steady boil.

The positions taken up by hard-liners are seized upon by moderates for reasons of political expediency, which makes it difficult to
parse the rhetoric for even a semblance of truth. However, there are
compassionate and fair-minded persons already playing a role on
the ground in the Middle East. In Washington, DC, where partisan
and highly vocal views dominate the debate, these other voices are
often overlooked.

Jewish Americans are some of the most proactive players in the
struggle to find an equitable solution for land distribution in Israel
and Palestine. Many of them oppose the Israeli army's de facto support for Jewish settlements on the West Bank and support the human
rights of their Palestinian neighbors. Though the US government
has often publicly opposed the mushrooming of Jewish settlements
on the West Bank, it has rarely—in recent years—attempted to use
its leverage as an aid donor (or its bully pulpit as a world leader) to
prevent the continued construction of these settlements. After a
meeting of Israeli and Palestinian groups in Annapolis, Maryland, at
the end of George W. Bush's eight years in office, the Israeli government immediately set about approving another twelve hundred new
housing starts for the coming year. As soon as the Obama administration came to office, officials heralded a new approach that sig-
naled Israel may no longer have carte blanche to keep building.

One of the most credible and dynamic of the Jewish organizations monitoring the West Bank and Gaza is Breaking the Silence, a
group of former Israeli soldiers who, through their own harrowing
experiences in the army, have been inspired to speak out against the
subtle and relentless violence perpetrated against Palestinians in the
so-called occupied territories. Their voices have gained instant credibility in recent years. Yehuda Shaul, the group's director and a
former soldier, sat at the front of a dilapidated minibus and clutched

a large, black microphone as he led me in the direction of the Hebron hills early one winter morning following Obama's election. Shaul, a heavy-set twenty-eight-year-old educated in the United States, was eager to show me the plight of the Palestinian shepherds who had traditionally lived in the caves of Soucia.

Since the early 1990s, these shepherds' subterranean homes and their tents had been ransacked by Israeli soldiers teaming up with Jewish settlers. Shaul narrated the tale of the Palestinian shepherds with the dispassionate, slightly ironic voice of a well-informed Israeli soldier. He said his fellow soldiers were mostly too obsessed with partying, doing drugs, and getting home to their girlfriends to care one toss about the plight of the shepherds, so he felt it was up to him to do the talking.

As we left Jerusalem, we passed through the immense walls that surround the city and entered a new maze of cordoned-off highways, concrete barriers, and designated routes. A young boy pushed his bicycle alongside the twenty-four-foot barrier wall, casting a tiny shadow against the sad, depressing concrete monstrosity. The barrier, located mostly inside the West Bank but also along the 1949 Armistice line between Israel and Jordan, restricts movement and access to government services. Israel maintains that the barrier has prevented attacks inside Israel proper, a contention that has more than circumstantial backing. Suicide attacks within Israel have been sharply reduced, and leaders of Palestinian militant groups have admitted as much in the press. Nevertheless, the wall remains a source of anger and dismay inside the West Bank and Gaza. (Though building has been curtailed, those sections already standing are not likely to come down anytime soon.)

As we passed beyond the walls of Jerusalem, it was easy to forget that Bedouins had roamed the West Bank for thousands of years, quietly—for the most part—tending their flocks and raising their families. They lived a stark and simple existence in the parched hills overlooking the ancient city of Hebron.

As Shaul pointed out as our bus wound its way up a hill, the

Israeli army regularly seizes high ground wherever it chooses in the West Bank, in order to carry out what it would like the world to believe is an innocuous type of military training. When our bus came to a halt below an Israeli military outpost, several soldiers raced down in a jeep from on high to question Shaul's permission to be there. He did not flinch. Fortunately, freedom-of-movement restrictions in the West Bank are harder to enforce against Israelis and Americans than they are against Palestinians.

"This is my training zone," Shaul quipped. "This is where I had my infantry training. One of the things we used to do is just ride over their wheat fields because these are just Bedouins who invaded our training zone!" Shaul assumed an increasingly ironic tone, pointing out how the Israeli forces maintain a relentless and self-justifying grip on the West Bank. "The idea is that soon you will be in training and since you will need to search a village, this is a great way to gain the experience." As he spoke, his skullcap flipped up in the wind, still attached to a bobby pin.

Shaul and a few other Israeli soldiers founded their organization, Breaking the Silence, with seed money from the lump sum they received upon leaving the army in 2004. The group, which would eventually publish a groundbreaking and stunning report on alleged Israeli war crimes and human rights violations during the 2009 assault on Gaza, began its work by assembling a startling series of photographs taken by soldiers in the field. These snapshots displayed graffiti reading, among other things, "Arabs to the gas chambers." Breaking the Silence's first exhibit sparked righteous outrage in Jerusalem's Jewish community and was later shown at the Israeli Knesset.

As a war correspondent for two decades, I now find the horrors of combat less shocking than the sinister machinations that ethnic groups everywhere use to justify their oppression of their fellow humans. I was particularly surprised in my time out with Shaul by the heavy-handed efforts employed by Israeli authorities to further their national claims on territory that the international community has long since agreed is not theirs.

After our brief run-in with the army, we drove down the hillside to a Bedouin encampment, where a row of plastic and burlap tents stood alongside lines of colorful clothes flapping in the wind. A mere thirteen families, out of a total of one hundred fifty families (including a thousand persons) who lived in Soucia in the 1990s, remained after their run-in with man-made Darwinian hardships.

The first official evictions of Bedouins from Soucia by the Israeli army began in the middle of the night in 1997. More evictions began in 1999, according to Shaul and Jewish lawyers for the Palestinian shepherds. Families were uprooted from their homes and they were forced down the road. Each time the Bedouins protested, but each time the number that dared return to their familial caves dwindled. In order to be allowed legally to roam in the hills above Hebron, the Palestinian shepherds are required to maintain "steady domiciles," insisted Shaul. As Bedouins, however, the Palestinians of Soucia traditionally move from one cave or tent to another cave or tent, tending their flocks. Therefore, they do not qualify under Israeli law as official residents.

"According to the agricultural seasons, they move," said Shaul. "So the state stood up in front of the court and said, 'Look! They are not permanent inhabitants here since they live here only six months of the year!'"

I was trying to keep in mind the fact that this same parcel of land, known as Soucia, would in theory become part of a future Palestinian state. The idea of a planned and US-sponsored statehood for these folks did not fit with the Israeli usurpation of land that was being described to me. It must have sounded even more ridiculous to the residents themselves.

In 2001, when hundreds of Jewish settlers had moved, alongside the Israeli army, into the highest hills above the caves of Soucia, clashes broke out between Palestinians and Jews. In the melee that ensued, an Israeli settler was murdered and the Israeli army moved in to "evacuate" the Palestinians.

"That was the turning point," said Shaul. "The next day the IDF

[Israeli Defense Forces] came here and conducted a very, very brutal evacuation." In order to make the evacuation more permanent, bands of Jewish settlers were unleashed on the Palestinians. At this point, Shaul popped open a laptop and showed me videotapes of several similar evacuations. (Though the settlers were not officially attached to the security forces, in one of these videos, angry, armed settlers could be seen racing down a hill with an extremist rabbi. The Israeli police did not appear to be in any position to restrain the settlers, one of whom slapped a Palestinian woman as another pointed a machine gun at her.)

In 2001, after the murder of a settler, about a thousand trees were uprooted in the Bedouin camps at Soucia and the tents were ripped down. Sheep sheds were demolished with the sheep still inside them, Shaul said. Israeli human rights lawyers intervened and forced the court to concede that the few remaining Palestinians actually resided on "private property" that belonged to them. A week later, the Israeli army returned and uprooted the Bedouins. This time, the Israeli government argued that—since the Palestinians had no building permits for their tents—they could not stay on. Like nearly 60 percent of the total land space of the West Bank, the Soucia caves—bulldozed and burned out by the settlers—fell under "Area C," a designation under which all legal permits, particularly building permits, are at the discretion of the Israeli government. As Shaul noted, the notion of "discretion" is a farce, because "no Palestinian receives a building permit." Indeed, along with highways criss-crossing the West Bank that are designated for Israeli settlers and IDF vehicles only, it becomes clear that even the Jim Crow laws against blacks in the Southern states, laws that lasted until the mid-twentieth century, did not approach the level of ethnic segregation sanctioned today in Israel.

Such operations as the ongoing intimidation and forced evacuations in and around the hills of Hebron are indicative of the slow-burning land war that is being fought daily in many parts of the West Bank. Every day brings with it new winners and losers. Deaths are usually kept to a minimum, and so stories of ongoing Israeli government–backed intimidation rarely make the news in the United States.

Almost as an afterthought, Shaul pointed down the hill to an "Israeli national park," in which people, under Israeli law, are officially forbidden to live. A modern Israeli subdivision was now under construction there. He chuckled knowingly.

Israeli forces seized the West Bank in 1967 and since the territory had never been part of a modern nation-state, its status continues to be disputed. However, international courts as well as the United Nations (UN) have held that the territory should fall within the official domain of a future state of Palestine. To that end, Europe, the United States, Russia, and the UN have all listed the lands of the West Bank as part of the future Palestinian state in the so-called road map for peace. That same peace proposal makes it incumbent on Palestinians to end all attacks on Israel and incumbent on Israelis to end their settlement and to dismantle the settlements that have been built in the West Bank and Gaza. Israel, while surrendering several settlements in Gaza during the rule of Ariel Sharon, has argued that its presence in the West Bank is justified because its eastern border is not officially defined and because what it refers to as the "disputed territories" have not been part of any state since the time of the Ottoman Empire. Prior to World War I, the area now referred to as the West Bank (since it sits on the west side of the river Jordan) was considered part of the province of Syria. Over two million Palestinians and nearly half a million Israelis now live in what is considered to be the West Bank, including the estimated two hundred thousand Israelis living in Israeli-annexed East Jerusalem.

✳✳✳

As in the former Yugoslavia, where I covered ethno-religious strife and the relations between freelance militias and the government, the symbiotic relationship between Palestinian government officials and several terrorist groups as well as the relationship between the Israeli government and militant settlers is deep and complicated. In the case of the Palestinians, Yasir Arafat's PLO's ties to the al-Aqsa Brigade and Islamic Jihad are well documented, as is the Hamas government's ties to suicide bomb squads. Indeed, in the case of Hamas, the group's leaders have boasted openly of their involvement in successful suicide attacks on Israeli civilians inside Israel, prompting Washington to condemn the group as a "terrorist organization."

Far less well known to the world, however, are the intimate ties that the Israeli Defense Forces and the Israeli government have historically maintained with illegal Jewish settlers inside the West Bank. In their detailed book, *Lords of the Land: The War over Israel's Settlements in the Occupied Territories, 1967–2007,* Idith Zertel and Akiva Eldar provide useful background on the origins of the relationship between the Israeli settlers and the government that has permitted the settlers to remain on occupied land for over thirty-five years.[3]

Zertel and Eldar trace the origins of this relationship back to 1936–39 and the security doctrine of Yigal Allon, the commander of the Palmach, the unofficial army of the Jewish community during the period of the British Mandate in Palestine. They note Allon's argument that "the integration of civilian settlement in the defense plan, especially for outlying locales and the vulnerable regions, will provide the state with permanent advance lookouts that save mobilized manpower and are able not only to warn of the start of surprise attack from the enemy side but also to try to stop it."[4] The policy had a name, "stockade and tower."[5] The first use of the idea after the Israelis' 1967 seizure of the West Bank came in 1968 in the region of Hebron, not far from Soucia, when a group of would-be settlers asked an Israeli general, Uzi Narkiss, head of the Central Command, to conduct a religious service and spend the night in Hebron. It was not long before the military rulers recognized the settlers as new, permanent residents. The settlers were given weapons with which to defend themselves, and one small settlement soon became many settlements, almost always situated on the highest ground in the West

Bank and almost always under the surveillance of the military. As Zertel and Eldar suggest, the new sites also "served the army as a training school for developing a special relationship between the state and the illegal settlers."[6] But the Israeli authorities did more than take the settlers under their wing. When General Rehavam Ze'evi was traveling regularly to settlements in the Valley of Jordan, he took up the habit of distributing teddy bears to newborns with the encouraging words, "Be fruitful and multiply, because this land is for your seed."[7]

Zertel and Eldar, both secular-minded Israelis with a particular distaste for the West Bank settlers, designate Ariel Sharon as the true godfather of the larger effort to populate and control the West Bank. They charge Sharon with setting up "scores of settlements in order to thwart any possibility of a viable Palestinian state."[8] In this way, argue Zertel and Eldar, "the man who had compared Arafat to Hitler and the Palestinian Liberation Organization to the Third Reich"[9] burnished his reputation as the nemesis of the Palestinian people.

Ironically, when Sharon feared US disapproval of further settlements in 1977, he suggested settlers be inducted as soldiers, an idea that was firmly rejected by the settlers' leaders, who considered the idea a threat to their rights to the land. Later, during the First Intifada (uprising), Jewish settlers proved useful to the broader Israeli military effort. They were encouraged to shoot their government-supplied weapons "for purposes of deterrence, in every case of stone-throwing."[10] Following the Oslo Peace Accords in September 1995, the Israeli Defense Forces created elite units from among the settler population and assigned them the duty of securing the roads that criss-crossed the West Bank. Militarization took on a deeper meaning when soldiers from the settlements were given detailed training in combating terrorism with the goal of achieving proficiency equivalent to that of fighters in the IDF special forces.[11]

Even as violence burned like a wildfire across the West Bank from March to August 2001, some thirty new outposts were established, all of them with approval from Israel's then defense minister,

Binjamin Ben-Eliezer.[12] *Lords of the Land* makes a cogent argument that every new road for the settlers that is paved and every new mobile home that is set atop a hill in the West Bank is carried out with the approval of the Israeli government and with the use of state funds. The authors designate the settlement movement as a kind of "Freudian 'unheimlich' that emerges from time to time from the depths of its [Israeli society's] subconscious to reveal its own dark side and irrationality."[13]

For the settlers themselves, however, the struggle for land has a deeper meaning, maybe best expressed by Settler Council member Yehoshua Mor-Yosef, explaining to a *Ha'aretz* newspaper reporter in 2001 why more and more settlements spring up in the wake of violence: "People almost go out of their minds when settlers are murdered, and the only way to vent the anger and distress is to build an outpost. For us, an outpost is a living memorial, and this is the only language the Arabs understand. They know that we cling to the land no less than they do. This is our best revenge. For every drop of blood, they will pay in land."[14]

My tour of the Hebron hills with Shaul would not have been complete without meeting Mohammed Nawaja, the patriarch of the last clan of shepherds at Soucia. He greeted us as he strolled up a rocky outcrop into his camp, where a pair of his grandsons played on a bicycle. The elderly shepherd sat down with us and offered us tea. Through a translator, he explained that his clan had been trying to obtain building permits for its tents from the Israeli government, but to no avail.

He pointed across a partially destroyed olive grove toward another large hill. "Little by little, the settlers have taken more and more of our land," he said. Earlier we had been shown a well into which Shaul said an Israeli bulldozer had stuffed a crushed and compacted car, which rusted and spoiled the water. Mohammed mentioned that a family member had had his skull cracked open six months earlier by a group of rampaging settlers. It was death by slow suffocation.

"I've heard of this man Obama," he continued, gesticulating and smiling as he spoke. "I believe he is surrounded by Jewish advisers, so what are we to expect? We are fed up with all governments—even the Palestinian authorities—because they have done nothing for us. We don't want to receive handouts and remain under occupation."

President Obama, upon taking office, took what has been called a politically risky step in denouncing the continued building of Israeli settlements in the West Bank. But was this politically risky or simply a reasonable and humane approach to making peace? When Jimmy Carter dared to use the term "apartheid" to highlight the plight of the Palestinians, Jewish groups in America demanded an apology and attempted to organize a boycott of Carter's speaking engagements. I recalled what young Shaul had said of his own work. "If I am not active against injustice, I'll be a part of it," he said aboard the bus. "Being silent is saying I know this is happening, but I prefer to have my big latte in Starbucks instead." This description could equally be applied to people in the United States who remain willfully or unwittingly blind to what their tax dollars are supporting. It could equally be applied to those who remain ignorant of what is happening in Darfur, Tibet, and Western New Guinea.

President Obama's sympathy for the underdog is well known. Even before his election to office, he stated in public that "no one is suffering more than the Palestinian people."[15] Later, in his Cairo speech, he pointed out that America's bond with Israel is "unbreakable" and "based upon cultural and historical ties, and the recognition that the aspiration for a Jewish homeland is rooted in a tragic history that cannot be denied."[16] There is no contradiction in the fact that Obama acknowledged the injustices perpetrated against Palestinians and the need to halt settlements while recognizing the horror of the Holocaust. In Cairo, he also said of the Palestinians that "for more than sixty years they have endured the pain of dislocation. Many wait in refugee camps in the West Bank, Gaza, and neighboring lands for a life of peace and security that they have never been able to lead. They endure the daily humiliations—large and small—that come with occupation. So let there be no doubt: the situation for the Palestinian people is intolerable. America will not turn our backs on the legitimate Palestinian aspiration for dignity, opportunity, and a state of their own."[17]

These are stirring words. Since Israel's founding, however, the United States has done little to actually improve the plight of the Palestinian people. In Jerusalem I met with Jeff Halper, a Jewish American anthropologist from Minnesota and an Israeli citizen, who heads a group fighting the Israeli Defense Forces' demolition of Palestinian homes. His group estimates that some twenty-five thousand Palestinian homes have been demolished in the West Bank, East Jerusalem, and Gaza since 1967. The Israeli army has said that the destroyed Palestinian homes belong to "terrorists." Indeed, the Israeli policy of bulldozing the homes of suspected terrorists and their families was imitated by the US Army in Iraq (to the great consternation of the Iraqis) for a time, early in the American occupation of that country. Halper contends, however, that most of the destruction—as in the case of the Soucia Bedouin caves—has been perpetrated with the intention of paving the way for new Jewish settlements.

Halper is a soft-spoken academic with a Santa Claus beard and a passion for his work. Though it might be best to refer to him as a realist, he remains a pessimist with regard to the likelihood of Israel's surrendering the West Bank anytime soon. He analyzes Israel's current activities in the West Bank down to the last detail. As a dual Israeli and American citizen, however, he also expresses concern about how those activities make the United States look in the eyes of the people of the broader Islamic realm. In other words, if the Israeli army is helping to perpetrate systematic violence against the inhabitants of the West Bank and the Israeli army is a close ally of the US military, America's reputation continues to be sullied by Israel's actions, he contends. The logic is inescapable.

Halper explained that one of his broader goals—in the effort to prevent the demolition of homes in the West Bank—is to highlight the significance of engaging in a sincere peace effort in Israel. He pointed out—I thought convincingly—that there was and is little alternative to a two-state deal, if for no other reason than to keep the two embittered peoples apart until they can come to terms with the need to live together.

"The Obama administration has entered into an entirely different international reality," he told me, lightly stroking his beard. "The world is much more multipolar than it was eight years ago. You have to reconcile with the Muslim world somehow. Even on a practical basis of getting out of Iraq and Afghanistan and dealing with Iran, you have got to do that. I believe that this Israeli-Palestinian conflict is a global conflict; emblematic in the Muslim world, and that this is not simply a localized conflict. The Israeli occupation is seen as an American one. It is clear that Israel could not sustain this without American support."

As an American and as an Israeli, Halper contended, he was drawn to examine the peace process from the standpoint of both American and Israeli national security. His view was that getting it right with the Islamic world is not a form of appeasement, as his critics would contend, but rather a sensible approach to security.

Those of us who want the United States to stand for human rights and maintain credibility when talking about our own ideals have little choice but to frown upon and, indeed, oppose oppression wherever it exists. This is not dissimilar to the defense of free speech. If we support restriction anywhere, it undermines our ideals and our credibility. In a newly globalized world, oppression anywhere stands out like a sore thumb, whether it be in Cuba, Guantanamo Bay, China, or Israel.

There is no right or wrong party in the Israel and Palestine crisis, but there are discrepancies in human rights, land distribution, and living conditions that would be corrected in a US-backed two-state solution. Some would be left to mend themselves on their own. Even today, however, Palestinians reside on what amounts to less than one-fifth of the entire land space in the current state of Israel. Since the Oslo Peace Accords, Palestinian lands have been further sliced and diced into some seventy noncontiguous "islands" cordoned off by walls and barbed wire. New, mobile Israeli checkpoints have been set up between these islands, not between Israel and the West Bank. What is worse, while Israel claims it faces violence from terrorists in Palestine—a legitimate and verifiable fact—its own settlers are armed to the teeth. In violent standoffs between Jewish settlers and Palestinians, the Jewish settlers have the upper hand, often wielding machine guns against sticks and stones. While forty-five Palestinians were killed by Israeli civilians between September 29, 2000, and December 26, 2008, compared to 237 Israelis killed by Palestinian civilians in the same period, the real violence is perpetrated by the Israeli security forces. In the same period (from September 29, 2000, to December 26, 2008) 4,791 Palestinians were killed in the West Bank and Gaza, compared to 245 Israeli security personnel killed in the two areas.[18] The only real game changer in the land struggle, which has served more to isolate the violence than to end it, has been the ugly concrete barrier that snakes along between Israel and the occupied territories, often dipping into these areas. Although attacks by suicide bombers in buses and other civilian environments have waned since the wall was erected, some Palestinian militant groups continue to launch rockets into Israel.

After meeting Shaul, I traveled to Ramallah, the paltry and inadequate "capital" of the West Bank, and met, among others, Dylan Smith, a young American lawyer who works pro bono for human rights in an effort to defend young Palestinians who are brought before Israeli courts. He explained that he was defending "kids thrown in jail for two years for throwing rocks at the wall—not even at Israeli soldiers." When you rule by the gun, there is no need for legal justice, as the young lawyer discovered every time he argued a case. "You go into court, and you've got five minutes before the judge," he said, detailing his own failed defense of scores of Palestinian detainees. Also in Ramallah, one of Palestine's top negotiators, Saeb Erakat, was making himself available to warn anyone who would listen that if Washington fails to actively goad Israelis and

Palestinians into making peace within a few years, disaster is sure to ensue. He put it starkly, openly expressing his worries as a father that his own son might wake up one day and decide to become a suicide bomber.

Erakat, a heavy-set, bespectacled, and feisty Palestinian intellectual, who has sought by the use of his own powerful rhetorical tools to goad US administrations into action for several decades, was in his element when we met. "And today, if the United States wants to involve itself in this peace process, they are not doing me a favor," he said, tapping his fingers on a conference table. "They are doing themselves the favor. They know that they cannot salvage Afghanistan and Iraq without a solution to the problem here. They know it, so it is the national interest of the United States to pursue peace between the Palestinians and Israelis. We don't intend to disappear. We are here to stay—so I dare American leaders to close their eyes and to walk me through the year 2025." Like a lot of other former Arafat allies, Erakat understood that support for a "moderate" Palestinian option was slipping. He also knew that Hamas had stolen the liberation struggle out from under his feet in recent years. Erakat's concerns are no exaggeration in a part of the world where hundreds of thousands of Palestinians are continually squeezed tighter and tighter into valleys and hilltops surrounded by cement and barbed wire.

While staying in Ramallah, just prior to the launching of Israel's December surprise in the Gaza Strip, I visited a Palestinian village a few miles down the road. It was one of several dozen villages that surround the capital of the West Bank, but to approach it, one has to drive through a checkpoint and around the back of an Israeli settlement strategically placed above Ramallah. As the sun spread an orange hue over the rocky, white hills and a muezzin called for prayer in the distance, I walked up a hill past several young boys playing in a paved alleyway. An old, nearly broken-down station wagon pulled a skinny horse in its wake. At the top of the hill, I found an older teenager—a plump young man with a slight goatee, maybe twenty years of age. He was a Palestinian American from New Orleans, who had moved back to the West Bank after Hurricane Katrina. His village was in what had traditionally been a stronghold of Yasir Arafat, the Palestinian Authority leader, but it had already begun to turn toward the militancy of the strongest Palestinian faction, Hamas.

The heavy-set young man spoke in broken English edged with anger. He told me—on camera—that he had given up on the idea of a negotiated peace with the Israelis. Talks had gone on too long in his mind. He told me he had reached his limit. "The only thing that can get us the right thing—what we need—is the war," he said. "To restart the war. Intifada again, bad Intifada. Bombs and all kinds of shit!"

I asked him if he thought that would really ever achieve anything.

"Well, if we stay here sitting down and waiting for them to give us our land back, we are never gonna make it."

These are not merely the sentiments of an angry, testosterone-charged Palestinian male. They are felt by a broader section of Palestinian youth than ever, and, as it happens, they are the sentiments of a young man who had lived for years in the United States. In a discussion I had several days later with Amirah, a Palestinian student who headed the Palestinian Students Organization at the American University in Cairo, I heard a similar sentiment. Amirah had recently fled the economic siege and humiliation of Gaza. "The reason that the Palestinian people in Gaza are suffering is because of the Israeli occupation," she told me. "So, yeah, why not Hamas? Why not the radical side? Why not the gun?" To hear a lovely young lady say those words was just a little bit heartbreaking.

✷✷✷

War is not a logical choice. It never is. During the Israeli Operation Cast Lead, carried out in Gaza before Obama's inauguration, Israeli forces destroyed 4,247 houses, according to a United Nations spokesperson. As a result of this operation, the attacks on Israel were temporarily stemmed, but at what price?

Just weeks before the operation, it was clear that Gaza, abandoned by Israeli security forces and settlers in 2005, was a target. It was not clear, however, what any attack on the small strip of land would actually accomplish. Hamas militants were already using the population both as their breeding ground and as a launching pad for their own attacks, which, while regular and sinister in intent, took only a limited toll due to the inaccuracy of their rockets (though the Israelis didn't look kindly at even errant rockets launched into their midst). Hamas was in charge of everything in Gaza, including the hiring of young men to carry out simple security tasks like traffic control and law enforcement with regard to petty crime.

The well-informed former deputy Israeli defense minister, Ephraim Sneh, explained Israel's plans for Hamas to me in advance of the operation as follows: "All of them will be dead," he said of the senior Hamas leaders. "They will not be alive on the day when we leave Gaza. All of them will be dead."

As a war correspondent, I knew that the chances that Sneh's bold prediction would be proved right—that they would all "be dead"— were nil. He sounded a lot like the Washington neocons who blithely predicted a quick victory after the 2003 invasion of Iraq. "This is unavoidable!" Sneh said, banging his fist on a table in the Marriott Hotel in East Jerusalem. "We will have to destroy the military force of Hamas in Gaza. We can do it only if we know how to get out, though. We can go out only if we have someone to hand the keys of Gaza to when the military job is done. The only one who can receive from us the key to Gaza is the secular [Fatah] government in Ramallah."

That was the theory. Unfortunately for the plan, the government in Ramallah had been dysfunctional for years, thanks to massive corruption and the lack of an equitable peace deal—and Sneh and his cronies knew that. (Analysts like Eldar believed that Hamas was essentially a Frankenstein created by Israeli policy and a lack of US initiative during the Bush years.)

The state of the Ramallah government didn't deter the Israeli hawks. At 11:15 on a Saturday morning, American-made F-16s screeched across the skies, dropping their bombs from ten miles high. Hamas, which won the US-backed 2005 elections and subsequently prevailed in street fights for the dominance of Gaza against its rival, Fatah, was caught with its pants down. The group's police chief was passing out awards to some eighty new police officers, who had been designated as traffic cops. Along with bombing a TV station and Hamas's Islamic University, the bombers blasted away at the ceremony, annihilating the young policemen almost instantly. It was the heaviest bombing since 1967, and the television pictures were, according to an old friend of mine, the BBC's Paul Wood, "too graphic and horrific to broadcast." They showed—among other images—a dead child on an operating table. Doctors at the main hospital in Gaza estimated that a third of the dead were civilians.

The result of Israel's extended aerial bombardment of Gaza and the brief ground assault would prove to be disastrous for the Israeli army. More than fourteen hundred Palestinians, including at least nine hundred civilians, were killed in the fighting, thousands of homes were destroyed, and Gaza's infrastructure was battered, according to Gaza health officials and human rights groups. International rights groups, including Human Rights Watch and Amnesty International, condemned the use of disproportionate force and the heavy civilian death toll. Earlier, the same human rights groups had accused Hamas of similarly blatant violations of the Geneva Conventions for firing rockets at civilian areas in Israel. United Nations investigators later charged both the Israelis and Palestinians with human rights violations in Gaza.

Still, the more graphic details of how the war was fought did not emerge for months. In a July 15, 2009, report on the actions of the Israeli army, Yehuda Shaul's group, Breaking the Silence, spoke with dozens of Israeli soldiers in order to find out what had really gone on in an operation that remained—to all intents and purposes—off limits to the international press corps. Israeli soldiers told Shaul's documentarians that they had accidentally killed unarmed Gazans as they were led into what the soldiers described as a "moral Twilight Zone," in which almost every Palestinian they spotted was assumed to be a threat.[19] (The stories were eerily similar to stories of what US forces had faced on their first blundering forays into Fallujah.) As early as July 15, the day the report was released, Israeli officials fired back with a rebuttal, insisting that the accounts had been provided anonymously and would be impossible to verify. In truth, the accounts had been given by Israeli soldiers who preferred, given the society they lived in, to remain unnamed. Speaking to McClatchy Newspapers, Shaul said the report didn't identify the soldiers by name because at least half the men quoted were young conscripts who could be jailed for speaking out. It is noteworthy that these same soldiers would probably not have confided the same information to the media as they did to their own former colleagues in arms. The work that Shaul's group had done was groundbreaking and stunning in its scope.

Earlier, news organizations like the BBC had spent hours gathering testimony from Palestinians who had witnessed the Israeli incursions. Details in the Breaking the Silence stories from soldiers dovetailed with much of the Palestinian testimony provided to independent news outlets. In one case, standing by the ruins of his home in Gaza, Majdi Abed Rabbo told the BBC how Israeli troops had used him as a human shield. "The Israeli soldiers handcuffed me and pointed the gun at my neck," he said. "They controlled every step." In this manner, Majdi Abed Rabbo said, he was forced to go into houses ahead of Israeli soldiers as they cleared houses containing Palestinian gunmen. The incident was also described by one of the Israeli soldiers who spoke to Breaking the Silence. "A Palestinian neighbor is brought in," he said. "It was a procedure. The soldier places his gun barrel on the civilian's shoulder."[20]

Such use of a civilian in an infantry maneuver tactic is a glaring breach of international and Israeli law. These tactics—once a common IDF approach to guerrilla war—were examined by Israel's

Supreme Court in 2005 and outlawed at that time. And the specifics of the Breaking the Silence reports could not be dismissed as "Palestinian propaganda," since they did not come from Palestinians. "Sometimes a force would enter while placing rifle barrels on a civilian's shoulder, advancing into a house and using him as a human shield," said one Israeli soldier with the Golani Brigade. "Commanders said these were the instructions, and we had to do it."[21]

Soldiers described incidents in which Israeli forces killed an unarmed Palestinian carrying a white cloth, an elderly woman carrying a sack, a Gazan riding a motorcycle, and an elderly man with a flashlight.

One soldier recounted that "the minute we got to our starting line, we simply began to fire at suspect places. You see a house, a window, shoot at the window. You don't see a terrorist there? Fire at the window. In urban warfare, anyone is your enemy. No innocents."[22]

In the case of Majdi Abed Rabbo, the man the BBC had found standing alongside the ruins, the Israeli military police had already opened an investigation, lending more credibility to the soldier who said the policy of using neighbors was part of a broader strategy. At the same time, Israeli officials contended that they went to extraordinary lengths to ensure civilians were not harmed in Gaza.

Both before and after the Israeli assault on Gaza, Hamas had training schools operating there, churning out suicide bombers. Prior to the Israeli attacks, my colleague, Wood, visited an Islamic Jihad underground locale engaged in just this activity. He interviewed and filmed a young woman preparing to die as her husband fastened a "martyr's" headband to her veiled brow. Beside her on a table lay her suicide vest, a pair of knickers rigged with explosives. The eighteen-year-old Umm Anas had nervously twisted her wedding ring as she spoke to Wood: "We were created to become martyrs for God," she said, her eyes burning with desire. "All the Palestinian people were created to fight in God's name. If we just throw stones at the Jews they get scared. Imagine what happens when body parts fly at them."[23]

But after the Israeli assault, Hamas and its affiliates in Gaza continued to openly promote and teach the usefulness and even necessity of suicide attacks.[24] For every traffic cop killed in the aerial assaults, several residents would now hear and possibly heed the fresh calls to martyrdom. Unfortunately for the Israelis, their state's military actions appeared only to have ensured Hamas a larger and stronger pool of suicide bombers to cultivate.

In an asterisk to the nitty-gritty work of documenting war crimes that Breaking the Silence has already performed, the UN's special investigator and South African judge, Richard Goldstone, dropped his own "bombshell" in September 2009. His UN report charged that Israel had "deliberately targeted civilians" and engaged in killing, torture, and inhumane acts during its military assault on Gaza. It charged Hamas with war crimes as well.

Mike Oren, Israel's ambassador to Washington, responded to the PBS's *News Hour* with the argument that Israel had not participated in the inquiry because it had been carried out in Gaza under the auspices and under the eyes of the Hamas government.[25] (To be fair, it would have been difficult for the UN to skirt the Hamas authorities.) Oren compared the investigation to being summoned to a court in which guilt is already presumed. He said Israel's own judiciary was that of a "democratic country." He added that the US government would—of course—not like to see similar reports on its own military conduct in Afghanistan.

In my view, Oren cited the wrong war. American attacks in Afghanistan, though they sometimes go awry and involve illegal actions (which have included clear cases of prison abuse), are almost always carried out with the intention of protecting and defending Afghanistan's national security, civilians, and sovereignty. On the other hand, the conduct of the US military during the illegal conquest and occupation of Iraq would—in some cases—have risen to the level of the variety of war crimes, of which Israel is accused (see chapter 3). In any case, the issue of war crimes is, to all intents and purposes, a moot point. As surely as the US military will not be standing trial anytime soon for war crimes, Israeli officials have little or nothing to fear from such accusations either, apart from the international condemnation they have already received. It is clearly, in this case, the words that hurt the most. It is worth pointing out that the Israeli veterans group Breaking the Silence, which did the most thorough documentation, did not rely on the Goldstone Report or on Hamas for any of its conclusions.

The conflict in Israel and Palestine cannot be isolated from America's counterterrorism efforts across the Islamic world; nor can it be seen as unrelated to America's efforts to calm tensions there. It bleeds outward in a number of ways, not the least of which is the string of refugee camps that pockmark the region with desperate young Muslims, most of whom feel angry toward the international community. Official United Nations statistics put the number of displaced Palestinians from the 1949–1950 conflict at seven hundred eleven thousand. A second major displacement occurred in June 1967, during the Six-Day War, when some three hundred thousand Palestinians fled the West Bank and the Golan Heights areas, many of them becoming refugees for a second time. If the international community had to worry about only one million Palestinians, it would be easier to solve the problem of their resettlement. Today, the United Nations Relief and Works Agency (UNRWA) cares for 4.62 million Palestinians, however.[26]

According to UNRWA's definition, nearly half of the total number of Palestinians in the world were refugees in the 1990s. The largest concentration of refugees was and continues to be in Jordan (three million), with over 1.5 million residing in the occupied West Bank and Gaza. More than four hundred thousand live in Syria, and another four hundred thousand live in Lebanon. Initially most refugees lived in camps established by the United Nations, but by the turn of the millennium some 2.7 million lived elsewhere, receiving various degrees of assistance from the United Nations.

Palestinian negotiators have insisted over the years that Palestinian refugees who do not live in Israel or the occupied territories should be allowed to return to their original homes. But this is seen by outside analysts as a bargaining position, which will remain in play until a peace deal is struck. An independent peace proposal by the Arab League, a body of mostly authoritarian Arab states, leaves aside the issue of the "right of return," in order to help promote the concept of a two-state solution. Until a deal is struck, however, members of the younger generation of Palestinians will remain political pawns in the stalled process. (Demographically, a Palestinian return to original homes, many inside Israel proper, would spell disaster for Israel's unique status, which arose out of the backing by US and European countries for the creation of an independent homeland for all Jews after the annihilation of six million Jews during the Holocaust.) Nevertheless, for now, the resettlement of Palestinians in a new Palestinian state or outside, preferably in developed Western countries where they might take advantage of educational opportunities, remains a pipe dream. If Palestinians aren't locked into the nightmarish living conditions of the occupied territories, they remain at the beck and call of militant groups that have no long-term interest in their resettlement.

Gaza, in and of itself, contains some 1.5 million Palestinians, who, according to the UN's special representative and former senior Irish military officer John Ging, are in dire need of humanitarian assistance. Ging, who served in Rwanda and Bosnia when genocide was being perpetrated there, says that violence, killing, and indoctrination have had a devastating impact on the minds of young Palestinians. He calls the policies aimed at the residents of Gaza "collective punishment" and warns that the world is running out of time if it intends to right the situation.[27]

Likewise, during a recent visit to Beirut's Shatila Camp, I discovered a wasteland of talented young Palestinians, many of whom had been moved around like pawns from one camp to another for years. Lebanese landlords were pressuring the residents to leave the camp, founded in 1949, even though under Lebanese law, these same residents are not permitted to work in most of the nation's well-paid professions. Young boys threw stones at one another and played hide-and-seek in empty oil drums.

The cramped and appalling conditions compared poorly even to the notorious slums of Cairo, where I've spent far more time. Some twelve thousand persons were crammed into the Shatila camp, whose dingy, wind-blown structures ran so close together in some alleys as to permit only a skinny man to pass between them. Sanitation was nearly nonexistent, and electric wires twisted helter-skelter from windows and through doorways. Everywhere the walls were pock-marked with bullet holes and shell explosions. Artists had painted pictures of "martyrs" killed by an Israeli aerial assault on the neighborhood in 2006.

Inside a hot and muggy classroom at the Shatila camp, visited in late 2008 before my trip to Israel and Palestine, my flirtation with "Obama-mania" in the Middle East came to a screeching halt. "We will not accept a two-state solution," said a seventeen-year-old in braces, standing beneath a poster of Fatah's deceased leader, Yasir Arafat. "We've been fighting since 1965, and they came from Russia, Ethiopia, Canada, I don't know where. They are killing even the boys who throw stones. This is racism. We need a solution, but the Israelis are unwilling, so we don't accept them to live on our land anymore."

This angry youngster held out no hope for a change in his own circumstances. He was particularly distressed that Barack Obama had made the glaring error of telling the powerful American Israel Public Affairs Committee (AIPAC) in June 2008 that "Jerusalem will remain the capital of Israel, and it must remain undivided." Although Obama's handlers had quickly corrected him at the time, suggesting that the final status of the Holy City was still under negotiation, the quote was still a burning point of contention for Palestinians in Shatila. "How can we believe in him when the first thing he says is that Jerusalem must be the undivided capital of Israel?" said the young Fatah supporter. Under most peace deals on the table today, Jerusalem would be divided and "internationalized." It was unclear how Obama could have made such a glaring error in such an important speech. Disenfranchised Palestinians saw it as less of an error and more of a Freudian slip.

Ironically, Palestinian youth locked in refugee camps outside Israel are—in many cases—as secular minded as, or even more so than, Palestinians who suffer occupation, virtually imprisoned in the West Bank or Gaza. Those in the refugee camps have more exposure to the rapid changes—particularly in fashions and global trends—taking place outside the West Bank. On this visit, I was particularly struck by two young women, Yazmeena El Khoudary, sixteen, and her older sister Layal, seventeen, both of whom recalled for me long nights spent in underground bomb shelters during the Israeli air raids of 2006. These youngsters had been raised by their loving father after their mother died of cancer at a young age.

Layal had just passed Lebanon's rigorous college entrance exam, but now her higher education aspirations came face to face with all the limits imposed by the national government. Layal's sister, Yazmeena, was a gifted artist and an aspiring news reporter. Already, though, she had been reprimanded at the UN-run camp for being "too political," particularly for calling both Hizbollah and Hamas "too moderate" for her liking.

Although they could turn out one day to be suicide bombers, neither young woman struck me as dangerous. Both were strikingly lovely and attired in blue jeans, blouses, and black-and-white plaid kaffiyehs. Neither wore anything approaching a veil. But they were worried about the future. "They only give the good ones scholarships," said Yazmeena, lowering her gaze. Yazmeena and her sister walked me out of the camp, and we passed several young boys playing with plastic guns, a common sight anywhere in the world, but one with far more dangerous potential consequences when considered against a backdrop of poverty and oppression.

From Beirut I drove north to Damascus, for an interview with Hamas's cofounder and political chief, Khalid Meshal. Syria remains a key to the peace puzzle in Israel for several reasons, not the least of which is due to Iran's overriding interests and influence. Israel also occupies the Golan Heights, legally part of Syria and constituting a strategic position that helps the Israeli army overlook southern Lebanon, where Hizbollah controls the countryside.

I had traveled to Syria on several occasions, but this time I took the time to wander through Damascus's back streets and discover the ancient layers of a five-thousand-year-old city, which projects a timeless, diverse atmosphere, not unlike that of Jerusalem. Some of the oldest churches on Earth are to be found here, and the artwork in them is equally impressive. All the splendid curves and spirals of the Arab world's ancient architecture are in evidence across Damascus, with its ancient hamams (Turkish baths), its Roman ruins, and its Ottoman archways that line the alleys and walls of the old city. The marketplace is rich with a wonderful and infectious vibrancy not found in most Western cities. Bright-eyed shop owners leap up to help an inquisitive foreigner and shoe-shiners swipe at your toes as artisans tap out silver filigree designs. At a crossroads, a boisterous young man in a red fez and a colorful vest serves up water to thirsty passersby from a long metal pitcher, his belt lined with rows of metal cups. Some women hide behind dark, black abayas, but most female fashions are as classy and sophisticated as anything in the Middle East; modest but seductive in their own way.

Syria is an anomaly in many respects—even within an authoritarian Arab world. The country is run by the secular Baath Party (which once had strong connections with Saddam Hussein's Baathists), but more specifically by the Assad family, currently led by the tall, earnest, and authoritarian President Bashir al-Assad. The al-Assad family, from the Alawite-Shiite grouping, holds together a volatile mix of religious and ethnic groups beneath the umbrella of a largely secular—and often brutal—dictatorship.

Hardly a radical haven in the 1980s or 1990s, particularly in comparison with its neighbors, Syria became a center of growing anti-American sentiment in the months before the most recent invasion of Iraq. Jihadist groups from across the region congregated there with the help of lax immigration regulations. They soon discovered that the desert roads from Damascus into Iraq were highly accessible. I had spent three weeks in Damascus just prior to the 2003 invasion of Iraq, talking to human rights activists, actors, and news editors about the coming invasion as well as the hope for a regional peace accord that would "liberate" Syria's embattled economy. It was hard to find a Syrian who was overtly anti-American, but nearly everyone I spoke to was vociferously opposed to the Bush administration's decision to invade Iraq. "We knew and understood his father," Fouad Mardoud, the editor of the *Syria Times*, told me. "The father had constructive ideas, and we appreciated the work James Baker did in forming the coalition against Iraq's invasion of Kuwait and talking about a road map for peace."[28] All that had been lost, however, insisted Mardoud. I was swept up in a massive but peaceful antiwar demonstration involving some one hundred thousand Damascenes a few days later, but my stay ended abruptly after I was arrested by the Mukhabarat (or secret police) while attempting to board a ferry boat into northern Iraq. I was held under house arrest for three days by two cordial members of the secret police, permitted to take walks in a park, and subsequently expelled for an earlier attempted "illegal exit."

Damascus is a city with a proud history and a reverence for its favorite sons. At the entrance to the tomb of Saladin, the Islamic warrior of the era of the Crusades, a bronze statue of the helmeted Damascene dominates a broad thoroughfare. At the height of his power, Saladin reigned over Palestine, Egypt, Syria, Mesopotamia, and Yemen. His glorious reign is cherished across much of the Islamic world as a serene and peaceful period. His rival, Richard the Lionheart, paid him a supreme compliment by referring to him as chivalrous. If, as Bernard Lewis says, "Islam is associated in the minds and memories of Muslims with the exercise of political and military power," Saladin embodied this and much more.[29] (Indeed, the fact that Mohammed was as much a political leader in his day as he was a spiritual leader has made it arguably much harder for Muslim societies to accept the separation of mosque and state.) On the foundation of Saladin's modern statue in Damascus, city-dwellers have carved their renewed calls for the "liberation of Jerusalem," the feat for which Saladin, who recaptured Palestine from the Kingdom of Jerusalem, is particularly remembered.

Nevertheless, one must be careful not to confuse Muslim or Damascene nostalgia for a glorious past—including a respect for martial prowess and professionalism—with support for Islamic extremism. For both Sunnis and Shias, Jerusalem's holiest sites, among them the Dome of the Rock and the al-Aqsa Mosque, are revered symbols that even moderates do not want to see surrounded by Jewish or Christian sentinels.

It is little wonder, then, that in Damascus, Saladin's hometown, there is still a place for the "holy warriors," whom most Westerners would not consider to be moderates. These individuals are seen to be striving to return some of Islam's most holy venues to the faithful. Hamas's most powerful leader, Khalid Meshal, lives under the de facto protection of the Syrian government, and his militant organization remains important to Syria and Iran as representing the Arab world's broader efforts to resist the Israeli occupation of Palestine. The political positions upon which Hamas has built its support—including the group's refusal to recognize the state of Israel—are focused on the aspirations shared by a significant percentage of Palestinians and other Muslims. Whether or not one labels Hamas as a "terrorist organization," as does the US government, there is no getting around this political reality. Although the group's founding charter commits the group to the destruction of Israel, in July 2009, Meshal told the *Wall Street Journal* that he was willing to cooperate with the United States in the promotion of a resolution of the Arab-Israeli conflict.[30] While this sounds contradictory, it is no secret that Hamas wants to increase its own political clout as an actor in the peace process.

Since Israel's secret service, Mossad, has not hesitated in the past to go after its enemies in Europe and across the Middle East (most recently in Dubai), any meeting with Meshal takes days to arrange. It occurs at an undisclosed location surrounded by heavy security. After getting a last-minute text message and wending my way through several back alleys, dark corridors, and weapons detectors, I arrived to find that the Hamas leader had already taken a seat in a tearoom whose walls were plastered with images of the Muslim Holy Land. Almost predictably, Meshal, who rarely grants interviews, handed me an inexpensive, gaudy wall hanging of the city of Jerusalem. The keepsake, which I discarded, was another reminder of the importance of that city in Islamic history and in his own group's struggle.

Although Hamas's guerrilla tactics, which have included suicide bombing and targeting of Israeli citizens, are reprehensible, Hamas is not seen as a terrorist organization across much of the broader Islamic world. The points made by Meshal in our interview needed, I believed, to be taken seriously, if for no other reason than the fact that peace remains beyond the scope of possibility today in the Middle East. This is due to the stubborn reluctance of all parties, including Washington, to sit down and discuss positions that otherwise remain set in stone.

While it was the dawning of a new era in Washington, the same could not be said for Damascus. Meshal chuckled at the idea that the Obama administration might take Hamas's positions seriously. He pleaded the hardship of making concessions. "Can you imagine when Israel has taken more than 40 percent of the West Bank, what will be left for a Palestinian state?" Meshal asked rhetorically. "Israel wants to keep her settlements and keep the whole line of the valley of Jordan. So, practically, we are left with almost no land where we can establish the Palestinian state."[31] There was a sense in Meshal's words that, even if he was committed to the destruction of Israel, he didn't believe that this was a feasible approach to the current situation. A handsome and affable George Clooney–like character with a quick smile and a friendly handshake, Meshal also stated, not for the first time, that Hamas is prepared to talk peace with Israel if the West Bank is put back into play. After my interview in July, Meshal clarified that his group was ready to accept a Palestinian state based on the 1967 borders, provided the Palestinian refugees could return and East Jerusalem would be recognized as the Palestinian capital.[32] In the ongoing and circular debate about the recognition of both Israel and Palestine, it is instructive to recall that neither the Palestinian authorities nor the Israeli authorities have shown—to date— through their actions much of a willingness to recognize the other side. On the contrary, they often do their best to destroy one another.

Although the Obama administration, like the Bush administration, appears to want Hamas simply to disappear from the scene, it cannot escape the fact that the group has risen to power in elections that the United States both funded and deemed necessary at the time. Even today, however, the United States and Israel prefer to attempt to manipulate internal Palestinian political differences in order to change the balance of power—largely because of a shared hostility toward Hamas. It is not clear whether this policy is having any impact, but there is evidence to suggest that it has bolstered Hamas's popularity. As the *Washington Post* reported on July 16, 2009, "US and Israeli strategy [toward Hamas] rests on a hope that improving the economy and security in the West Bank will undercut popular support for Hamas and strengthen Palestinian moderates."[33] The way events are moving today, however, that could take decades —decades that no one has.

Washington's almost complete failure to deal with Hamas since its 2005 election victory remains an impediment to any future peace deal. Recognizing that peace is a powerful diplomatic endgame that can pacify and placate enemies is not a weakness as the fearmongering commentators in the United States and Israel would have us believe. It is common sense. The alternative is not just conflict but war on an increasingly global scale. A more legitimate Washington approach to Israel and Palestine would be to push for peace and—at the same time—to attempt to induce further moderation. A two-state peace deal does not mean that Hamas's pool of recruits will evaporate, but it does diminish the likelihood of more young Palestinians taking up arms. A radicalized Hamas will only grow stronger in the absence of peace.

Additionally, and despite our recent ineptness, which included insisting that peace in the Middle East goes through Baghdad, not Jerusalem, a two-state peace deal for Israel and Palestine remains the one straw that can break al Qaeda's proverbial camel's back. It would help to foster peace not just in the Middle East but across the Islamic realm, whose inhabitants represent about 20 percent of the world's population.

For the Obama administration, making peace in Israel and Palestine will require immeasurable courage and political risk taking. The first step, officials decided early on in the president's first term, was to turn off an American green (sometimes yellow) light for settlement construction. After Israel's election of right-wing leader Benjamin Netanyahu, during the new prime minister's first trip to Washington, President Obama told the Israeli leader the bad news. In a news conference he explained this. "And so what I told Prime Minister Netanyahu was that each party has obligations under the road map," he said.[34] "On the Israeli side those obligations include stopping settlements. They include making sure that there is a viable potential Palestinian state."[35]

This simple, direct language came as a shock to Israeli officials, and for weeks they probed for loopholes in what sounded like a categorical statement from President Obama. In late July 2009, Israel's deputy prime minister, Dan Meridor, had the audacity to say that the Obama administration's call to freeze West Bank settlement construction flew in the face of past agreements. "We had an agreement with America," Meridor told a group of foreign correspondents. "The agreement we had with Americans is binding on us and them. … They should keep to the agreement."[36] But even as Meridor spoke about an American betrayal, the building of new Israeli homes in the West Bank was continuing apace.

Clearly, Netanyahu and his closest government advisers believed they could defy the decision and that they were entitled to do so. According to Eldar, an author and columnist for *Ha'aretz*, the liberal Israeli news organ that is also popular in the United States, the attitude stemmed from George W. Bush's ham-handed dealings in the region, which had served to "spoil his father's legacy." When I spoke to Eldar in a seaside resort not far from Tel Aviv, he had nothing but praise for the determination of Bush senior to stand fast, using his leverage against settlement expansion. "Bush senior laid down the law," he insisted. "He said either you stop the settlements or you don't get the money" for assistance in resettling Ethiopian and Eastern European Jews in Israel proper. "Bush [junior] gave Sharon a letter [written by US Ambassador Dan Kurtzer] indicating that he accepted what had taken place on the ground for years, even though these settlements were illegal under official American policy."[37]

Eldar alleged that Kurtzer, a Bush appointee, had made it abundantly clear that Israel should feel at liberty to keep building and expanding its presence in the West Bank. Ambassador Kurtzer expressed approval for the "retention by Israel of major Israeli population centers [in the West Bank] as an outcome of negotiations," Eldar told me.[38] This would explain the Israeli position, that they thought they had a deal. Kurtzer's letter had only further emphasized what President Bush had said a year earlier, that any future peace deal should reflect "demographic realities" on the West Bank.

But Kurtzer fired back in June 2009, writing in the *Washington Post* that a Charles Krauthammer column titled, "The Settlements Myth," published some days earlier, had merely perpetuated Israeli interpretations of a deal he had never made and, thus, one the Israelis had never had. He stressed that the road map for peace was the operative agreement and that it required in no uncertain terms that Israel "immediately dismantles settlement outposts erected since March 2001" and freezes all settlement activity.[39]

In a telling sentence, Kurtzer admitted that when he was the ambassador, "Israel began to act largely in accordance with its own reading of these provisions, probably believing that US silence conferred assent." He added that "Throughout this period, the Bush administration did not regularly protest Israel's continuing settlement activity."[40]

It would not be the first time that the Israelis had taken US silence and lack of condemnation as a green light to continue with policies that exacerbate tensions in the Middle East. Kurtzer, nevertheless, now a professor at Princeton, wanted his reputation back, and he continued in his rebuttal of the charge of his own complicity in the growing problem that "despite Israel's contention that this letter allowed it to continue building in the large settlement blocs of Ariel, Maale Adumim, and Gush Etzion, the letter did not convey any US support for or understanding of Israeli settlement activities in these or other areas in the run-up to a peace agreement."[41]

To his credit, Kurtzer did not hesitate to take on the "nonsense" put forth by Charles Krauthhammer, one of several right-wing commentators in Washington who can never manage to discover anything wrong with Israel's abuses in the West Bank. Krauthammer had written in "The Settlements Myth" that the Obama administration was against the right of Israeli settlers to have babies and charged the administration with the intention to "undermine and destroy these towns [settlements]—even before negotiations."[42] Kurtzer responded: "No one suggests that Israelis stop having babies. Rather, the blessing of a new baby does not translate into a right to build more apartments or houses in settlements. The two issues have nothing to do with each other." He added that "Since 1993, when Israel signed the Oslo [Peace] Accords, Israel's West Bank settler population has grown from 116,300 to 289,600. The numbers in East Jerusalem [have] increased from 152,800 to more than 186,000."[43]

Obama's firmer stance has not yet ushered in a new era of peacemaking between Israel and Palestine. Obama's own secretary of state, Hilary Clinton, set the effort back substantially in October 2009, when she said that Israel had made some "unprecedented concessions" toward freezing new settlements in the West Bank, a statement she quickly explained away to her Arab peers.[44] (To be fair to Clinton, she had made her point on "concessions" in the context of Netanyahu's near complete intransigence on the issue prior to a minor concession in talks with another envoy.)

In Obama's first year in office, his line on settlements has sent a message that has been understood by almost everyone except the people who needed to "get it," namely, Netanyahu and his advisers. "Over the past fifteen years, settlements have gone from being seen in Washington as an irritant, to the dominant issue," Georgetown University Middle East expert Daniel Byman told Washington blogger Laura Rozen, who was with *Foreign Affairs*. Rozen (now with *Politico*), who carefully monitors the nuances of diplomatic change in Washington, noted that Byman also pointed out that key figures in the Obama administration, including Special Envoy George Mitchell and National Security Adviser General Jim Jones, were also firmly behind Obama's decision to draw a line in the sand against more settlement activity.[45]

But has Israel's own broader policy of militarily beating down the Palestinians been discontinued since the Obama administration took office? On July 16, 2009, the *Washington Post* reported that Yuval Diskin, head of Israel's internal security organization, Shin Bet, had said at a closed briefing in May that he thought "Israel would ultimately have to overthrow Hamas in Gaza" in order to move ahead with the peace process.[46] Diskin's words reminded me of my chat with Israel's former defense chief, Ephraim Sneh, who said virtually the same thing before the most recent invasion of Gaza, which took place in December 2007 and January 2008. It is not only Israel's preferred approach, but it is part and parcel of an Israeli strategy that has been—no doubt—well articulated behind the scenes. It is also a strategy that is doomed to fail.

Obama's new push against settlements does not alter the big picture, particularly with Israeli settlers still openly defying Washington's wishes. As Neil MacFarquhar, who covered the region for two decades, contends, "Palestinian self-determination is a legitimate grievance that the US has allowed to infect all manner of other issues by not applying itself to its key role as the designated mediator, the only mediator with the means to knock a few recalcitrant heads together."[47]

Knocking heads together hasn't even been tried of late. Eldar, the *Ha'aretz* columnist, believes that the US government—as a guarantor of Israel's long-term security—has far more leverage to use than it has used to date. He makes no bones about his disgust with the tens of thousands of Jewish settlers who have vowed to fight back if anyone tries to remove them from their "promised land" of Samaria and Judea, the Israeli names for the West Bank. He predicts that President Obama will have to act decisively in order to stop the settlers and their well-placed allies from rudely interrupting progress toward a two-state peace deal. "They will certainly try to undermine any efforts to remove them," he said. "They were traumatized by what happened in Gaza." (Back in the summer of 2005, Ariel Sharon did move several thousand settlers out of that small stretch of land.) "They don't believe their rabbis and leaders, who told them that if they pray strong enough, it will not happen. It happened and they were evacuated—so they will be prepared this time."[48]

Whether we like it or not, US policy toward Israel and Palestine in the past three decades has created an impression in the Islamic world that the United States—through direct military assistance and silent nods of approval for Israel's current policies—is aiding and abetting attacks on Muslims. Polling data across the Islamic world in recent years has given this view further credence.

In a part of the world where perceptions are as important as or even more important than facts on the ground, current US policy makes the United States appear to be subservient to the political interests of another nation. Whether true or not, this is precisely what George Washington warned Americans sternly against in his Farewell Address of 1796, insisting that, instead, it should be America's "true policy to steer clear of permanent alliances with any portion of the foreign world."[49] He understood that choosing one brother over another turns the shunned brother into an enemy.

While Washington insisted that America should remain aloof from foreign entanglements, he also highlighted the benefits of neutrality, noting that "our detached and distant situation invites and enables us to pursue a different course."[50] Some historians would argue that Washington was attempting to promote isolationism in American foreign policy, but "independence" is probably a more accurate word. In this global era, it is America's ability to avoid taking sides that will help it lead by example, promote democratic and universal ideals, and, at the same time, help foster peace. Notably, this does not exclude defending the right of all states to exist.

"The name of the game for the United States in the Middle East is engagement, not disengagement," Eldar told me. "The Israeli people will sacrifice their lives in war with the Arabs, but they won't sacrifice anything to surrender their relationship with the United States. They know that the most important thing is that 'we can trust the Americans,' and if there is a prime minister rocking the boat, he will be punished." By this, Eldar meant, among other things, that the settlements in the West Bank were expendable, not crucial to Israel's continued existence. He and other open-minded Israelis believe that this is the path to peace and reconciliation and that US foreign policy need only follow their lead. Eldar believes that the United States is as valuable to Israel as an honest broker in the Middle East, as the United States is crucial to Israel as a guarantor of military might.

The seasoned columnist described the future of the region as "a deadlock; like a couple in the middle of a divorce: both of them want the house and custody. You need a good lawyer, a divorce lawyer, not a rabbi or a priest. We need a lawyer and it has to be an American lawyer. And Obama is a Harvard Law School graduate—right?"[51]

A final peace plan for Israel and Palestine still looks to be a long way off, but what is the alternative to peace? I recalled the words of Saeb Erakat when Akiva Eldar said to me, "You can't reach stability in the Mideast as long as this conflict is open and raging. So it is *not that I am asking the USA to do me a favor* and invest the energy and goodwill and maybe even some money into making peace in the Middle East. It is in your own interest as Americans." Even when a peace deal is struck, the US government will have to continue acting as an impartial mediator. There will be the need to "send in a technician" when someone or some party needs service, said Eldar.

This is also the right thing to do. It would be hypocritical for the United States to stand by as oppressors run roughshod over the rights of others. While America was not precisely born in blood, as Obama said in his Cairo speech, "We were born out of revolution against an empire. We were founded upon the ideal that all are created equal, and we have shed blood and struggled for centuries to give meaning to those words—within our borders, and around the world."[52] These words, spoken in the heart of the Middle East for every Muslim to hear, are far more than a modest rejection of the status quo. They argue for peace.

Chapter 3
WHAT BECOMES
A TERRORIST MOST

For over a decade I've been obsessed with a few basic questions: What is the genesis of what we refer to in the media as "terrorism"? And what factors motivate individuals to turn to violence as a perceived means to an end? As a journalist working in predominantly Islamic states since 1995, I know that my investigations have still not provided me with a conclusion that I'm comfortable with. I suspect they never will. There are just too many contributing factors.

On an individual level, young men and women in the Islamic realm are influenced by socialization and peer pressure. Dr. Marc Sageman, a clinical psychologist at the University of Pennsylvania with long experience working for the Central Intelligence Agency, has set out a kind of mental road map for the new kind of insurgent that he believes the US government should be concerned about. He says such persons exhibit some similarities:

1. They have a sense of moral outrage.
2. They view their anger as a part of a "war on Islam."

3. They believe their grievances are consistent with everyday grievances.
4. They mobilize through networks.[1]

Not all of the young fighters who join Islamic insurgent groupings are obsessively religious, says Dr. Sageman, who worked for the CIA in South Asia starting in 1984. Many join in search of adventure and to root their lives in greater meaning. Sageman—correctly in my view—sees global, societal, and local environmental factors as contributing to the rise of what we in the West like to call "Islamic terrorism." He has engaged in a heated and public debate with the Rand Corporation's Bruce Hoffman about what the US government should focus on: whether on the phenomenon of new terrorists being born, as Sageman suggests, or on al Qaeda's growing terrorist network, centrally based in South Asia, as Hoffman prefers.

A debate about whether to attack organizational structure or motivations is worthwhile, but the debate must also—in my view—look at the vast global forest and not just the trees. The heated dialogue between Hoffman and Sageman remains relevant, however, because it can give the American public and its representatives—whether military, legal, or diplomatic—a more refined idea of how to allocate crucial and expensive resources in the struggle to pacify the Islamic realm.

Still, the definitions often obscure the issues. Just as "terrorist" is a broad and overly general term, so too is the phrase "war on terror." Most of us still use the phrase, but it is counterproductive in that it sets America at war with a concept. Moreover, it does not help us understand that our strongest and least expensive remedies for the problems we face across the Islamic world can be provided by changes in our own approach, particularly in our foreign policy.

In order to accomplish this, our best strategy is first to place ourselves in the shoes of others. As University of Michigan professor Juan Cole points out, "Although most American observers view the conflict between Israel and Palestine through Israeli eyes, so [that] the main issue is the Palestinian terrorism, most Muslims see the Palestinians as victims of Israeli ethnic cleansing campaigns and of continued occupation and brutality at Israeli hands."[2] We ignore this opposing perspective at our own peril, which is one reason why I have focused on it, probably to the point of appearing biased to many American observers. (In my defense, I've risked my life to enhance my own understanding, and terrorists have attempted to kill me on more than one occasion.)

Viewing the conflicts in the Middle East and beyond from all perspectives, even through the prism of angry Muslim men and women, is useful in the effort to arrive at new strategies to tamp down violence and help pacify the Islamic realm. I chose to begin *My Brother, My Enemy* with a discussion of a few of the outstanding issues in Palestine that drive and catalyze a broader Islamic sense of humiliation and animosity. In many respects, Palestine remains a litmus test for the enormous rage that still exists in the Islamic realm. While it does not explain the broader patterns of terror, it is the foundation of a great deal of learned and historical animosity toward the United States. A twenty-five-nation Pew global attitudes survey, published in July 2009, found that attitudes across the world had improved dramatically toward the United States, due in the main to the election of Barack Obama.[3] The survey suggested, however, that animosity toward the United States runs deep in Palestine and Pakistan. In what some might consider an incorrect or less than useful comparison, the survey also suggested that in Egypt, Jordan, and Indonesia, there is now more confidence in the US president than in America's nemesis, Osama bin Laden. In contrast, however, a majority within the Palestinian public said that they trusted bin Laden "to do the right thing" in world affairs. In their fight against Israel, a majority of Palestinians still support the use of suicide bombings. Interestingly, other surveys have shown that most Muslims support the Palestinian right to engage in such bombing, but that this does not translate into sanctioning it for their own use. It is easy to see how the use of suicide bombings becomes associated in the minds of many Muslims with the plight of the Palestinians.

It is difficult, indeed, to parse the results of recent polling data or even see how comparing bin Laden to the American president can be useful in the long run. It has become clear to me, however, that, while Americans still believe that aggressive Islamic radicals are out to get them, most Muslims believe that they are obliged to support a "defensive jihad" against American and Israeli aggression, though definitions of such a jihad vary considerably. Most Muslims don't see the world through our eyes, nor should we expect them to—at least until we show a willingness to see it through their eyes as well. While there may well be two divergent views and "never the twain shall meet,"[4] it is worth examining the genesis and evolution over the past three decades of jihadist movements, all of which have developed from what are viewed, in the main, by Muslims, as defensive struggles against outside aggression.

AFGHANISTAN: THE ORIGINAL GLOBAL JIHAD

The first and most obvious case study begins in Afghanistan, where the CIA avoided direct involvement, preferring to work through third and fourth parties. Pakistan's intelligence services handpicked Afghan leaders, often strict fundamentalists, to be funded, armed, and trained in a war against Soviet aggression. Both the Carter and Reagan administrations boasted of their roles helping to assist an Afghan insurgency that began with sixty-year-old British Enfield rifles and ended with guerrilla bands of "freedom fighters" shooting down hundreds of Soviet flying machines with heat-seeking Stinger missiles. Thousands of Arab volunteers, mostly young Muslims looking for adventure and a chance to help fellow Muslims liberate themselves from foreign oppressors, streamed into the fray.

These foreign fighters included young men from Egypt, the Arab world's most populous country, and from Saudi Arabia, the birthplace of Islam. Among the Egyptians who arrived in South Asia were Dr. Ayman al-Zawahiri and the blind sheikh, Omar Abdel-Rahman. Together with Osama bin Laden, they founded Maktab al-Khidamat (which still operates openly along Pakistan's border with Afghanistan), the humanitarian wing of an organization that would one day morph into al Qaeda, or "the base."

Egyptians from both Islamic Jihad and al-Gama'ah al-Islamiya had earlier come together in an assassination plot aimed at President Anwar El Sadat, whom they blamed for signing a peace treaty with Israel that did not guarantee the sanctity of Muslim holy sites or the return of Palestine. The regime of Egyptian President Hosni Mubarak—in a blithely ignorant act of "good riddance"—freed many of the leading conspirators from jail on the condition that they would leave the country and carry on their business elsewhere. This was tantamount to the export of international terrorism.

In a case of strange bedfellows, these individuals already had in common their anger over the continuing issues surrounding Palestine and Israel. They now found common ground with both the US government and independent—often Christian—groups who decided to make Afghanistan a graveyard for Soviet soldiers. Democrats and Republicans in Congress raced to join the cause. As this successful "war of liberation," which in the eyes of many was also a war against "infidel aggression," ran its course, bin Laden and his Arab associates in Afghanistan also openly railed against Israeli aggression in the West Bank.[5] Though little attention was being paid by the West to these often anti-Semitic rants, in the minds of the men the West dubbed "freedom fighters" the struggle in Afghanistan was also about throwing off the yoke of oppression elsewhere.

While it is often argued that bin Laden seized upon the liberation of Palestine as a struggle that was secondary to his own war against the United States and oppressive regimes, it is worth keeping the above history in mind. The Egyptians who took on senior positions within bin Laden's new jihadist movement were instrumental in forming his views. The idea of liberating Jerusalem from American and "Zionist" imperial rule has never been far from bin Laden's central message, and he has not hesitated to reiterate this in his hundreds of statements, sermons, and writings since the victory against the Soviet Union. (This may be one explanation for the fact that even in 2009, after bin Laden had been underground for years, the Palestinians, more than other Muslims, still looked to him to do the right thing in world affairs.) Bin Laden, ironically, had found his own voice as a leader in a US-backed struggle, one that most Americans identified, however, as a war of liberation from oppression.

YUGOSLAVIA: MUSLIM OPPRESSION IN EUROPE

Throughout the 1990s, several small wars erupted that were also overlooked by both terrorism analysts and the broader American population. These battles had distinct parallels in the minds of Muslims with what had gone on in Israel since 1948. Holy warriors, nearly invisible to America's Cold War machine and already inspired by their successes in Afghanistan, rallied to these new struggles. It wasn't long before their cause captivated popular opinion in parts of the Muslim world. They fought in Chechnya, Kosovo (which sparked off much of the later Yugoslav violence), and Bosnia, among other places. I arrived in the Balkans in 1994, as NATO hesitated and fretted about how to stop Serbian forces from slaughtering Bosnian Muslims. In the Balkans, I witnessed some of the most horrific war crimes that I have seen as a correspondent. Most the dead that I saw were Muslims, although there were Serbs and Croats as well. But there were also nonviolent moments that permitted me to see why many Muslims were so disappointed with Europe and the United States.

On one occasion, I spent a day in Sarajevo's main hospital interviewing disabled children and traumatized youth. This medical facility had a psychiatric wing that had once served as work space for Serbian Dr. Radovan Karadzic. In addition to the tens of thousands of individuals killed in the war, Bosnia ended up with some eighty thousand maimed in the war, 20 percent of them teens and children. One fifteen-year-old, Mirza Alihodic, impressed me no end as he explained how—despite his paralysis—he often dragged himself across the floor at night to help his fellow trauma patients. He had been shot by a Serbian sniper as he played football in a back alley a year earlier, in 1994. His personal will was unbroken. He gave me an explanation that only a child can provide for a complex situation, while sitting in his wheelchair with his arm around a desperately traumatized twelve-year-old girl abandoned by her grief-stricken parents.

"You see, it was Dr. Karadzic who wanted this: He was the crazy one," he said, identifying Dr. Radovan Karadzic, the president of the neighboring Serb Republic, who would remain on the run for years afterward, finally turning up disguised as a "New Age" medical doctor. As if to highlight the absurdity of it all, a few weeks later I watched Dr. Karadzic quietly walk through the portals of an Orthodox church in a town where Italian NATO troops were on regular patrol. It is little wonder that this war created growing outrage across the Islamic world—even as the world's superpower remained frozen in time.[6]

The war in Yugoslavia was not necessarily preventable, but the slaughter surely could have been staunched in its early stages with quick, concerted Western intervention. One of NATO's largest bases was just across the Adriatic in Italy. Instead, the conflict was allowed to drag on, producing horrific images of Europe's indigenous Muslims under constant fire in downtown Sarajevo and other major enclaves, culminating in the mass murder of some eight thousand Muslims at Srebrenica. The moments before that slaughter were caught on videotape, with European generals and the United Nations essentially caving in to the domineering will of Serbian General Ratko Mladic.

As the war progressed through the early 1990s, Western nations had turned a blind eye as Iran and other Islamic nations poured weapons and assistance into Bosnia. This represented a diplomatic cop-out in favor of our archrivals, but the press paid little attention to this part of the story. This is not to say that the press corps didn't expose war crimes and cry out against the apparent genocide. But Iran, America's professed rival, spearheaded an arms pipeline to the Muslims in Bosnia between 1993 and 1995 as Clinton administration officials in Croatia simply turned a blind eye. Although the US president expressed overwhelming sympathy with the plight of the Muslims, the lack of action spoke louder than words. Although it was hard to find an American mercenary anywhere, hundreds of Muslim fighters streamed in by land, sea, and air from Iran, Syria, Saudi Arabia, Libya, and Egypt, some of them young men in search of meaning and adventure and others strict adherents to fundamentalist forms of Islam.

I sat in a safehouse one day in Zenica, Bosnia, and spoke with Dr. Tafi de Suhiel, a Syrian dentist, who had organized a safehouse for dozens of these fighters, many of them from Saudi Arabia. He was outraged that these rogue warriors were even there to be housed. "If the US and Europe had helped us in a timely way back in 1992 and 1993, none of [the] bad elements would be here today," he told me.[7] De Suhiel was referring to a group of local Egyptians and Libyans (not living under his roof) who had gained a reputation for enforcing their strict codes of morality, which included full veiling and forced marriages, in surrounding villages. When I left the dentist's home, I stumbled, coincidentally, on a video shop that was selling graphic, frontline videos of "holy wars" in Chechnya, Somalia, Afghanistan, and Bosnia. The war in Bosnia wouldn't be the first or the last war that would become grist for the jihadist propaganda mill. The appearance of the videos marked the beginning of a viral phenomenon that would help spread the idea of holy war to the most distant corners of the Islamic world.

An American officer on patrol around Zenica in 1996 as the war came to an end complained to me about the animosity he experienced as a Western soldier in that part of Bosnia. "They [the Middle Easterners] stood around us waving their big knives in the air and drawing them across their neck, saying, 'I'll kill you after the elections, you Jewish pig!'" US Lieutenant Bill Ferrer told me that these holy warriors were doing all they could to intimidate the locals, often subjecting them to whippings and beatings when they did not adhere to Islamic law.[8]

Iran's ambassador to Bosnia, Mohammed Ebrahim Taherian, had no time for complaints about what he termed his country's efforts to "stop genocide." He told me in a rare interview over cashew nuts and tea, "If they [the United States] had stopped us, they would have been facing their own citizens asking, 'What are you doing applying pressure when you are not helping yourself?'"[9]

What the ambassador said sounded logical on the surface, but I'm not sure he was correct. As a journalist covering that conflict, I am not convinced that our leaders did enough early on to enlighten the US public either about the wanton slaughter of innocents or about the clandestine assistance that they were receiving from those who were described as our foreign foes. (Recall that this was not many years removed from Colonel Oliver North's unfortunate dealings with the same foe and the infamous Iran-Contra scandal.)

There is a stark lesson to be learned from what happened in Bosnia, however. Due to our negligence and our lack of attention to the evolving situation there, Iran was able to strengthen its hand in the region as it had already done across the Middle East. Our blindness to Iran's Balkan ambitions allowed Iran's theocracy to enhance its reputation at our expense. It wasn't the first time and it probably wouldn't be the last time. In the end, even the most secular of Bosnian officials were intensely grateful. "Iran helped Bosnia in the worst moments of our tragedy, and our people don't wish to forget that," Mirza Hajric, a senior Bosnian official, told me. "Many people believe that without some shipments of arms coming from that country or arranged by that country, we wouldn't have been able to continue fighting."[10] Hajric, a secular Muslim, suggested to me the idea of a drowning man offering a rope. If America had been the first to throw the rope, it would have had far less to worry about in the long run.

YEMEN: R & R FOR HOLY WARRIORS

By the turn of the millennium, sympathy in the Islamic world toward a global jihadist struggle—not necessarily led by Osama bin Laden but helped along by his declarations of war against America—had reached critical mass. As a journalist based in Cairo, Egypt, I was able to keep a close eye on the growing threat, mostly through the prism of Arab views on the rising violence in Israel and Palestine. But there was another storm developing, one that could be heard only in remote corners of the Islamic world: the distant melody of a shepherd's flute in the howling Arabian wind.

In the spring of 2001, I traveled to Yemen to look into the difficulties that the FBI was having with its investigation into the October 12, 2000, attack on the USS *Cole*, which had been carried out by suicide bombers in a rubber raft that rammed the hull in a massive blast and killed seventeen American sailors and injured thirty-nine others. Yemen, formerly termed Arabia Felix, is a fascinating country with an ancient history to rival that of almost any Islamic nation. Christians who remember the story of the "three kings" believe it to have been the origin of the frankincense carried to the manger. Modern Yemen, the homeland of the bin Laden clan, has a complex tribal structure whose clan-based rivalries mirror what one finds in Afghanistan. It exhibits the easy-going tempo and temperament of the old Middle East and still boasts a small yet vigorous Jewish community, mostly of silversmiths, who have remained an integral part of the culture by virtue of their expertise in making the Yemeni dagger, or *jambiya*—an ornate knife kept in a scabbard, usually attached to the waist with cross straps or a sash. Such knives are mainly for show, pulled out for use only in rare cases when a Yemeni male feels that his honor has been violated. The *jambiya* has become redundant, simply a showpiece, largely because almost every Yemeni also has a machine gun these days. For a foreigner traveling to remote parts of the country, it is highly advisable to take several bodyguards along to ward off would-be kidnappers and brigands.

Apart from this, however, the country's male population is oddly relaxed, due to a long-standing tradition of chewing the narcotic leaf qat in sitting rooms with neighbors on long and garrulous afternoons. The ritual is not unlike the British 4 p.m. tea-drinking tradition in its civility but more akin to hashish parties in other ways.[11]

In Yemen, I traveled north to the edge of the Rub al-Khali, or empty quarter, where the vastness and aridity of the Arabian desert stretches out as far as the eye can see, extending into substantial portions of Saudi Arabia, Oman, Yemen, and the United Arab Emirates. Through a local sheikh, Dr. Omar al-Faid, I arranged a visit to the Dar al-Hadith school, a religious madrassa, which sat in the southern corner of the Arabian desert just south of the Saudi Arabian border and outside the town of Sadah, in Yemen. Here I would uncover a world of intersecting jihads that provided hints of the long struggle ahead.

The school, which we approached early one morning, consisted of a series of brick buildings connected by walkways. At the time of our arrival, most of the students had gathered at a teahouse beside their mud-brick dormitories, where they sat with their machine guns at their side, softly discussing verses from the Koran. Their living quarters were little more than hovels made of mud bricks with small windows opening onto a vast, desolate, windblown desert marked by a ghostly stone fortress in the distance that resembled a crumbling sandcastle.

Assisted by Dr. al-Faid's kind persuasion, we located a young instructor who agreed to open a classroom so that we might sit with the students and discuss their views of the world. To my surprise, a young Caucasian from Manchester, England, and a black American Vietnam War veteran from Baltimore immediately introduced themselves and welcomed my inquiries into their lives and motivations. Soon, the conversation took on an uneasy feel.

Our talk began slowly with some light joking. "It is our nature sanctuary," said Ismail Ibn George Gordon, the tall, lanky Brit with a straggly beard. Soon, however, he began to sound slightly condem-

natory. "We do everything in conformity with the Koran here, and if
you don't do the same you will burn in a hell sixty-nine times hotter
than this desert," he said, reminding me of the cultish-sounding "fire
and brimstone" preachers I had met on the walkways at the two large
public universities I had attended. A few questions of my own
proved provocative enough to elicit a sharp rebuke for my tight
white pants and unnatural posture. "You have to cover yourself!"
snapped Gordon, pointing to my trousers. "Men who wear tight
pants do not respect the Koran. You are a Christian, and you believe
in three gods—the Father, the Son, and the Holy Ghost. Who are
you gonna call when your house is on fire?" I wanted to say "the fire
department," but I held my tongue as the encounter began to border
on the absurd.[12]

I shouldn't have been as surprised, I suppose, by the turn in the
conversation. Before my northern foray, American diplomats had
warned me that the school's founder, Sheik Muqbel bin Hadi al-
Wadie, had nothing but scorn for Americans as "Zionist lackeys"
responsible for the "slaughter of Palestinian innocents." It is worth
remembering that this animosity toward the United States was not
new. It was only now boiling up to the surface at the crossroads of
intersecting holy wars.

Several fellow students, particularly the Arabs in the room,
reminded Gordon that I was their guest and that he ought to accom-
modate my unusual ways. Over the course of the next few hours, I
was able to determine that almost all the "students" at Dar al-Hadith
had served some time in a war zone and were now attending class to
catch a break and increase their knowledge of the Koran. Although
there was a firing range out back, the school itself bore few signs of
being a formal military training center.

Students and teachers from Yemen, Somalia, Britain, and the
United States described their own concepts of "jihad," but they were
careful to insist that their ideas were within the bounds of Islamic
principles, which, they said, specifically banned terrorism. The
African American veteran of the Vietnam War said, "I think we've

got to make clear that we preach only 'right' jihad—and that excludes all forms of terrorism."

A young Yemeni added, "We only learn the fundamentals of the Koran here, and only after that do we strive for the final victory." Like other scholars, he was not pleased that Westerners had accused the students at his school of sending fighters to help with the attack on the USS *Cole*, so he quickly turned the tables on my queries, preferring to talk about the struggle in Palestine.

"Western leaders could easily bring justice to Palestine, but they are either hesitating or engaged in a conspiracy," said Sheik Turki Abdullah Muqbel, a young cousin of the school's founder. This was a common view expressed in conversations around the Middle East in the lead-up to the attacks on the World Trade Center as well as in its aftermath. Arabs would tell me that my efforts to probe the nature of Islamic terrorism were laced with hypocrisy because of the distortions created by US foreign policy, which they insisted favored Israel.

Yemen, a country of twenty million residents, happened to be home to more militants than many of its Arab neighbors. As one British diplomat had joked in advance of my trip to Sadah, "Most species of Mideast terrorist are alive and well and living in Yemen." Yemen was so obscure in international affairs that I am sure few Americans would be able to find it on a map or have any inkling that hundreds of jihadists had returned there or arrived there in the 1990s and sided with the government in its efforts to put down a southern secessionist rebellion backed by current and former Communists.

That put the government in a bind. "We're not happy that these groups exist, but our hands are tied," Faris Sanabani, a spokesman for Yemeni President Ali Abdullah Saleh, told me. "Even when we crack down on cells in once place, suspects pop up someplace else."[13] Sanabani complained that his government had been left to deal with Western policy failures in places like Afghanistan and Chechnya that had left many Islamic holy warriors from Egypt, Libya, and Saudi Arabia looking for an adoptive homeland. "It has been up to us to take these people in," he moaned.[14] Yemen stood in contrast to Egypt, which never let its own Afghan jihadists return, or if they did, hunted them down.

Stephen Day, a British expert on Yemen whom I met in the capital, Sana'a, said Yemen was already fertile soil for global jihadist interests. Prior to another bloody civil war that broke out in Yemen in the late 1960s, Day had served as a colonial administrator before Britain's final departure from Yemen in 1967. In recent years, he said he had seen the anti-Western sentiment rising and claimed that the US government had been naïve to moor its warships off the coast after the embassy bombings in Africa, knowing what it did about the jihadist elements in Yemen and their anti-American leanings. "These schools get used for political reasons when there is a motive," he insisted.[15]

Of course, hindsight is often twenty-twenty. The Americans in Sana'a had insisted, in any case, that the Sadah school was a training ground for Islamic fundamentalists. On that front they were correct; the result of US policies from Palestine to Afghanistan to Chechnya was hell to pay.

BIN LADEN: THE MAN AND THE MYTH

In response to the attack on the USS *Cole*, the Clinton administration unleashed cruise missiles on bin Laden's training camps in Khost, Afghanistan, but to no avail. Indeed, the failed attack—like others before it and others after it—would serve only to enhance the legend of the Islamic world's leading holy warrior. At the height of his popularity, in the wake of the 9/11 attacks, the tall, slender Saudi, whose billionaire father had immigrated to Saudi Arabia from Yemen, would attract greater admiration across the Islamic realm than the commander in chief of the "free world," George W. Bush. For America, that represented an astounding loss of international prestige, a loss that continues to grate in Washington as a new administration desperately attempts to right the ship of state. Even at the height of the Cold

War there was no Communist figure who approached the stature of bin Laden in the lands from Casablanca to Jakarta.

Bin Laden's rapid rise in fortune coincided with the Second Intifada, or uprising, against Ariel Sharon's crackdown in the West Bank. Although in the United States that conflict was not perceived as having risen to the level of a major conflagration, in the Arab world the scenes of bloodshed and images of running street battles were seen before 9/11 as reflecting a full-scale war. Bin Laden's full arrival on the international scene (particularly in Islamic circles), apparently invincible to American military might, was greeted with glee in the streets of Palestine and across much of the Islamic world.

It was bin Laden's name that I now heard echoing like a siren's call from the deserts of Yemen to the slums of Cairo. There was nothing humble about bin Laden's approach to the fight. A recording of his view of the destruction of the World Trade Center (WTC) presented him as the cold, calculating son of an engineer, curious as to how the airplane attacks succeeded in melting the center's metal beams. Yet the Saudi's piety and his willingness to stand up to the world's only superpower, in the face of what most Muslims perceived as US-backed Israeli aggression in Palestine, made him an instant hero in the heart of the Middle East. Mohammed Ali Sauti, a Yemeni student, told me, "Osama is a hero because he is the only one who stands up to the US—who is not afraid of them. He will prevail if Allah wills it."[16] Two floors above my apartment in a wealthy district of Cairo, an erudite businessman agreed: Bin Laden had finally given the United States—"the real source of terrorism and racism"—its comeuppance.

In the wake of the attacks on the WTC and the Pentagon, Pakistan and Afghanistan buckled in the turmoil of this new sentiment. Bin Laden was able to capitalize on the enigmatic nature of his own rise to power. For a dollar in Peshawar's Bazaar of the Storytellers, you could purchase the book *Who Is Osama bin Laden?* in which the author, Abni Atta, explained how the Saudi had traded in his "princely life" for the austere life of a guerrilla in the mountains of

Afghanistan.[17] On my regular visits to that market, before the Khyber Pass opened up to a stream of CIA-backed warlords, vendors could be seen doing a brisk business in T-shirts reading "Jihad Is Our Mission," purportedly signed by none other than the al Qaeda chief himself. The affection for him in Pakistan and Afghanistan also had a great deal to do with the notion that he had survived all efforts to capture and kill him. He was still bathed in the mystique of a successful game of hide-and-seek when other al Qaeda leaders were being rounded up left and right, his survival being due, in some Muslims' eyes, to the protection he had from on high.

Few members of the illiterate classes in Egypt or South Asia believed, initially, that bin Laden had been capable of the attacks in New York and Washington, but when they discovered that this one man had been the mastermind, many of them were overjoyed and amazed by his skill and audacity.

Bin Laden was protected by his fellow Muslims. In South Asia, where he lived a remarkable life on the run, he was the grateful beneficiary of an ancient code of hospitality, which Pashtun tribesmen were bound to honor. If someone had made sacrifices for you and yours, you were obligated to honor him with your protection.

"It is misleading to believe that most Pashtuns consider bin Laden to be a hero," said Professor Ghulam Bongash, chairman of the history department at Peshawar University and himself a Pashtun.[18] "They do find him possessed of a practical bravery, however. After all, he fought alongside them against the Soviets. The Pashtuns are a people who think 'if you do me an unselfish favor, I will remember that forever.'"[19] Residual love for the valorous combatants of the war against Soviet aggression still resonated in the badlands of Pakistan.

Admiration was one thing, but accident another. Many of bin Laden's own fighters were pathetic, hapless types who had arrived in the region to fight one war and ended up—through an accident of history—fighting another. One of the more revealing discussions I had with these mujahedeen took place when I happened upon a US-funded team of Afghan bounty hunters two months after covering the battle of Tora Bora in November and December 2001. From the bowels of a dungeon, anxious to get a reward from the CIA for their handiwork, they dragged out Haji Mohammed Akram in shackles attached to a chain that resembled a heavy dog's leash. Akram had arrived in Afghanistan years earlier to fight the Soviets because, as he explained while eating an orange, he had a "great devotion to Islam and holy shrines and the idea of fighting for the freedom of Muslims."[20] The Saudi, who had once been sent—all expenses paid—by bin Laden to Detroit for special medical care, had taught the Koran and occasionally cooked for bin Laden, serving up what he called "the sheikh's favorite meal, stuffed quail."[21] Now, the hapless holy warrior, whose bloodied nose was stuffed with cotton, begged me to somehow get him to Guantanamo, where he said he hoped to receive better treatment from his captors. He tried his best to suggest to me, in hope of escaping the cruelty of his captors, that he was a bin Laden follower by accident, not by admiration. I suspected it was a little of both.[22]

EGYPTIAN JIHAD: THE POLITICS OF SUICIDE

But if bin Laden and his al Qaeda movement were taking advantage of fortunate tides of history, they were also—in the remarkable attack on the World Trade Center—capitalizing on a growing sentiment across the Islamic world that was siding increasingly with the Palestinians in their struggle against what was described as Israeli aggression. This was not a small-scale phenomenon, despite the limited press it received in the United States. It was best exemplified by the growing spite expressed in popular Arab culture. Since the start of the Second Intifada, Egyptians had been boycotting Israeli goods and lavishing praise on a previously unknown country singer whose song, "I Hate Israel," quickly rose to the top of the popular charts.

The singer, Shaaban Abdel-Rahim, had been hired by McDonald's in Egypt to promote the new "McFalafel" but had quickly been dropped after an insistent outcry from US-based Jewish groups. At the height of the controversy, Abd El Nasser Aziz, a McDonald's executive in Egypt, told me that Abdel-Rahim was a man that "you either hate or love, but most Egyptians love him." Apparently unrepentant, the executive said that despite the cancellation of his contract, he had sparked amazing sales for the new sandwich.[23]

Far more worrisome than the falafel foolishness was the growing approval in Egypt—across class lines—for the idea of suicide bombing. In the week prior to the attacks in America, I met with an up-and-coming young Egyptian actor, Amr Waked, who lived in a houseboat across the river Nile from my own apartment. I had been to see a movie that he starred in, *Friends or Business*, and I thought it was an interesting story: a possible window into the way that Egypt itself was being transformed by the Second Intifada.[24]

Cairo has for decades been a barometer for the Arab world's views. Even as Egypt's Palestinian neighbors embarked on the Second Intifada, though, Egyptian theaters stayed full of giggling audiences obsessed with chubby comics who generally avoided mentioning anything remotely political. Comic relief was one of the means that Egyptians used (and still use) to deal with their plight. After all, Egypt with its amazing ports and energetic young generation had missed the boat in terms of economic progress. Egyptians suffered from poor economic management and had a stultified, greedy political leadership to blame for that.

As the Second Intifada—generally believed to have begun when rioting broke out in the wake of Ariel Sharon's heavily guarded visit to the Temple Mount—unfolded in Israel prior to 9/11, the Egyptian government began to loosen its censorious grip on television and radio discussions of suicide bombing.

Both the screenwriter for the movie and the young actor, Amr Waked, who played a suicide bomber insisted that the movie was not meant to inspire similar attacks. "I don't think their low-budget movie should encourage suicide bombing as much as make a state-ment about why it exists," the actor told me, sitting on the balcony of his houseboat as the muddy waters of the Nile swept past us.[25]

Yet the audiences that I had spoken to as they were leaving a showing of the film clearly sympathized with Waked's character. The movie awakened deep sympathy—empathy if the audience members were displaced Palestinians—and made them think about the motiva-tions of oppressed Palestinians. Wiping tears from his eyes, twenty-one-year-old Adel Mogazy said: "I thought the movie was great. We Egyptians are aware of Israeli cruelty, but this puts us more in touch with the agony and feelings of the Palestinian people. We, as Egyptian youth, want to go and help to stop Israel's policy of slaughter, and if I get a chance, I'll go too and give my life for Palestine."[26]

Walaa Aly, nineteen, wearing a yellow head scarf, her neck draped with a red necklace, expressed similar sentiments: "There is nothing like this bomber. If I have the chance, I'll do the same, because Palestine is ours too. I wouldn't mind sacrificing myself. Ever since this problem began, I've felt...basically helpless, and I want to find a way to act."[27]

These were not the sentiments of would-be bombers, but if you found a pool of a hundred Arabs with similar views, one or two—maybe those who were the most bitter and down on their luck—would likely emerge as prospects for a suicide mission. If only one in a thousand took on a mission, it would become a problem. Israeli officials whom I contacted about the movie were dismayed that Egyptian authorities had permitted the film to be shown at all.

"This new praise for suicidal martyrdom has run parallel to a growing streak of anti-Semitism in the Egyptian press and is being encouraged through the state press," Ayellet Yehiav, an official in Israel's embassy in Cairo told me over the phone. She condemned the movie as "mere propaganda," and accused Egyptian government cen-sors of deliberately ignoring its potential as incitement to violence.[28]

Anger was to be expected, but what outraged Israeli officials was the movie's narrative, which appeared to work as an advertisement for suicide bombing. Filmed in southern Lebanon, the movie opened with a friendly gang of Egyptians producing a game show, which featured trivia questions about Western singers. Looking to inject substance into the daily fare, the young producers decided to take the show on the road to the Palestinian territories. They hopped into a minivan and sped off to Israel, where they confronted sneering, red-headed Israeli soldiers. The producers were assisted at a border crossing by "Jihad," a Palestinian, who took them to his village.

While they filmed their game show in the hills of Israel, their questions grew increasingly irrelevant, as the day turned into a festival of brotherhood and unity with Palestinian brothers and sisters they hadn't been aware of while in Cairo. Then the celebrations were interrupted by the funeral of a martyr and by a riot. Israeli soldiers gunned down children. Horrified by the killing, Jihad decided to martyr himself. Just before he walked toward the Israeli checkpoint, he explained on camera why he was about to make the ultimate sacrifice. There was a sad farewell, and, moments later, he was dead. Back in Egypt, a senior television network executive, apparently representing Arab complacency, forbade the team to air the footage. But the producers defied him by airing the show on satellite TV, exposing the Arab world to the realities of the Palestinian struggle.

Both the film's writer and its director insisted they made the movie to awaken Egyptians from their zombie-like stupor and blind acceptance of Israeli atrocities. In truth, the fact that the movie had slipped past Cairo's usually vigilant censorship board suggested that Hosni Mubarak's regime was attempting to divert attention away from its own wretched economy and its own political oppression by highlighting an external struggle. This did not make the growing and disturbing sentiments less real, however.

The subsequent 9/11 attacks forced many Muslims to contemplate in what circumstances they would support the idea of a suicide attack. Meanwhile, street demonstrations in Egypt intensified, and the regime's complicity as a player in the ineffective peace process, now seemingly put on hold by George Bush and his colleague in arms Ariel Sharon, came into question. The Egyptian government, equal to the challenge and wary of the growing anger, attempted to ride out the protests.

By the late spring of 2002, it was increasingly clear that Egypt's president had given the country's top religious leaders tacit permission to advocate suicide bombing as a legitimate tactic for the Palestinian people to use against the Israeli military. As surely as the world had changed for Americans after 9/11, the Islamic world was now being transformed by events, being reshaped beyond the comprehension of the handful of neocons who were ignoring Israel and Palestine in favor of continuing to steer the Pentagon and the State Department toward Iraq, which had had only a negligible impact on the larger issue of terrorism. When Secretary of State Colin Powell arrived in Morocco in early April, King Mohammed VI, a staunch US ally with long-standing ties to Israel, had the audacity to ask him in public, "Don't you think it was more important to go to Jerusalem first?"[29]

In Egypt, Powell faced the prospect of growing anti-Americanism as protesters torched US flags and chanted "Burn, burn the flag of America!" In his public statements, however, Powell demonstrated that he was neither deaf nor blind to the sandstorm blowing across the region. Emerging from a meeting with Mubarak, Powell said, "I think that it is up to all of us to recognize that the suicide bombings, all of this, has to be brought to an end."[30] He went on to implore Arab nations and Palestinians to condemn the practice of suicide bombing. At the same time, he refrained from harsh denunciations of the Israeli military's heavy-handed tactics in the West Bank, essentially ignoring the crisis that was driving young Arabs into the arms of recruiters.

In Egypt, the rabbit was already out of the proverbial hat, as I discovered in making the rounds to meet several senior religious leaders. It is worth mentioning here that Egypt's secret police, or the Mukhabarat, keep a close eye on all religious figures, from firebrand preachers in the slums to senior clerics in the most hallowed institutions of Islamic learning. Members of the secret police are there to listen and to intimidate when necessary. In other words, almost nothing is said by religious leaders, hardly even in a whisper, that is not closely monitored by the central government.

Government-appointed clerics were now pointedly reversing their positions toward Palestinian suicide attacks against Israeli targets, an astounding development considering that Egypt was still one of the signatories to a peace deal with Israel from the time of Jimmy Carter and Anwar Sadat. The increasing radicalization of young Muslims made past peace agreements worth little more than the paper they were written on.

I sat down in a sunroom on the perimeter of Egypt's most sacred mosque with the government's top religious adviser, Mufti Ahmed al-Tayyeb, who was himself surrounded by a small entourage of interpreters and government advisers. The mufti did not mince his words. He called it "the right of the Palestinian" people to attack civilians, pointing out that all those in Israel—women, men, and children—are considered an occupying force. "The faithful are being martyred to force the Zionist occupiers to reconsider their plans," he told me, adding a rhetorical question for the British readers of the *Daily Telegraph* in order to hammer home his point: "If the Germans invaded London, wouldn't the British people support the idea of self-sacrifice?" It wasn't a fair comparison.[31]

Egypt's senior government spokesman, Nabil Osman, had presented an only slightly watered-down version of the same view to me a day earlier, when he insisted that "To put civilians in harm's way, either Palestinians or Israelis—is definitely the wrong policy. But we must look at the root causes of such attacks. If there was no occupation, we would not be talking about suicide bombing."[32]

In the past, Syria and Iran have rarely concealed their support for suicide strikes against Israel, but the carefully articulated views from Egypt's hierarchy represented a sea change. Western journalists, in my view, too often focus on the suicide factories run by Hamas and other militant organizations without examining the broader recruiting pool and the implicit approval for suicide bombing that still pervades parts of the Islamic world, assisted in part by the rain-makers for the perfect storm in Washington and beyond.

Indeed, the new mood of defiance that developed post-9/11 across the Middle East represented a bizarre moment in relations between the East and the West. Now, even moderate Arab leaders were indirectly backing what the US government defined as "terror"—suicide bombings by the Palestinians. These attacks were seen by some Arabs as a means to an end: a means to bring about an Israeli pullout. Unsure of how far the Egyptian authorities, who were themselves increasingly unpopular, wanted to take this, I arranged a meeting with Sheikh Mahmoud Ashour, a senior Egyptian imam at Al-Azhar University. He presented me with a definition of terrorism that provided the flip side of the broad-brush view of the issue put forth by the Bush administration. "Terrorism," he began, "is when you threaten people who live in security and usurp the rights of others. Jihad is when people resist those who usurp their territory. The prophet Mohammed says that those killed without their land, money, or [honor] are true martyrs. If it [suicide bombing] will lead to the end that Israel will acknowledge the peace and human rights of the Palestinians that they have usurped, the attacks are justified."[33] He insisted that Israel had "breached all Islamic and Christian values."[34] At the same time, US officials were accusing Arab citizens and regimes of breaching "Islamic values."

Ashour went further; he placed the moral burden of bringing about change squarely on the shoulders of the United States. The suicide bomb was ticking, he suggested, so Washington would have to act. "As soon as the US forces the Israelis out of the occupied territories [of the West Bank and Gaza], we will be committed to peace again," he said.[35]

There were other, more reasonable, voices to be listened to in Egypt, albeit not in cahoots with the government, which was being funded by US taxpayers to the tune of $2 billion annually. Hala Mustafa, an astute political and social analyst, was disturbed by all the efforts by senior clerics to justify the use of suicide bombers. In the wake of 9/11, Egyptian youth were being forced to make a choice. They could push for change on a secular and political level or wallow in the mire of a growing religious debate, which, in the end, was leading them nowhere. "The whole region is far more militant than it was," she confided in me. "Religion, as never before, is playing the main role in mobilizing people—both Palestinians and their Arab neighbors. And because there is no real Arab army as such, Arab youth and demonstrators feel that they have no other way except to fight back through militant groups. In Syria, the population supports Hizbollah; and in Palestine, they support groups like Hamas and Islamic Jihad."[36] Even women were jumping into the fray. Wafa Idris, the first Palestinian female bomber to launch a suicide attack inside Israel, on January 27, 2002, had fast become a new heroine for Egyptian women, who were filling the streets with their own cries of jihad.

✳✳✳

Former *New York Times* Cairo correspondent Neil MacFarquhar points out that those who argue that the word "jihad" carries absolutely "no implication of violence are glossing over the fact that for some zealots, jihad means only one thing: an armed fight against the enemies of Islam that they believe they are destined to carry out in perpetuity."[37] He also highlights the fact that—given the predominant view in Islam that all learning derives from the Prophet— "there is no one authority to settle an argument," and so the idea of when and where to wage holy war "has been left ambiguous in the Islamic world."[38] That means jihad, including ideas such as self-sacrifice in wartime, is often left to the interests of politicians to define within the context of their own goals.

It was precisely this ambiguity that bin Laden and his cohorts, who slipped the noose at Tora Bora, were seeking to exploit for their own ends. Even leading Saudi Arabian scholars say that many in the predominant sect, Wahhabism, believe that a state of constant warfare is the duty of Muslims. They use the life of the Prophet, a life in which he successfully spread Islam across the Arabian peninsula, as an example for their own lives.

✷✷✷

Islam is not an inherently militant religion, as some ill-informed "experts" in the West insist, however. It is a modern and dynamic faith that satisfies the spiritual needs of 1.2 billion people. Yet it can hardly be disputed that Islam began as an insurgency, as a struggle against the status quo of another era, and it is against this historical backdrop that prominent Muslim guerrilla leaders now operate—often using parallels from another age to rationalize their own struggles.

Mohammed is justifiably revered as a fiery guerrilla leader who led the Arabs to victory and prosperity. Indeed, had it not been for his martial skills, his religious prophecy would surely have been lost to posterity. The pagan world in which Mohammed rose to prominence was one of idol worship, tribal rivalries, and blood feuds. Between 622 and 632 CE, Mohammed spent time organizing a growing Muslim community in Medina, which eventually engaged in open warfare with the Meccans. Along with his Muhajir, or followers, the Prophet succeeded in spreading his new religion across the Arabian peninsula. Mohammed is known to most Muslim scholars as a reluctant warrior, and a warrior who often succeeded through the use of persuasion and diplomacy where others might have attempted to use military might. The Koran proclaims that the oppressed can and should fight back, however: "Permission to fight is given to those who are fought against because they have been wrong. Truly, Allah has the power to come to their support, those who were expelled from their homes without any right, merely for saying, 'Our Lord is Allah'" (22:39–40).[39]

Mohammed's own life illustrates a spirited rise from humble beginnings and a will to fight for what he believed in. Orphaned at an early age, Mohammed was raised by Bedouins in the desert, but he eventually ingratiated himself with the moneyed classes by proving himself a polite and reliable professional. Over two decades, he gained an intimate knowledge of the tribes and desert terrain around Mecca and Medina as a manager of camel caravans.

Expelled from Mecca for condemning idolatry, Mohammed fled to Medina with his followers. Seven months later, he launched his first guerrilla foray: an attack on a caravan under the control of Meccan merchants. His knowledge of distances and travel times proved useful, but it was his knowledge of the local human terrain that would play the major part in assisting his rise to prominence.

Until Mohammed became their prophet and leader, Arab tribes, mostly nomads living off the land, had known war on their own terms and for their own purposes.[40] For them, conflict was less a matter of ideology than a means of survival in a Darwinian world. Nor did war require a fight to the death—for martyrdom and an afterlife—as Mohammed would eventually promise. Instead, desert raiding parties engaged in classic hit-and-run attacks on fellow nomads, which added up to a regular exchange of goods and slaves, depending on who had the greater skills in horsemanship and fighting.

The Prophet's earliest raids against Meccan caravans, however, altered the nature of the Arabs' raids, for Mohammed was not an ordinary raider. Rather he was a messianic visionary who believed himself to be the keeper of God's word. It was his ideas that set him apart and earned him a reputation as a formidable warrior among the tribesmen. As the military historian Richard Gabriel points out, "From the very beginning, Mohammed's raids were intended to achieve the political objective of winning the hearts and minds of the Bedouins."[41]

With promises of salvation and shares in the loot, Mohammed exhibited prowess and won favor in the badlands between Mecca and Medina. In his first major engagement as a religious leader, the battle of Badr, the Prophet's Muslim warriors had been seeking to take back possessions that they had earlier abandoned in Mecca. At this famous battle, Mohammed managed to draw Mecca's best and brightest out of their urban (idolatrous) lair and onto a desert battlefield. He dealt a harsh blow to the old establishment and—according to his scribes—gave no quarter to his captives. Battle reports and rumors assisted in the growth of the Prophet's legend, which was often associated in the minds of his followers with his martial efforts.

Although Mohammed infused Arab warfare with a new ideology that forever changed the rules of conflict, he also evolved, through his own experiences—including numerous failures—into a revered strategic thinker. Summing up his view of conflict, he once remarked to his lieutenants that "all war is cunning," mirroring what Sun Tzu, author of *The Art of War*, had said: "All war is deception."[42]

Westerners who attempt to write off Islam as a violent religion, however, would be advised to read the Koran in its entirety. Just as ancient Christianity burned its way into the global psyche through warfare and threats of fire and brimstone, Islam rose to prominence in the same way, albeit in a different era and with a much faster pace of conquest.

A tolerant and all-too-often silent minority in both religions is well aware of this commonality. It is disingenuous to say that Muslims can resolve their conflict by looking within themselves—or discuss the violent versus peaceful aspects of their faith—and not, at the same time, ask that Christians and Jews look within themselves and do the same. Thoughts of violence, often dressed up institutionally in terms of martial prowess, bring out the worst in all religions. When it comes to warmongering, we are all in the mix, as we have been for centuries. Jerusalem, which was the crucible of medieval religious violence, plays a similar role even today, which suggests that the faithful on all sides still have not escaped the violent traditions of the past. Strife in Palestine and Israel, even after 9/11, feeds the flames of conflict across the globe. Particularly adept at capitalizing on this strife is al Qaeda, "the base," which melds legend and fact carried from the sands of Saudi Arabia in the sixth century to Palestine early in the twenty-first century.

Bin Laden has successfully targeted both the naïve youth in the streets of major Islamic capitals, including Cairo, and the intellectual elite that longs to see Islam reassert itself on the world stage. To learn more about the latter phenomenon, I ventured to visit the terror chief's "godfather," Mahfouz Azzam, whose legal offices sat on the thirty-seventh floor in a plush corner of a high rise overlooking the Nile.[43]

Azzam was the uncle of Dr. Ayman al-Zawahiri, a man often described as "the brains behind bin Laden," who had practiced as a pediatrician before being convicted for his involvement in the conspiracy to assassinate President Anwar Sadat. Al-Zawahiri is remembered in Egypt less for his extended rants on Al Jazeera but rather for his cries of injustice from behind the bars of a small jail cell sitting awkwardly inside Cairo's main courthouse. Azzam had defended his nephew and, in the end, al-Zawahiri had been released and permitted to travel to South Asia after less than a decade in prison.

Amid moth-eaten books and mildewed stacks of legal papers, Azzam, who still held power of attorney for bin Laden, denounced Americans for their complicity in keeping Islamic lands under Israeli law. "Any American civilian who serves against our cause to liberate Islamic lands—defends, helps, or pays money to keep Israel in control—deserves to be punished," he said, answering a question I put to him about the attacks on the World Trade Center and the Pentagon.[44]

It was a common refrain that one could hear in parlors from Cairo to Islamabad after the September 2001 attacks in the United States. It was what Westerners might call historical revisionism, in that it promoted al Qaeda's leaders as the "good guys" and US officials as the "bad guys." (In fact, similar rants against American-backed Zionist imperialism were to be heard well before 9/11, but it was only after the attacks that these voices resonated in the media.)

Azzam, a polished and respected lawyer in Cairo's mainstream, went on to defend al-Zawahiri, lamenting the "legitimate" political reasons that had forced his beloved nephew to give up a career as a "marvelous, intelligent, and very good doctor." He said he longed to see his nephew again. "Millions of Muslims in the world are proud of his words and they all have the same cause, which is the liberation of Palestine," he said, adding that "Muslims feel that the US is an aggressive country—a superpower without morality."[45]

In truth, the Egyptian doctor had begun his career as a member of the Egyptian Muslim Brotherhood at the early age of sixteen. He had played a highly secretive role in helping to recruit Islamic dissidents from within the Egyptian military. Later, al-Zawahiri had been instrumental in al Qaeda's own efforts to train sleeper cells in Afghan camps and disperse them across the Middle East.

Al-Zawahiri, whose grandfather was the first secretary-general of the Arab League, wrote in his memoir, *Knights under the Prophet's Banner*, that "in the training camps and on the battlefronts, our Muslim youth have developed a broad awareness and fuller realization of the conspiracy that is being weaved against them."[46] It was left to al Qaeda to highlight all the conspiracies against young Muslims in order to persuade them to sign up for the global jihad. After surviving and escaping the US attacks in Afghanistan in late 2001, al Qaeda was attempting to exploit the disconnect between authoritarian Muslim states, like Egypt and Saudi Arabia (which were being propped up with American military assistance), and a growing wellspring of internal hatred of both the United States and these same regimes. Al Qaeda's efforts would be checkered with successes and failures.

So powerful were the forces backing al Qaeda in Egypt alone, however, that one of the organization's top critics in Egypt, Montasser al-Zayat, a former jihadist and prison mate of the doctor, had agreed to remove his book, *Ayman al-Zawahiri, As I Knew Him*, from Cairo's bookshelves until a time when al-Zawahiri would be in a position, as al-Zayat told me in an interview, to "properly respond directly to the criticism."[47]

"All these groups, including Egypt's Muslim Brotherhood, insisted that I should wait until conditions improve for Ayman," al-Zayat said, using the doctor's first name.[48] Sitting in a swivel chair across from his young daughter in his central Cairo office, he insisted that he was not "physically" threatened by those who insisted that he should pull the book, but that, in all fairness, they told him, he should wait until President George Bush had left office in the United States to resume his critique. Al-Zayat described his "old friend" al-Zawahiri as a stubborn and determined man, driven by a desire to right the wrongs committed against Islam. Although al-Zayat had broken with his old friend in public, his private thoughts were less easy to read.

✳✳✳

In November and December 2001, I had borne witness to al Qaeda's cunning escape from beneath the wings of US B-52s at the battle of Tora Bora in eastern Afghanistan. Although many Western terror analysts have speculated that bin Laden had been surprised by the ferocity of the US-led attack, bin Laden himself subsequently made clear that his attacks on New York and Washington were meant to "lure the tiger from its lair." His lengthy preparations for the battle of Tora Bora, which I documented in *Al Qaeda's Great Escape*, also suggest that he carefully chose his foothold in the White Mountains of eastern Afghanistan with the intention of slipping out the "back door" into Pakistan when the time was right. Like any accomplished tactician, he was prepared both to fight and to flee.[49]

In Afghanistan and later in Iraq, Islamic insurgents managed to drag conventional-minded militaries into long, protracted, and exhausting struggles. Despite the middle-aged vanity and demagoguery often attributed to bin Laden, the puritanical Saudi sheikh did not see his main role as that of a new caliph, or ruler of all Muslims, but as that of a classic guerrilla leader—a key player in a global Islamic resistance that was attempting to institute religious and social reform. For this, he earned a modicum of respect from anyone across the Islamic world who felt duty bound to do the same.

What bolstered bin Laden and his top lieutenants more than the poorly aimed US aerial attacks in the White Mountains of Afghanistan, however, was the constant verbal barrage launched by the United States. Al Qaeda was built up as a larger-than-life organization that posed an existential threat to the future of Western civilization, instead of being seen for what it was.

Bin Laden cherished the spotlight but managed to maintain an aura of humility in the Arab street. He and his closest followers aspired to walk and fight in the footsteps of their Prophet. And in order to keep their struggle alive in perilous terrain and against the world's most potent conventional military, the jihadists adopted the cunning of their mentor and adapted it to the modern age. Al Qaeda or its trained affiliates would appear in a province or country in one month and vanish from the field in the next. CIA directors were quick to suggest that the Islamic insurgency was on the decline and would never rise to the level of its earlier successes, but they were advised by men who insisted that al Qaeda's leaders were not as smart as they were.

Even if these men weren't as smart as the best and brightest America had to offer, they were certainly just as determined and focused. In order to understand its foe, the US government would have been better advised to think of bin Laden and his ilk as diligent and devoted students of guerrilla warfare. There is no evidence that al Qaeda had studied Sun Tzu's *Art of War*, yet the network and several of its affiliates appeared to closely follow Sun Tzu's advice that "Even though you are competent, appear to be incompetent. Though effective, appear to be ineffective."[50] Both bin Laden and al-Zawahiri understood that both appearing weak and appearing strong were suitable for use as the situation presented itself. They were good at both.

Indeed, American strategies did not reckon well with the adaptive and disappearing qualities of their enemy. In the winter of 2001–2002, the Taliban and al Qaeda fled from Afghanistan and eventually regrouped in Pakistan. In doing so, they followed al-Zawahiri's advice in *Knights under the Prophet's Banner*.

At the same time, the Pentagon embarked upon a broader, unfocused war. This in turn aided and abetted the underground expansion of an Islamic insurgency whose cadres (and cousins) saw Washington's vague policy as a broader war on Islam—one of the key ingredients in Dr. Sageman's recipe for a jihadist.

Bin Laden and his associates expressed their public relish at the idea that the United States—while falsely believing it had obliterated its foe in South Asia—would then invade Iraq to rid itself of an ancillary enemy. After all, Saddam Hussein had been a longtime enemy of fundamentalist Islam. (Ironically, while US General Tommy Franks had said he would not invade Afghanistan with a massive force because he did not want the US military to get bogged down "like the Soviets," he was quick to accept orders to push into Iraq with one hundred fifty thousand US troops.)

Bin Laden and his ilk must have chuckled to think that the government in Washington was selling the war on Iraq to the American masses on the basis of bin Laden's nonexistent ties to Saddam Hussein, an old enemy. As bin Laden stated in a videotape before the 2004 elections in the United States: "All that we have to do is to send two mujahedeen to the furthest point east to raise a piece of cloth on which is written al Qaeda, in order to make the [US] generals race there to cause America to suffer human, economic, and political losses without achieving for it anything of note."[51]

IRAQ: IN SEARCH OF MONSTERS

In 2003, our conventional forces—with myself in the rearguard in a Mitsubishi Pajero—flooded into Iraq. Although we swept through Baghdad, US strategists failed to foresee or plan for the reappearance of our unvanquished foe. Early on, the military attempted to tackle the al Qaeda conundrum in the framework of a "zero-sum game"—a game in which the interests of the opponents are always taken to be diametrically opposed to our own and in which the killing of an enemy is considered to leave one less chess player for the opponent to wield. In asymmetrical warfare, however, such calculations simply don't apply.

In *The Forever War*, Dexter Filkins described the circumstances surrounding the alleged drowning of an Iraqi man by US forces in the fruit orchards and palm groves along the Tigris River on the outskirts of Balad, a large town north of Iraq.[52] Filkins detailed the circumstances in which one of West Point's most trusted young officers, Lieutenant Colonel Nathan Sassaman, eventually lost his position in Iraq because he instituted a system of punitive measures against Iraqi villagers whose relatives had openly revolted against the American occupation. In keeping with a vague order from US Maj.-Gen. Ray Odierno to "increase lethality," Sassaman called in air strikes on houses suspected of sheltering insurgents and ordered bulldozers to destroy others. For a lesson in how war changes the best of men and turns them into brutal disciplinarians, Filkins's insightful tale on the Tigris is highly instructive. Sassaman, the son of a Methodist minister and a former quarterback for the West Point football team, told Filkins in the field that "with a heavy dose of fear and violence, and a lot of money for projects, I think we can convince these people that we are here to help."[53] Filkins describes how the colonel's forces, responding to a growing insurgency, cordoned off villages and placed bags over the heads of Iraqi suspects before carting them off to Abu Ghraib prison, where they disappeared into a netherworld. A father of eight, standing beside a razor-wire cordon set up by US forces, is quoted as saying: "Where is the Iraqi freedom? We are just like the people in the Gaza Strip."[54] Such words became almost predictable when the United States instituted a policy of bulldozing homes, a practice the Israeli military had made famous across the Islamic world, if not in America, during the Second Intifada. The parallel between the United States and Israel was an easy one to see for any Muslim who had a TV set and was under occupation by a foreign army. What is maybe even more shocking than the actual practice of using bulldozers, however, is that it was a tactic chosen from the Israeli Defense Forces' playbook. Israel had already been accused of engaging in "collective punishment" by destroying the livelihood of an entire family, often when only one of the family members had committed acts of terror. In using this approach to counterinsurgency, Pentagon planners and Sassaman's chief, Major-General Odierno, were proving themselves utterly unaware of the way in which their actions might be perceived across the broader Islamic world. Indeed, their actions were seen as little more than a mimicking of Israeli strategy in the West Bank.

During the second of my several reporting stints in Iraq, I had the opportunity to see the world Filkins talked about, but from an entirely different perspective: the Iraqi point of view. I settled down for several weeks in the same palm groves and fruit orchards in which Lieutenant Colonel Sassaman's forces had operated. Iraq's anti-American insurgency was just beginning to find its legs in the so-called Sunni Triangle, and the region offered a window into just who was signing on to fight. With my trusted interpreter, Mohammed Tawfeeq, who would later become a senior producer for CNN in Baghdad, I managed to get to know several Iraqi families on both sides of the river, in an area that the US forces jokingly referred to as the "Redneck Riviera." This particular corner of the Sunni Arab heartland was given this nickname because it is the area where many of Saddam Hussein's military commanders grew up. It had a reputation for stubborn farmers and gun lovers, many of whom prospered under Saddam and were promoted by him.

Mohammed, twenty-six, was one of the politest interpreters I had ever come across in my years of reporting overseas. He was easygoing and, on our first foray into the Riviera, he made friends with an interesting family, one that became more intriguing with each passing day. One of four sons in the family, Abu Jabbar, took a liking to Mohammed and invited us to several Sufi ceremonies in which young men would perform feats like walking on a bed of nails or sticking a sword through both their cheeks while a group of males urged them on. (This was not a form of trickery and is common in Middle Eastern and Islamic Sufism.) These ceremonies served as a source of communal bonding but also included a strong spiritual theme. The participants made me—an outsider—feel like an honored guest and witness. Though I never witnessed the feat, Abu Jabbar boasted that he had a friend who could shoot himself in the belly with a Kalashnikov, wipe the wound, and walk away.

Abu Jabbar's mother, Um Hossam, an extremely large and affectionate woman, who always dressed in black with a dark headscarf, adopted Mohammed and me as her "sons" and soon began asking us, after a long day of work, to stay the night as the family's house guests. In the early morning hours, as the river birds twittered in the chilly air, she would wake up to bake bread and recite epic poetry that, as it turned out, she wrote herself. She had endless woes to pen because her husband, a driver, had been transporting a truckload of grapes two months earlier when an errant American bomb had landed in the road and killed him instantly. For this reason, Um Hossam, a Saddam Hussein loyalist, would gently curse the Americans and chant that the "blood of Iraq's sons will flow like a river" in revenge for her husband's death.

As we spent time with the family in their rustic, ranch-style home on the Tigris, we gradually discovered that at least two of Um Hossam's sons were active participants in the anti-American insurgency. Abu Jabbar himself, the first member of the family to befriend us, was a police officer by day, allowing insurgents' weapons supplies to pass through his checkpoint, even as US forces looked on unwittingly. At night, Abu Jabbar, tall and lanky with pock-marked cheeks, would gather with friends in fruit orchards and launch attacks—on foot—against US patrols. One evening, he described an attack in which he had nearly lost his life. As he was speaking, he indicated that his colleagues were mounting an attack and—like clockwork—we heard rockets firing in the distance.

He opened up to us and described an earlier attack in which he himself had participated and the leader of his band had been killed. "We stepped out of the orange grove and confronted the tank with our rockets," he said. "We fired and ran." In a lengthy radio feature I did for National Public Radio, Abu Jabbar said, "Most of my group ran in another direction and I found myself alone, so I dove into a muddy ditch. I heard the footsteps of the American soldiers coming toward me. I knew that if I stayed I would be dead, or if I ran I would also be dead. So I said to myself that it is better to kill as many of the Americans as I can before they kill me. I threw the grenades and ran for my life." He fled deeper into the orchards and into a palm grove, eventually finding shelter in the home of a relative.

This lower-middle-class Iraqi family had prospered under Saddam Hussein and the family members' fears of disenfranchisement though a foreign occupation—along with the death of their father—created a visceral reaction.

I was with Abu Jabbar and Um Hossam a day after Saddam Hussein was dragged out of a "spider hole" hideout in a farm farther to the north. Um Hossam cried incessantly at the knowledge that her hero had been brought to heel by the US military. "He was a brave, strong leader of the Arabs," she said, sobbing. "He shook the world and now he is dead. I am really sad—more sad than when Abu Khalid [her husband] died."

Abu Jabbar had two other brothers; one of them was in the army, and another, Ra'ad, was a gun runner. Over a lunch of fresh greens and chicken prepared by Um Hossam, Ra'ad begged his younger brother to stop running around the fruit orchards with his small band of insurgents. Abu Jabbar bridled at the suggestion and insisted that he was duty bound to fight the American occupiers. (Fortunately for me, Mohammed had thought ahead and convinced our hosts that I was a Bosnian Muslim news reporter from Sarajevo. This was of course untrue, but it was also the only hope I had ever had of being treated like a reporter and not an invader.)

One evening at sundown, Abu Jabbar took Mohammed and me

for a short motorboat ride on the Tigris with a neighbor who was a fisherman. We went up the river past a line of dairy cows, and the neighbor pointed to a steep embankment. He insisted that two US soldiers had handcuffed two Iraqi men atop the embankment and forced them into the chilly waters below, where they drowned. The idea startled me, and so I asked Abu Jabbar a second time to tell this story, which Filkins would later detail in his book. When Filkins had asked Lieutenant Colonel Sassaman why he had not come clean during the army's investigation and admitted his battalion's policy of throwing suspects into the river, Sassaman had said: "I wasn't going to let the lives of my men be destroyed. Not because they pushed a couple of insurgents into a pond."[55]

Further up the river, there was a pontoon bridge that locals had cobbled together from floating oil drums. It led across the Tigris in the direction of the larger town of Thuluya, which Abu Jabbar insisted held a much larger group of insurgents than his own small band of Sufi fighters. He offered to introduce me to an insurgent cell, which he said had its base in a small Salafist Sunni mosque that sat just to the right of the bridge as we crossed on foot. First, however, we came across a band of young guys on motorbikes, who quickly agreed to take us out to a graveyard where they said they regularly organized attacks on US patrols. The youths were lighthearted high school students, Arab teenagers, and there was little to distinguish them in appearance or demeanor from any of the Egyptian students I had met in Cairo while pursuing other stories. In the graveyard, however, their faces became serious, and they spoke of fallen colleagues. What was it precisely that bound these young men together in opposition to the US military? Had it been the bulldozed homes? Had it been the anger aroused by watching their colleagues trucked off in the backs of vehicles with bags over their heads?

(Weeks later, I would witness directly the absurd treatment of Iraqi suspects in what the 3rd Armored Calvary Regiment referred to as "the Cage"—an immense barbed-wire holding pen on the Syrian-Iraqi border. Stoic-faced soldiers from Fort Carson, Colorado, wielded wooden clubs as they pulled back prisoners' blind-folds and began their interrogation. As they worked, several US sol-diers joked that they had front-row seats at the "Super Bowl of jihads." It was the kind of undisciplined wartime behavior one would have expected to see in the Balkans, but not from a professional Western army.)

With Abu Jabbar as our guide, we rode on motorcycles to the home of three brothers, who, he said, would tell us about the deep-ening insurgency in Thuluya. At the home of Abu Farras, a local Salafist, we parked behind an eight-foot-high metal gate in a small yard and were invited in for afternoon tea. Abu Farras, a tall, thin-bearded man, explained what he was doing to help his older brother, Abu Ali, organize the insurgency. This was in the immediate after-math of the capture of Saddam Hussein, and the young Salafists were elated that their arch-nemesis had been brought to heel. "His power was based on material possessions alone," said Farras. "As for Osama bin Laden, whose principles are spiritual, no one I know believes that his followers will ever betray him. Salafists protect each other."[56] Farras's oldest brother was a *khatib*, a preacher in the mosque, and he had explained to his younger brother that there was a growing group of men within the local Salafist movement that favored stepping up the jihad against the Americans. Farras said that some in the movement had warned against rising too soon against a stronger force. With the capture of Saddam Hussein, however, all bets were off.

"I can tell you that the jihadis are clearly winning this internal struggle," Farras said. "Those who don't stand up to the USA are insulted by their soldiers. They suffer humiliation and are weak."[57] On another level, I sensed that fighting the Americans was also quickly becoming a matter of hometown pride.

Suicide missions were just starting to disrupt the American occupation of Iraq. Bombers were entering the country from Saudi Arabia, Jordan, and Syria, leaving Damascus, an immense city not far from the border, to serve as a key gathering point and first stop for many of the foreign fighters. Farras was not pleased to have to tell us that most of the would-be martyrs were coming in from the outside. He was actively attempting to encourage more Iraqis to take part in suicide missions.

"We are fewer and weaker in firepower than the Kafirs," he said, clinking his cup of green tea down on a coaster. "So martyrdom attacks are the only way for us to move ahead in this struggle," he argued. "This has been the trend in Palestine, and without these tactics, they [the Palestinians] would be in a far worse bargaining position."[58]

Analysts can disagree with that logic, but the similarity with Palestine was constantly mentioned, suggesting that many of the insurgents considered that the Americans were playing the same role in Iraq as the Israelis did in the West Bank. Pointing out the similarity also gave even Iraqi insurgents a sense of fighting in a global conflict.

Farras explained the delicate nature of leading suicide bombers into Iraq from the Syrian border. "Every time we are involved in a mission, there is the risk that we will compromise cells within our own movement. But we can't stop them from engaging in jihad since that is their holy mission." He said that Iraqi insurgents had a means of identifying their allies in arms from outside through "coded responses from them for the purposes of identification. If they are committed to an attack, we lead them to their target as soon as possible. We provide them with one Iraqi guide and a safehouse."[59]

We drove that same afternoon to the home of another young man, whose father had been a senior government official in Saddam's regime. We were back with the group of insurgents from the graveyard, and this time they showed off glistening machine guns and rocket launchers. Across the water we could see the home of Um Hossam. The Tigris River area was at its most fertile here, the river being lined with groves of date palms as far as the eye could see. With the reeds and trees waving in the winter winds above the muddy waters, the scene might have come from another conflict, decades earlier in Southeast Asia.

The group of young men we were with pointed to a house farther north on the same side of the river. It was the home of a father whose son had led American forces into Thuluya in an effort to root out insurgents. Locals told the father that—in return for his betrayal of the tribe—his entire clan would be killed unless he killed his son. He was given only one choice. Anthony Shadid, a Lebanese American who won a Pulitzer prize for his coverage of the war in Iraq, would interview the father after he had killed his son with his own hands. "Even the prophet Abraham didn't have to kill his own son," the father told Shadid. "There was no other choice." Shadid's story hinted at the societal forces that work to hold together an insurgency.[60]

✳✳✳

The capture of Saddam Hussein represented a moment of immense satisfaction for the Bush administration, which bordered on gloating. Paul Bremmer, the leading diplomat in the country at the time, stepped up to a podium before the entire press corps on the day Hussein was caught and said, "We got 'im!" as though reciting a line from an old Western. In truth, the capture of the fugitive president was a watershed moment; not for the better but for the worse. It marked the moment when popular reverence for the old regime collapsed and groups that had been persecuted by Hussein rose up to seize control of the insurgency with an immense influx of Gulf money to help them complete the takeover. "We got 'im " would turn out to be a "gotcha" moment not unlike "Mission Accomplished."

For several weeks after the capture of Saddam Hussein, party loyalists up on the Redneck Riviera looked devastated. Abu Jabbar told me he had contemplated suicide and his brother Ra'ad was as sad as Um Hossam. Across the river, Farras and his brothers, on the other hand, saw the capture of Saddam as a golden opportunity. "Our dead will become martyrs, and more and more young people will embrace our creed," he told us as the Tigris swirled past.[61]

It was not until I was able to arrange a meeting with Farras's older brother, Abu Ali, however, that I would understand the extent of the planning and the intensity of the ideology that was behind the growing anti-American insurgency. Several days after we met Farras, Mohammed, my interpreter, received a phone call asking us to return by car to Thuluya for a meeting with Abu Ali, the "manager" of the largest Salafi insurgent cell in the region. We drove to a barren cliff along the Tigris, which provided a wide-angle view of the date palms and orange groves in and around the Redneck Riviera.

Abu Ali was waiting for us, squatting contemplatively on his haunches, kneading a string of black worry beads. In the distance, low, undulating hills surrounded a field between two hills that insurgents called the "Valley of Death." It was a low point on the horizon that any American unit had to pass through if it planned to patrol the peninsula jutting out into the Tigris at Thuluya. The landscape of lush green fields and irrigation canals was the kind of terrain that any guerrilla would long for.

"With the demise of Saddam and the Fedayeen, you will see our parties unite," he said. "We will form alliances with anyone ready to attack the Americans and force them into retreat. We are happy that Saddam has been arrested. In fact, this makes it easier for us. We can now convince people that the fight was never about Saddam. The aim is to kill Americans. There may be mistakes. Muslim innocents who are killed in these attacks will become martyrs."[62]

Abu Ali and his brother Farras, both well educated, spoke the language of the international jihad. In their broad aspirations and sense of duty I heard the ambitions that I had heard in the northern reaches of Yemen at the Dar al-Hadith school. The brothers mentioned ancient and modern ideologues but no specific mentors or leaders. Even bin Laden served as an inspiration, one of many, but he was certainly not their leader.

Far more important to Farras and his brother Abu Ali than any modern jihadist was Ibn Taymiya, an outspoken Muslim cleric who led the resistance to the Mongol invasion of Damascus in 1300.[63] In 1306 and again in 1308, Taymiya was held captive in the citadel of

Cairo, later moving on to Damascus, where he was also incarcerated for his views. Taymiya's austere rejection of traditional Islam's reverence for saints and their tombs became an inspiration to the puritanical-minded Salafists in Iraq and many other Islamic nations. Taymiya attempted to steer the faithful away from false idols and toward the worship of Allah and Allah alone. Rather than seek common ground with detractors, he furiously denounced his fellow Muslims for treating saints as protectors or benefactors. Taymiya also openly advocated war against foreign occupiers and anyone—in his case the Mongols—who did not strictly adhere to Islamic law but followed "man-made laws." In this respect, he preferred to follow closely the life of the Prophet and his earliest followers. It was their form of worship and their teaching that could provide, in Taymiya's view, an infallible guide for living. It was their stubborn asceticism that had set Iraq's Salafists at loggerheads with the gaudy and prideful reign of Saddam Hussein. As I wrote in *Time* magazine in 2004, "Many of the indigenous jihadists in Iraq practice Salafism, a stringent brand of Sunni Islam that was brutally repressed by Saddam's regime after it began gaining adherents in Iraq a decade ago."[64] The last thing that Saddam had wanted was a religious challenge to his iron-fisted reign of glory. And while he was in power, the Salafists had been imprisoned and often murdered. It was a wonder that the war planners missed that, but then, as the president had said, we didn't "do nuance."[65]

Over the next month, I cultivated a relationship—which I hesitate to call a friendship—with Abu Ali and his brother. Both of the young men were highly educated, far more so than Abu Jabbar and his Sufi brothers. Compared to Um Hossam and her earthy poetry, however, they were a bit cold, like New York intellectuals compared to southern farmers. They were also well connected and extremely ambitious. Abu Ali had served as an official in the Ministry of Education (where he had kept his religious views to himself) under Saddam Hussein and still worked in Baghdad in the same office, which gave him a base to help organize the growing insurgency in

Thuluya. I visited him in his Baghdad office, and he also would drop by my hotel. Our relationship continued until I discovered that he had been following me about the city on certain occasions, which raised suspicions in my mind that he might have an interest in kidnapping an American, though he still, as far as I knew, believed I was a Bosnian Muslim from Sarajevo.

He was always polite and surprisingly forthcoming about his own views. More important to Abu Ali than bin Laden was the Saudi sheikh's own mentor, Abdul Azzam. When Western terrorism analysts downplay the influence of the Palestinian struggle on bin Laden's global jihadist movement, they often overlook the origin and influence of Azzam, who was both a scholar and a theologian. Azzam's own life melded the idea of defensive jihad in Palestine with other Islamic liberation struggles around the world. In this regard, he is one of the founders of the modern global jihad. Born in 1941, Azzam first studied Islam at Cairo's Al-Azhar University, where he befriended both Dr. Ayman al-Zawahiri and the blind sheikh, Omar Abdel-Rahman. As a Palestinian by birth, he became a member of the Palestinian Muslim Brotherhood, which was dedicated to the liberation of Palestine. But he became a global activist after receiving his doctorate and accepting a teaching post in Jeddah, Saudi Arabia, where he is believed to have met Osama bin Laden for the first time. In 1979, Azzam issued a fatwa, or religious edict, equating the Afghan and the Palestinian jihads as defensive jihads against foreign occupation that all Muslims were obligated to support. He famously said that "every Muslim on Earth should unsheathe his sword and fight to liberate Palestine," adding that "the jihad is not limited to Afghanistan, 'jihad' means struggle. You must fight in any place you can."[66]

To that end, Azzam made plans to train Hamas fighters in Afghanistan, who would be given the expertise to return to their homeland and continue the jihad there. Like several other modern Islamic scholars who were influential in the Afghan jihad, Azzam believed that a "clash of civilizations" with the non-Islamic world was both inevitable and necessary.

Although Abu Ali read what I wrote, I sensed that he was more comforted by my knowledge of wars in the Balkans, where I had spent five years, particularly when I made a point of mentioning—as a means of drawing him out as an interview subject—the persecution of Muslims there. He claimed to know several Bosnian Muslims currently living in Baghdad, and he mentioned the names of two Arabs, Anwar Shaban al-Masri and Salah Halibi, who had been killed fighting Serbian forces loyal to President Slobodan Milosevic. One day, Abu Ali came to my room to tell me that a week earlier he had organized a mortar attack on the base at Balad, an attack that had killed one American officer. He described the attack matter-of-factly and then divulged to me that he had served in an Iraqi army commando unit when Saddam had invaded neighboring Kuwait. Though he objected to that invasion, he said the experience he had gained had been invaluable.

Abu Ali, forty, helped to organize a cell of fighters in Thuluya known as the Mujahadi al-Salafia (Salafist Warriors), most of them between the ages of twenty and thirty. He said his fighters had indirect contacts with a better-known fundamentalist group, Ansar al-Islam, and a new group of al Qaeda fighters, but that they operated independently, as did a myriad of other insurgent groups that sprang up in 2004, all with the common objective of fighting the "occupation." He said his own group had made overtures toward disaffected former Fedayeen, members of Saddam's own paramilitary units. "If anyone asks to work with us, we try to provide them with the principles and belief structures they will need to put aside their old fight and understand our liberation efforts," he told me. "That person must convince us that he has changed his ways and he must pray with us. When someone in the Baath Party wants to join our struggle, I am personally responsible for their introductions. The circle is complete now and Saddam is no longer a player. Many in our country are already aware of his close ties with Donald Rumsfeld and other American diplomats. Clearly, the Americans have finally found it in their interest to get rid of him, but this is to our advantage, not theirs."[67]

Abu Ali made it clear that he was against everything he believed

America represented in Iraq. "We are against crusaders who try to destroy Islam," he said. "This includes all kind of individuals, people, contractors, companies, and anyone who deals with the US and tries to help them, including the media that burnishes their image."[68]

Our ideological discussions went on in depth, and Abu Ali mentioned names I was familiar with and some that I had only a vague knowledge of, including several Arabs he knew who had fought with the Chechens in Russia. He asked me to go on an attack with him in Balad, but I refused because I did not want to witness the killing of my own countrymen. Other reporters in Iraq—at the time—did take insurgents up on such offers and argued, convincingly I thought, that real war reporting often requires a cold heart and appalling moral choices. (I think that a useful rule of thumb is to report both sides of the story from both of the front lines and to always refuse a gun to defend yourself.)

I had listened closely to the warnings of CIA officials about how a US invasion of Iraq would play into the interests of Islamic radicals (and I had reported their warnings in my preinvasion news stories). Subsequently, I became appalled at the way the US military had treated Iraqi citizens, particularly in the first two years of the war. None of Lieutenant Colonel Sassaman's soldiers spoke Arabic, and almost all of them believed that they had come to Iraq to "liberate" the Iraqi people, yet so many behaved with wanton brutality toward them. Sassaman was no exception, however. After the war, he told Filkins that that everything he did he had been ordered to do by his superiors—all except lying about it when events went wrong.[69] It was a comment on his character that—with an education at West Point, an institution that places such value on "the truth"—that he could excuse his own lying to a reporter. Unfortunately, his moral character left a lot to be desired on several other fronts as well.

Almost everything that Abu Ali said made sense and, while I did not see the world through his eyes, the essential (and cold) logic of his struggle became increasingly clear. It was sad but true that Islamic fundamentalists had projected their own duty-bound struggle onto a need to kill Americans. There was also another spiritual motive grounded in their homeland and faith that interlopers like me could never fully understand, but that I was able to sense. Abu Ali said that his cell, Mujahedi al-Salafia, was gaining new recruits by the day, because "Allah is on our side."

In support of this point, he explained that the Iraqi Red Cross had returned the body of a local holy warrior, Majid Akhmed, who, he said, was a courageous young fighter who had been captured alive and taken six weeks earlier to the Abu Ghraib prison. (As I'm writing this story now, it is worth noting that these events occurred before the scandal of prisoner abuse at this now notorious prison became public.) Abu Ali said that his friend Majid had protested against the conditions inside the prison and was present in the prison when US forces had attempted to put down an uprising there.

"Majid took two bullets in the abdomen and was left untreated with his hands tied until he died," said Abu Ali. "When the Red Cross delivered his body this week, he still had the burn marks on his hands where he had been tied by the Americans. But even after forty days of being dead, he was still bleeding hot blood and he had a wet forehead. His body smelled sweet as though he was still alive."[70]

I suspected that US military undertakers had likely done a quick embalming of the body before handing it over and allowing his relatives to return it to his home village. In any case, I also had no doubt that Abu Ali and the citizens of Thuluya saw Majid Akhmed as both a miracle and a martyr; one that would surely inspire others to follow in his footsteps.

✴✴✴

It is foolish to predict winners and losers in war. In the end, all the participants emerge dead, injured, or mentally undone. To my dismay, I had borne witness to the emergence of the insurgency in Iraq and—as a result—the strengthening of the global jihad. I was witness to a process: "What becomes a terrorist most."

Bin Laden's declaration of war on America in 1998 was intended to draw the US military into an unwinnable conflagration, and there were now irrefutable signs across the Islamic world that this goal was being achieved. I was dismayed that the United States had left the fight unfinished in Afghanistan by conjuring monsters in Iraq where none had existed—but where they then appeared almost as a rude afterthought to satisfy our expectations.

In the Bush years, the war that we paid billions to win had less to do with Islamic ideology than it had to do with perceptions of an American and Israeli aggressor. In keeping with bad karmic principles, force rose up to meet force on both sides of the equation. I traveled to Tunisia and Morocco in the wake of suicide bombings there, only to find more young men inspired by the likes of Abu Ali to fight against perceived Western aggression. In a slum outside Casablanca, a small clan of Salafists, also inspired by fighters with Afghan connections, burst onto the scene with a string of attacks on Western and Israeli restaurants and clubs. In Tunisia, ideologues targeted one of the few remaining Jewish communities in the Middle East outside Israel. All these occurrences were very similar in motivation, and also rather predictable, given the storm that was raging.

Dr. Sageman's road map for how and why young men turn to violence was being followed, with the assistance of the United States government. Washington, through its own hyperventilation and military blundering, heightened the sense of moral outrage across the Islamic realm and created the impression—true or not—that the United States was at war with Islam, which is one of Sageman's keys to radicalization. Conflicts that might not be local were linked to local grievances through a process of globalization, with networks of insurgents working over the Internet and on the ground to mobilize young men for the fight. In creating the moral outrage, of course, Washington had the help of its favorite monster, Osama, at every turn, with his propaganda machine hinting at every possible conspiracy theory.

One of the more insightful investigative reports on young Arab men turning to violence was written by *Newsweek* reporter Kevin Peraino, who used information obtained from computer files in Iraq to show that, out of 606 foreign militants recorded as entering Iraq to fight the Americans, fifty-two of them—most destined for martyrdom—came from a single town on the Mediterranean coast, Darnah. As it turns out, Darnah in Libya has a long history of conflict with the West, particularly the United States, beginning in 1801 with the capture of an American frigate, USS *Philadelphia*, by pirates, who put the ship on display in Tripoli's harbor. Darnah's old city was eventually overrun by General William Eaton, who marched across the desert from Alexandria, in Egypt. Peraino notes that "Libyan schools teach the capture of the *Philadelphia* as a great national victory."[71] Later, people in and around Darnah fought against a brutal Italian occupation that decimated the local population between 1912 and 1933. The struggle against the Italian occupation is the stuff of legend, and Italian tactics, Peraino discovers, included the use of concentration camps, deliberate starvation, and executions. "The hero of the insurgency was a charismatic, white-robed Muslim holy warrior named Omar al-Mukhtar," writes Peraino. "The Lion of the desert was a disciple of Senussis, a secretive and deeply conservative order of Islamic ascetics," who "honed a strict, yet almost evangelical, variety of Islam that spread quickly through eastern Libya."[72] In a sense, he was the bin Laden of his day.

What also helped drive many of the young men in Darnah to Iraq were the modern images of carnage seen on Al Jazeera and CNN; a reminder to them that Islam was under attack in Iraq. One is left to wonder, when reading about the ideology that inspired and continues to inspire resistance in Darnah and places like it, whether it is really Islam that drives these young men into battle, or something deeper within human nature. Other ideologies, after all, including Christianity, have provided the same impetus to fight that ascetic Islam provided for the resistance in Libya. The imagined need to resist foreign intrusion, whether in one's own backyard or elsewhere on the globe but within one's cultural boundaries, is probably, in the end, as important as or even more important than any inspiration that religion can provide.

Chapter 4
ISLAM IN THE SHADOW
OF DEMOCRACY

Inside Jakarta's main football stadium, a leather-clad rock 'n' roll band had just finished playing, and now the officials were piping in, oddly, the theme song to Bruce Willis's movie *Armageddon.* Several rough-and-tumble militants in black and blue spun down through the skies, twisting a rope from three hundred feet above the crowds on the top deck. A troop of drummers in batik shirts and bandanas kept the beat for nearly one hundred thousand Indonesians, who had turned out to rally in favor of something few of them knew much about: the imposition of Sharia, or Islamic law.

Hizbut Tahrir Indonesia, a global Islamic organization founded by a Lebanese scholar, Taqiyuddin al-Nabhany, had organized the rally and its vitriolic lineup of speakers, which, at the last minute, excluded the firebrand leader Jemaah Islamiya's Abu Bakar al-Ba'asyir. Al-Ba'asyir is widely accused by Western governments of "inspiring" the Bali bombings. Nevertheless, the sentiments of the massive gathering of Indonesians were palpable and clear. Speakers fervently denounced the United States for what they alleged was America's role in starting a war against Islam after the events of 9/11.

As a grand, dramatic display to end the day's festivities, an on-field skit brought together flag bearers representing both Muslim nations and Western "aggressor" nations. I watched as the aggressor nations symbolically beat down Muslim nations, specifically Afghanistan and Iraq, hammering them with the butts of their flagpoles. This was not necessarily the end of the story, however, as hundreds of black- and white-clad actors revealed another possible ending to the conflict. As the skit concluded, the audience of men, women, and children writhed in human waves. Muslim nations could be seen rising up against Great Britain, Australia, the United States, and Serbia—among others—to fend for themselves and throw off the yoke of US-led oppression. Literally, the Muslim nations chased the bad guys off the field.

It was late 2007, and I had returned to Southeast Asia for the first time in seventeen years. It was an exciting time. A lot had changed in the region since I had covered the Burmese and Chinese uprisings of the late 1980s. I had spent five years reporting in Southeast Asia, covering civil wars, environmental issues, and economic development. I had visited Indonesia twice at the height of General Suharto's "guided democracy," a fancy term for dictatorship. Back in 1990, I had looked hard in Indonesia for the kind of news-making violence that was so easy to find along the Burmese and Cambodian borders, but I had failed to turn up much obvious strife. The best I could do as an aspiring young war reporter was to cover the fate of a Stone Age tribe in the Balliem highland jungles of Western New Guinea whose members were trying to shoot down Indonesian army helicopters with bows and arrows. Meanwhile, Christian missionaries, intent upon putting pants on the same naked tribesmen, who preferred penis gourds, dropped Nike jogging shorts from airplanes. The shorts had quickly been made into headdresses by the natives. Indonesia, while suffering only limited strife, was still one of the more unpredictable and entertaining countries in the world, with a vibrant economy to boot.

On the other hand, free speech and civil society as we knew it in the West were severely restricted in Indonesia. Like a lot of other autocrats, General Suharto guaranteed his power by oppressing his opponents and limiting debate. Soon after he seized power in 1966, the strongman had burnished his reputation as an advocate of the history of his native Java and its indigenous faith, components of which were animist, Hindu, and Buddhist in nature, embellished and held together by principles of moderate Islam. He kowtowed to American interests but gradually, under increasing criticism at home and abroad, empowered Muslim radicals in a last-ditch effort to guarantee his authority across the vast archipelago. None of this worked. The Asian markets crashed and terrorism raised its ugly head, revealing the region as fertile soil for al Qaeda's global operations.

Yet as I watched the events inside the stadium unfold on that muggy day, the stunning cultural diversity of the region all came back to me in a rush. Traditional dancers and wide smiles lightened the stern, anti-American fare. After the event concluded, I managed to corner the organizers as well as the Indonesian rock band that had played. Leo, the group's violinist, who had his hair tied back in a pony tail, wore a tiger's tooth necklace and a black shirt laced with white. He told me the group's own "jihad," or struggle for Sharia, was performed through its music. "We all have the same fight, we are just doing ours through art and culture," he said, as dozens of lightly veiled women streamed by. The group's guitarist, Ali Shefi, looked amused in a floppy black hat as he puffed on a cigarette. His day job was that of a legal counsel. He did not see any glaring irony in playing American rock music, which was also prized by drug-crazed, decadent Western youth. "I love the spirit and fire of rock music," he said. "We respect our Western brothers." Leo hadn't finished having his say yet, and so he added, "what people were trying to say here today is that every person must have their own filter. Before you take up a religion, you have to be human first. We don't hate Americans; you guys show a lot of humanity. It is just the way that you live, which is in conflict with our own culture and religion. We don't have to push each other. That can be your culture and this can be ours."

The language he used included hints of the postindependence Indonesian ethic of strength in diversity as well as the state's promotion of vague but useful ideas like "civilized humanitarianism and social justice."[1]

But there were other forces at work inside this vast stadium. I wanted to believe a Hizbut Tahrir campus agitator in a snow-white gown when she told me afterward in delightful broken English that "What we are trying to do is something—peace for everyone. We want to say Islam is peace. Islam is something very beautiful, very nice." She made the prospect sound almost idyllic, with her wide smile and lovely white headdress.

On the other hand, I knew more about Hizbut Tahrir than the music and the positive message. The group had been banned from Egypt, Pakistan, and Saudi Arabia. Jane Perlez of the *New York Times* had described it as calling for "a caliphate in Muslim countries, the end of Israel," and the withdrawal of all Western interests from the Muslim world. She cited analysts who said that Hizbut Tahrir represented the interests of "soft jihadists."[2] A noted American scholar of Islam at the University of California, Muhamad Ali, had written in the Jakarta newspapers at the time of my visit that the group was promoting a sort of "Muslim papacy" consisting of a caliph, a single man who would control the entire Islamic realm. The group did not deny this.[3]

But there was also a Southeast Asian context that could not be overlooked. Indonesia was still a young nation, defining its own identity and—to be fair—the Hizbut Tahrir group had only acted as the facilitator of this massive meeting of divergent groups. Democracy had hit some rough waters, and the undefined vision of Sharia was little more than a political device offered by Islamic leaders who sought to provide a sense of order against a backdrop of conspicuous consumption, governmental corruption, Javanese mysticism, and varied interpretations of Islam. Furthermore, Indonesians were not used to having ideas imposed on them from abroad.

Islam did not arrive in Indonesia on camelback, on horseback, or by the sword. It came across the ocean currents on the lips of mild-mannered Arab traders and melded with a rich indigenous culture to create an extremely tolerant brand of what is known as "syncretic" Islam. This archipelago of 235 million inhabitants with a literacy rate of 90 percent was not an obvious home for radical Islamic groups. The radical Islam that had arrived on Indonesia's shores had been imported from the Middle East in measured doses over decades. The 1980s and 1990s had witnessed a fresh influx of stricter strains of Islam—aided in part by wealthy Muslim charities in oil states of the Persian Gulf. These ideas arrived against the backdrop of a successful Iranian revolution and a gathering of global jihadists—some of whom were Indonesians—in Pakistan and Afghanistan that ended up defeating the mighty Soviet empire.

In the late 1990s, the fall of the corrupt and embittered President Suharto, who was estimated to have acquired over $10 billion in personal assets, coupled with the demise of the Southeast Asian nation's strictly controlled social and political life, beckoned in a new era. It promoted a rekindling of Islamic interest in Indonesia, the world's largest Muslim nation. More recently, the US-led war on terror had had a ripple effect on an increasingly devout culture. Indonesia, once a reliably pro-American nation, wavered and turned bitter toward US foreign policy. Polls conducted by the Pew Research Center in Washington had recorded 70 percent of Indonesians as viewing the United States favorably in the year 2000, but only 15 percent seeing it that way in 2003, and 29 percent seeing it that way in 2007. By 2009, when Barack Hussein Obama took office, the slide in public opinion would be quickly reversed, however, with 63 percent looking favorably on the United States.[4] George Bush's war on Islam had morphed into something entirely different, particularly when the United States now boasted a president who had spent part of his childhood in Indonesia and whose mother had been a doctoral student of Indonesian culture and had literally married into the country.

Indonesian public opinion was in a state of flux, and the jury was still out with regard to the path its people would choose. There were several questions I hoped to address through interviews and reporting in the three months that I would spend in Indonesia in the summer of 2007. Through my meetings with academics, diplomats, and young Indonesians, I wanted to determine if there was a critical mass of anti-Americanism that posed any kind of existential threat to the Western world, including the United States. I wanted also to understand the broader implications of US foreign policy in the Islamic realm and the way US policy impacted the radicalization of young Muslims in Indonesia. More important, possibly, was the issue of whether the advancement of stricter forms of Islam posed a threat to Indonesia's own democratic development.

Before I traveled to Indonesia, I had already spoken to Dr. Steven Kull of the University of Maryland, whose WorldPublicOpinion.org Web site had conducted extensive focus group polling across Indonesia in 2006–2007. Kull explained to me in an interview that he had discovered a growing sense in Indonesia that "after 9/11, the USA made this decision to go after Islam itself . . . that the war on terrorism is really a war on Islam."[5]

One particularly worrisome influence was developing in the form of the mass media, mostly in the form of Arab news channels, that were beaming pictures of mayhem and violence from the Middle East, both from Iraq and Israel. It was becoming hard for Indonesians to distinguish one violent military engagement from the other. More than anything, Indonesian youth, who represent the majority of the population, were receiving mixed messages about the nature and causes of strife across the Middle East.

My first few weeks in Indonesia would be spent talking to university students, mostly young leaders of Islamic organizations who had an interest in global politics. Indonesia had a modern history of student militancy, and I would soon discover that such militancy had not disappeared. Later, my journey would take me to the far reaches of the archipelago, to the Moluccan Islands, where Muslim and Christian groups had butchered one another earlier in the decade in a conflict that had all the color of a local land dispute and all the flavor of a larger global struggle.

Indonesia is about as distant from American shores as any land on Earth. Its volcanic soils are home to vast jungles and rice fields, above which palms and banana trees sway in the Pacific breezes. Its people are short and hearty, often lovely in complexion, a measured mix of dark skins and curly hair alongside lighter skins, oval eyes, and straighter hair.

Whatever one says about the brutality of past dictatorships, the occasional crackdowns on dissent, and the legacy of Dutch colonial rule, a love of education and economic advancement is infectious across the vast nation. While talking to Indonesian students, I discovered many of their concerns to be similar to those found on American campuses. At Jakarta University, a large, sprawling campus built partially with US assistance, I arrived just in time to witness the orientation sessions for new students. Unlike students at a large European or American university, students in Jakarta were dressed in uniforms and willingly subjected themselves to a disciplined indoctrination of sorts. Second- and third-year students were taking the newcomers through the paces of daily campus life, which included a strong dose of religion, with Muslims required to pray five times a day. (Muslims make up some 88–90 percent of the population in Indonesia, with Christians coming in second at about 8 percent, Bali's Hindus at 2 percent, and Buddhists at 1 percent.)

New students enrolling at Jakarta University are required by law to list a religion, with no exceptions for atheists or agnostics. It is an unusual regulation that highlights the state's long-standing requirement of belief in one God, a concept that hasn't sat well with Hindus and Buddhists. The requirement is a legacy of the policies of Suharto's predecessor, President Sukarno, who was overthrown in a military takeover.[6]

My guide on campus was a young journalist, Enrico Aditjondro, who specialized in religious and environmental issues and displayed the same kind of lively intellectual curiosity as nearly everyone else we met in this highly literate nation. As the students filed by in yellow shirts and blue pants, some of the women in colorful head scarves, a Cat Stevens (now Yusuf Islam) song about Islam and love was already blasting out across the manicured lawns and asphalt footpaths. The upbeat lyrics—in their original English—stressed that Islam is a peaceful religion. In a crowded cafeteria, we met Tigor Dalimunthe, the head of a campus Islamic group known as the Forum for Islamic Studies. His job was to help with the orientation and to organize events.

Tigor led us around a bit as we peered into the prayer rooms for males and females and watched as the new students turned in military formation to march up a hill for their next set of instructions. On one side of an open classroom, young male students genuflected, and on the other side, women in white gowns, looking a bit like Halloween ghosts, did the same. "It is prayer time," Tigor said, ushering us down a path. "We pray five times a day." Just as a Christian leader of an evangelical society might look after new recruits on campus, Tigor was counseling anyone interested in sharing ideas about Islam. His audience was all ears. He said that an interest in Islam had grown stronger on campus, particularly since the outbreak of war in Iraq, which he said gave everyone a "sense that fellow Muslims are under attack."[7]

We strolled across the verdant hills—not unlike those I recalled at Tigor's age from my own pleasant campus in Berkeley, California—and moved to his group's office on the second floor of a set of classrooms nestled neatly in a grove of palm trees. I asked him why he or anyone else felt they were under attack from the United States: "After the 9/11 attack, it becomes real," he said. "It becomes clear that whenever the US [that is, its politicians] talks about terrorism, the US also relates this to Muslim countries. It is unfair. As a Muslim, if we get one Muslim being hurt, it is like every Muslim being hurt."[8] He suggested that American officials were promoting guilt by association, not unlike the process of racial profiling, in the United States.

As Tigor spoke, beside his head was a stuffed owl with spectacles and a graduation cap, a reminder that he was only nineteen years old. He insisted that the war on terror had created a bad impression in the minds of Indonesian students. "They think rationally and they can assess what is right and what is wrong," he said, as if he intended to remove my doubts. Though he described his Forum for Islamic Studies as an "apolitical" organization that concerned itself with cultural and economic issues, he said that he had helped to coordinate several pro-Palestine rallies in downtown Jakarta, intended to pressure the United States and its allies to make good on their promises to push for a two-state solution.

Tigor merely chuckled when I mentioned Osama bin Laden and asked whether he had any supporters—or any future holy warriors—on campus. "Most of us do not have sufficient information to be for or against him," he said, adding that he did not know anyone who had gone to fight in Iraq or Afghanistan against the United States.[9] In interview after interview at Jakarta University, I heard the calm and cogent expression of political opinions about the wrong-headedness of George W. Bush's war in Iraq and the crisis in Palestine and Israel. Any real animosity was, for the most part, buried behind friendly sentiments or nonexistent, and I saw no overt sign of militancy.

But the global conflict was front and center in the minds of many of the young students Enrico and I would meet. They believed, as well, that it was their responsibility to know and understand these broader issues. In *Indonesian Destinies*, Theodore Friend, a seasoned writer and former president of Swarthmore College, highlights the young student revolutionary groups, *pemuda*, which, he says, have inspired successive generations.[10] Although the Indonesians' struggle against the Dutch was less bloody than many other colonial wars, Dr. Friend points out that "from the society at large sprang up all kinds of laskar [paramilitary] and struggle groups—fighters with various orientations and motivations." These fighters, he states, were "not regular soldiers but youths willing to put their lives on the line for a democratic republic, or a communist republic, or an Islamic republic," and most of them were also expected to be "pioneers of ideological war."[11] In an interview, however, Dr. Friend downplayed the threat of Islamic militancy in modern Indonesia, while, at the same time, acknowledging that there were still many idealists whose intention it was to "rescue Indonesia through Islam."[12]

Enrico drove me everywhere around Jakarta on the back of his motorcycle. It was the logical alternative to being stuck in traffic for hours. When you become a part of the motorbike traffic in Southeast Asia, you come to terms with both the vastness of humanity and the prevalent sense of egalitarianism, at least among the young.

At Jakarta's Islamic University, however, the opinions were decidedly sharper and more critical of the United States. In the offices of another student leader, Hissan Sobar, a slender and soft-spoken young man with a slight goatee, we sat on the floor. A number of young women, who were on their way to a choir practice, joined us. Later they would assemble nearby and start singing in sweet, mellifluous voices. One of the themes that emerged from our discussion was that contradictions in US foreign policy were causing unease and dissonance within the student population on campus. This did not translate in any way into animosity toward me as a reporter, however.

"The United States supports democracy in language, but in reality that is not what they are doing," Sobar said. "Though the US talks about democracy and human rights, its overseas operations do not appear to be democratically designed, and certainly the result is far from promoting human rights. Look at Guantanamo. Even the media is kept at bay, suppressed and not permitted to show what is going on."[13]

"We hear the US talking all the time about Islam and terrorism in the same sentence, but the US public is not stupid, they seek out answers and information for themselves," he added. Behind him, Sobar had what I would describe as an overtly militant poster of the Hamas founder and of masked gunmen defending holy sites in Jerusalem. I asked about Abu Bakar al-Ba'asyir, the leader of Jemaah

Islamiya, the fundamentalist-leaning Islamic group that is believed by most terrorism experts—even in Indonesia—to represent the Southeast Asian wing of al Qaeda. "I think Abu Bakar is a good person," Sobar said, offering me another cup of tea. "He would not recommend conflicts or clashes. He is simply fearful of what the US is creating with its power—a dangerous atmosphere in the world—and for that he is being blamed."[14]

On our way back to the city center, Enrico and I dropped into a university bookstore, where a used copy of Richard Clarke's *Against All Enemies* sat on display beside *God's Call Girl,* a story of about the horrors of prostitution and the moral choices involved in choosing the right path in life. Other texts, full of what we might consider radical ideology, glorified the lives of global jihadists. Indonesia was a country of contradictions, but I wondered if it would be better to curtail the free flow of information in bookstores or, instead, to make an effort to tamp down the real motives for radical thought? In Southeast Asia, after the failure in Vietnam, American values, including the value of an open marketplace of ideas, had prospered far beyond our expectations. If the United States ever changed course and insisted on a new crackdown on that same marketplace (which we did not insist on in our own country), would it create a backlash and hand extremists further ammunition? And what about the participation of Islamic groups in the democratic process? Was that not also a "marketplace" of ideas?

For answers, I traveled with Enrico to the city of Solo or Surakarta, the heart of Java. As the home of al Qaeda associate Abu Bakar al-Ba'asyir as well as the site of Indonesia's most violent recent history, this city of half a million inhabitants is considered a litmus test for the nation's changing character. The city has a large percentage of Christians, and so my first visit was to the offices of a Catholic priest, Father Mardi Widayat. He provided a history lesson, stressing that Javanese culture today owes a great deal to pre-Islamic animism and Hinduism despite the predominance of Islam in the modern era. For centuries, Hinduism and Buddhism coexisted in

Java, giving rise to two of the ancient world's most splendid temples, the Buddhist Borobudur and the Hindu Prambanan temples. As author Sadanand Dhume points out, even in the modern era, "The Javanese retained their own history and architecture, their own names, their own dress and dance and music, their own rituals at birth and marriage and death, even their own conception of the afterlife."[15] The country's first president, Sukarno, an internationally renowned playboy and an avid student of Western culture, owed much of his own charisma and national popularity to his ability to inspire the masses through references to the "wayang [shadow theater] heroes from the mythic past."[16]

Father Widayat lifted up a *Homo erectus* skull saved from wild rioting in the city in 1998, which he said targeted the local Chinese community, most of whose members are Catholics. "Java Man," who can be traced back to 1.7 million years ago, is believed to have roamed the banks of the nearby river, Sungkai, forty thousand years ago along with *Homo sapiens*. Widayat bemoaned the violence of the recent decades. Prior to the fall of Suharto, he said, he suspected that elements in the Indonesian government had found it politically expedient to work closely with the Islamic fundamentalist leader, Abu Bakar al-Ba'asyir, whose group ran schools and organized militant Muslims across Java, who often targeted Christians.

Widayat warned me that tensions remained high, so high that he said it was best for the government just to leave al-Ba'asyir alone, so as to allow him to stew in his own juices, and not put him on any kind of pedestal. "If the government cracks down directly on Abu Bakar, he will only get stronger," said the priest, lifting up another skull, that of a Javanese tiger, apparently to illustrate his point. "I've met with Abu Bakar myself, and he admits that he wants to build an Islamic state based on strict Islamic law."[17] The priest, a small, soft-spoken man, who is considered an "uncle" by most of the Catholic students in town, said that Christians in Solo were trying to live low-key lives amid the city's ruined palaces, reminders of an ancient, more tolerant past that is not likely to return anytime soon. He set up a roundtable discussion for us with a group of Catholic students, many of whom had recently dropped out of campus groupings that—they claimed—had turned militant in the past decade.

One of their leaders, Vita Manaan, twenty-two, was, to my surprise, highly critical of US foreign policy, which she said had stoked local tensions by aggravating Muslim students into projecting their anti-American aggressions onto Catholic students. She said that during student union meetings, Muslim students had attempted to force Catholic students to read in Arabic from the Koran to open the meetings. In the end, Vita left the university's union because she felt as though she was just a prop for a group that professed tolerance but did not practice it.

She and her fellow Catholic students described several other incidents that they said were indicative of the tensions surrounding the so-called war on terror. In one instance, Catholic students in a dorm room had attempted to paint over a mural of Osama bin Laden, but they were prevented from doing so. One young woman described how a pamphleteer had come around to Catholic students' dormitories and asked for students by name before dropping off a leaflet. "It said that Jesus was a Muslim and would pray five times a day like Mohammed," she said. "We did not read this until the pamphleteer had left, but we were very upset."[18] A young man nodded and said that if things did not change, Solo would surely "erupt with a big conflict."

In villages across Central Java, religious tensions remained high, with serious incidents often going unreported in the media. Catholics were lying low, but they maintained some strength in numbers and influence within local government structures. Protestants, on the other hand, many of them evangelicals attached to smaller churches, were more vulnerable. Islamic youth groups in and around Solo had strengthened their ranks and were targeting nightclubs in which both alcohol and prostitution were often found, in addition to targeting new churches.

Since the demise of President Suharto, Indonesia has been suffering from a prolonged identity crisis. Although Indonesia was identified in the 1980s as one of Southeast Asia's up-and-coming "Tigers," its economy imploded in the 1990s and left a lot of young Indonesians searching for work. The currency plummeted and then recovered. Since the economic crisis, the country has witnessed the rise of a new professional class that has power and politics on its mind.

We were to meet with Mohammed Farisy, a young Chinese banker in Solo, the local spokesman for the Prosperous Justice Party (PKS), the country's fastest-rising Islamic party. This party favors the implementation of an undefined form of Sharia and is a prime example of the way in which Islamic forces have emerged as important players on the democratic front. Although critics have been fast to lash out at the party's hardliners, a more liberal younger generation of leaders has led the party to recent victories at the polls. Dr. Mark Woodward of Arizona State University, a leading Western academic studying Islam in Indonesia, warned me in an e-mail message months later that "It is increasingly clear that this [the PKS] is not a 'liberal Islamist' party, but a political party that shares a Sharia-based agenda as other Islamists. They deny this, and yet their behavior indicates that they are practicing dissimulation, denying who they are, for political reasons."[19]

Unlike Jakarta, a bustling behemoth of mass marketing and treeless boulevards, Solo is a city of about a million Indonesians with verdant palm-lined parks, bicycles, and strollers that retains ancient and elaborate palaces, unspoiled churches, and ornate mosques. It has some of the modern aspects of Jakarta but maintains the timeless flavor of an older era. Farisy, dressed in a thin rugby shirt and wearing gold-rimmed spectacles, met us over a lunch of dim sum in a downtown Solo hotel where Toyota taxis competed for customers with cyclo drivers in wide-brimmed straw hats. After lunch, he took us over to his party's local headquarters, a few rooms in a house off a busy street where everyone sat around on the floor discussing global politics and strategy. Farisy was quick with his critique of the US government and claimed, like Tigor, the more moderate university organizer, that Islam was being unduly maligned. "I think that the United States and the US military are pushing Muslims to admit that Islam is bad, that Islam is a kind of terrorism," he told me.[20] This is a logic that might escape an outsider, but it is prevalent across much of the Islamic world. Young Muslims say they are not happy to be associated with the word "terrorism," particularly when they consider it to be a universal problem, often associated with Western soldiers, shadowy groups, and spy agencies.

Though Indonesia is officially the largest Muslim country in the world, its distance from the Middle East, a notorious rumor-mill, has assisted in fostering a sense of confusion about what is perceived as an undefined US-led war on terror. Conspiracy theories abound. Many of the young Muslims I met in Indonesia did not even connect Osama bin Laden to the attacks on the Pentagon or the World Trade Center. So whereas many young Indonesians said they admired this so-called holy warrior, they did not think he had committed any heinous crimes against the United States, a country they still admired in a broader cultural sense.

When I pressed Farisy on the issue of his party's alleged support for Sharia—would hand-cuttings and hangings be all right, for instance?—he demurred, insisting that he was not a legal expert and did not really understand the law. This fitted with another point Dr. Woodward made to me: that Indonesian "Islamists treat the term as if it refers to a formal legal code," whereas in the history of Islam, "there is no such thing and never has been. The term is so broad that it can be read in almost any way one wants. The question is who defines and uses the term."[21] In parts of Aceh that impose a fairly direct interpretation of the law, a person missing Friday prayer three times is subject to three strokes from a four-foot rattan cane. A person caught alone with an unrelated member of the opposite sex (outside of marriage) is to be punished with three to nine strokes.[22]

As it turned out, the PKS was helping to sponsor a student rally for Palestine that same afternoon. We drove together with Enrico to the rally and gathered around a gaggle of motor scooters on the state university campus. In the violent 1960s, the name of the university in Solo, translated as "March 11," 1966, reflected a date that came to be etched deeply in the minds all Indonesians. Indeed, it was the date on which Suharto seized formal authority over the nation, taking it away from President Sukarno. Sukarno was described by Dr. Friend as "a poetic romanticist, a mixture of South-Pacific D'Annunzio and indigenous mystagogue," who "was smart enough to dress his presumptive divinity in democracy."[23]

Bizarre occurrences had begun a year earlier when the Indonesian army's top generals were mysteriously murdered. The bodies were dumped in a well. General Suharto, not a participant in the murders, then seized power and—in an era when pressure from the CIA was at its height in Southeast Asia—launched a nationwide purge of suspected leftists, assisted by a list of Communists provided by the US embassy.[24] As Sadanand Dhume points out in his travelogue, *My Friend the Fanatic*, Suharto proceeded to "preside over the annihilation" of the PKI (the Communist Party of Indonesia) and "the slaughter by death squads of an estimated half a million people, most of them in Java and Bali."[25] Under Suharto's watch, the army, not unlike the people who inspired Rwanda's genocide, "broadcast concocted stories in which PKI cadres had gouged the murdered generals' eyes" and castrated them.[26] The lies were designed to incite mayhem. What occurred in the wake of this incitement was more than the British-Malaysian word "amok" can describe. Indeed, Dr. Friend makes the case that the killing was systematic and points out that "the fact that Islamic righteous jihad and Sivaite [referring to the Hindu God, Siva] destructive purification existed alongside historical passivity is not contradictory."[27] This does not, however, excuse the religious and political leaders who ordered their minions to engage in mass slaughter during what Sukarno dubbed "the year of living dangerously."[28]

In 1965 and 1966, some three hundred thousand to eight hundred thousand alleged Communists were rounded up, most of them by paramilitary youth gangs—many with Muslim affiliations—

under military direction, and slain. The campaign of terror was the region's bloodiest series of events until the Khmer Rouge rose from the ashes of war in Cambodia in the following decade. President Sukarno was placed under house arrest, where he died in 1970, an embittered former independence hero. Suharto would be elected unopposed six times in a row.

Providing proof that history's lessons don't last long, the student leaders who Farisy introduced me to found no irony in the fact that their school remained named after the very date that marked Suharto's formal rise to power during the time of the slaughter of their countrymen. Instead, it was the persecution of their fellow Muslims in distant lands that most concerned them.

An associate of Farisy, Joko Pitoyo, an official in the school's student union, explained in an interview that the situation in Israel and Palestine was a rallying point for young Indonesians. This was not a new phenomenon, I noted, however, as Suharto had encouraged pro-Palestinian rallies as well as public outpourings on behalf of the Bosnian Muslims at the height of their own persecution.

Pitoyo spoke in a clearing surrounded by a eucalyptus grove. "The US is involved with Israel in a massive arms trade across the Middle East and is determined to give Israel the upper hand against her enemies," he said. "Foucault said that the United States wants to dominate Palestine because it is a symbol for Islam. Iraq was about oil, but Palestine is about defeating the symbol of Islam," he insisted. "To do that, the US and Israel use all kinds of brute force and violence, combined with gross human rights violations."[29]

Fundamentalist leader Abu Bakar al-Ba'asyir had been out of an Indonesian prison for less than two years when I visited Solo, but as I now learned from Pitoyo, he had already taken the time to meet with young Muslim leaders across Java to clarify his own anti-American views. The public relations effort undertaken by the spiritual leader accused by Western politicians of inspiring the Bali bombings in 2002 was making inroads within the ranks of Indonesian youth.

"Ba'asyir isn't what he is made out to be—he is just a humble Islamic leader who believed the world would be more peaceful with a little unity," said Pitoyo, a tall, strapping young man who was at ease with a reporter. "He was not involved with any of the Bali or Jakarta bombings."[30]

"How do you know this?" I asked.

"I met with him and he told me this himself," he said. "He explained all the difficulties he has been having with the law. Conditions must be met before any of us picks up a gun to carry out jihad. Jihad is not all about fighting with arms, either. Other methods can be used. But when there is heavy oppression—as in the case of Palestine—we must use these methods to fight back against injustice."[31]

It was clear that al-Ba'asyir, whom I soon hoped to meet, was testing the political winds, trying to burnish his reputation as a scholar and influence the direction of his country, not just the direction of his terror network. He had managed—through the force of his own preaching—in many cases through high-profile interviews in the media, to present himself as a viable alternative to Western leaders in some youth circles. That was astounding, considering the militant origins of his group and its less-than-secret ties to al Qaeda. Al-Ba'asyir, once described by Australia's foreign minister, Alexander Downer, as a "loathsome creature,"[32] is descended from a prominent Yemeni-Malay family. His Arab clan came from a part of Yemen (also known in the twentieth century as Arabia Felix) called Hadraumat, a desert valley marked by ancient multistory towers. This corner of the Arabian desert, which borders the so-called empty quarter, also happens to be the home of Osama bin Laden's father.

Founded in 1993, Jemaah Islamiya (JI) did not engage in overt terrorist attacks until 1999 and 2000. Early on, however, the group pledged *bayat* or allegiance to bin Laden for the purpose of sharing resources, primarily in terms of finances, intelligence, and recruitment efforts.[33] The group's founders, al-Ba'asyir and Abdullah Sungkar, met bin Laden as well as other senior al Qaeda leaders and

pledged their cooperation. In 1999 and 2000, Jemaah Islamiya cobbled together like-minded militants—with the help of al Qaeda's
advice—into two militant wings, Laskar Mujahideen and Laskar
Jundullah.[34] These groups became the fighting wings of al-Ba'asyir's
powerful Mujahideen Council of Indonesia (MMI in Yogyakarta).
The MMI was an umbrella organization that embraced humanitarian endeavors, politics, and militancy. When fighting between
Christian and Muslim factions broke out in the Moluccan Islands in
1999, these forces were deployed in earnest, often with a wink and a
nod from elements in the nation's military.

After my chat with the student leader and with Enrico on a
Al-Ba'asyir and his associates were now carefully watching the
rise of young Farisy's PKS, the country's fastest-growing Islamist
party, which had won only 2 percent of the vote in 1999 but captured 8 percent in 2004. Just as PKS downplayed its own strident
calls for the implementation of Sharia law, the Jemaah Islamiya spiritual leader downplayed his own final agenda, which was to set up an
Islamic state with strict implementation of Sharia. That was astute
politics in any country.

After my chat with the student leader and with Enrico on a
motorbike beside me, I leapt on the back of Farisy's scooter and
headed off to what had been billed as the "One Man, One Dollar"
rally for Palestine. It was being held, I was told, as a thank you to
Palestinians for recognizing Indonesia's own independence struggle.
We swerved through a mass of scooters and moved on in the direction of Solo's city square. Although Indonesia is a country that is
about as far from the strife in Israel and Palestine as one can get, I
saw—I must say—an impressive show of people power. In a city of
only half a million persons, about ten thousand young Muslims
gathered together for several hours, most of them wearing bandanas
over their faces and checkered black and white scarves around their
necks in solidarity with their Palestinian brethren. I jumped off the
scooter and watched the sea of humanity pass by. I was probably the
only foreign journalist in town, and it wasn't entirely clear to whom
these young Muslims on a distant island in the Pacific were

appealing. But they were expressing solidarity with a cause they believed in, and they were raising money for it.

On a large flatbed truck with megaphones pointed in all directions, young men, their faces also covered, were screaming at the top of their lungs. A band of exceptionally tall men passed by— members of a sports club—and raised clenched fists to the sky, shouting "Allahu Akhbar!" The largest numbers of flags at the rally, next to those of the black, white, red, and green banners of the Palestinian state, were those of the PKS, in black and yellow.

High school kids climbed up into nearby trees to see what all the fuss was about. Farisy, twenty-seven years old and a rising star in his party, explained to me the significance of what I was seeing. "We are meeting because we think that Palestinians have a right to independence, like most nations in the world," he said.[35]

And what about the support for Hamas at the rally, I asked. "Do you think that raises a red flag?"

"No," he said. "Hamas's popularity is really just a sign of the times. It frames the two-faced policy of the United States government. On one hand, you support democracy all over the world, but as soon as Palestinians use democracy to choose their leaders and Hamas wins, the US does not recognize them. It is a kind of bullshit."[36]

"You mean hypocrisy?" I asked.

"No, bullshit will do," he replied.[37]

There were plenty of secularists in Indonesia who wanted to keep Islamic parties like PKS at bay. The party's elders, its *ulema*, were trained in the Middle East, and for years they had had to lead underground cells, during the repressive early Suharto era when Islamic political forces were banned outright.

A PKS leader attached to the House of Representatives made a plea in the *Jakarta Post* (at about the same time as the rally) to critics who wanted to limit the participation of religious parties in Indonesian politics. The leader, Zulkieflimansyah, denied that his party's view of the future was limited to the strict interpretation of Islamic law. He said that young leaders—I assume he meant young men like

Farisy—were coming to the fore with new and dynamic interpretations. Only through political participation, however, "can space be
accorded to the movement so that the necessary reforms and
learning can evolve from within."[38] It was a reasonable argument for
an inclusive democracy, particularly one that might well keep
Islamists from resorting to other means to assert themselves.

Yet open up the democratic system to all voices and some become
louder than others, potentially drowning out the minority voices. I was
reminded of a teacher I had had in Moscow who explained that the
first ever Russian voting had taken place when groups were asked to
stand on one side of a river and shout out in favor of their interests to
someone on the other side. The loudest voices, those of the majority,
would prevail. But Indonesia had only just embarked on its path
toward democratic change, and the danger was that its delicate bal-
ancing act to date could quickly be undermined by groups intent on
changing the laws and creating a stricter Islamic state in place of a
more secular entity that was still struggling to come into its own.

The student union at March 11 University had already been
taken over by Joko Pitoyo and his gang, who openly admired al-
Ba'asyir. Their public rallying cries clearly emanated from abroad,
not from at home.

Over the course of several days, Father Widayat directed me to
several Protestant leaders who described both the bureaucratic difficulties they were running into and the attacks on their efforts to start
up new Christian congregations. These attacks were increasing in
and around Solo. Pastor Thomas Hwi, an aging evangelical leader,
said that a marauding group of radicals had prevented him from
laying the foundation stones for a new church. "Three truckloads of
firebrands came to my house," he said. "They were very angry. They
broke down my door, slammed a spear into the coffee table and said,
'Let's see you fight George Bush's crusade now!'"[39]

He continued, explaining that "They swore at me and hammered
my dining room table, forcing me to kneel before them. They
demanded my identity card and I brought it. Then a local police

officer arrived, but they shouted him down and told him not to inter-fere. He was asked to step back and turn off his walkie-talkie, for fear that he might record what was about to take place."[40]

Next, the young militants tossed down a pen and paper and said, "Start writing," according to Pastor Hwi. "I was forced to write a letter [saying] that I would never open a church."[41] This kind of low-level intimidation gave Islamic militants in and around Solo something they could feel proud of. It suggested that their demands for "tolerance" went only one way. With such confrontations, often bloodless, their leaders put young Muslims on the front lines of militancy and also gathered strength for a longer war. Like the policeman who stepped back from the fray in an effort to avoid bloodshed, Indonesian authorities have often taken a laissez-faire approach to these kinds of confrontations. They have remained reluctant to clamp down unless such incidents turn into open fighting. In a sense, they are keeping a lid on a boiling pot while doing nothing to extinguish the fire beneath it. While repression continues, violence will have to be confronted in the long run.

✳✳✳

Many Westerners, particularly Americans, will find nothing troubling in the tensions between religious groups in a country as distant and remote as Indonesia. Indeed, such tensions usually make headlines only when Westerners become direct targets. In truth, however, what happens in Indonesia has an impact on issues of sta-bility across the Islamic world. The country's new and inclusive political environment—an experiment that the Obama administra-tion and other Western governments are encouraging—may well turn out to be a bellwether for other Muslim countries flirting with reform. Indonesia will also test the limits—in the future—of the US government's encouragement of peacemaking and democracy on the one hand and security on the other.

Indonesian academics and politicians, like Western governments anxious to see democratic inclusiveness prevail, remain intensely concerned, however, about the impact of events in the Middle East on reforms in their homeland. In Jakarta, I met with Dr. Imdadur Rahmat, an international relations expert concerned with the flow of radical ideas from the Middle East to Indonesia. He had investigated the US-led war on terror's indirect effects on the radicalization of Indonesia's younger generation. He explained that Indonesians have had an on-again, off-again love affair with American ideals, with large numbers of political and business leaders having obtained training at prestigious US institutions, including Berkeley and Harvard. In Indonesia's early years as a nation-state, American ideas were the currency of academic and political discussion.

Dr. Rahmat said that the very meaning of democracy in Indonesia, however, had changed considerably during the administration of George W. Bush. "You can also see the effect with the mainstream Islamic groups in Indonesia," he told me in his study, which was cluttered with academic papers and computer drives. "Early on, these groups were advocating all kinds of ideas from the United States and the West. The concepts of pluralism, democracy, human rights, religious freedom, and civic rights were all promoted as great ideas. That has changed, however. Due to US policies since 9/11, leading Islamic groups have become far more critical of the United States. You can see all these groups from left to right demonstrating against so-called US aggression."[42]

By virtue of the United States' perceived policies in the Middle East, the larger and bolder ideals that the United States stood for were now being shunned. This was partly attributable to the Indonesian press's emphasis on American militarism. Indirectly, this was also acting to radicalize Indonesia's younger generation, Dr. Rahmat said.[43]

I was reminded how difficult it is to influence minds when words don't match the videotape. One of the young radicals, Khalid Saifullah, who had recently served time in jail for attacking Western-style nightclubs in Solo, arrived at my hotel to discuss a book he was writing about alleged abuses against Muslims perpetrated by Indonesian police and security officials. He charged that the abuses were committed by US-backed counterterrorism police, set up in the wake of 9/11.

Saifullah worked out of a small room above an Islamic library that was supported with funds from Middle Eastern charities. A brief tour of this library revealed several upbeat books about the life of Osama bin Laden as well as more serious texts about the benefits of Sharia law. As I spoke with Saifullah over several days, the young ideologue with dark eyebrows and a quick smile struck me as a person determined to make an academic point first and a militant statement second. He was excited to engage a couple of journalists, one American and the other Indonesian, in a serious debate about right, wrong, and the future of his country. But clearly there were darker influences on his thinking. In his office above the library, he showed me several videotapes of clashes between Muslims and Christians in the Moluccan Islands, a chain of heavily populated islands on the eastern perimeter of the archipelago. These tapes were striking for their graphic depictions of the violence, offering some of the most shocking video material I've witnessed in my decade-plus of covering the current global conflict.

Saifullah contended that the US government was backing an Indonesian government effort to crack down on Sharia law advocates. Indonesia did have a horrendous record—across the board—for police abuse, but that abuse did not appear to be specifically targeted to any religious grouping and was not directed more at Muslim extremists than at anyone else. In 2008, Amnesty International's briefing to the UN Committee against Torture suggested that in just two years between 2003 and 2005, over 81 percent of all arrested persons in certain detention centers were either "tortured or ill-treated" by the police. Interrogations alone accounted for 64 percent of the abuse, but little of the reported abuse was directed at specific religious groups.[44]

Saifullah was convinced in his own mind that a broader conflict, which he said had been predicted on all sides, was now unfolding before our eyes. He said that the United States was acting in ways that British academic, Samuel Huntington, author of *The Clash of Civilizations*, had suggested that it would.[45]

"The United States is reacting to what Samuel Huntington predicted," Saifullah said. "After the fall of Communism, the greatest threat to American power would be Islam. This is why the US has now launched a war against us and why we are fighting back."[46] Huntington's views are probably better known and digested in Indonesia than they are in the United States. In *My Friend the Fanatic*, Sadanand Dhume reports on a similar conversation with a young Muslim, in which Huntington's name figures prominently. Ela, a young woman Dhume meets on a ferryboat, cites Huntington's contention that Islam is in competition with Christianity and the United States. She speaks about the rise of Islam: "If we see terrorism, there are connections with Palestine. So it's the main cause. WTC was predicted. Osama bin Laden said the world is silent about Palestine."[47]

For Saifullah, however, jihad was and is an international struggle to apply Islamic law. He insisted to me that Sharia should be implemented in full, not in part as, he said, some secular regimes, including Indonesia, preferred.[48]

"I don't have a sword, so all I can use now are my words," he said. "This is my obligation, for silence is a betrayal. As long as the US maintains its policies as an international terrorist, Indonesians will be urged to fight using their capabilities, either physically or through information technology. Our last two presidents have been very pro-American. They have acted as puppets, following whatever the US wants them to do."[49] I had heard that Saifullah had been imprisoned for attacking nightclubs, and he admitted to this. He said, however, that when he had finally been captured he had been held only briefly and then as "an honorable prisoner, treated well." That didn't sound so bad, I told him. (Later that day, we visited the offices of one of the leading militant groups in Solo that had been engaged in regular attacks on Western-style nightclubs. However, the young militants fled down a back alley and refused to talk to us.)

It was not easy reading the tea leaves in Indonesia, where major hotel and resort bombings punctuate the laid-back, tolerant atmosphere from year to year. Were the Islamic leaders driving the radicalization in Indonesia, or was the violence more a result of outside influences, particularly the United States' foreign policy and misadventures in the Middle East? I was learning more about the war within Islam, as well as the external influences that affected this internal struggle.

Enrico now informed me that we would have our sought-after interview with the man who is alleged to have provided his ideological support to the Bali bombing in 2002, which killed over two hundred people, most of them young Western tourists.

Our entry into the Nagruki school, where Abu Bakar al-Ba'asyir served as director and headmaster, was facilitated by our driver, who happened to have both fought in Afghanistan and been educated at the same boarding school. Yasir, forty-one, short and pudgy with a spiked goatee, had served as a foot soldier for al-Ba'asyir's field commanders in the Moluccan Islands just as al-Ba'asyir's group was receiving fresh funding from the Arabian peninsula's more famous holy warrior, Osama bin Laden.[50]

Typical of concerned Muslims across the Islamic world who signed up early for the "global jihad" against Russian infidels, Yasir arrived in Peshawar, Pakistan, in 1987.[51] Later, he entered Afghanistan, where he spent some months training for guerrilla warfare and fighting alongside a group of other Indonesians who would eventually come to make up the core of al-Ba'asyir's terror network. He had been twenty-one, and he told me he had felt "fortunate ... to join the battle on the front with the Afghan mujahedeen against the Communist Russian forces," where he befriended Arabs, Afghans, and numerous Asians of Malay descent. In 1999, as Muslim-Christian violence spread like wildfire across the Moluccan Islands, Yasir was able to put his weapons training—particularly his bomb training—to work.

Yasir had several brothers who had also attended Muslim boarding schools. His father, Achmed Kandai, had belonged to Darul Islam, a fundamentalist Islamic organization, and boasted to his sons about attempting to assassinate Indonesia's president Sukarno in 1957. Yasir also had an uncle, Nasir, who had worked closely with Abu Bakar when he founded the Nagruki school in 1972. Along with his brother Abdul Jabbar, Yasir had driven a car bomb to the home of Leonides Caday, the Philippine ambassador to Jakarta, on August 1, 2000. He had been captured, convicted, and imprisoned for several years, but he was now our driver—an extraordinary fate, I thought, for someone who had taken part in cold-blooded murder.

Yasir was a curious character, even joking at times about how he had driven bombs around Jakarta. I believed he was kept under close surveillance by Indonesian police, and there were suggestions that he had already been "turned" into an informant. Oddly, he had expressed his dismay when Khalid Saifullah, the young activist, suggested that "US military agents" had carried out the Bali bombing. Yasir even thought the suggestion was part of a smear campaign against JI's bombing capabilities, of which he himself was proud.

Although earlier in the week we had been told that the interview with al-Ba'asyir would not be possible, the tone of al-Ba'asyir's assistant had changed, and we were welcomed for a lengthy chat.

The school itself consisted of several nondescript two-story concrete blocks, with shoes neatly lined up on concrete steps beneath fast-peeling painted walls. It was hard to believe that nearly every recent terrorist attack in Indonesia had been attributable to a student or an associate of the school.

Abu Bakar al-Ba'asyir, dressed in a plaid waist wrap and a plain white shirt, greeted us warmly.[52] He gave us a quick explanatory tour of the school, pointing out that it had been a Socialist commune in the early 1960s. Al-Ba'asyir struck me as a solemn man who believed in the righteousness of his cause, but he also displayed a wide smile when discussing his school and its storied history. He was clearly proud of his limited empire, however ideological in nature.

Our interview took place as several of the young bombers who attacked tourists in Bali in October 2002 were awaiting execution and had refused to make an official request that they should not be executed, on the grounds that their attack was religiously justified. (One of the bombers, Imam Samudra, insisted that he wanted to die by the sword, as prescribed by Islamic law, rather than by a government firing squad. His request was refused.)

Al-Ba'asyir spoke carefully. He knew just how to couch his diatribes to avoid the appearance of directly inciting fresh attacks. But he left no doubt in my mind as to the war he wanted to fight. His was a personal struggle, driven primarily by words that would inspire others to take up work as foot soldiers for his brand of intolerant extremism.

On a couch in a small, enclosed wooden sunroom, he gesticulated and chuckled on occasion as he spoke.

"America has been instigating a war of ideas and, therefore, we are fighting back with our own war of ideas," he said. His recognition that his own long war was a battle for the hearts and minds of Indonesian and Muslim youth struck me as astute. A war of ideas, after all, is not a zero-sum game: It is a nuanced rhetorical struggle carried on in classrooms, in Internet cafés, and on the mean streets of inner cities. The talent to persuade, in the end, is the firepower of final victory.

"What we try to do is counter the lies, break down the lies," he told me. "We want to uncover the truth that the Koran teaches. This activity in and of itself is much more productive and efficient than bombing, because just by doing this—preaching the truth—I am being called all kinds of things." He bragged about the fact that he had avoided being dragged out of an Indonesian prison and sent to Guantanamo, where he said the American government wanted him to be. As he spoke, it seemed that he relished the idea of being a successful bête noire to his American nemesis.

The mentor of the Bali bombers, born to a Hadhrami Arab and Javanese family in 1938, said he was confident that time and Allah were on his side. He said that events across the Islamic world were conspiring to destroy the crusade of his greatest enemy, the United States. As he reclined in his boarding school, he laughed at the idea that the West did not fully comprehend where it stood in what Pentagon officials liked to call "the long war." He insisted that temporary setbacks would not stand in the way of final victory, and he called the Bali bombers young men with good intentions gone awry.

As he carefully answered each question that I put to him, I could not help but recognize the language of the global jihad—a way of talking about the struggle in many of the terms that I had already heard in the Middle East and South Asia, as well as Southeast Asia. He represented the essence of the global jihadist viewpoint. His group had already spread its tentacles across most of Southeast Asia. His struggle was always the same, against a US and Israeli conspiracy to oppress Muslims. "The United States is a tool for the Zionists," he said. "The United States has a program and has a crusade that is being carried out in an unfair way—spreading the message that there is Islamic terrorism in this world. It says all the enemies, all the terrorists, are Islamists and all the people who fight for Sharia law. Everyone who is active is left with the stigma that they are terrorists. They are being arrested and imprisoned." This was a commonly held view that I had already heard in Islamic youth circles across the archipelago. It was often repeated like a mantra.

I asked al-Ba'asyir if he had rethought the initial approval he had given to the Bali bombings. "Yes, there are cases when some persons in some Islamic groups have carried out bombings here in Indonesia. It is also unfortunately the case that they are bombing places that are relatively safe. It is easy for them to become prey to US efforts to stigmatize all Muslims." In other words, as I interpreted his answer, the blame should fall on the stigmatizers. He did not take responsibility for encouraging the bombings.

Knowing that he was making a point of meeting with youth leaders—and, indeed, had begun his own career as a student leader—I asked al-Ba'asyir if he felt that Indonesia's young were inspired to continue the jihad, or struggle.

"Among the youth, many want to fight the United States because of the aggression in Iraq and Afghanistan," he said. "And in Indonesia they attack US interests, but I think it is a mistake to do that here in Indonesia against US interests because Indonesia is a safe place, a safe country, safe from conflict." I dislike disingenuous equivocators, so I asked him if he was "condemning the Bali bombers."

"No," was his answer. "The bombers are actually counterterrorists because they are opposing US terrorism. They are mujahids." Didn't he think that was really just encouraging more of the same? From his answer, it sounded as if he was still encouraging the bombers: "They are not terrorists," he insisted. "They are not instigating terror; that is not their intention. They want to fight terror. I don't think that by saying this that it will encourage them. Only the method is wrong. But it is not right to call them terrorists. Theirs is a reaction, not an action."

His reply was not utterly nonsensical. Indeed, he was again appealing not for Muslims to go on the warpath but for them to "defend" themselves from what he saw as US and Israeli aggression. This interpretation of the world and the forces at work against Islam essentially gives the green light to any method of what its adherents see as fighting back.

"Many people think that students who have attended your school here have taken their inspiration from Osama bin Laden," I continued. "What kind of an influence has he been on students in your school and on young people in Indonesia?"

"Generally, the influence of [bin Laden] is good," replied al-Ba'asyir. "His intention to fight the United States is good. However, the methods and steps that he uses are not necessarily to be applied here in Indonesia. Some young Muslims here clearly idolize him and others do not. There are also students who have quit the school, my school, because they would not necessarily agree with his teachings."

That was a sharp way of putting it. It was another way of saying that if you don't agree with bin Laden and al-Ba'asyir, you always have the option not to listen to them. He called bin Laden an inspiration, someone who "is trying to teach, to pass on jihad against the United States," adding that the Saudi "opposes US terrorism against countries. Jihad can be done through arms and can be done through words as I'm doing now—by preaching." They—al-Ba'asyir and bin Laden—were two peas in a pod.

Did this mean that al-Ba'asyir was out to force conversions across the United States in order to create world peace?

"In Islam, you cannot force someone to convert to Islam," he said. "It is quite possible to have peace with the United States, but the United States has to distance itself from Israel or decide not to be used as a tool by the Zionists. But peace is the objective of Islam—to live in peace."

Al-Ba'asyir walked a fine line between supporting terrorism and denying any personal involvement. He recognized the line between the information war and the fight. There were really two wars out there—one of words and one of bombs. It was an important distinction. Nevertheless, Indonesia's own successful antiterrorism efforts, often far less bombastic and brutal than those of Western powers in the Middle East, had given al-Ba'asyir and his associates little to cheer about. While the Indonesian government had allowed arguably too much leeway in the sphere of words, it had gained immense amounts of intelligence since 2002 on the activities of al-Ba'asyir and his associates. This in turn had turned up a better communications trail to terrorist plotters and prompted more arrests.[53]

But while al-Ba'asyir's Jemaah Islamiya radicals have been sidelined politically and ostracized in Indonesia for their role in inspiring the Bali bombings, al-Ba'asyir's reemergence as a spokesperson for jihadist struggle was a worrisome development. (Ironically, I could be sure his admirers would read my interview with their mentor in the *Asia Times* and interpret his words from their limited perspective.) Though he spent over two years in prison after a judge said he had given his spiritual blessing to the Bali bombings, al-Ba'asyir was now a free man. After his interview with me, he unleashed a sermon denouncing scantily clad tourists in Bali as "worms, snakes, and maggots" who deserved to be beaten.[54] Later he called on young Indonesians to charge to the "front," to die "as martyrs" in a struggle in which "all your sins will be forgiven."[55] I noted that even Christian evangelicals urging US soldiers to war in the aftermath of 9/11 didn't go quite that far.

Al-Ba'asyir's basic line was already accepted doctrine for many young Indonesian males, including Saifullah, who had espoused a similar hatred toward Israel and the United States while touting a need to crush their influence locally by attacking nightclubs that represented "Western decadence." With his ideas germinating anew in the minds of young Indonesians as well as old jihadists like Yasir, al-Ba'asyir had much to smile about.

I was still confused about how Indonesia's own efforts to tamp down angry sentiments were coming along, so I decided to travel to the farthest reaches of the archipelago to examine the historical, biographical, and sociological origins of some of the bloodiest Christian against Muslim violence that had ever taken place in Southeast Asia. Maluku, also known as the Moluccan Islands, had been the earliest proving ground for JI's efforts to help fight a so-called defensive jihad against so-called external enemies. The conflict itself, however, sprang from a variety of land, ethnic, and political issues that produced an environment ripe for a jihadist incursion.

Chapter 5
SPICE ISLAND JIHAD

After two flights and a seven-hour ferry ride to the Banda Islands, the heart of the "Spice Islands" and the original home of nutmeg within the Moluccan chain, I put up for the night in the tattered Hotel Maulana, a storied waterfront mansion. Across from the small, bustling port; a bubbling volcano; and a coral reef teeming with colorful creatures; I had landed for a few days in the "Mick Jagger Suite"—a faded reminder of the better times of this 1970s hotspot, to which both Princess Diana and the Rolling Stones had come to escape the paparazzi.

In the Roman era, Arab, Chinese, and Bugi (Sulawesi) sailors had descended on these coral gardens, tranquil inlets, and luxuriant jungles to trade in the most lucrative products on the high seas: spices, including the all-purpose European elixir, nutmeg. In the sixteenth century, after a race to the Spice Islands ushered in Europe's age of exploration, Dutch merchant traders took over from the Portuguese and gained a monopoly in the trade, imposing their religion and murdering uncooperative natives. After a small British fleet seized one of the islands and a high-stakes war ensued, the Dutch—

desperate to maintain their grip on the spice trade—agreed to hand over the small North American island of Manhattan in return for one of the Spice Islands, a move that temporarily restored the Dutch monopoly.[1]

Today, the impoverished island chain struggles to maintain strong ties with Jakarta and promote its own economy, which still consists mainly of spices and textiles. The islands, situated in mostly calm Pacific waters, west of New Guinea and east of Sulawesi, are about the last place on Earth anyone would expect to encounter a genuine holy war. Nevertheless, the mayhem that engulfed the island chain between 1999 and 2001 is a good prism through which to see the tensions that punctuate a world in which Islam and Christianity exist side by side as globalization intervenes. On the first evening of my stay in late 2007 at the Hotel Maulana, I learned of the unpleasant fate of the last of the Dutch spice plantation owners, Wim van den Broeke. The hearty planter of old colonial stock had survived until a Muslim vigilante assault on his compound in April 1999.

The violence began as a territorial dispute between Christians and Muslims and escalated into a series of killing sprees, assisted in some cases by modern weaponry, that left hundreds dead or maimed. Western and Indonesian academics have since engaged in heated debate about whether the violence, which left some five thousand to ten thousand dead and another seven hundred thousand homeless, was an international or a unique and localized matter.[2] Once the islands had been the center of the *pela*, blood-pact, tradition in which Christians and Muslims pledged lifelong loyalty to each other and helped each other with church and mosque raisings. When disputes arose, the Indonesian government failed miserably to oppose the violence and, in some cases, even sided with jihadists or Christian militias.

Long-standing competition over government jobs between indigenous Muslims and Christians, the latter having been favored by and loyal to the Dutch colonial government, as well as strong Christian resentment about being overrun by large numbers of

Muslim immigrants from elsewhere in Indonesia, boiled over when a Christian bus driver and a non-Ambonese Muslim (that is, not a native of the Moluccan Islands) clashed.[3]

By May and June 2000, Muslim and Christian communities were at each other's throats with swords, homemade guns, and bombs. Into the fray flew Dieter Bartels, a German-American anthropologist with a Dutch-Moluccan wife. Bartels landed in Ambon's small port-side airport just in time to see the island chain go up in smoke, and as an academic who had studied the islands for over three decades, he was well placed to analyze the root causes of the strife. What he saw and then documented suggests that the conflict had international as well as local and national ingredients. Indeed, on the airplane from Makassar, Sulawesi, Bartels sat next to the Yemeni Jafar Umar Thalib, the chief of Laskar Jihad, who, along with al-Ba'asyir's Laskar Mujahideen, was sending hundreds of trainers and fighters to the remote chain. Thalib, while from a competing jihadist group, had fought in Afghanistan and had Yemeni descent in common with al-Ba'asyir and bin Laden, whom he had already met in South Asia.

"There were hundreds of Laskar Jihad members at the airport waiting before our arrival," Bartels said.[4] "We engaged in small talk, and I did not know who I was sitting next to until he was greeted by a group of South Asian mujahedeen in the airport's arrival lounge. They looked like Mexican fighters out of a Pancho Villa movie strapped with all their bandoleers and weaponry." The main city of the island of Ambon, which is also called Ambon and is the capital of the island chain, was already engulfed in heavy fighting and daily destruction. Bartels found himself stranded at the airport, forced to take a small speedboat that could outrun militant vessels to the Christian side of the capital across the bay, where he took up residence with a pair of middle-class government workers whom he had never met but whose hillside home, high above the bay, overlooked the largest mosque in the city, where Islamic groups were massing at night to launch attacks across the city. But the national and international jihadists had arrived late in the struggle and the Christian militias had proven superior in the rough-and-tumble jungle and urban fighting that had spread across the small island chain. The young jihadists arriving with Umar Thalib had almost no fighting experience. Christian forces, gathering near their own places of worship and inspired by the Indonesian version of "Onward Christian Soldiers," held the line against jihadist attacks and inflicted heavy casualties on the jihadists. Bartels characterized Umar Thalib's adherents as "untrained and naively fanatical youth from Java, most of them well-educated kids from urban areas."

In Southeast Asia in the late 1980s, I tramped through paddy fields with Khmer Rouge fighters and witnessed Buddhist monks in kangaroo courts ordering the beheading of Burmese military officers, but never in my travels had I seen Muslims and Christians butchering one another, as Bartels saw it in the summer of 2000. Bartels notes that Hajji Yusuf Ely, a former navy officer and at the time of the violence the Muslim commander at the Al-Fatah Mosque, later boasted that on a single day he had decapitated at least eight Christians with one stroke of his sword.[5]

Bartels managed to creep up on an attack on the Christian university in Ambon, where he filmed Laskar Jihad fighters destroying the house in which he had once lived and setting most of the university buildings on fire. Christian youths defended the campus by shooting back with bazookas.[6] Jihadi mobs celebrated with shrill howls even as Bartels's Christian host family huddled around a television set to watch a popular Indonesian soap opera, in order to distract the children from the slaughter going on outside. Meanwhile on a nearby street, Bartels witnessed child soldiers praying with a Protestant minister before being dispatched to the fight.

Refugees fled to the main Al-Fatah Mosque and a neighboring Christian redoubt at the Silo Church in the capital. As deaths mounted, embattled Muslim and Christian enclaves formed, and the war took on further religious implications. Retaliatory killings spread to neighboring islands, for example, to the picturesque village of Sirisori on the nearby island of Saparua, where Muslims and Christians lived at opposite ends of a road shaded by palms and clove trees. Just as Bartels had done in 2000 in order to visit his in-laws, I took a boat ride from Ambon out to this tiny island, which had been the scene of some of the most intense fighting. I remained there for three days in a beachside hotel exploring the nature of the strife.

Shooting had first broken out when Muslims allegedly caught a Christian man intentionally damaging their clove trees. In the island's interior, I found David Liklikwatil, an elderly Christian pensioner, who claimed that—at the height of the fighting—he had fled into the jungle. "They burned our houses and so we had no choice but to try to defend ourselves," he insisted, sitting in the charred remains of his home. "We made shotguns out of old pipes and retreated to the forest." The old man waxed nostalgic about the colonial era in which he had grown up, a time when, he said, "people didn't lie and they respected the government."[7]

Further north, I discovered an abandoned Muslim village, Iha, which had been surrounded and ethnically cleansed by Christian militias, the survivors of mass executions having been forced to swim out to the coral reef surrounding the island, where they had been saved by waiting military vessels.

During the Ambon troubles, which lasted nearly two years, the small, efficient jihadist group known as Laskar Mujahideen, which had been gathered together by Jemaah Islamiya, was instrumental in turning what had started as a local and regional dispute into a major conflagration. This is the group with which my driver Yasir Kandai had fought. Its commander, Haris Fadillah, alias Abu Dzar (a Robin Hood–like figure), was killed in October 2000 in Saparua.[8] Abu Dzar, a human smuggler and gangster (*preman*) who operated out of a villa in West Java, was the father-in-law of a top al Qaeda operative, Omar Faruq, who also fought in the Moluccan Islands and was subsequently captured and extensively interrogated by the US military and the CIA at Bagram Air Base in Afghanistan. (I interviewed the US prison guard from Fairfax, Virginia, Damien Corsetti, who befriended Faruq in Bagram and was later accused by the US military of assisting in his abuse, which included hanging him from chains suspended from the ceiling.[9] This is a digression, but it goes to show that terrorism even in the remotest places often has intimate ties to a more global struggle.)

According to Yasir, Laskar Mujahideen went to the Moluccan Islands with a clear plan of action.[10] Fighters would destroy churches and target Protestant ministers and Catholic priests. Machine guns, grenade launchers, and antipersonnel mines were smuggled in by ship from Surabaya and handed to friendly fishermen. Some arms shipments were brazenly unloaded in the Muslim-controlled harbor of Ambon City, the capital. Weapons caches were set up in secret locations across the capital. Small groups of fighters arrived, until the Laskar Mujahideen forces totaled some five hundred fighters, many of them with experience fighting in the Philippines with the Moro Islamic Liberation Front, or MILF. (On July 12, 2007, MILF militants in Basilan in the southern Philippines killed fourteen Filipino marines, beheading eleven of them.) In 2000 and 2001, some twenty foreigners, Arabs and Malays with Afghan experience, helped train local Moluccan Muslim youth to fight the Christians.[11]

Yasir told me that his own bomb-making training in Afghanistan had been useful in the Moluccan Islands. I asked him why the struggle there had become important to veterans of the Afghan war, and he said that it epitomized the persecution of Muslims by Christian and "international forces." He saw the battle there as a struggle against what he called a "foreign Satan." Al Qaeda, which already had a reliable corps of Malay followers, found the struggle in the Moluccan Islands compelling enough to send its own leading military commanders to the front with funds and words of inspiration. Mohammed Atef, bin Laden's most senior military commander at the time of the 9/11 attacks, who was killed in late 2001, had deemed the Moluccan struggle important enough to visit on a mission of his own in June 2000.[12] Most of the tell-tale signs of intense international jihadist interest in the struggle are ignored by academics who claim the Ambon fighting was a local and national issue only. Bartels is not among these academics. He sees the struggle as having begun as a series of local disputes, and having been aggravated by government transmigration policies that provided tens of thousands of mostly Javanese with new homes in the Moluccan Islands, thus upsetting a fragile Christian and Muslim ethnic balance in the islands and tipping it toward confrontation. National efforts to stem the violence failed, in Bartels's view, when military and police reinforcements sent from Jakarta took sides in the struggle.

Historically, the local people who converted to Christianity from five hundred years ago maintained an advantage over the local Muslims, who were sometimes maligned by their Dutch rulers and kept from obtaining a Western-style education. Still, there is strong evidence that the ancient tribal bonds between Christian and Muslim Moluccans far outweighed any ties to the Western interlopers.[13]

In a tale that is as profound and exotic as any in the South Pacific, the Ambonese believed that their civilization descended from a single mountain on the largest island in the chain, Seram. The bubbling Mount Nunusaku was thought to be the redoubt of God, Upu Lanite. Traditionally, the islanders saw Islam and Christianity as two alternate but equal paths to God, whom the Christians also address by the Arabic term "Allah," using the metaphor of climbing a mountain on two different paths but ultimately reaching the same goal.

The myth of Mount Nunusaku thrived in the Moluccan Islands, according to Bartels, largely because the islanders were generally uninterested in "dogma and ideology and relatively unaffected by, or even ignorant of, any historical enmity between Muslims and Christians" elsewhere on the globe. Effectively, it could be said, what these islanders (in this would-be Garden of Eden) did not yet know was not yet killing them. In keeping with their beliefs, the two groups developed a system of blood pacts between villages, which Bartels traces back to headhunting times. Over time, the alliances adapted pragmatically to changing social and economic needs.[14] In ritual pacts between villages, often one Muslim and the other Christian, tribal elders drank from a cup of palm wine mixed with their own blood in which spears and swords had earlier been ceremonially dipped. It was believed that, should the pact be broken, the weapons would mysteriously turn upon the offender in punishment for his betrayal. Illness, death, and misfortune would befall any offender. Around this *pela* system, an elaborate set of commendable traditions sprang up, including the custom in which local Christian villagers placed the *kepala*, mosque top, on the roof for their Muslim neighbors before the mosque opened its doors to worshippers. The whole process of social interaction had taken on added meaning, which persisted even during colonial rule, and thus became, as Bartels explains, a "core identity maker." Locals believed that neglect of the social bonds would lead to catastrophe, which, in the end, would prove terribly true.

With his in-laws still living on one of the worst-hit islands, Bartels has kept a close eye on the reconciliation process that has taken place across the Moluccan Islands since the massacres. Christian and Muslim religious leaders have come together to reinterpret their ancient traditions and attempt to set them in a more modern context, one more akin to what one finds, as Bartels suggests, in Jean-Jacques Rousseau's *Social Contract*, with an emphasis on tolerance and respect. He hopes that perhaps the Ambonese can again succeed in seeing each other as true brothers and sisters after the traumatic experience of the internecine strife.[15]

However, the divisions that sparked the violence in the tiny island chain are part and parcel of a larger problem witnessed in the globalization of both Islam and Christianity. Local mythologies in small places are not built to weather the onslaught of the mass media. Whereas Islam in the Moluccan Islands had been largely decentralized, even atomized at the village level, outside influences have forever altered that dynamic today. Indeed, Christians, many of whose relatives live in European cities like Amsterdam, believe they are more civilized because they have adopted Western values, Bartels said to me in a series of phone discussions. Moluccan Muslims have also strengthened their ties with outside Islamic groups, including those with radical and fundamentalist leanings. After the massive bloodshed and the outside meddling, Christians and Muslims on the island chain now view one another less as brethren than as Kafirs, or unbelievers.

Importantly, recruitment for the fight in the Moluccan Islands and later in Poso on the island of Sulawesi gave groups like Laskar Mujahideen and other affiliates of Jemaah Islamiya (JI) the opportunity to further cultivate the minds of the youth across the vast archipelago with regard to future holy wars. Speaking to investigators from the International Crisis Group (ICG), young JI members recalled striking up conversations with boarding school students, many of them already undergoing intensive religious training. Recruiters would then ask young Indonesians to come and watch a video about the fighting in the Moluccan Islands or elsewhere. The screening sessions were intended to spark outrage at the brutality of the Christian side in the struggle, but the videos that I obtained of the violence in the Moluccan Islands, many of them available from market stalls, also put on display the heinous actions of the jihadists themselves. In one video, which introduces the struggle in Indonesia as a classic example of the persecution of Muslims, a young Muslim man is seen chasing a Christian with a sword, with dumbfounded uniformed Indonesian police officers looking on but doing nothing. A mob cheers on the assault.

The video is cleverly made, and the videographer is perfectly placed to watch the hunting down of the Christian. The astounding access of the videographer, in this case, suggests that a kind of non-fiction "snuff" movie was being made with the intent to inspire jihadists. The scene is so graphic, however, that the young man's head is split open and part of his skull is sliced off as he flees through the heartless crowd. In the end, the young man is carted off in a police truck, apparently half-dead. After watching such scenes with students, JI members (or their brethren in the Laskar Jihad group) would invite their potential recruits for further religious study sessions to help them make sense of what they had seen.

According to the 2002 International Crisis Group study of the recruiting networks, students were told that "what Muslims had to fear most was a government enslaved to infidels."[16] This type of brainwashing in itself made the fight that the participants would later join in the Moluccan Islands more than just a local and ethnic matter. Furthermore, the study sessions stressed the origins of Islam and the original struggle of the Prophet in Mecca when "Muslims were being persecuted." The students were also urged to help rid the faith of idolatrous practices by joining directly in the struggle. Further jihadist military training included the use of machetes and knives.

Since the eighteen-month killing spree, the Spice Islands have returned to being a semitropical paradise. Only sporadic violence occurs. Nevertheless, the origins and the nature of the conflict provide important lessons for students of world peace. In Ambon, I met with an antiterrorism investigator in the local police force, Frans Yusak. He said that the extremist groups in Ambon had not disbanded but remained under intense government surveillance. "We know where they are, and we basically maintain an element of control over their movements and activities," he said over a meal of fried chicken. "We still don't know what motivates them, but we know they still want to use Maluku to grow their organization."[17]

Kirsten Schulze, a senior lecturer in international history at the London School of Economics, has argued that the violence in the Moluccan Islands was "a social conflict rather than a religious one."[18] She points out that on both sides of the conflict, groups turned to their respective creeds to explain the difficulties they were facing, that Christians promoted talk of Christian persecution just as Muslims emphasized the persecution of Muslims. Bartels believes, however, that Christian fears of a large-scale ethnic cleansing were warranted in this case, particularly as chaos engulfed the island chain after the fall of Suharto. He says he witnessed Muslim militias that had the clear backing of military forces already stationed on the islands. As thousands of civilians were killed in the fighting, it was not clear when and how the violence would end, he said. It was not the first time that the military and Islamic militants had cooperated in their mutual interest.[19]

Since the end of colonial rule, it has never been easy to keep the lid on growing tensions. It had been President Sukarno, overthrown in a coup d'état by the military in the 1960s, who had first attempted to create a system that would provide equilibrium in one of the world's richest repositories of religious and cultural diversity. Sukarno set in place the philosophical foundations of Pancasila, which set forth as sacrosanct, albeit rather vague, a belief in one God, democratic deliberation, and social justice. This ideology, announced in a speech in 1945, attempted to set to the side the differences between Muslims, nationalists, and Christians through the promotion of a state "based on the belief in the one and only God."

One can argue that the eventual disharmony that religious radicals tapped into in the Moluccan Islands and beyond had some parallels with the mayhem that erupted across parts of Yugoslavia after the fall of Josip Broz Tito, also a strongman who did his best to tamp down ethnic differences. But there are significant differences, and it is the international flavor of the conflict in Indonesia that keeps the flames alive. The Indonesian case shows that globalization has forever made local conflicts global.

Indeed, militant Islam is both a product of local conflicts like the conflict in the Moluccan Islands and also a broader phenomenon. Academics who look with a magnifying glass at small, regional issues often miss the big picture that war, violence, and mayhem are breeding grounds for further terror across the globe. One of the key moments of inspiration for future JI leaders came at the battle of Jaji in Eastern Afghanistan's Paktia Province in 1987, when Indonesian mujahedeen fought alongside none other than Osama bin Laden.[20] The core (or skeletal) global component of Indonesia's terror network remains intact, albeit spread out across the islands and subject to increasing government scrutiny.

I asked Yasir, who trained in eastern Afghanistan at a time when few Americans suspected the global nature of the phoenix that would rise from those camps, what had ultimately turned him against the United States. In other words, what had allowed the transference of his enmity to the superpower that was providing the most funding to the anti-Soviet insurgency in which he had once fought?

"In my view, after Communism fell, we started to hear noises in the US and elsewhere that the next great threat would emanate from the Islamic world," he said. "A lot of Muslims who fought against Soviet aggression felt vilified and betrayed, as though we had just been used by America to defeat Communism and nothing more."

But for Indonesian jihadists, like Yasir, another turning point came when they could see their own struggle in the context of a larger global effort launched by bin Laden's 1998 declaration of war on the United States from a camp not far from Jaji, Afghanistan. Later, the attacks on the WTC and the Pentagon and the American response to them helped to solidify Yasir's views. "When Osama became a target, we wanted to fight for him, and because Bush mentioned the 'crusade,' that only inspired us further," said Yasir, stroking his small goatee. "Since then we've heard more and more statements referring to Islam as a radical religion and that terror is identical with Islam. That feels like a direct American intervention in our lives. Not only must we fight for Osama, we are obliged to fight for him." On the surface, Yasir's own interpretation of why he was fighting sounded counterintuitive, but it was, after all, our founding father, George Washington, who told a friend at Valley Forge in 1778 that "the most certain way to make a man your enemy is to tell him you esteem him such."[21]

The impact of the US-led war on terror is not easy to judge in a land as distant from the Middle East as Indonesia. Indeed, trying to understand why and how Indonesian perceptions of the United States have moved on a roller coaster from great admiration to disdain and back to a modicum of respect in the Obama era is also a difficult endeavor, as these changing perceptions are tied to a wide range of social, political, and even psychological issues. Nevertheless, my research in Indonesia suggested to me that the younger generation, although it wants to believe in an American "ally," remains deeply suspicious of US intentions toward Islam and of US goals both in Indonesia and in the Middle East, namely, in Palestine.

Even before the Bali bombings, as the United States ratcheted up its threats against Saddam Hussein, extremists like al-Ba'asyir were gaining popular support. "Millions of Indonesians are angry at the US for the war in Afghanistan and for perceived support for the Israeli offensive on the West Bank," wrote Dan Murphy.[22] "To them, the frail, pious Ba'asyir is more credible than what they see as the American bully."[23] When this is combined with the success of JI's grassroots organizations in rallying jihadists to join in local conflicts against "Christian crusaders," we see that the hands of the Islamic terror network have been strengthened from both within and without.

Al Qaeda, for its part, has maintained its presence in Indonesia in precisely the terms dictated by a senior ideologue, Abu Musab al-Suri, who argues in favor of autonomous cells, operating in a leaderless resistance.[24] In other words, al Qaeda cells, many of them with similar ideological and military training backgrounds, have embedded themselves within other networks so as to make themselves invisible to police investigators.

JI's own efforts have mirrored al Qaeda's and taken advantage of the government's tolerance for humanitarian work. Al-Suri contends that "Al Qaeda is not an organization, it is not a group, nor do we want it to be: It is a call, a reference, a methodology."[25] In a similar manner, JI's leader even denies his organization's existence. He prefers, instead, to embed his followers in broader activities aimed at the creation of an Islamic state and the recruitment of young militants for the long fight ahead.

Al-Ba'asyir's MMI, whose very name, Mujahideen Council, suggests overt militancy, continues to operate openly across the country, even being mistaken at times for a force for good by well-meaning Western humanitarian organizations, including the United Nations.

Jemaah Islamiya's tenacity illustrates why providing Islamic political groups space to operate in a democracy and helping a young generation of Muslims express themselves through democratic means, while worthwhile in principle, are also fraught with peril. In New York City, a few months after my most recent journey to Indonesia, I met with Professor Zachary Abuza, one of America's most incisive analysts of Indonesia's internal struggles against terrorism. Abuza teaches at Simmons College in Massachusetts and has written extensively on Jemaah Islamiya's efforts to project itself as a humanitarian-minded national movement concerned with the welfare and well-being of fellow Muslims. He worries that beneath the surface, al-Ba'asyir's organization is still running a covert terrorist operation that feeds off its image as a social welfare provider. "What we really see that JI is doing is twofold," he said. "They are going back and fomenting sectarian violence in the outer islands as they did from 1998 to 2001, and they are also engaging in this overt social work and civil society work that the Indonesian government is actually encouraging them to do. They are really starting to adopt the social welfare paradigm of an organization like Hamas, where a small, covert cell is underground but the larger presence is distributing social services and goods."[26]

That description of JI's nefarious efforts almost works for me, but I see an element of apples and oranges as well. The Hamas militants I had seen in Palestine and Damascus were operating more above ground (albeit under cover from Israeli strikes) than the JI terror cells in Indonesia. Hamas was struggling against a foe on its own soil, while the only "foes" JI was managing to find—for the most part—were tourists, Christian villagers, and a handful of foreign businessmen in Jakarta. In any case, I understand Abuza's argument about JI's bifurcated approach, and it serves to highlight several points that al-Ba'asyir made in his interview with me. Above the surface, al-Ba'asyir was all about peace and preaching the good word, but beneath the surface he was espousing hate and encouraging attacks on symbols of so-called Western dominance.

Abuza, narrowly focused on Southeast Asian terror networks, brought a moral tone to his analysis. "What bothers me," he continued, "is when the Islamists want it both ways and they engage in extralegal violence and intimidation, and then the Indonesian government is afraid to crack down on such behavior. In some areas, JI issues death threats against people who want the country to maintain a tradition of syncretic Islam, a faith that is largely secular and pluralistic."[27]

In a paper entitled "Jemaah Islamiya and the Inverse Triangle," Abuza also discusses the group's "broadened definition of defensive jihad" as well as its cadres' insistence that the Indonesian state "has abdicated its responsibility by not coming to the defense of the Muslim community" in places like the Moluccan Islands—even in a country that is already 88–90 percent Muslim.[28] (Even when the military worked with militant groups in its own interests, it was accused of not fighting hard enough with the militants.) The cadres' argument was one I had heard from Saifullah.

Abuza suggested that JI and its affiliates still maintained an advantage in the battle for the hearts and minds of the broader public in Indonesia. He said that the point of JI's social initiatives was—first and foremost—to garner good press. "This infrastructure is essential to JI's terrorist operations, and will make them more durable over the long run," he writes in his paper, going on to analyze a particularly embarrassing moment for the United Nations as it spearheaded food aid operations for the Yogyakarta earthquake in 2005.[29]

Since JI had suffered several high-profile arrests, Abu Bakar al-Ba'asyir's MMI, run by a close associate of his, was looking for a way to burnish its image as a welfare organization when it was lucky enough to become one of the World Food Program's eight partner organizations selected to distribute ninety-five tons of food on the ground, as part of a $536-million program. Australian officials, whose fellow countrymen had been slaughtered in Bali and who were enraged that an organization close to JI should receive UN foodstuffs, protested vehemently over the contracts, to which the World Food Program's spokesperson in Indonesia, Barry Came, replied: "We don't pick groups to distribute aid based on their religious or political beliefs. We choose based on the ability to deliver, and so far they've performed up to standard."[30]

Some days later, however, Came would have to climb down and admit an astounding error: "Unfortunately, at the time and in the heat of the moment when there was such a rush on, and some considerable confusion, we didn't realize MM was the same as MMI and affiliated with Abu Bashir, and in light of that, as of yesterday, we canceled the contract."[31]

The incident highlighted several outstanding issues that complicate cracking down on extremism across the Islamic world. First of all, the Indonesian government had licensed MMI to carry on its humanitarian endeavors, which it continues to do so despite the knowledge that this burnishes the image of JI and can lead to accidental funding for terrorist operations.

I was able to discuss the World Food Program incident directly with a senior UN official involved in food distribution in Southeast Asia, who asked to remain anonymous. He suggested that there were far deeper moral issues underlying the question of allowing religious groups to participate in humanitarian operations. To my surprise, he also brought up the case of Hamas and the Israeli government's heavy-handed crackdown on so-called terrorist networks. Given all the injustices in the world perpetrated against Muslims, he argued, what is the harm of having these groups engaged in good deeds, if that is all they are doing? "We've seen similar groups working across Asia and—as long as they are helping and not hurting anyone—what harm can that do?" he asked rhetorically.[32]

The debate went to the heart of the issue of political space, and it returned my thoughts to the stadium in Jakarta packed with one hundred thousand would-be supporters of Sharia law. If these folks are not given a public outlet and a democratic forum in which to express themselves, will their aspirations be forced underground toward a more violent approach? I believe I would prefer to see these folks rally for whatever they want in a public stadium. However, as an American taxpayer I would not want my country's contributions to the World Food Program going to support an organization run by Abu Bakar al-Ba'asyir.

✳✳✳

The Ritz-Carlton and Marriott Hotels in downtown Jakarta are two of the most obvious symbols of Westernization in Indonesia. Their glitzy exteriors stand out even in a city of flashy skyscrapers and wide boulevards. On visits to Indonesia, I have dropped into both hotels. Both are the scene of a bustling nightlife, which includes an unlikely number of liaisons between Western men and Indonesian women. Mistere, for example, a chic club in the basement of the Ritz, is not unlike several other night spots that cater mainly to a wild Indonesian love culture, not unlike what one would find in New York City or Paris. For anyone who is interested, in *My Friend the Fanatic*, Indian writer Sadanand Dhume gives a hint of the flavor of the sexual escapades to be found in the club life of downtown Jakarta.[33] There is no specific evidence that the nightclubs in either hotel have become direct targets for bombers, but their presence is no doubt an added magnet for ultraconservative Islamist ire. In Solo, the young radical Saifullah had boasted to me of his own less deadly attacks on similar Western-style fun spots. Many of the young Islamists I met in Indonesia, both male and female, felt it was their duty to condemn what they saw as lasciviousness.

The American-owned Marriott Hotel chain has been attacked on several occasions since 9/11, most prominently in Jakarta in 2003 and in Cairo in 2005, and then again in July 2009 in Jakarta. On July 17, 2009, the Ritz and the Marriott were hit with bombs within five minutes of one another. Three of the seven dead were Australians, two were from the Netherlands, and one each was from New Zealand and Indonesia, suggesting that Westerners, not Indonesians, were the intended targets of the blasts.[34] The audacity of the attacks, carried out by suicide bombers who checked themselves in as guests and assembled the bombs in their own rooms, startled regional terrorism analysts. Investigators also determined that the bombers probably had help on the inside as well, from hotel staff members or others who had brought in supplies through a back entrance. At the

Ritz, the insider was apparently a florist who had been delivering flowers to the hotel for three years.

Analysts suggested that the bombers returned to a hotel that had already been attacked once to prove they could still attack in any place and at any time.[35] In the Marriott, the bombers, mere country boys who did not understand how to flush a modern toilet, disassembled a television set to obtain electrical components for the bombs. The bomber himself, caught on a security camera, emerged from an elevator with the bomb in a backpack strapped to his chest, pulling a larger airplane carry-on bag and making a beeline for the lounge. A meeting of a small number of members of the Jakarta business community, hosted by James Castle, president of a branch of the American Chamber of Commerce, was going on at the time of the blast.

Seasoned Jakarta-based Southeast Asia reporter John McBeth pointed out that a plan of the second Bali bombing, obtained from a laptop computer in eastern Java, said that "The deaths of foreign businessmen will have a greater impact than those of young people."[36] Jihadists' Web sites provided predictable explanations for the bombings, including the argument that the two hotels were a center for Christian and Jewish business activity in Jakarta.

In both the 2003 and the 2009 bombings, Indonesian investigators cited the participation of a former JI member turned rogue operative, the Malaysian-born Noordin Mohammad Top. (As one last insult added to injury, it may have been no coincidence that one of the bombers in the July 2009 attack had checked in under the name "Nurdin.")

In the aftermath of the bombing, the Indonesian government was immediately accused of timidity for not dismantling the educational institutions involved as well as, according to the *New York Times*, "uprooting the culture that breeds extremism."[37] The International Crisis Group's leading Indonesian analyst, Sidney Jones, commented in the same article that "everybody knows where these schools are. but there's been a sensitivity in dealing with them because people don't want to see Islamic education stigmatized."[38] Southeast Asia's preeminent expert, Rohan Gunaratna, criticized Indonesia for being "too focused on catching operators when they need to be tougher on actually preventing terrorism," adding that "they should take the boxing gloves off."[39]

Then, in mid-September 2009, Special Detachment 88 of the Indonesian police, aided by US and Australian know-how, killed Noordin Mohammad Top in a raid turned shoot-out at a home in Central Java, not far from Solo.[40] When the police announced the successful takedown at a large press conference, a cheer of relief went up from the Indonesian press corps. Indeed, the cool, calculating police work that had been going on behind the scenes made Western criticisms of Indonesia's antiterrorism efforts look over the top.

In the broader analysis of Indonesia's own antiterrorism efforts, however, few counterterrorism analysts have begun to connect the dots between radicalization and the international issues that impact public opinion, particularly the views of the youth. As long as the United States is not seen to be making progress in pushing for peace in the Middle East, conspiracy theorists, including al-Ba'asyir, will have grist for their propaganda mill. Dieter Bartels makes the point that millions of non-Muslims in Indonesia believe that Washington's actions in the Middle East will mean a great deal to their nation's long-term stability.[41] Certainly it is not easy to relate the persecution of Muslims outside the nation to the ongoing problems in Indonesia, but, as I was able to see by engaging Indonesia's younger generation, conspiracy theories resonate, and al-Ba'asyir has continued to burnish his image as the leader of a so-called resistance. He spins his lies in a vacuum created by a lack understanding of where the West stands on resolving conflicts elsewhere in the Islamic world.

On the other hand, the tide appears to be turning in favor of America's ability to project so-called soft power in the form of its own democratic ideals. Theodore Friend, author of *Indonesian Destinies*, told me in an interview that he viewed Obama, whose mother raised him in Indonesia for several years (a story Obama details in his own book, *Dreams for My Father* [42]), as a "great potential lynchpin" in relations between the United States and Indonesia.[43] "Obama has pretty well got it," he said. "His own mother, a highly creative thinker in her own right, was probably a big part of his views" about Islam and the East.[44] (On the president's father's side, he still boasts a plethora of Muslim relatives.) Obama and his envoys are favorably inclined to work with the Indonesian government, a government that has been elected twice by democratic means.

As soon as the Indonesian government receives more help from partners pushing for a broader peace in the Middle East, it will have less to fear from new inspired Islamic parties entering the political fray in Indonesia. Even in the islands of the South Pacific, ideas and images of a war a world away have a profound impact. Indonesians caught in the rhetorical crossfire say that it is fear—both of the intentions of a traditional ally, the United States, and of the machinations of radical enemies—that continues to stoke tensions.

Chapter 6
GOOD SHEIKH HUNTING

To hover over Timbuktu in an aging twelve-seat Antonov with a Ukrainian pilot at the controls is to understand why the city is synonymous for some with the "end of the Earth." In a sandstorm, our aircraft hugged the Niger River, which snaked north through the tropics into the grasslands and then into the Saharan desert. Immense sand drifts were blown into golden crests in the morning light above the muddy river bank lined with wooden fishing boats, their tattered sails made from a patchwork of rice bags. As we approached the once-booming metropolis, the river swerved to one side of the town with its Moorish sandcastle mosques and crumbling adobe homes. Surrounding the city was a series of Bedouin encampments where goats and camels had been tethered to sprawling acacia trees. From the north, Saharan drifts edged down, threatening to engulf the city. When I arrived, an unexpected plague of locusts had devastated most of the surrounding watermelon patches. As the Antonov circled to land, I watched nomads, their faces swathed in indigo turbans, slouched on the backs of their camels, hurrying to get to the city center, where there was nothing left for the pests to munch on.

Downtown, smugglers, truck drivers, and desert travelers, exhausted, barefoot, some begging for a bite to eat, meandered about the shabby marketplace. One turbaned hustler, wearing a silver sword with an inlaid ebony handle, sold T-shirts of Osama bin Laden and another reading "Timbuktu, the Mysterious." It was early in the year 2006, and here was one of those rare cities that—at least in the modern era—carried more recognition as a name than as an actual place. Timbuktu still traded on its rich history, and rightfully so. It represented the idea of a lost epoch that scholars are just now getting to know better. More than the gold bars, salt, ivory, hides, and nuts that passed through the hands of traders, it was the Arabic language, an international currency of sorts, and an emphasis on learning that set Timbuktu apart from the desert wastelands that surrounded it.

Language was the currency of religion, and when Malian Sultan Mansa Musa arrived by caravan in the city in 1325, he ordered the famed Granadan architect and poet Abu Ishaq al-Sahili to build a mosque to match the magnificence of the city's bazaar and its wondrous mix of Moors, Bedouins, and Jews. The Jinjere Ber Mosque, still standing in all its glory, transformed a growing oasis into a leading attraction for trans-Saharan travelers. When Ibn Battuta, a famed Arab explorer and scribe, visited the city two decades later, he was both amused and appalled at the way West Africa had mingled its own customs with Islam.[1] Stranded in a Saharan village to the north for several weeks, he described the salt lick where he stayed as the "most fly-ridden of places." Later, he met the sultan, whose followers emerged with spears, bows, drums, and "bugles made of elephant tusks." Ibn Battuta expressed disgust with "female slaves and servants who went stark naked into the court for all to see; subjects who groveled before the sultan, beating the ground with their elbows and throwing dust and ashes over their heads," as well as "royal poets who romped about in feathers and bird masks." The seasoned Arab writer also remarked on the devoted children of Islam, youngsters made to memorize the Koran in full. Ibn Battuta also described the mud-walled homes with domes of timber and reed that I would enter upon checking into the Hotel Colomb late in the year 2004. Even the food was virtually the same, with meals of millet served with yogurt.

Timbuktu was ideally situated along several leading caravan thoroughfares that criss-crossed the Sahel from North Africa to West Africa. It quickly became a center of wealth and learning. In 1526, African explorer Leo Africanus, commissioned by the Medici in Italy to write a survey of the region, sketched a city of one hundred thousand citizens living in "huts made of clay covered wattles with thatched roofs."[2] In it lived a king who "greatly honored learning," Africanus said, adding that "there are more profits to be made from books than from all other merchandise." Ideas generated industry and prosperity. A professional class of tanners, leather workers, metallurgists, calligraphers, illuminators, gilders, and scribes sprang up to support the thoughts of men. For centuries, scores of private libraries in remote Timbuktu served as repositories of scientific knowledge, at a time when Europeans cringed in superstition and fear of the plague. Modern scholars have been left with their heads spinning as they have discovered a lost treasure of Arabic texts and poems in and around the old city. Several of the biographical tomes are amazing in their scope. For example, Ahmed Baba's biographical dictionary, written in the city, documented the lives of notables from Arabia, Egypt, Morocco, and Central Asia.

My first evening in Timbuktu, I sat on the roof of the two-story Hotel Colomb with one of the city's most prominent librarians, Sheikh Abdel Kader Haidara, who has for three decades been intent upon rediscovering Timbuktu's lost heritage. Haidara, a tall, rounded man with a goatee hinting at erudition, was bursting with optimism about the changes possible in West Africa. He told proud stories of a lost era and described for me the unexpected arrival of Professor Henry Louis Gates, director of African American studies at Harvard, who had traveled to the city in 1997 to look into stories of ancient, long-hidden documents. "I opened the doors to the books and manuscripts piled up in a dusty back room by the thousands, and Professor Gates broke down in tears," said Haidara, chuckling softly in the dim light.[3] "He started to sob and said he had grown up all his life believing that Africa had no written heritage of its own."[4] (This, I realize in retrospect, was a far different image of the professor whose tirade against a Cambridge police officer earned him an invitation for beer at the White House after he was carted off to jail in 2009.)

As Haidara told the story, I contemplated the howling of the sands to our north. Whereas ideas once moved in step with the languorous camel caravans, the pace had certainly picked up in the twenty-first century. Timbuktu now had three dingy Internet cafés, some of the keyboards covered in sand, from which I worked to send stories to the *International Herald Tribune* on the locust plague and illegal migration. News from the Middle East that took months to arrive in Timbuktu even in the last century now arrived via the Internet the same day, quickly spreading in the city's bazaar by word of mouth, just as tales had been spread seven hundred years ago. The desert caravan routes, largely neglected after the growth of maritime trade, had again become attractive for businessmen, mostly in shiny four-by-four trucks. With armaments, cigarettes, and drugs in demand across West and Central Africa, there was also a ready-made capital market to fit just about any smuggler's interests. (Unfortunately, even a limited trade in human slaves still existed.) All you needed was a satellite phone, preferably with text messaging, and a good set of wheels to become a master of the Saharan sands. Even without a good GPS system, you could still, if you were trained, follow the ancient routes—tracking them from one star to the next.

I was reminded of the words of Dr. Hamidou Magassa, a gentle religious scholar I had met in the Malian capital, Bamako. He said that the "desert should not be looked at as a frontier, but rather as a kind of virtual society, a means of communication between humans. It offers only artificial borders, and everyone living in the desert has close, very close relations. Just to stay alive, people need to help each other."[5] He spoke of the paradox of wide open spaces: everything is so far away, yet—in the desert—everyone is so dependent upon everyone else.

After just one night in town, I fell into the company of Hama, a tall, fidgety young man who had been driving an American aid worker around in his four-by-four Toyota Land Cruiser. He looked strong enough to defend me from just about anything that might come our way. Since he was by his own account desperate to find a "tourist" to replace the one he had just lost, I volunteered, giving him the impression that I just wanted to tool around a bit in the desert. I made appointments to see the mayor and several leading scholars upon my return to Timbuktu, but first I was itching to see the desert.

Almost immediately, we came face to face with the elements in the form of the machine gun–like splatters on our windshield caused by three-inch-long grasshoppers. As we rolled out of Timbuktu, the skies darkened with millions of flying locusts, some of them as long as a man's finger and bent on a feast of biblical proportions. The swarms, I was told, rode the Saharan drafts, circumventing aerial spraying and eating the equivalent of their own weight in a single day. With their pink heads and speckled wings, the pests descended on us with a muted drone, battering our windshield like a hailstorm and targeting everything in sight, including rice and millet fields, fruit orchards, and vegetable patches. Trees in full leaf were gnawed down to skeletons. There were reports of new swarms amassing on the Algerian border to which we were heading.[6]

Hama put a pinch of snuff under his bottom lip at midday. He looked undaunted as we tore off beneath a set of rosy sand dunes and through the last of the savanna, past a herd of several hundred wild elephants. We had a blowout and we crossed paths with gasoline, cigarette, and milk smugglers from Algeria as well as several wild ram hunters, invariably Saudi royalty in shiny, new all-terrain vehicles. The expanse of tiny pebbles and undulating sand dunes gave way to a vast flatland that stretched as far as the eye could see.

We fishtailed past the rib cages of dead camels and the rusting hulks of old jeeps. Tuareg families, guided by men in long blue robes with brightly clad women on mules and camels, marched along in single file behind braying goats.

At dusk we stopped briefly outside a desolate police post, a crumbling mass of sand set on a small hill, to deliver a pair of blankets from the police at a post we had passed earlier—and to ask for directions. When I returned from the police post, I saw that Hama had plopped down in front of our Land Cruiser with his arms crossed. He looked up, snorted twice, and spat in the sand.

"Qu'est que c'est?" ("What is it?") I asked Hama, a muscle-bound twenty-four-year-old, who was now apparently refusing to budge.

"I don't trust these Arabs," he complained. "They will rob us and kill us."

"Come on now, this is what we agreed to," I retorted. "Besides, they aren't Arabs, they are Tuaregs, Berbers, and they are Malians, right?"

"Why did they change the route of the Paris-Dakar race last year?" he snapped rhetorically. He already knew the answer to his question. The dangers of Algeria's continuing strife, particularly the growing threat of kidnapping, had long since spilled across the Sahel in all directions, with al Qaeda cells and their associates now spreading their tentacles down into West Africa's Guinea coast. While these terrorists represented little immediate threat to local governments, the Paris-Dakar competitors, most of them wealthy, white Caucasians, stood out as highly visible Western targets. The French authorities had thought better than to run their race near to Timbuktu this year. Hama and I argued back and forth for several minutes until a gendarme in a tattered green uniform walked down the hill and entered the debate on my side. Hama agreed, albeit reluctantly, to drive on.

As we drove into the heart of the Sahara toward the border of Algeria, the swirling sands and heat waves on the horizon obscured our vision. The road ahead offered a smuggler's paradise of winding tracks that veered off in all directions, many leading north into

Israeli musicians in Jerusalem's old town.

Israeli musician rates Obama. He says he came from down low and has risen to "on high."

Israeli policemen on patrol (on horseback) in Jerusalem's old town near King David's Gate.

Damascus water boy provides water to thirsty residents in ancient and bustling market.

Young men walk near the spice market in Damascus.

Damascus Café. Young, pro-Western Syrians favor a warming of relations with the United States.

Young ladies watch the world go by in Damascus's old town.

Khalid Meshal, Hamas's foreign relations chairman and cofounder, speaks in Damascus.

Jewish clerics at the Wailing Wall.

Palestinian shepherd near the Soucia caves explains his plight.

A Palestinian boy clings to a meal and a toy gun in Beirut's Shatila refugee camp.

Egyptian bartenders at Luxor's Winter Palace. They miss the days when Winston Churchill stayed here.

Sunset in Maluku.

Author, Philip Smucker, in Indonesia's Spice Islands with kids on a boat off the island the British traded to the Dutch in exchange for Manhattan.

A young child on Saparua Island in Indonesia's Spice Island chain. Outside agitators helped destroy an ancient Christian-Muslim harmony.

Young Muslim children on Seram Island in the Spice Island chain. Christians and Muslims mingle here near bubbling Mount Nunusaku.

Timbuktu's ancient libraries are turning up treasure chests full of knowledge and insight into Islam's mediating and peace-making role in African history.

Young Muslim "adventurists" seek a future in Europe by travelling through the burning sands of the Sahara.

Sheikh Kounti saved his family's treasured books in this leather sack. His pupils are now discovering their lost history.

In the Sahel, the mayor of Inhalid, a small town on a human smuggling route to Europe.

African elders in the Sahel have adapted fundamentalist Islamic principles to African realities.

An Afghan child hopes for peace and stability.

An Afghan boy carries wheat husks in Kunar beneath the fight raging in the Korengal Valley.

Taliban relax near poppy fields in southern Afghanistan.

Afghan warlord in bandolier. US counterinsurgency policy hopes to empower locals.

Lekshan Bibi, a leader of the Kalash in northern Pakistan, says that a jihadist onslaught has imperiled her people's ancient way of life.

Kalash girls in northern Pakistan. An ancient and embattled way of life.

A Pakistani Shepherd carries a tired lamb over the mountains.

Afghan elders in southeastern Pakistan's Paktika Province gather to talk to US forces. The Taliban controls the night.

US forces on patrol in eastern Afghanistan.

Lieutenant Kerr addresses concerned elders in the Dangam District of Kunar Province, Afghanistan.

Ha'aretz columnist Akiva Eldar. He believes that firm US pressure will convince Israeli leaders to surrender their dreams of a "greater Israel."

Algeria. The desert leading to the Algerian border was so flat and barren that it was possible to race ahead at speeds of seventy and eighty miles an hour. At dusk we arrived at a man-made oasis on the Algerian border, a wretched, mud-brick town with drifting sand creeping up cinder-block walls and hundreds of smugglers and travelers hanging out in roadside diners lined with rusted refrigerators. Inside, the dark faces revealed bloodshot eyes and glistened with perspiration, the faces of men and boys overworked in the Saharan sun. Outside, at sunset, the devout—heads bowed to the grainy winds—recited verses from the Koran. It wasn't long before we caught wind of the work being done by the town's lone medic, Dr. M. Hamzata, with Médecins du Monde.[7] He was a skinny yet energetic Berber, horrified at the conditions in which he had been sent to work. When he discovered that I was a reporter, he quickly offered to show me the plight of the town's most desperate people. We drove past mud-brick factories—the only visible sign of industry in the town—and discovered a sign in the sand marked by three old tires. It read, "Voyagers welcome, sleep for the night at the Restaurant Bienvenues!" Inside a courtyard with ten-foot walls, amid the swirling sands, several dozen emaciated young Africans, many of them shoeless, sat at a picnic table eating their only meal of the day, a plate of rice with vegetable oil. A young boy in rags immediately approached the doctor and complained about suffering from chronic dizziness. He was eating one meal a day and working in a brick factory to earn money for his journey to Morocco and on to Europe. Dr. Hamzata did what he could and asked the boy to drop by his clinic. "These are stubborn children," he told us. "They won't listen to reason, no matter how the dangers are described to them."[8]

Although some of the boys spoke English, most of them, like the doctor, spoke French with a heavy African accent. Baterna, a twenty-three-year-old Senegalese man with a bloody and bandaged left foot, claimed he was headed to Europe in order to send money back to his family in Dakar. "Once I get into Algeria, I'll almost be in Morocco and once I get to Morocco, I'll almost be in Spain," he said. For many of the young men, the journey offered hope for the future, an escape from the West African economies of Senegal, Nigeria, Cameroon, Mali, and Liberia. Daouda Badji, thirty-four, a Senegalese father of two, was nearby in a yellow robe. He squatted on a straw prayer mat where he would sleep later that night.

Badji, known appropriately in French as an "adventurist," had a sad but typical tale to tell us. As he was riding north, Malian policemen had sprung from the acacia trees and ordered him out of the small minibus he was traveling in. Stripped to his underwear and robbed of the several hundred dollars he had been saving to get to Europe, he was taunted by the cops. "They told us, sure, we know you are going to Europe," he said. Germany, his final destination, was still months if not years away. "This journey is like a book you read and you just don't know how it will end," he told me. He offered me a poem he had just composed, entitled, "Weep for the Lost Sons of Africa!" It was a tale of desperation but also of hope for a better life. I hauled out an old *National Geographic* map of Saharan and North Africa that I was carrying, and we traced a finger over the route that Badji hoped to take.

Inhalid, the border town where we had stopped for the night, was teaming with young men trying to get out, most of them already robbed of the little money they had brought with them. From the city of Gao, a few hours to the south, for $120, a large sum by local standards, drivers linked the "adventurists" up with smuggling teams along the trans-Saharan routes, teams that, in turn, brought the travelers over the pink dunes to what was virtually a prison camp here on the border. With some four hundred thousand illegal immigrants entering Europe every year, the European Union had just stepped up its efforts to stem the influx of illegals. It was very much the Europeans' own version of the "Mexican immigrant issue," except that the travelers in this case had both the Saharan desert and the Mediterranean Sea to cross before arriving anywhere near to their final destination.

The entire town owed its existence to human smuggling, as we quickly discovered. Groups prospering from the trade maintained links to rings inside Algeria. For an insider's perspective, Dr. Hamzata introduced us to the town's mayor, Lamin Ag Ilbak, a local Tuareg, a member of a nomadic, pastoralist Berber group, not to be confused with several Arab groups that also inhabit the region, mostly in the north. A short, robust man, Ilbak had a deep brown complexion, pleasant rounded cheeks, and a quick laugh. He insisted we photograph him alongside his favorite camel as he smiled at us with a set of crusty teeth, the same yellowish-green hue as his charge. "This is an open frontier," he said. "Anyone who arrives here is free to move in any direction—provided he has a good vehicle. With a bad vehicle, you'll end up dead. If you stray from a known route, you can also die. I've pulled dead travelers out of the sands myself." Ilbak said he had heard talk of the central government wanting to close down his town in order to curtail illegal trafficking. "If they did that, we would be swallowed up by the Sahara," he said, suggesting it could never happen on his watch, and besides, his distressed sub-Saharan minions weren't about to vanish anytime soon. Each night, Ilbak organized illegal departures into Algeria. He had actually founded the town a dozen years earlier in an effort to help the UN high commissioner for refugees repatriate young Malian men to Mali. They had been in Moammar Qadhafi's Libya, where they had been trained in guerrilla warfare. "In 1992, there were three houses in town; now there are over one hundred," he boasted.

All this smuggling of humans and goods was not lost on US military and intelligence officials, who had become obsessed in recent years with what they referred to as "al Qaeda's new desert playground, the Sahara." Well, at least the region had the makings of one, according to General Charles Wald, who was at the time the deputy commander of the US military forces in Europe. He applied an analytical Westerner's logic to the matter. "A Europe obsessed with human rights protections and an Africa devoid of any laws at all both—in their own ways—afford ideal environments for terrorists to plot, plan, incubate, and execute," he told me over the telephone from Germany in a lengthy interview.[9]

I had come to the region to examine these concerns, which, military officers and counterterrorism officials claimed, posed a "threat to regional stability." Of course, "regional stability" was a relative term and—in the next few months of travel in West Africa and the Sahel in 2006 and 2007—I discovered nothing that could rightly be identified, at least from a Westerner's viewpoint, as such. What I did find, instead, was an evolving and ancient Islamic tradition that was—for the most part—helping to keep a lid on excessive violence, even offering elements of hope for regional development.

✶✶✶

After a night sleeping in Hama's jeep to defend it from "Arabs" and mechanics who might try to steal parts, we turned and headed back downwind to the ancient city of Gao. Here we sought out Sheikh Ben Hamada al-Kounti, a low-profile Tuareg scholar who hailed from a clan of desert wanderers known for their sagacity. He was the headmaster of a school for impoverished children. Through the entrance of a mud-walled courtyard, I spotted a crowd of barefoot and ragged children sitting cross-legged beneath a burlap awning reciting verses from the Koran written in charcoal on wooden tablets. This was the kind of memorization by rote that one witnessed in the madrassas, or religious schools, of Pakistan, but here it was not accompanied by any injunctions to kill foreigners. The boys looked underfed, a gang of urchins brought in out of the baking sun, but they were all pleasant enough and apparently pleased to be studying.

The sheikh himself, noticing guests at the gate, disappeared into a back room to find his slippers and emerged hooded and squinting from an afternoon nap. I explained that I was interested in both his family history and the future of the region. He turned around, reentered his home, and returned, dusting off an ornately decorated leather sack full of ancient texts. Like many other intellectuals in the Sahara, al-Kounti had obtained a good education among the camel wells, palm trees, and rocky outcroppings. "I first studied these documents in my father's tent by the light of a candle," he told me. He fidgeted with the crusty bag and appeared slightly uneasy at my unannounced arrival at his gate. (I had apologized and mentioned the apparent lack of a phone service.)

Al-Kounti's tribe, the Kounta, were descended from a distinct group of fair-skinned Berbers who roamed what is now Mauritania, Algeria, Mali, and Niger. The sheikh's nomadic ancestors, many of them intellectual and spiritual leaders, served as the thread that connected believers and merchants for centuries. My host was particularly proud of the account of how his great-great-great-grandfather Sidi al-Mukhtar al-Kounti had managed to restore peace in Timbuktu early in the nineteenth century. He left the room, returned with a moth-eaten text bound in calfskin, which he carefully spread before us, even as the pages crumbled in his hands and grains of sand fell onto the table. He crossed his legs on a prayer rug as he began to read the story of how Sidi al-Mukhtar had mediated between warring factions during a siege of the city sparked off when residents killed two nomads. Citizens on the verge of starvation—already having consumed much of the local canine population—were ready to make a deal.

"Sidi al-Mukhtar asked the inhabitants of Timbuktu to hand over ten horses, one thousand formal robes, and one thousand pieces of gold," he explained. "The opposing nomad leaders reluctantly accepted the gift despite a strict ban in their own culture on blood money. Later in life, Sidi al-Mukhtar negotiated an end to a spate of highway robberies and acts of terror carried out by two desert tribes against travelers in and around Timbuktu. Another kinsman, Sheikh al-Bakkay al-Kounti, had petitioned the ruling sultan of Masina to spare the life of German explorer Heinrich Barth on the grounds that non-Muslims should not be banned from traveling in the Sahel. Barth owed his life to al-Kounti's kin. For this and similar actions, both of his kinsmen were dubbed "saints" in the Sufi order that al-Kounti espoused—placing them amid the pantheon of some 333 similarly venerated holy men, or "marabouts," in today's Timbuktu.

Al-Kounti explained that his kinfolk had fought hard against French colonialists to preserve their unique way of life. When French forces arrived in the Sahel in the middle of the nineteenth century, most of al-Kounti's family declared war on the foreign invaders and fled to the Adrar-n-Iforas, a low range of rocky outcroppings and caves along the Algerian border. They took their dearest possessions with them. Here they hid their texts and rallied the locals to join in a "holy war" to oppose foreign occupation. It was a holy war in name, but a war of liberation in actuality.

The French strategy to control West Africa, known as *la politique musulmane*, was a new approach to an old Western strategy: "divide and conquer." Administrators attempted to build local alliances with Muslim scholars and would-be jihadists. Almost immediately, however, they faced a series of smaller jihads, referred to as the Marabout Wars, which spread from Senegal to modern Mali and Niger. As with the mistakes made across Africa by other European colonial powers, trivial disagreements between Frenchmen and Africans sometimes ended in outright massacres of tribesmen.

Fear of an unfamiliar culture and the unknown threats it posed to colonial expansion drove French policy. As the colonial rulers viewed it, the flow of traffic, camels, humans, and ideas posed a direct challenge to their own economic and political interests. They restricted traffic in the belief that by regulating the circulation of ideas, they could impose their own. To this end, French spies spread their tentacles across the desert from Senegal to Chad. American academic Dr. Ben Soares, whom I met with in Bamako, would write in *Islam and the Prayer Economy* that "the French attempted to identify in a systematic way all Muslim religious personalities," a process that got fully underway in the second decade of the twentieth century.[10] Soares, a senior researcher in West Africa for the Afrika-Studiecentrum, a Dutch institute, noted that the French recorded such key information as each Muslim religious leader's lineage, library holdings, and sphere of influence. It was profiling by another name.

Peripatetic preachers in some regions of the French territory were branded "charlatans" and "vagabonds" and dealt with severely. Officials came to define the threat of pan-Islamism as "any attempt at interterritorial communication for religious purposes."[11] Needless to say, this was a broad-brush approach that pushed many into the arms of the jihadists. One demanding French administrator, cited by Soares, advised his colleagues that the "policy to follow with regard to Muslims is simple. It can be summed up in a few words. No useless harassment of marabouts who prove to be correct, but severe repression of all subversive propaganda."[12] Judge and jury were one in the same. At this time, despite the efforts of the French, Islam continued its inexorable spread across French West Africa even as officials sought to restrict it. One reason: improving transportation. Africans in the Sahel, together with everything they wrote and talked about along the way, circulated in larger numbers and faster than ever before. Islam—as it had been for centuries and is even today—was part and parcel of daily communications in the Sahara.

In the wake of World War II, French rule in most of Africa was doomed. With fewer men and means to monitor charismatic personalities and their ideas, French authorities came to terms with their loss of control and offered to lift their harsh restrictions on the freedom of travel and communication. They set conditions but opened the floodgates, and the region began a massive transformation. West African Islam's distinctive flavor—an amalgamation of Koranic belief with tribal custom held together by strong local personalities, often drawn from Sufi mystical traditions that stress charms and hexes, characterized by a cocktail of tongues, chicken's feet, and lizards, remained, but simpler and more direct forms of worship also made their way to West Africa. Along with tens of thousands of new pilgrims making their way to and from the annual hajj, new versions of Islam made inroads, particularly those funded by charitable contributions from the Middle East.

Pilgrims returning from Mecca advocated more puritanical and egalitarian approaches to religion: a direct interpretation of the Prophet's teachings and a new effort to walk in his footsteps. The newer and more austere interpretation of Islam advocated an end to what was perceived as the undue exaltation of the human form. Leaders of new Middle Eastern–influenced sects accused some Sufi leaders, often with reason, of working hand in hand with the French authorities. As they had in Egypt's anticolonial movement, the more puritanical followers of Islam seized the militant and nationalist mantle. Among other changes, they advocated advanced and wide-spread education in the Arabic language, which French authori-ties—always keen to have the world speak a language they knew well—actively discouraged.

As the militant tide rose higher, the French, facing revolts across North and West Africa, aimed their old repressive measures at the new importers of strict Islam, backing malleable Sufi leaders in their efforts to restrict the rise of fundamentalism. Nationalism super-seded new forms of worship or religious ideology, but also molded and incorporated Africans in the spiritual rejection of French authority. The fury was strongest and bloodiest in Algeria, the lynchpin of French colonial rule. Algerian rebels found safe havens, among other places, in Mali, near to Gao. By 1961, the year John F. Kennedy took office, nearly 1.5 million Algerians and thousands of Frenchmen had been killed in the rebellion and the internecine war-fare across the region. Gen. Charles De Gaulle, with the ghosts of Dien Bien Phu fresh in his thoughts, capitulated, ending a war rife with atrocities and allowing France to reduce its presence with a few shreds of goodwill still lingering.

Unfortunately, the French hadn't stopped meddling. They briefly toyed with the idea of helping to found a Tuareg state in the Sahel. Instead, black African leaders rushed to assert their control. In their haste—both in Mali and Niger—these leaders ignored local custom and sparked off revolt across the Sahel—often against a Marxist-nationalist ideology that grated against the authority of the Tuareg tribal chieftains. Then, in 1968, the first in a series of severe droughts struck the central Sahel, lasting so long that at one stage the Niger River simply stopped flowing. Families of all ethnicities, but mostly

Arab and Berber, sent their young sons north, some to Algeria and more to Colonel Moammar Qadhafi's Libya. The wily colonel quickly gained a reputation as a master manipulator of African liberation movements. He entertained the wild prospect of opening up a corridor through the Sahara in the direction of Timbuktu and other key Sahelian cities with his Islamic Legion, a force of young Africans united by pan-Islamic and anti-Israeli sentiments.

The colonel promised fighters a chance to take back their homeland from "brutal oppressors," but did not see the ethnic complexities inherent in his new force. Desert nomads rejected the imposed discipline of Arab officers. The colonel's attempts to foster pan-Islamic unity failed. In the end, many factions, all trained in Qadhafi's military schools, returned on their own and without the colonel's guidance to make trouble in the Sahel. They used their Libyan training to enable them to become rogue warriors. (Among these unsavory characters were the leaders of the Janjaweed, wild fanatics who now regularly engage in the ethnic cleansing and rape of their enemies in the Darfur region of southern Sudan. In a mirror image of the colonel himself, his former protégés, armed with bogus ideals, behaved in their own self-interest.)

Today's Sahel, a semiarid savanna area that runs from Mauritania in the west to Sudan and Ethiopia in the east, remains a disorganized mix of ethnicities. The Sahel south of Algeria, particularly in Mali and Niger, is populated by black African farmers and herders living alongside nomadic Arab and Berber merchants. In some districts of northern Mali, more than 60 percent of the population are descendants of former African slaves, most of them of mixed blood but mostly dark skinned. (In Mali, part of the animosity between Tuaregs on the one hand and blacks on the other arose from the astonishment and humiliation that the Berber nomads experienced, as they felt they had been conquered by a race of black men that they had previously been accustomed to employing as household servants.)

After Qadhafi's failed experiment, Berber and Arab youth returned to the Sahel from the north embittered toward black rule and anxious to stake out their future. They revolted against their central governments and eventually won varying degrees of autonomy. Amadou Ag Ilene, a Malian human rights lawyer, advised me to look upon the Malian government's concessions to the Tuaregs in Timbuktu and elsewhere as something akin to mafioso allotments of turf to former rebels. The concessions could, in turn, be used by both corrupt government officials and Tuaregs to extort taxes and monopolize north-south smuggling routes. There was something in the deal for all parties. "This entire area has become ideal territory for smugglers—including terrorists from Algeria," the lawyer warned. "It is a bad, chaotic place where cancer cells can grow and mutate." Everywhere you looked around Timbuktu, swirling sands and heat waves abounded. The roads were winding tracks that veered off in all directions, many leading north into Algeria, where over one hundred twenty thousand civilians and soldiers had died in warfare since 1992.

Some might see a terrorist haven in the making in the Sahel and parts of North Africa, but for this to occur, more than mere poverty, corruption, and chaos will be required to stoke the flames. By local accounts, the US government's decision to invade Iraq provided plenty of grist for the terrorist mill. In Africa, as in Asia and the Middle East, it is not so much the truth that matters as the perception of events on the ground. An independent Tuareg radio director near the Algerian border told me what I had already guessed at— that "the war in Iraq reinforced fears that the United States is engaged in a war against Islam, not a war against terror." He added that many in the region had found their worst suspicions confirmed in the photographs that emerged from the prison cells of Abu Ghraib. The wide publicization of these photographs is not surprising unless you consider the remoteness of the region and the lack of Internet facilities and even phone lines.

To the north, Algeria remained a lynchpin—or tinderbox, depending on your predictions—largely held together with Western military assistance backing authoritarian rule. The government in

Algiers has begun to get a grip on what has been a terrifying civil war. The terrorists helped out by shooting themselves in the feet—read, committing more atrocities—a few more times than their equally brutal government counterparts. Nevertheless, underground Islamic groups were still on the make. An al Qaeda affiliate known as the Salafist Group for Call and Combat has already morphed into something called Al Qaeda in the Islamic Maghreb (AQIM).[13] A low-ranking government official near Gao told me that AQIM associates, some previously schooled in al Qaeda's Afghan camps, were secretly recruiting by stoking fears based on the annual visits of American Special Forces, who are now training regional armies in counterterrorism. "Al Qaeda [AQIM] is trying to gain recruits, just as the Americans are training them," the official, Ahmed Moussa, told me, suggesting a kind of symbiosis between the two efforts.

The American diplomats and generals I spoke to appeared to be at least vaguely aware of a disturbing metaphor—the footprint of the ten-thouand-pound American gorilla. American petroleum companies were expected to invest some $60 billion in the region in the coming decade. If that goes unmatched by diligent US development assistance, the sense of greed it generates could be disastrous, warned public officials. "Al Qaeda will use this as a recruitment and convincing tool as they proselytize," General Wald told me. "There is a retaliation element to their strategy as well as whatever they can do to hurt American interests." At the time he spoke to me, Wald was in charge of a $300-million trans-Saharan counterterrorism initiative that embraces a dozen countries in North and West Africa. It all looked like a logical Western approach to a problem that was still in its nascent stages. I couldn't help but suspect, however, that we were setting ourselves up for disaster by singling out the "enemy" in advance. The imagined fight on the horizon might soon become a fait accompli, according to my Timbuktu friends, but more on that later.

General Wald said he was aware that a vast parasitic business of terrorism run by Osama bin Laden and his affiliates was already setting itself up as an alternative to what many in West Africa see as just more of the same: US materialism and militarism encroaching on the sacred soil of Islam. At the same time, General Wald and the United States looked hard-pressed to stop bin Laden and his affiliates from presenting themselves as the better alternative.

To its credit, the Obama administration has stepped back from the Bush administration's moves to militarize US African policy; it has not retreated in terms of military strategy but is stressing development first. It is difficult, after all, to fight poverty with guns. Nevertheless, given militant Islam's patience and persistence, Western strategic planners have a lot to ponder amid the swirling sands and parched grasslands of Saharan and Sahelian Africa. Given the public relations problems that have devastated the American image in the Muslim world since 9/11, a heavy-handed approach could quickly backfire. The International Crisis Group's regional expert based in Dakar, Senegal, Mike McGovern, worries that heightened US militarism without a massive increase in Western economic assistance could lead to increased turmoil and new terrorism across West Africa. "If you come down hard, then the Islamists become martyrs, or if you go easy they tend to take advantage of the extra space," said McGovern.[14] "If you try to get terrorists and end up bombing caravans of cigarette smugglers, you lose the regional battle for hearts and minds."[15] In any case, as the French found out several decades ago, Islam is likely to steer and alter its own direction regardless and in spite of Western efforts to tame and channel it. The real trick may be how we manage to remain aloof enough *not to encourage* the fringe and militant elements in Islam. For, as we know in Afghanistan, a country from which we will not quickly extract ourselves, once we are in the fight, we are in the fight come what may.

For now, the lid is still on the Pandora's box in the Sahara and the Sahel, although some elements of al Qaeda remain hidden, agitating for recruits on an unrestricted information and desert highway. For six decades now, fundamentalist Islam has been making inroads in the region, but most of the region's "fundamentalists"—who represent as much as 10–15 percent of the population in some West African countries—remain about as outwardly threatening as an Amish farmers' village in Pennsylvania. They may be back-to-the-earth fundamentalists, but most of them have not morphed into militants.

Outside Gao, on the way back to Timbuktu, Hama and I hitched a ride across the Niger on a ferryboat in the direction of a Saudi-influenced Wahhabist village named Kadji. Nomads in turbans and flowing robes shoved their spitting and kicking camels to the back of the barge, as Hama slammed on his brakes, to dislodge us from the shore and launch us forward. Several sets of eyes glared at us from beneath black and indigo wraps. On the opposite bank, we drove over a hill past burlap tents and through a lush, green ricefield. A grandfatherly figure bathed in a warm inlet alongside white egrets, striped woodpeckers, and long-tailed blue birds. Off the barge, our car became lodged on a sandbar from which the Niger's waters had only just begun to recede. A gang of skinny kids rushed over to help shove us of and we arrived in the village center, where we were greeted with handshakes, smiles, and offers of tea.

The village headman, Sheikh Hafizu El Maadi, sixty-two, greeted us warmly. He insisted on walking us to the edge of the rice paddies, where he stroked his beard and bemoaned the damage done by the swarms of locusts that had only just left Kadji. "Now we're being plagued by something almost as bad—flocks of small birds that eat the rice stalks before they mature," he said. "Listen to the children beating their tom-tom drums to frighten off the birds." We listened and heard the faint patter of a goatskin drum from somewhere deep in the paddy, and we observed a couple of brightly attired scarecrows with bamboo arms and straw hats.

El Maadi had the misperception that I represented my own government, despite my protestations to the contrary. He politely suggested we visit an adult language school for women, which was already in session when we arrived. In a barren room with a plastic tarpaulin for a roof and no proper windows, women sat cross-legged on the floor looking up at a blackboard and reciting vowels. The students, some of them mothers, were dressed in black, but none of their faces were covered. This was a tame version of Saudi Wahhabism, indeed. As had been the case through history, Saharan and sub-Saharan Africans were loath to implement the most conservative aspects of Middle Eastern Islam, particularly strict Sharia punishments like execution and hand amputation, but also full veiling, which is rare in the Sahel. In other words, the Africans had incorporated the basics of the religion but preserved their African traditions. The term "Wahhabism" as it is applied so loosely in West Africa was actually a French colonial-era misnomer for almost all African interpretations of fundamentalism. (The term that the US ambassador to Mali was using when I met with her, "Salafism," was also an inadequate name for the inroads being made by some strains of Middle Eastern fundamentalism.) The dissimilarity between local African Wahhabism and the Wahhabism that was practiced in the community Muhammad ibn Abd al-Wahhab founded in Arabia in the late 1700s, and that dominates Saudi Arabia today, is comparable to the difference between a "soft " interpretation of Marxism by a French or Yugoslav Socialist and a "hard" interpretation of the same ideology by a Russian Stalinist.

In a circle under the largest baobab tree, beside a small, dilapidated mosque, gray-bearded elders with red checkered scarves drawn across their white skull caps beckoned me to sit with them on straw mats. Once I had explained that I was an American journalist—not an aid worker as they had hoped—the imam, Sedu Idrisa, agreed to discuss some of the world's problems. We spoke for an hour and most of the elders listened without a word. "For us, religion is a path chosen by the individual worshipper," the imam said. "If outsiders intercede and try to prevent a Muslim from doing this, it is right for him to defend his way of life. For instance, if someone with arms attacks you, it is the people's right to struggle against this—even if it means taking up arms."

It was a classic recital of Islam's version of a defensive jihad, the notion that all Muslims are prepared to live and let live with their neighbors across the world, except when their right to practice their religion is infringed upon by an outsider. If couched in terms of "freedom to worship," this view is not so different from the view that America's founding fathers set forth in the Bill of Rights. It is not by accident that freedom of expression and freedom to worship were subsumed under the same item: "Congress shall make no law respecting an establishment of religion, or prohibiting the free exercise thereof; or abridging the freedom of speech, or of the press; or the right of the people peaceably to assemble, and to petition the Government for a redress of grievances."[16] Unfortunately, the prevailing view is also in keeping with the basic rationale that bin Laden has long since incorporated into his own anti-American propaganda game—that it is the right and duty of any good Muslim to fight back against anyone seeking to inhibit or restrict the "free exercise" of religion.

The simplicity of life in Kadji was striking and also oddly reassuring, given the frightening rumors I had heard repeated in American diplomatic circles about the spread of Saudi-inspired "extremism." Undoubtedly, these fundamentalists had their differences with traditional African Islam. They strongly objected to the local African mix of totem and spirit, the use of amulets in worship, and the reliance on mysticism, including spirit possession. Just as German Lutherans and American Puritans ridiculed idolatry and the outright worship of saints in Catholicism, so the new forms of Islam in Africa attacked perceived diversions from the simple and righteous and path to God. One could hardly blame impoverished Africans who traveled on a pilgrimage to the developed world, witnessed a simpler and less hierarchical practice of religion, and then sought to imitate it at home. Many were mere followers, as are most devout persons the world over.

Fundamentalism, for Kadji and other villages across West Africa, had become a pragmatic alternative to the status quo, not least because it was subsidized by Middle Eastern charities. (People like those in Kadji were arguably too poor to turn down any assistance.) A legal scholar and development consultant for the US government in Mali told me that "the fundamentalists are able to offer a brand of

Islam that appeals across the traditional caste system, from the poorest former slaves to the richest businessmen. Whereas, for an elaborate Sufi wedding, a young Sahelian might fork over several dozen camels and pay the local imam exorbitantly for the music and ceremony, Wahhabists eschew musical performances and prefer simple, no-frills ceremonies." In terms of sheer marketing, the Middle Eastern brand of Islam had the appeal of a Target or Walmart, in contrast to Saks Fifth Avenue.

Basic morality has also played a role in the inroads made by fundamentalism. In Gao, while visiting Sheikh al-Kounti, we had spent the night in the Tizi Mizi Hotel, owned by a prominent former mayor, a Christian. The whitewashed, ranch-style hotel with a wall encircling it also served as a short-stay brothel, not an uncommon phenomenon across rural Africa. The owner, Sedou Diallo, who said he counted himself as a good "friend of the American ambassador" to Mali, was a rotund man with a thick gold chain around his neck. Diallo's hotel, in addition to being the annual residence for the US Special Forces, who train local troops in counterterrorism tactics, also offered short-stay rooms for a disco just down the road, where young women offered their services on the stoop. Diallo, not surprisingly, blamed the local "Islamic fundamentalists" for inspiring fear and social conservatism, and he said they thought he, Diallo, was the devil incarnate.

In contrast, the humble and impoverished residents of Kadji maintained an optimistic, wholly tolerant outlook. "You'll find that there isn't much difference between any of the Muslims around here," said one fifty-four-year-old father, sipping on a Coca-Cola. "We all pray and follow the same God, though our techniques and some of our values are a little different. For instance, we don't like our women going about in tight jeans. It is too much of an enticement for the young men—especially with this AIDS thing." I wondered if Islamic fundamentalism's inroads in West Africa should really be considered alarming within a social structure so devastated by disease, poverty, and neglect. Fundamentalism did offer some basic solutions.

Across much of Africa's Islamic belt, so-called Salafists and Wah-habists hold out a collective appeal that offers an apparent antidote to the failed nationalism—even the lingering racism—that plagues Africa from Liberia and Sierra Leone to Algeria and Egypt. Whether we in the West like it or not, these groups have been around for decades and are already carving out a distinct place for themselves in Islam's future. It may be that both moderate and extreme interpretations of Islamic fundamentalism will provide varied degrees of cohesion on rapidly changing religious, political, and economic fronts across Africa. West-erners taking sides risk ending up on the wrong side of history. The best we can do in Africa is the best we can do in our own country—defend tolerance, justice, and the freedom to worship as one sees fit.

Dr. Hamidou Magassa, the author of a recent social survey of the modifications in Islamic practice in the Sahelian region, had reminded me in Bamako that the new strains of fundamentalist Islam made reli-gion increasingly accessible to the masses. "Islamization is no longer something that happens from the top down with someone powerful or rich bestowing the fruits of religion on the masses," he said. "Unlike the Sufi big men, the Wahhabist and other fundamentalist leaders don't try to use their finances to make a one-man show and gain the largest following. They work in more subtle ways."

Well, at least some of the time. Many West Africans still spurn the new fundamentalist ideologues, for both their wealthy creden-tials and their often elitist view of what is good for the masses—as I would learn on my return to the forgotten city.

✳✳✳

On our return to Timbuktu, we had spotted Imam Ben Essayuti strolling through the dun-colored sands in downtown Timbuktu, leading an immense wedding party amid the jingling of tambourines and the beating of tom-toms. Children skipped along behind his procession, laughing with joy. A wedding like this made a Wahhabist ceremony seem like a trip to the justice of the peace.

The next day, I made my way over to the imposing Jinjere Ber Mosque. With its towering fired-brick walls and nine geometric naves, it was a seven-hundred-year-old meeting place of astounding proportions. If it was the fertility of the Nile River that had allowed Egypt to prosper earlier and become a center for world civilization, it must have been the adventuresome spirit, devoutness, and good-will of Muslim traders that had created the former wealth and prosperity in this city that now, on the surface, had so little in Western material terms. The grand mosques of Timbuktu served as centers of mediation, arbitration, and learning. Imams, judges, and scholars opened the mosques' doors and declared them sanctuaries that could not be violated. Islam and knowledge also gave the region's African monarchs a seat at the table with Arab traders in search of African gold. In addition, Islam and knowledge provided a passport to any destination, from Marrakech to Baghdad.[17]

Jinjere Ber's early links to Andalusia's financial and intellectual renaissance—which preceded the equivalent in the rest of Europe by centuries—made it a prime target for Moroccan invaders at the end of the sixteenth century. The elders of Timbuktu met the marauding Moroccans with gentle rebukes. No one in Timbuktu could find a reference in the Koran that would permit one Muslim nation to invade and enslave another. Unimpressed, the Moroccans shackled the city's intellectuals, mounted them on camels, and packed them off to Marrakech. It marked the beginning of the end of Timbuktu's regional dominance.

I met the mosque's head imam, Ben Essayuti, informally the next day. We sat on the floor of his vestry and sipped green tea. (My father had been a minister and I had once served as an acolyte, though I could not remember my own house of worship ever providing this pleasant informality.) Essayuti expressed a real worry about rising tensions between traditionalists and Wahhabists, couching it in terms that made it sound like a small schism in the making. "Timbuktu people have a broad understanding of philosophy, religion, and human rights, but we are in danger of losing that with these Wahhabist mosques springing up all over," he complained. "They don't even understand the significance of celebrating Mohammed's birthday. They must understand that problems cannot be resolved with the force of arms."

But apart from those employed by the desert smugglers in their four-wheeled, air-conditioned caravans, the immediate threat of arms was hardly apparent to an outsider. I had to wonder if the imam was trying to play on my sympathies, knowing I was an American interested in local politics. There were religious and personal rivalries in the air here that no reporter could ever fully understand. Essayuti added, however, that "talking down violence" had become increasingly difficult, given what he referred to as "America's war on terror." A jocular and rotund pillar of the community, Essayuti appeared in to be no immediate danger of losing his own following. Each year, thousands of locals, many young boys and girls included, showed up for a communal mud-packing party, attacking the walls of the ancient mosque with handfuls of earth, its best defense against the encroaching sands. The imam praised an effort within Timbuktu's High Islamic Council to put an end to the construction of new fundamentalist mosques funded with money from Gulf states.

The holy man also mentioned an unusual move afoot to censure a local Wahhabist imam for his harsh denunciation of a common belief in Islam that the prophet Jesus Christ will return to Earth one day. The Wahhabist imam had been wrong, he insisted, and Jesus would return. He suggested that an official reprimand was the only answer to such treachery. It was an irony not lost on me—a mere interloper—that such a lively dispute could arise out of the question of Jesus's second coming in a city that was 99.9 percent Muslim. (Although I was aware that Jesus was admired within Islam as a genuine prophet, it sounded like the kind of dispute any Westerner should avoid at any cost.)

We had two more stops in Timbuktu, to meet with the city's senior librarians and to witness some of the city's efforts at a cultural revival that—with some luck—would become an example for other remote corners of Africa. Outside the neat offices of Sheikh Abdel Kader Haidara, who had earlier told me the story of Professor Gates, several homeless families slept on burlap under the stars, living off the handouts of the kind scholar. The young sheikh ushered me into his library, where he showed me a new set of bookshelves held together with chicken wire that he had constructed to hold texts that are hundreds of years old, some of them containing writings in Yiddish by Jewish merchants who had once worked and lived in the city. He flipped through some pages to display the marginal annotations of successive generations of African scholars. As he turned the pages, however, I flinched as paper and gold leaf crumbled to dust in his hands. Praise be to digital technology, I thought, as a belated form of preservation.

We returned to the roof of the Hotel Colomb and he had a green tea, while I ordered an Elephant beer. Something was bothering the sheikh, as I learned that evening on the veranda as locusts buzzed in the skies beneath a full moon. He feared that the region's historical tolerance and openness could soon be lost amid all the talk of the war on terror. "All you have to do is look at the proliferation of terrorist Web sites on the Internet," he said over dinner. "There are new militant groups out there, including al Qaeda, that don't share the values we have known here." Abdel Kader insisted that the US government was—for now—engaged in a Sisyphean struggle against terrorism because it is facing off so starkly against al Qaeda, almost with blinders on, while ignoring the opportunities to help West Africa build on its storied past. "Even when bin Laden and his people put out this militant nonsense, we always see officials in the United States, sometimes even the president, jump to respond. The US needs to stop reacting with a jerk of the knee to everything bin Laden and his cohorts put out. You might better start with the premise that most Muslims, particularly those of us here in Africa, are tolerant and moderate by nature."

It was dawning on me, even as Haidara spoke, that sometimes foreigners in a foreign land search their own paradigms for answers to questions that actually become clearer with a little local digging beneath the surface. "If you come to Africa with a military man's view of the war, you will find what you want," McGovern of the International Crisis Group had told me.[18] "There are clearly not a lot of people screaming for US blood, but they are wearing Osama bin Laden T-shirts."[19] He and others believed that the US approach to Africa is skewed toward "American interests," and mostly consists of defensive posturing against an unknown "threat." In the Bush years of the early twenty-first century, the US government spent— on average—$450 billion on defense and under $20 billion on development assistance across the globe. That was an astounding juxtaposition of priorities, when you consider it.

In Africa there is still time and a surprising amount of political capital in reserve, particularly now, with an African American president at the helm. "Our chance here is that we have an ancient culture to preserve," said my host. "We have a wealth of knowledge at our fingertips. This is a point of convergence and attraction for all groups." What he was saying, I think, is that the real struggle is not so much that of facing down the fundamentalists but rather the more subtle choice of supporting openness and building anew on an old foundation. That sounds like a safe bet for American development interests.

In the sandy streets and barren courtyards of Timbuktu, I had heard small children reciting Arabic poetry and learning tales of conflicts solved and wars averted. Sand, wind, insects, and flames had frayed the pages of Timbuktu's texts, a mother lode of some one million individual texts. Nonetheless, old books had been turning up in many places since the French colonialists abandoned the region a few decades ago. Some have been found beneath homes, others have been found stashed in desert caves, and still others have been spotted straddling the backs of camels.[20] Ironically, some of the families that had taken it upon themselves to hide and defend these ancient texts were now illiterate, victims of fear and stubbornness.

Timbuktu today, thanks to the interest of American scholars like

Gates at Harvard, is in the throes of a revival, which, along with donor funding, now coming primarily from the United States, might just blossom into something more enduring for all of us. Increasingly known as a repository of Africa's intellectual heritage, the city is attracting Western scholars who are partnering with Africans to seek out, rediscover, and preserve its ancient texts. Particularly relevant, as black African and Arab scholars point out, are accounts of how the African interpretation of Islam helped regulate the affairs of men, resolve disputes, and provide a model of tolerance. Buried in the crumbling manuscripts of Timbuktu and neighboring cities, scholars are finding evidence of wars averted, sieges ended, and lawlessness put to rest.

The effort has been a long time in the making. In 1967, UNESCO had provided money for a manuscript conservation center in Timbuktu, but until recently progress was excruciatingly slow. Then, in 1997, recalls Haidara, director of Timbuktu's Mamma Haidara Library, Gates arrived. Gates got in touch with the Andrew Mellon Foundation, which agreed to finance a small restoration project for the Arabic-language documents in Haidara's family library, some of them 850 years old. The foundation and several European Union aid groups have since begun the meticulous process of restoring the ancient texts of Timbuktu. Money has also been provided to build several libraries.

In the Malian capital, Bamako, I met Stephanie Diakite, an American scholar who works closely with African scholars. She is the kind of Peace Corps liberal one finds in strange places doing great, unheralded deeds, without which the "US presence" would be confined behind immense embassy walls. Diakite told me that "a select group of scholars is aware of the African model of Islam found in these ancient texts," which, she said, "reanimate an old model of thinking."[21] In one aid project, Diakite and local librarians in Timbuktu are finding families with ancient skills in manuscript writing and bookbinding to get them involved in the text preservation process. "Some families have kept bookbinding tools in their homes for centuries and haven't known what they were used for,"

Diakite, a legal expert who is a certified binder, told me. "We are locating these families and training men and women in the art of conservation, adapting old book-writing and bookbinding skills to the necessities of the modern age."[22]

Workers are scanning pages of the ancient texts and creating digital images of the works. As I had witnessed on my visit to Sheikh al-Kounti's school, entire libraries of African texts—mostly written in Arabic but often transcribed from local African languages—had been handed down from father to son over the centuries. In the end, it wasn't the hunt for books but the stories in them that had the most remarkable impact.

In the Fondo Kati Library, to which Diakite directed me, I met with Ismael Diadie Haidara, a soft-spoken, eclectic scholar who claimed Germanic, Jewish, and black African ancestry. (Ismael Haidara was not a direct relative of Sheikh Abdel Kader Haidara.) Ismael Haidara's Andalusian paternal ancestor had fled from Toledo, Spain, in 1468, in the opposite direction from that of the young men now fleeing through Inhalid in search of a better life in Europe. "Timbuktu was a melting pot for centuries," he said. Ismael Haidara had written several books, including a volume on the Jews of Timbuktu, who flourished centuries ago and built a synagogue that lasted through the nineteenth century. "Our work is both urgent and necessary as a means of recovering our collective memory," he insisted, sitting in his well-preserved Moorish-style abode, partially rebuilt with Spanish funding.[23]

Although few Malian youths these days can read Arabic, Ismael Haidara and Diakite had also begun a program designed to involve Timbuktu's young people in recitations, particularly poetry readings on themes of openness and tolerance. Along with the half-million books and manuscripts that Diakite says she has seen in recent years, there are, she added, "thousands of wonderful poems," many reflecting a lost culture that now has a chance to be rediscovered. I guessed the most important lesson—out of many—to be learned from Timbuktu is that sometimes the future is buried in the past.

Chapter 7
ALONG THE WATCHTOWER

Puffs of smoke appeared on the jagged horizon, and two Apache helicopters whipped through the skies overhead. As the choppers approached the firing line, Sgt. Wayne Amos called for his men to cease fire and allow the choppers to home in on their targets. He gave verbal instructions to the pilots to mark a mound of stones between two smaller hills. "Higher, higher! The next hill over! Yeah. Right there." A series of explosions blasted the boulders, sending stone flying and white puffs of smoke floating into the breeze.

Amos, the RAGE platoon leader in charge of security for the provincial reconstruction team (PRT) in Kunar Province, also narrated the fight as it unfolded.

"We just got hit," he cried. "It is crazy now; we took one RPG [rocket-propelled grenade], a lot of small arms. They are kickin' up now."

"Ten seconds and on the enemy!" Amos screamed. The "tat, tat, tat" of a 50-caliber machine gun rang out from the turret of a Humvee. Shell casings popped and spun through the air. There were no enemy faces, just the loud, gut-wrenching clap of ammunition rattling through guns and pinging off the side of the vehicle. The 50-caliber fired rounds for cover, and a single soldier dashed into the dirt road, kneeling to fire a TOW missile launcher up into the hills. The back thrust from the missile rocked the squatting soldier back on his heels.

As was often the case, the insurgents soon melted away into the rocks, and the fighting came to a halt when Amos determined that only his men were still shooting. The Americans and the world's best-protected military were safe in the valley, another "skirmish with unknown elements" to report back to base.

Amos had a sparkle in his eye as if he knew a little about warfare.[1] But I didn't know anything about his origins, and so I said in an off-the-cuff way, "Looks like Indians and cowboys," in order to set the Afghan guerrillas in the role of Indians taking on—as it were—the US Army's mounted cavalry. I'd met a direct cousin of Colonel Custer in the province of Khost a few months earlier, and so this did not seem to be a far-fetched analogy.[2] Well, when I finally sat down with Amos, he informed me that he was actually a reservist cop from the White Mountain Apache Tribe in New Mexico. He was a six-and-a-half-foot tall, full-blooded American Indian. My jaw dropped. I guessed again and figured he probably knew a great deal about insurgencies—at least in the historical sense.

Amos was part of a motley crew of eighty US fighters, engineers, and commanders who in 2008 made up the provincial reconstruction team charged with the unrewarding task of fighting off al Qaeda and its affiliates and creating a semblance of stability in war-torn Kunar Province. All of the dozen or so US-led PRTs in Afghanistan consisted of a navy-led or air force–led civil affairs unit, which was assigned two army combat platoons for the purpose of providing base security. Each provincial team was in charge of a multimillion-dollar annual humanitarian aid budget provided by the US Department of Defense.

First Sgt. James "Grumpy" Spears was the Kunar team's spiritual leader. He was one of about five hundred US Army veterans who, in the Pentagon's struggle to keep the services intact and functioning, had been called back from a happy retirement. As far as Grumpy, age fifty-six, knew, he was the only retiree sent by the Pentagon to stand guard on the Afghanistan-Pakistan border, just across the mountains from the suspected lair of Osama bin Laden. Cupping a mug of coffee one morning, he unleashed one of his curmudgeonly gripes as I stood by his side: "I can't tell you why they haven't caught him [bin Laden] with all their gee-whiz toys!"

As the grizzled "human resources manager" for the PRT in Kunar, Spears played a key role with his stentorian cries across the mess hall and quiet, reassuring chats in his office. Shot down in the Vietnamese highlands in the early 1970s and still in the mix today, his mere presence on base was reassuring to the young soldiers, who had been pulling fifteen-month deployments for several years on end. In Spears's view, the long extensions were starting to weigh on the minds of the young soldiers and sailors in the PRT. "I'm really afraid that some guys and girls will snap," he confided to me between puffs on his cigar and talk of his golf course back in Mississippi. Both his sons had served in Iraq.

The actual head of the PRT was Commander Larry LeGree, a Naval Academy graduate and a nuclear engineer. A blue-eyed native of Michigan, who grew up on Lake Michigan dreaming of the navy, he was all that was smart, pragmatic, adaptable, and idealistic in this mission rolled into one package. (He also happened to be a concert pianist.) At the age of thirty-six, LeGree had been the navy's youngest commander, and after his twelve months in Afghanistan, he would be in command of the newest and most modern of the navy's vessels. For now, the closest he would get to a maritime engagement was shooting across the rushing Kunar River at al Qaeda's Taliban allies. Every evening, at the end of the day, LeGree's team held a meeting to assess the day's accomplishments. Invariably, to needle his army cohorts, he would have one of the navy's largest ships projected on the white wall as the first shot in the evening's PowerPoint presentation. He knew every engine room and broom closet in the ship.

In 2007 and 2008, the US 173rd Airborne Brigade's Combat Team had set up dozens of small operating bases across some of the most remote terrain on Earth. These were the same high plateaus and steep mountains that had served through history as an obstacle to foreign intrusion. Indeed, Alexander the Great and Tamerlane both stumbled through this terrain on their way to conquer India.

In his memoir, Tamerlane, the fourteenth-century Turko-Mongol conqueror, mused about the way he had had to submit to being passed down mountain slopes and over gorges in a chair. When his men tried to do the same for their horses, they slipped out of their harnesses and plunged to their deaths on the rocks below.[3] Back then the land had been called Kafiristan, after the Kafirs, or infidels, who inhabited it. Now the only Kafirs were the foreigners on a special mission that few of the natives recognized as any kind of an end in itself, called simply "stabilization."

I was no stranger to Kunar Province when I returned to it in 2008. I had been there on several occasions and would return yet again in 2009 for more reporting. Most recently, I had spent two weeks in the province in 2007, looking at things from the Afghan government's perspective. Along with an interpreter from Kabul, I had lodged in the governor's guesthouse and paid the governor's guards an exorbitant amount to drive me across the province, where I met with various officials. In addition to meeting the commanders of the PRT, I had been to meetings in the west and the far north of the province. At one point, my driver had been seized from the front seat of our taxi and beaten at the side of the road by a police officer who was upset that the driver had run a checkpoint without paying a bribe. Not much had improved on that front: four Afghan road workers had been beheaded on this same road on the day of my return to the region in January 2008.

This time, I was back in Afghanistan to observe how our efforts were changing—or not. Afghanistan, run by one-time American presidential antiterrorism poster boy, Hamid Karzai, was fast slipping into full-scale warfare. Despite or perhaps because of our faltering efforts to fight demons of our own choosing—and some would say our own making—in Iraq, al Qaeda central had reconstituted itself inside Pakistan and now had a safe haven from which to attack US forces at will. With security deteriorating, a new malaise had set in across Afghanistan. The 2001 US-led invasion had brought with it high expectations, most of them based on promises from the international community. Billions of American dollars had been committed to Afghanistan, but little of that money had found its way outside Kabul or beyond the deep pockets of the US-allied warlords who ruled the hinterlands. Afghans rightly wondered how—with over fifty-five thousand foreign troops in their country—security could have deteriorated substantially between 2002 and 2008. NATO had belatedly expanded its operations in the hinterlands, where an insurgency fed off local dissatisfaction with a foreign occupation and a corrupt government.

There was a rising sense that America's war on terror was an imported conflict—something that did not *belong* to the Afghan people. It was not the US failure to capture Osama bin Laden and his chief lieutenant Ayman al-Zawahiri (both of them being in Pakistan) that worried Afghans. "For Afghans, the 'global war on terror' was something for the rest of the world," said Sanjar Qiam, the young general manager of a leading national radio station.[4] "For Afghans it was about getting rid of the Taliban and getting rid of the Northern Alliance, but we still have both of them, and they seem to be getting stronger by the day. That is disheartening."[5] Afghans had not embraced America's war as a means to an end. Indeed, the very idea of an ongoing war conflicted in most minds with ideas of peace and stability.

In the six weeks that I spent with the crew of Kunar Province's reconstruction team, I saw constant reminders of that sad state of affairs. However, I also saw positive signs that some in the military were rethinking the long struggle ahead.

Within a day of my arrival, I was up on the landing pad filming choppers zipping down through the blue skies. They looked like toys in the distance and then, as they approached landing, they looked like the aged behemoths from the Vietnam War era that they really were.

I mused about the contrast with the abysmal US military operations at Tora Bora, when General Tommy Franks had vetoed any significant influx of US infantrymen to avoid the not-so-long-ago Soviet scenario of getting bogged down in a foreign land. What Franks was really saying was that the world's most powerful military was not going to get trapped in a xenophobic Afghan nightmare.[6] In 2001 and for several years more, US operations in Afghanistan had been rather conventional in nature—characterized by large bases, heavy bombing of suspected targets, and little interaction between infantrymen and Afghan civilians. That posture reflected the unfortunate reality that the US military had simply buried its own counterinsurgency manuals in piles of bureaucracy after the abysmal failures in Vietnam.

As I watched the incoming choppers, two old T-55 Soviet tanks, noticeably without treads, were being fired alongside a pair of Katusha rocket launchers in a show of force by the ragged Afghan guards. They had been assigned by American officers to provide protection at the base, also known as Camp Wright. An Afghan fighter dressed in an oily jogging suit quickly handed me a pair of earplugs. As far as I could see, the tanks didn't appear to be firing at any specific targets, other than a large mountain across the valley. For the sake of the few hundred Afghans living in the valley—whom we were now shooting over—I hoped that the old Soviet weaponry was in good repair. Not long after I had started filming these fireworks, a Special Forces commander came over to me and told me to "cease and desist." The pictures would no doubt be something of an embarrassment to the Pentagon should they reach the evening news.

Nevertheless, Kunar Province was an ideal prism through which to view US military efforts in Afghanistan. The province straddles the border with Pakistan's tribal areas, al Qaeda's center for global operations. It was also notorious—as was much of the rest of Afghanistan—for venality, tribalism, and warlordism. A classified US government report (which I obtained from US servicemen) on Kunar's former governor, Asadullah Wafa, who ruled the province in 2005, described him as "ill tempered, easily frustrated," and one who "routinely walked out on development meetings." A senior officer on the PRT base—who knew the former governor and had remained on base for a second tour of duty—described him to me as "a hash smoker and an ornery son-of-a-bitch." I knew him myself from a couple of meetings. I ran into Wafa in Helmand Province in 2007, wearing his signature *karakul* cap while he was openly bribing local journalists—I filmed him doling out fistfuls of money—to keep up reporting the "good news" and to bury any suggestions that he might be involved in the province's rampant narcotics trafficking. (According to impartial accounts, the narco biz was his fiefdom.) The word in Kunar on Wafa's promotion to Helmand, a much larger province, was that he had allegedly been so good about funneling illicit logging revenues back to Kabul from Kunar that he was receiving a percentage of Helmand's drug profits as his reward.

The next Kunar governor, Haji Mohammed Didar, who had been in power during my last visit and who had been ousted in November 2007, proved to be almost as bad as Wafa. Described kindly in US reports as "lacking administrative skills" and maintaining ties to insurgents fighting US forces, he became infamous for spending half a million dollars in Western aid money on giving away five thousand goats to bolster his popularity. (The donors were scratching their heads at the idea of a goat costing one hundred dollars in rural Afghanistan.)[7]

Didar had only recently left for Dubai in the United Arab Emirates, where he expected to start a new business with his unofficial earnings. An American officer had set up a dinner with Didar in Kabul prior to his departure, so that the soldiers could surreptitiously take back a two-hundred-thousand-dollar armored car, one of four that the US government had supplied to the governor's office. After a cordial goodbye from his former American patrons, the governor emerged from the restaurant where he had dined, shocked to find that he would have to hail a fifteen-year-old Toyota Corolla taxi to get him to the airport.[8]

Within a day of my arrival in Kunar, I linked up with Captain Jason Coughenour, who had had the honor of taking back the stolen property. An energetic, highly strung, red-faced character with a penchant for dealing with the strange nuances of local Afghan politics, the thirty-five-year-old captain was a key player in the US government's efforts to bolster the government. Coughenour had signed up to return to the army in the immediate aftermath of 9/11 and had been verbally pilloried by his superiors at the Department of Housing and Urban Development (HUD), who had seen no reason for a patriotic American to abandon a good, altruistic-minded HUD job for a war zone. Six years later, Coughenour, though he had managed to keep his civilian job, was still serving his country. He was a short and garrulous man, and I soon noticed that he had something of a Napoleonic complex. He irritated at least some of his fellow soldiers, who told me, "When we get Jason out of here, we're going to have to pop his head with a pin." For a journalist with an interest in everything that was going on in Kunar, however, Coughenour was a godsend and a refreshingly open book. He quickly offered to show me the US military's efforts to bolster the local Afghan government.

As it turned out, he was something of a one-man show and was setting precedents as he went. As we mounted up for the first of several missions in downtown Asadabad, I noticed that Coughenour moved with an interpreter and two armed guards but with no US military backup. He was also dressed as a civilian, concealing his pistol in a holster beneath a woolen Afghan jacket, which he had purchased locally. I felt relieved not to be in a US Humvee, particularly in the area where we were—hard up against bin Laden's Pakistani sanctuaries. Though our car was armored, other than Coughenour's baseball cap, which had the letters "PRT" stenciled on the front, we gave no indication that we represented the US military.

At the gates of the governor's compound, half a dozen bearded guards in brown blankets greeted us with shy smiles and rushed to open three pairs of metal gates that—once entered—left us in the inner sanctum of power in Kunar. They opened our door and one spat a wad of tobacco juice on my shoe.

Coughenour's difficulties became clear to me as we made the rounds together that afternoon. As we moved between meetings, we saw that the sidewalks were lined with flowerbeds, weeping willows, and fruit trees, also paid for by Uncle Sam. One of the curious attributes of Afghan men is that while they are great warriors they are also proud gardeners. They were maybe a little trigger happy, but they also had amazingly agile green thumbs. It was still February and already the scent of spring had invaded Asadabad.

We were on our way, Coughenour explained with a straight face, to see "democracy in action." Inside a high-ceilinged meeting hall decorated with stars and arabesques, a gaggle of Afghans sat cross-legged on the floor. On one side of the room, Pashtun men in pajama-like shalwars sat in contemplative poses, stroking their long beards, and on the other side a group of women in sky-blue burqas sat, reaching out like cartoon ghosts to grab the wrists of whining children. Through the tiny window woven into their garment, I guessed they were also keeping an eye on proceedings, but that was impossible to know. The center of attention was a drawing of a tree, roots exposed. This was known as a "problem tree" and was designed to help the community get to the "roots" of problems.[9] Coughenour squatted down beside the district headman as a bearded gentleman kneaded a set of red prayer beads, flipping them along a string with his thumb and forefinger. The circle's leader, Dr. Mohammed Shahid, a broad man with glasses and a knitted brow, explained the rules of the procedure that had been devised to help everyone in the room brainstorm about what was holding them back.

"This shura is sitting together to formulate the DDP—district development program," he said, speaking in fluent English.[10] "We have to find the core problems. So far, the main one is weak social services. We think this core problem has four main causes."[11] Even as he spoke, one of two literate women without veils wrote down her own take on the issues on small pieces of paper, which were pasted to the roots of the tree. Dr. Shahid continued, "There is also a lack of coordination on a local level with the security forces."[12]

That was a modest, polite way of saying that Afghanistan was still at war and that the late-night visits of insurgents to villages was an issue, particularly when the police showed up for work only at dawn—or not at all. Without cops loyal to a central government, these small villages were also subject to sudden US bombing raids, which often had the undesirable impact of hitting "friendly" homes and missing fleeing insurgents. Despite seven years of similar incidents, the rate of such errant bombings had not significantly decreased. Indeed, classified documents on errant US bombing runs in Kunar that I had obtained suggested that irregular US-government blood money was being paid to injured families. On the other hand, with regard to the larger strategic issue—including the thousands of angry Afghans created by each accident—not enough was being done to address the real causes of the mistaken aerial strikes and the concerns raised by them. In Washington, however, the work of the Campaign for Innocent Victims of Conflict had already gone some way toward forcing a change in the US military's outlook toward its overuse of air power.[13]

Just outside the meeting hall, Coughenour gave me a rundown on what to expect. "Tomorrow, we'll move into the next phase, the actual resolution of problems—the main one being the lack of access to good government services," he said. "Without a central foundation for good governance, it is impossible to deliver what is needed."

Coughenour admitted to me that he was "a little disappointed with the female participation that we got for the problem tree meeting. We are really looking to get older women involved, you know, the mothers whose sons are fighting-age males. Given, it is difficult to find enough educated women for these kinds of meetings, but we are trying to get women with more clout in their own communities." That was a tall order in Afghanistan.

As if on cue, we next paid a visit to Mariam, the deputy director of a local women's group. She was one of the few women in Kunar willing to remove her burqa in the presence of a strange man. Her cheeks were rosy pink and her beauty was disarming, especially because usually you just didn't see women's faces in Kunar at all.

Coughenour wanted Mariam to participate in the district development meetings as a kind of coach for other women who were not familiar with the process. He told her that the US military had paid for a secondary school to be renovated, the one that sat just outside the window where we were chatting. "I would like to do the same for your women's center," he said, addressing Mariam. "But I also need your help in these district development meetings."

The way Coughenour put it could have been interpreted to mean that he was using a material incentive to coerce her to participate. It sounded crude on the surface.

Mariam's reply, "I'll be there because I care," threw the suggestion right back at him. She likely felt that an American, however well meaning, was not going to bribe her or any Afghan into taking an interest in her own community. The risk to her life and limb by just talking to him was something he could not adequately comprehend. The Taliban executed women for lesser violations of their social code.

Coughenour was acting as an unofficial authority within the provincial Afghan government. The Pentagon was giving his team a lot of money to play with—with the ultimate goal of curtailing the rising insurgency. We were providing tiny Kunar with about forty million dollars a year in development assistance. That was the equivalent of about one hundred dollars per person, which, if it had been cash in hand, would have almost doubled the province's GDP. That could be a boon or a bust, depending on how it played out over time, particularly if the "trickle down" was not working well. On the one hand, as an American taxpayer I appreciated the captain's concerned oversight; on the other hand, I knew that as long as the US government was playing the role of honest broker (or broker of honesty) inside the Afghan government, we were going to be engaged indefinitely in a twenty-first-century American occupation. International officials working in development are often accused of letting corrupt third world officials run roughshod over their beautiful plans. Yet crack the whip over corruption and you are accused of paternalism or worse, imperialism. This is only one reason why nation building is such an unrewarding endeavor and probably another good reason why Americans don't do it terribly well.

✳✳✳

Coughenour was a Texan, and due to this he was a little too direct for some of the Afghans he was dealing with. He made up for his occasional ineptness, however, with sincerity and a knack for befriending the locals. At our next stop, at the dilapidated gates of a small, two-room shack not far from the governor's elite mansion, half a dozen old men, some of them on crutches and others missing arms, greeted us warmly. Most were victims of the war against the Soviets. Their modest lodgings, heated by a potbellied stove, made me feel as if I might be entering a pool hall in South Philly populated by a disheartened band of Vietnam veterans—minus the bar, the antlers, and the pool tables, of course. In Afghanistan, which lost well over a million men in the war against the Soviets in a country an eighth the size of the United States, there was enough posttraumatic stress for several nations. It was there, but you did not always know it, because the Afghans are a tremendously stoic people. That there weren't even more crazies on motorbikes and in suicide vests whipping about the streets of Asadabad was always a surprise to me.

We stooped to pass beneath a wooden beam over a door and sat down in a circle of couches. Green tea was offered and Coughenour joked that he'd only be able to have a single cup if he was going to keep up his appointments about town and not have to make too many pit stops. The men chuckled.

Our discussion focused on a new rehabilitation center that Coughenour said he had asked the US government to fund—a request that he assured the men would most likely be granted in short order. He explained to me: "They depend on a miniscule monthly pension, but hopefully they'll be able to generate a little income as soon as we start building."

These men—according to Coughenour—were of special interest to al Qaeda and its brother insurgent groups across the border in Pakistan. He wanted to get a rehab center up and working before his competition could persuade some of the most down-trodden veterans to go back to war—this time even more focused on the ultimate sacrifice.

"This is the group that the Taliban targets when it comes to recruits for suicide bombing," Coughenour told me. "Some of them live such desperate lives that they are more than willing to strap on a suicide vest. For al Qaeda and the Taliban, this is one of the most accessible segments of the population. So what I am doing—in setting up this center—is robbing the enemy of access to a vulnerable population and at the same time providing jobs for thousands of men who should be key breadwinners in their family."

It was hard to think of a rehabilitation center as a key aspect of a counterinsurgency strategy, but that was precisely how Coughenour had sold the idea to his own government. He was our man on the ground, and either folks in Washington trusted him on this or they didn't. After six years of watching the Taliban making a comeback, some in Washington were finally tuning in to the larger battle for hearts and minds that required attention if the United States was going to help stabilize Afghanistan. Humanitarian assistance had risen from about twenty-five dollars per person per annum in the first two years of the invasion to closer to one hundred dollars per person in the last two. A veterans' center here and there went a long way, despite all the caution over misspent US dollars.

Direct aid was fast becoming part and parcel of a broader counterterrorism effort. As Sun Tzu affirms in *The Art of War*, it is better to prevent a fight than to go looking for one. In other words, if you can win without a fight, do so by all means, but don't expect to be a hero for it. No one was giving out medals for setting up veterans' centers in Afghanistan.

✳✳✳

There was nothing new or unusual about peacemaking in Afghanistan—and it didn't require a PhD. It was about reaching out and helping Afghan friends who in any case had made some amazing sacrifices on behalf of the "free world" fighting the Soviets. But it also meant assuming a role that did not come naturally to most American soldiers. Coughenour had switched from wearing a uniform to wearing civvies months before my arrival. "There are places that I would not go in this province without a flak jacket and helmet on," he told me. "That said, I discard them whenever possible. It would be the same concept used in community policing in any community in the US. If you show up in the full metal jacket of your SWAT team gear on a street corner, people are likely to be intimidated by your presence. It would be awfully hard to connect with the local population. What I'm trying to do is remove the visual perception that I am a military officer and that I am here for the fight first. I take that away and leave them with a blank slate, so they can see me as a caring civilian first."

Dropping one's guard was essential in dress and demeanor, he said. Protecting oneself with "gear" presented the same dilemma, however, as protecting oneself inside the confines of a military base with four rings of security. There were risks and rewards and a fine balance to be struck. (Even if Coughenour was an exception to the rule, however, the rest of the US presence in Kunar was still heavily weighted toward the militarized approach to peacemaking.)

I learned that Coughenour had arrived at his decision to assume civilian attire out of the most practical of experiences. "Foreign nongovernmental agencies would not even meet with us because of the weapons we carried," he said, reflecting on his early difficulties working in Kunar. "I am the only one [who] operates this way, but I can tell you that it is effective. I move within one of the most dangerous provinces in Afghanistan and with a small footprint. It allows me a rapport with the civilian population that the military needs here to be successful."

It was also necessary because no one else appeared ready for the job. When I visited Kabul, as I did regularly, I found hundreds of international officials, aid workers, and private contractors with life insurance policies that apparently forbade them to travel into the war zone. Instead, they were living it up in exotic restaurants and Dionysian watering holes that rivaled those in most big Asian cities. If Kabul had been safer, it would have qualified as a "Hedonism II" resort.[14]

I followed Coughenour on his rounds the next day, and we had the opportunity to dine with the new governor, Sayed Fazlullah Wahidi. According to Coughenour and Commander LeGree, Wahidi had all the right stuff—albeit he was untested in a province renowned for kickbacks and corruption. Wahidi was, they insisted, one of the new and improved lot of provincial governors touted by President Hamid Karzai's government as viable partners for progress. The new governor's résumé, long on development work and low on military heroism, also suggested that he was a person who might be able to help channel US-led assistance for Kunar in the right direction.

Wahidi, chubby and graying, struck me as a warm, grandfatherly figure. He did not suffer fools well but tolerated his American patrons because they managed both his security and his province's economic well-being. He was accompanied by a bubbly, somewhat bulbous nephew from Australia, who was fresh from receiving his MBA and was now serving as a kind of governor's assistant. His name was Rohan, and he was unnerved to be in Afghanistan, which made me feel better about my own trepidations. He longed to return to his days as a rugby player in Australia. We sat down beside the governor in a long dining hall with a dozen of his deputies, including the supervisor of education. A lavish Afghan meal of lamb, chicken, and mixed vegetables was set before us and, as is the Pashtun tradition, we mostly ate with our hands (our right hands) as Coughenour and the governor, as was the ritual, discussed the day's affairs.

The talk centered on everything from how to win a government project for a new dam to security problems. Toward the end of the meal, I asked the governor about the state of affairs in Kunar. "We are small, we are poor, and we are behind the mountains," he said, noting that larger provinces received more attention in Kabul than did his own. "Our main security issue is with the border and the insurgent infiltration. Al Qaeda is everywhere—literally."[15]

Not long after our lunch, Coughenour and I visited the provincial jail, which was situated within the governor's compound. The guards hadn't permitted me to take my camera in, and once inside I understood why. A pair of Frenchmen from the International Committee of the Red Cross (ICRC) was already inside talking to some thirty-five prisoners who were bemoaning the fact that their kitchen was a sanitary disaster, that they all shared a single toilet, and that they had no sink or shower. Put thirty-five men in two small adjoining rooms without proper showers, and you can produce a stench that will stay with you the rest of the day and into the night. It will, of course, also linger in your mind indefinitely. "It is disgusting!" an ICRC official whispered to me. We both spoke to the prisoners, who seemed in decent spirits, but I was—I realized—ashamed as an American to be standing alongside my European colleagues and ashamed to be visiting prisoners in such a state. Since the US military had been on the ground in Asadabad for several years already, it was something of a shock for me to see the state of the provincial jail.

I sensed that Coughenour was also a little embarrassed at what we were seeing. Given the prison abuses that had taken place in other Islamic countries—both with US assistance and without it—in the wake of 9/11, you might have expected proper prisons to be an American priority in Afghanistan. Coughenour reassured me that he would try to use the report that the ICRC was about to file to bolster his own argument to the US government that a new facility was needed. Given, however, that the US military had been responsible for preventing the same pair of ICRC investigators from obtaining access to the facility in the past, I wasn't reassured that the problem would be at the top of the US agenda. Expanding the existing facility—at least by two rooms while another was being built—didn't require two generals, a colonel, and three majors; it just required a contract, a plumber, and several local bricklayers. Financially, it was a drop in the bucket out of the forty million dollars that the US military's PRT had to allocate to Kunar.

At lunch, Coughenour had mentioned his idea for a new jail to the governor, who appeared anxious to move ahead with the idea. Indeed, over tea in the early afternoon, the governor produced a detailed plan for a large prison, the plan of a prison that had been installed in the Bamian region and that he felt would work well for Kunar. Coughenour was a little unclear as to why such an extensive facility might be necessary. "We have at the moment eight hundred persons we would like to put in there," Governor Wahidi mentioned.[16]

Coughenour looked confused. "Where are they now?"

The governor's tummy began to shake and he broke into a grin and began to chuckle. "On the mountaintops!" said the governor pointing to the snowy white peaks that divide Afghanistan from Pakistan. "If we ever catch all those bad guys, we'll have to have some place to put them."[17] It was nice to hear the governor use US military's own broad-brush label for insurgents as "bad guys" and manage to turn it into a pleasantry. (To the US military's belated credit, a year later they would complete a new facility.)

✳✳✳

I admit that, despite misgivings over his occasionally brusque style, I was already impressed with Coughenour's modus operandi. Ten years ago, the fast-track US colonels and majors would have referred to his work as "mission creep." The captain's colleagues in Afghanistan still sported machismo T-shirts, bought at Bagram Air Base, which read: "The Taliban Hunt Club."[18]

For several years after the US invaded the country in 2001, economic and political development played second fiddle to the hunt for al Qaeda and the Taliban. "Nation building," President Bush had famously said before taking office, was not something our military did. So—for several years—an ugly pattern played itself out as a kind of B-movie backdrop to the exciting and enthralling hunt for bin Laden. Villagers looked on as US soldiers shot and literally "bagged" their foes, and then turned a cold shoulder to the populace. (To be sure, "secret" interrogations going on in the detention centers of Afghanistan were sending a far meaner and more undemocratic message than this. My own interviews with former US prison guards who moved on to set up and operate notorious facilities in Iraq suggested a systematic abuse of power authorized from above.)[19]

At the same time, the Pentagon had disparaged the very idea of setting up a new nation, even though they knew Afghanistan was—in UN parlance—a "failed state." Rumsfeld himself had famously presented the conundrum that he was unable to solve in Afghanistan. In October 2003, he wrote one of his famous memos to senior US commanders on the global war on terrorism (GWOT):

> The questions I posed to combatant commanders this week were: Are we winning or losing the Global War on Terror? Is DoD changing fast enough to deal with the new twenty-first-century security environment? Can a big institution change fast enough? Is the USG changing fast enough?
>
> DoD has been organized, trained, and equipped to fight big armies, navies, and air forces. It is not possible to change DoD fast enough to successfully fight the global war on terror; an alternative might be to try to fashion a new institution, either within DoD or elsewhere, one that seamlessly focuses the capabilities of several departments and agencies on this key problem.
>
> With respect to global terrorism, the record since September 11th seems to be: We are having mixed results with al Qaeda, although we have put considerable pressure on them—nonetheless, a great many remain at large.[20]

In retrospect, this memo underscores the frustrations of a military giant unable to adjust to the realities of asymmetrical warfare and nation building. A final Rumsfeldian question—presumably for himself and everyone else concerned—was whether the United States was killing more bad guys than the enemy was churning out. The fear inherent in the question was that the answer would be "No."

With wealthy al Qaeda and Taliban financiers still waiting in the wings to lure young Muslim men to battle with pay and promises of martyrdom, the ability of the US military and NATO to engage the Afghan public in activities and employment had, nevertheless, become the real key to quelling the insurgency in Afghanistan. What Rumsfeld and his protégés did not understand was that this wasn't even a war in any classic sense of the word and that their actions were likely creating more insurgents than would otherwise have risen up to fight the US presence. In Afghanistan, 50 percent of the entire population was still under fifteen years of age. These people were learning more about US intentions every day.

The new, fledgling US efforts at nation building in Kunar were at the tip of the spear of this new strategy, which had yet to produce results. But if the strategy was to have any hope of working, it would require a call to service and the participation of the American public—something that the Bush administration had failed to recognize and deliver early on.

✳✳✳

As we drove through town in an armored sports utility vehicle on our way to visit the director of religious affairs, we passed by Asadabad's largest mosque, which was still unfinished after two decades of work. The mosque had been started with Gulf charity funds tied to the jihad against the Soviet Union. But the project had been taken over by Abu Ikhlas al-Masri, an Egyptian fighter who had known links to Osama bin Laden. By virtue of his own ties to charities in the Middle East, Ikhlas had become the sole financier of the unfinished mosque. He was a well-known personality across Kunar, and various religious leaders had maintained long-standing ties with him until the arrival of foreign troops after the 9/11 attacks.[21]

In the 1990s, Afghans, particularly Pashtuns in the border areas, had publicly glorified jihadists and held them in the highest esteem. Ikhlas was no exception. As an Egyptian, he was well placed to move within senior al Qaeda circles, which were still full of his fellow countrymen—some 50 percent of al Qaeda's top leadership in 2001 was Egyptian—many of them rebellious young men who had left the country under the persuasion of Egyptian Dr. Ayman al-Zawahiri, bin Laden's right-hand man. Ikhlas's own role and the role of Middle Eastern religious conservatives were mirrored across Afghanistan's Pashtun belt, which the West, particularly the United States, had largely abandoned after Afghanistan's victory over the Soviets. They had filled a vacuum in Afghanistan at the same time that foreign jihadists had crept into Bosnia to fight for that imperiled population. Immediately after the Soviet withdrawal, these jihadists had been almost entirely ignored by the State Department and Pentagon as a potential future threat. From all my conversations with senior commanders in Kunar, I gathered that the US government was still downplaying the foreign jihadists' affinity with the locals and the strong influence they retained. As had been the case at the time of the initial invasion of Afghanistan, when CIA operatives knew little about local ties on the ground in eastern Afghanistan, the influence of major figures with long histories in the area still went unnoticed.[22]

Coughenour and his colleagues recognized, however, that without some kind of outreach to the religious community, Soviet-era heroes like Ikhlas would continue to plot and organize. The Egyptian financier was currently roving the mountains, even as American commanders held him responsible for being involved in several major attacks on their forces.

Passing the mosque, we were on our way to meet with Kunar's director of religious affairs, who was also in charge of organizing the annual hajj. He arranged the pilgrims' journey to Mecca. (In some cases, their pilgrimage was still funded by charities linked to global terrorist outfits.)

Apart from a few sporadic newspaper accounts, the US government's efforts to coax and persuade local religious leaders and to influence Islam in a way that would be favorable to Washington's interests was a well-kept secret—and for good reason. While there are some people in Washington who now see the importance of winning over religious leaders across the Islamic world, the issue of spending US tax dollars to influence the religious debate in any way, shape, or form is controversial for reasons quite apart from the money it costs. It smacks of having Uncle Sam's long arm engaged in religious affairs, which breaks with American traditions, both internally and externally, of keeping government and religion separate.

If some Americans think that injecting God into domestic politics is a violation of the sacrosanct divisions between church and state, almost anyone may view messing around with Allah in our foreign affairs as fraught with peril. In any case, what I experienced next provided a window into this world of spirit and mirrors.

The setting for our meeting was outside in the shade on a bend in the Kunar River, where it widens into a rocky bed of pebbles. We sat on a bank, several meters above the waters and on a grassy lawn attached to the offices of religious affairs. I found Coughenour's explanation of his intentions innocent enough. "The government sometimes has a hard time connecting within itself, so I am kind of acting as a conduit to connect different players with the same goals," he said. "I am hoping that by sitting down with the director of the hajj and other religious elders that I can jump-start some of the religious dialogue in Kunar."

My journalistic instincts made me wonder, however, what business it was of Coughenour and the US military that the mullahs should have a dialogue among themselves. How exactly was ingratiating oneself with religious leaders, given the Afghan sensitivity to foreign intrusion, a good use of US tax dollars?

Coughenour was leaning back, wearing his dark sunglasses,

waiting for the director to show up, and enjoying the Afghan sun on his face. His explanation of what he was up to had some logic to it. "Even ministers in the US have meetings and talk about common themes and issues," he told me. "So there may be some topics that are discussed in madrassas that aren't making their way back here. Voices aren't being heard in Asadabad because of some difficulty in their traveling here from small and remote villages. So we are hoping to support meetings where mullahs can come where they can discuss their own issues, including issues they are having with us."

But would the US military's support—even minimal support—be seen as an attempt to keep tabs on what was said or not being said in the local religious community? In other words, was it not also likely that locals and Afghan tribal leaders would see the outreach effort as a subtle form of intelligence gathering by an interested foreign party?

Coughenour did not appear to be worried about that perception as he stretched his arms beneath a willow on the riverbank. "The PRT might be able to subsidize some level of transportation for them to have that meeting, that being our only role in it—of course," he told me. I asked him if some religious leaders hadn't already been accused by religious hard-liners of being lackeys for the Americans (I already knew that such accusations were being made in at least some quarters).

"I think there are some issues. That said, I can't really be effective in bringing together the tribes and bringing the government together with the people unless I also reach out to religious leaders as well. This is consistent with a lot of places in the US—like the Bible Belt." In that respect, he was correct. Community organizers used religious institutions all the time to rally constituents to their political causes, but these organizers were generally not government or military officials.

As he spoke, the director of religious affairs, a short man with piercing eyes and dressed in a long chemise and pants, arrived. We stood up to greet him. Coughenour asked about the director's family and mentioned in a roundabout way that he was here to help. "But I don't want this to look like the PRT is pushing this—a meeting of the mullahs, you know," he said, sounding self-conscious. "We want to work with you and have you take credit for the fact that you are bringing these meetings together." In other words, Coughenour wanted to be sure that the event had an Afghan face on it, even if it would be American financed.

At this point, however, Coughenour introduced another revealing tidbit. "Right now, we are paying for something like fifteen mosques to be repaired across the province." He mentioned this more or less as an offer of even more help. In other words, he was saying that we are doing this much and we can do more. It was a way of coaxing more interest, which, as it turned out, he did not really need to do.

Coughenour asked the hajj director if he wanted to come by and talk at the PRT sometime, but that brought a quick reply. "If I just visit the PRT one time, that will be the end of my authority in this town," he said. Many locals felt that penetrating the four layers of security surrounding the US base was not only intimidating but guaranteed that everyone in town would know they had sought out the Americans—which, of course, could get you shot, or worse. It was another irony of the US military effort that the heavy security meant to protect American lives (and intelligence) was also an immense impediment to community outreach. It was an immense obstacle that went hand in hand with trying to build a nation and fight a war at the same time.

Coughenour quickly reassured the director that it was only his own humble presence that the director would have to cope with. "That is why it is just me and these two gents on the waterfront," he said, pointing to the two armed guards, who had been requisitioned from Governor Wahidi's own security detail. "We understand that success starts with the mosque and conversations that people are having at the mosques. We know how important it is to have the support of the mullahs—to make sure that our schools are used and that children are allowed to go to their school, not just allowed but encouraged. And the mullahs can encourage the use of our clinics and roads."

In my view, calling the schools "ours" was an unnecessary conceit; a suggestion that these institutions would not exist but for the kindness of Uncle Sam. The meeting continued, and the director accepted the offer that Coughenour was making, to pay for mullahs and religious teachers from across the province to come to Asadabad and share ideas. Though Coughenour had sounded—on the surface —a little authoritarian if not vaguely imperialistic in his approach, the olive branch he offered to help local religious leaders was, nevertheless, accepted.

The director then opened up and explained that Afghanistan was in great need of a spiritual revival. "Afghanistan is not just a country destroyed on the outside—its buildings and roads—it is also a country destroyed on the inside," he said. "We need to work on the buildings, but we also need to rebuild our tattered spirits and broken minds."

When you heard that kind of frank admission, it was hard to begrudge the Afghans the help Coughenour was offering. Remaking a strong nation had as much to do with the human spirit as it did with roads, bridges, and schools. Afghans needed help whether or not we could deliver it with any real competence. Surely if the US military did not somehow address the realities staring it in the face, its enemies would undoubtedly find a way to do so.

Back on base, Coughenour loosened up. "What I do here is essentially similar to the job that I do in the United States," he told me over a US mess hall special dinner of sirloin steak and Alaskan crab legs back at the base. The mess hall, incidentally, had been built by Halliburton. Coughenour continued: "You have to take the view that Afghanistan as a whole is like a disenfranchised community that has been ignored and isolated by its own government for years and years. One of the major surprises for us in our efforts to bolster local government has been the participation of women and other underrepresented groups." That was the kind of talk that some men, and women, in the US military still weren't comfortable with. It was the kind of talk more familiar to a social worker or community organizer. But, as I had seen elsewhere in the developing world, it was also the bare bones of development and democratic enfranchisement.

The US PRTs in Afghanistan clearly needed motivated experts like Coughenour, but how would talent be brought on board? In Kabul, there were already dozens of qualified professionals, but they were unwilling to get anywhere close to a US military jeep, as such vehicles were proven magnets for al Qaeda–backed attacks.

Coughenour had ideas of his own on this subject. He didn't think Europeans or Muslim professionals from other Islamic nations should or could be lured to work for (or with) the US military. He also doubted that the US government was doing a good job of channeling its own talents. "The only people who can meet this mission will be brought on board through the Department of Defense," he told me. The Pentagon was facing a crisis in leadership because mid-level civilian leadership was not available. "The Pentagon needs to adapt, and right now there is still a great deal of resistance in senior ranks to the changes in recruitment that are necessary to get the talent on board." Even among the Pentagon's top brass, "closing with and killing" the enemy took priority over all else. Adding civilians to that mix was like trying to stir water into oil.

In the spring of 2008, Coughenour was leaving the US Army as a captain to return to work with HUD. But he was advocating a total revamping of the recruitment program in order to draw in experienced professionals from civilian ranks, who would be able to take on the work of good governance and nation building. The young, energetic captain wanted the military to consider letting down its guard and providing major professional incentives that would allow lawyers, urban experts, and social workers to assume ranks within the military. This would give them a seat at the table—where they would not serve at the beck and call of colonels and generals obsessed with combat operations.

But that got back to the essential problem of building a nation in a war zone, which occurred to me again one evening at twilight back at the base. Camp Wright had two outposts on the mountains above the base. Both provided standard protection from guerrilla attacks.

At one of the outposts, known as Bull Run, half a dozen US fighters with 50-caliber machine guns monitored the jagged passes that led into the base. A few weeks earlier, a sentinel team had spotted a group of insurgents traveling like mountain goats in the rocks several hundred meters to the west. The soldiers called in an air strike just as the sun was setting in the west. Upon hearing that the payload had been unleashed from above, the fighters began to roar with pleasure, anticipating the hit.

"Sweet Mother of God!" barked one gunner, as he monitored the radio traffic.[23]

"Thirty seconds till splash down," shouted another.

As a red flash spread fire across the mountainside, another shouted "Dammmmmn!" in a long and drawn-out scream as a colleague started to laugh uncontrollably.

The commander interrupted to make another—now moot—point: "Holy God, gentlemen, that was a five-hundred-pound bomb!"

✳✳✳

The scenery on the border was stunning. One day, we traveled in a convoy to Naray, the northern tip of Kunar, with Grumpy, our aging gunner and only Vietnam vet, keeping an eye on two helicopters—small Kiowas—overhead. The birds provided surveillance and warnings of insurgent activities ahead. I was wired with a headset for the occasion. Grumpy smoked a cigar, chatted with Commander LeGree, and aimed his 50-caliber at the immense boulders in the distance. LeGree had had some dealings with the Balkans, and when I told him how I had hiked into Kosovo from Macedonia during the NATO bombing in 1999, he told me a long story of how he had managed to buy a rare, classic piano through his sister, who had been in Macedonia at the time on a mission to provide medical relief for war victims. He also told me about his uncle the police sergeant, who had worked in the same Michigan town were I grew up and gained a modicum of fame as the singing sergeant. It was a small world, indeed.

The green Kunar River rushed along to our right as we dipped around bends and slipped down toward the river to attend the dedication of a new bridge project. Several hundred villagers squatted on the side of the mountain, staring down at the governor and shouting, "Allahu Akhbar!" as he cut the ribbon. Further up the river, young boys pulled themselves onto a raft, made from thatch, bamboo, and inner tubes, that would have made Huckleberry Finn proud. About twenty elders stepped aboard for the ride.

Next, allies of the governor hijacked our party and insisted that we attend a feast in the governor's honor in the town of Naray, which sits at the northern tip of the province on the Pakistani border. Upon our arrival, members of a small mountain tribe, the Gujers, were already preparing the meal. They stirred the food in giant, three-foot-high, Ottoman-style pots. In the distance, the Himalayas released their waters in wild torrents, and a crescent moon rose in the red-hued skies. As the governor stood on a podium and spoke about bold plans to bring development to the remotest corner of the province, I struck up a conversation with a young police chief, Hajji Mohammed, who had gone out of his way to befriend me a year earlier and insist that I remain as his guest for a night. He had been the target of numerous assassination attempts due to his cooperation with the Americans. "Now is the time in the early spring, Philip, for the US and Afghan forces to seize the high ground from the Taliban and al Qaeda," he told me now. "If they don't do it now, by July and August they'll be swarming all over the province."[24] The only problem was—and he knew this when he said it—half of that high ground was in "no go" Pakistan, where even "hot pursuit" of the enemy was next to impossible due to the rules of war.

Several days later, we assembled again around the flagpoles at the PRT for a trip into the hinterlands that—I was assured by

LeGree—would introduce me to the local "three cups of tea" phenomenon.[25] As we drove out, we passed several bulldozers and at one point had to dismount in order that one of them could carve out the side of the mountain sufficiently to allow an oversized American jeep to pass. The soldiers dismounted and took up positions that provided a line of sight to the hilltops that surrounded us. Innocent-eyed children gathered in the hills, amused at the spectacle. Their curious faces were devoid of the suspicions their elders showed toward the US Goliaths.

I was reminded of the conversation I had had with Rory Stewart, the former British diplomat and author of *Places in Between*, back in Kabul before this trip. Stewart, who was running the Turquoise Mountain Foundation in Kabul, had framed the incongruities of nation building in a war zone rather succinctly: "Right now, NATO soldiers are flying ten thousand miles to maneuver through Afghan villages in full body armor and a tank. Villagers just think, 'Yes. And the Taliban are trying to kill you, and you are insisting that you are just here to build a girls' school?'"[26]

In the village itself, a road crew of several dozen men was fast at work digging around a streambed. One of the workers looked like Osama bin Laden or his first cousin. He noticed that I was taking his picture and stared back at us with a look of curious defiance.

Lieutenant Commander Alan Moore, another native of Michigan and an engineer who designs automobile factories in his civilian life, led us through the village and up a rickety ladder. A group of a dozen elders had already taken up seats inside a small, mud-walled room. The hospitality was overwhelming. Within moments, we were cherished guests, our safety in theory guaranteed by the local elders. Despite their waning faith in America's good intentions, Pashtun tribesmen, touted in the Western press as fierce, misogynistic warriors, remained outwardly friendly. It would have been insulting to them for Moore and his colleagues to hold nervously to their guns and not surrender their security to the Afghans in exchange for the help they were giving the province. The

US soldiers and sailors set their guns aside, though they did not remove their boots. This was a violation of basic custom, but the Afghans forgave it, acknowledging that their American guests might—after all—yet have to make a run for it if shooting broke out.

Moore unveiled plans for a new school. The elders said they welcomed the idea. They just wanted the US government to consider the purchase of a small parcel of land to put the school on. Moore was prepared for that. "You see, when I put in a school, it usually costs us between one hundred sixty thousand and two hundred thousand dollars." Moore spoke as cups of tea were poured for the circle of elders and the US officers. "So we ask that the communities donate the land in order to make this school possible. The last time we were up here there were only a couple of mortars fired at us and we hope that—as this school goes forward—the relatively peaceful conditions continue."

The elders insisted that those had not been mortars but dynamite blasts from mining work. True or not, the last thing the elders desired was that their district be tagged as a trouble spot undeserving of development funds.

I counted about one and a half cups of tea consumed before the elders informed Moore that they had just "designated a parcel of land for the school." They did not insist on payment, after all. Moore had the green light, but only because of the sit-down, face-to-face discussion, which put US troops in danger but also reassured the Afghans of their commitment. The road was also moving ahead, despite Afghan concerns that it would bring more fighting into their region. "Unfortunately, since we are military people, the Afghans sometimes see it as us trying to further our road so we can push into areas and maybe fight with the insurgents," Moore told me in a frank aside. "In fact, we see these roads and schools as economic investments in development. These are schools for Afghans, not anyone else."

It was hard not to be impressed when you saw what the US military did well, particularly building schools. It should be mentioned here that almost every senior US officer in the Asadabad PRT had read *Three Cups of Tea*, the bestselling tale of Gregg Mortenson, the American school builder. Although the price of one of Mortenson's schools was still only about 20 percent of the cost of a US military–built school in Afghanistan, the essential lessons of the book had been well taken. Schools were the building blocks of trust and progress, an essential element of "stabilization." Afghans and Pakistanis in the tribal areas are more accustomed in many regions to educating only boys and sending them to inexpensive boarding schools where they focus almost exclusively on religious studies, often with a religiously inspired curriculum with an emphasis on jihad.

Each new school was a small success and a victory in and of itself. The difficulty lay in the fact that the US government's (and the UN's) definition of nation building was still vague and undefined. I sometimes thought that if the United States concentrated just on what it did best—building roads and schools—the mission would go much more smoothly. Some of my associates agreed: "By talking so much about democracy and propping up warlords without delivering serious progress, we have managed to discredit a lot of our basic notions in the eyes of the Afghans," said Rory Stewart, the British author and former diplomat. With a vast agenda of "gender equality, civil society, open media, democratic transformation, capacity building, counternarcotics, and religious tolerance," high-minded Westerners had bitten off more than they could chew, he insisted. "The more of these agendas we take on, the more we doom ourselves to eventual failure." It is worth pointing out that Stewart, as a visiting professor at Harvard starting in 2008, became a leading voice in the debate within the Obama administration when it came to reassessing the US mission and, indeed, scaling back some of the boldest ambitions. By 2010, Pentagon spokespersons and leading generals were again refraining even from mentioning the term "nation building."

✳✳✳

Some of the new PRT-sponsored roads were clearly designed as part of a new economic backbone, whereas other roads were essentially tracks into some of the most dangerous insurgent redoubts in Afghanistan. This illustrated the schizophrenic approach: attempting both counterinsurgency and development at the same time. In order to better understand the politics of roadbuilding, I joined Commander LeGree and a large Humvee convoy on a road inspection, driving into a known insurgent redoubt. We dismounted, and I walked with Commander LeGree over to a single-room school that was in session on the cramped front porch of a small home. An instructor scribbled on a broken chalkboard made of slate as small boys stood up to recite from the Koran. On the dirt track running past the schoolroom, a US Humvee stopped in its tracks. Outlined in black letters on the turret of its 50 mm gun was the word "RAGE," the name of our combat platoon. The gunner set his gun heavenward, slipped his gloves under the plated turret, and passed out handfuls of candy. Such scenes in the presence of heavy US firepower with helicopters hovering overhead could be deceptive. When the US forces were not present, the Taliban often distributed literature, known as "night letters," disparaging the Americans and warning of swift retribution against anyone caught working with them.

I asked LeGree if his men had any idea where the province's most notorious al Qaeda operative, Abu Ikhlas al-Masri, might be. "We don't know where he is," he admitted. "But as you can see, we are pushing up into areas where the enemy is operating freely. We are determined to take away their population base. If they don't have the population to lean on anymore, their fight becomes irrelevant."

I knew that LeGree, as a senior naval officer, had a special interest in what had happened here in June 2005, when a team of four Navy SEALs had been surrounded. A Special Forces chopper that had come to their rescue had been shot down, killing a dozen more servicemen. A single SEAL had survived on his wits, stumbled down the mountain, and found comfort in the arms of a Pashtun elder, who, despite threats from insurgents to slit his throat, vowed to protect the soldier's life. It was an example of how far the ancient Pashtun code of hospitality, *pakhtunwali* (the practice of honoring a guest) could be taken. Ironically, the same code also guaranteed that enemies like bin Laden would be protected by Pashtun villagers on the Pakistani side of the border.

I wondered if the strategy that Commander LeGree was overseeing in this particularly dangerous valley had just a little to do with the Navy SEAL incident—either repaying the elders or punishing the insurgents. In a nearby valley, US forces were hell-bent on attacking a foe that was as anxious to fight back as any insurgent force on Earth.

LeGree's demeanor gave little away. He exuded a keen naval officer's confidence in the course of action that he had embarked upon. Nevertheless, as we continued up the road in the direction of the Korengal Valley, the scene of some of the worst fighting in the previous two years in Afghanistan, LeGree's own soldiers started to express second thoughts about moving forward. The driver of the Humvee I was in said that the bases we were approaching were "hit on an almost daily basis" and were littered with shell casings. "If it was up to me, I wouldn't go any further," he said, adjusting his mouthpiece. "But then, I'm not in charge." Beside him on a computer screen was a map with GPS coordinates that pointed out presumed enemy redoubts as well as our own current position. It was the kind of technology that warriors in Vietnam could have only dreamed of.

I recalled that on the day I arrived at the PRT to take up residence across the hall from LeGree's office an intelligence report on a road incident was read out at a team meeting. As mentioned earlier, insurgents loyal to al Qaeda had attacked a road crew, beheading workers and leaving a note: "This is what happens to you when you work for the Americans!"

As we returned to our vehicles, LeGree took a radio call from a lieutenant who warned him that he was entering a free-fire zone for insurgents. The soldiers spun on their heels and pointed up into the rocks above. It wasn't the first time LeGree had come upon a dangerous pass in the road. Weeks earlier, his convoy had been trapped at a hairpin bend, and two rocket-propelled grenades had hit the cliff face above the hood of his vehicle. His convoy had backed around a bend and dismounted to take on the enemy.

LeGree was undaunted, but as a jaded war correspondent I couldn't help but see him as one of those eternally optimistic American characters out of a Graham Greene novel. Nothing could deter him, for the roads—all of them—were a commonsense means to an end—the hoped-for conquest. He told me that he knew through US intelligence sources that al Qaeda and other insurgent groups paid their fighters $5 a day to attack US and Afghan soldiers in these parts. "So I pay the road workers $5.50 a day to work on this road," he said as his chief engineer spoke to a group of armed Afghan men assigned to protect the workers. "If the insurgents start making $6 a day, I'll pay $6.50. We prefer several dozen manual laborers to a bulldozer because we really are not in any great hurry. Young men, who might otherwise be fighting us, are employed. We are driving a wedge right into insurgent territory—in a slow, agonizing way for our enemies." As we moved along, Afghan workers swung pickaxes and wielded shovels, slowly chipping away at a solid rock face.

LeGree wasn't reckless, just determined, and he had wanted me to see the front lines of his own mission, warts and all. "I'll tell you right now, the threat that the Taliban and al Qaeda fear the most are the schools and health clinics we are bringing to these remote areas," he said as we strolled on foot up the road into the Korengal Valley. "It means they are losing out on the hearts and minds of the local population. Meanwhile, we are tapping into a pool of poor, unpaid men in a warrior culture who will fight if not given another alternative." If it were a game of numbers alone, I'm sure the odds would have been on LeGree's side.

Ideally, the macadam roads circumventing the peaks, some of which made the Rocky Mountains look like Appalachian foothills, would lead to economic prosperity and separate the enemy from his base. I asked LeGree about the incessant fighting in the valley we were now walking into—one that many combat soldiers referred to as the "Valley of Death."

"In the specific case of the Korengal, this is a very isolated area where there are a lot of foreign fighters and they choose to fight us here," he said. "But the general population is just as open to our counterinsurgency efforts as elsewhere in the province."

LeGree explained that by building a road into the redoubt, famous from the Soviet era as an excellent hideaway, he would be "able to fracture some of the existing tribal dynamics that support the insurgency."

The problem with this theory was that it was not in line with the rest of the counterinsurgency strategy across Kunar Province, which was geared more toward empowering Afghans, building up the local government, and expanding its reach. A stronger government would attract support and repel insurgents. LeGree now aimed to "fracture" the opposition in the toughest insurgent redoubts. He was placing the US military in a new role, beyond that of nation builder. I had spent hours back in Asadabad talking to officers and some civilians who vehemently opposed the current push into the Korengal Valley because they saw it as an "adventure too far" for the US military. It was a logistical nightmare, but it was also a thrust into a part of Kunar occupied by the Korengalis, cousins of the Nuristanis to the north, who simply despised anything foreign and would resist the US military's best efforts. Those who opposed the push took the line that America should be helping those who want help and leaving the troublemakers to their own devices.

This argument against pushing headlong into the Valley of Death had its own logic: let the economic success and good relations in the main valleys become an example for the wild hillbillies who refused to cooperate. (Captain Coughenour, incidentally, was a major proponent of this approach.) Eventually, they would "see the light" and end their resistance. Notably, when the Kafirs (unbelievers) in this area had been converted forcefully through jihad to Islam at the end of the nineteenth century, their land had been renamed Nuristan, or "Land of Light." Even in the twenty-first century it could not boast, however, that it had become the "land of the enlightened."

There was an essential disconnect within the American thinking. Our enlightened optimism had few limits when it came to the most remote and difficult terrain on Earth. The problem with actually putting an end to efforts in places like the Korengal Valley was that the US military is an institution that fights wars (and, in military theory, never loses, unless politicians get in the way). Although I had heard grumbles about the Korengal policy, no one in the PRT or in any of the combat units stood up at the secret strategy meetings I was allowed to attend, to say, "We can't do that. It is simply too ambitious." Taking no for an answer—especially when it came to an area rife with "bad guys"—was still considered a psychological surrender to evil forces.

American counterinsurgency efforts in Afghanistan in the waning years of the Bush administration remained a work in progress—an effort so new (and innovative) that the lessons learned hadn't been written down, much less digested.

A few days after my patrol with LeGree, I learned that I was being authorized to fly by air into the remote Korengal outpost for a reality check inside that embattled outpost's rocky walls. Before I left, Sergeant Amos, the affable Apache Indian, showed me some more short videos from trips that his RAGE platoon had made into the Korengal Valley. He showed them in my chambers, adding a narration in a hushed voice, and I couldn't help looking at him—in an odd way—as a distant cousin of Big Chief in Kesey's *One Flew over the Cuckoo's Nest*. We watched a group of soldiers coolly observing an air attack on a house. There had been a direct hit, and a huge cloud engulfed the hillside. What was left of the house must have been shards and stones. "What a plume!" a young fighter roared in satisfaction. A colleague chirped in, "Won't anyone be fightin' outa that son-of-a-bitch anytime soon!" These were the voices of war—the kind I knew all too well from the Balkans and other combat zones: cynicism oddly laced with elation, brought on by death and destruction. I had learned long ago that it was futile to look for silver linings in mushroom clouds.

I was traveling with Carter Malkasian, a young Oxford PhD who directs the Stability and Development program at the Center for Naval Analyses in Virginia.[27] Also at our side was Sergeant Justin Faulkner, a student of ethnography, who had been assigned by LeGree to study the "human terrain" in order to understand why the fighting in the Korengal Valley was so intense. My own understanding of the challenges posed by the US military's activities in this isolated pocket of the province would be greatly enhanced by my opportunity to sit in on the briefings that the two would receive.

The chopper flight whisked us a mile and a half up into the highest ridges of Kunar. As the Chinook beat ever harder at the thinning air, I could look down through an open gunner's window and see mountain goats and men in turbans engulfed in dust, running for cover with their eyes burning. We landed on the side of a mountain, literally. Atop the narrow valley was an operations center and barracks made of plywood with aluminum roofs. On the perimeter, overlooking pine trees and shrubs, were a series of guard towers, placed to provide 360-degree fields of fire in the direction of the ground below.

A young ROTC graduate from the University of Colorado, Boulder, met us at the landing pad and walked us up the mountain. We were to keep our helmets and flak jackets on at all times. The blond officer provided a quick briefing as we moved briskly up the hill. He explained that foot and air patrols had been unable to pinpoint a large Russian machine gun, a Dishka, which was shooting rounds into the outpost on a nightly basis. Insurgents had carried the large gun in one piece into the surrounding mountains some weeks back, and each time it fired down on the outpost, they would bury it and melt into the wilderness as shepherds, leaving it up to a foot patrol with a metal detector to get lucky one day. The heavily wooded terrain punctuated by huge boulders for fighting cover was more than ideal for guerrilla operations. It was heaven at two miles above sea level for al Qaeda and its affiliates, mostly consisting of local tribesmen. Even thermal-imaging technology meant to pick up heat signals seemed to malfunction at this altitude.

In the operations center, five real-time video screens of the surrounding terrain were up and running. The monitors provided an eagle's eye with a zoom lens on everything in the immediate vicinity of the base. "Sometimes you'll see a group of five of them [insurgents] running down the hill, and then—'blam!'—they are dead," Sgt. James Himrod, a soldier assigned to the valley, told me. His name for the real-life video game was "Kill TV."

At the Korengal outpost (also known to the solders as the KOP), there were upward of one hundred US fighters and a contingent of freshly arrived Afghan soldiers. These forces were concentrated near the landing pad, although smaller units had hacked their way into adjacent mountainsides to set up additional observation posts. According to the acting commanders, all of them anxious to talk but none of them over thirty years old, LeGree's road project (which rose to an elevation of about a mile and a half here) was in serious danger of collapse. A group of local Korengali elders, angered that the war had intensified in their area, had forbidden the road's surveyors—most of them locals—to continue their work. The elders' main interest was in getting back their sons, who, they complained, had been randomly taken captive by American soldiers.

LeGree's roads were intended to create a firewall against the infiltration of insurgents from Pakistan. That translated into regular ambushes or firefights for the foot patrols that left the outpost at night to uphold the "wall." Although the US soldiers' night-vision goggles gave them an advantage in the woods, the guerrillas used the terrain to their own advantage, particularly at full moon. Nearly three dozen US fighters had been killed in these woods in the past two years when on foot patrol.

Even gathering intelligence from villagers was fraught with peril. The US foot patrols were being lured into traps by locals in civilian garb. "The other day, we had an old guy who asked us to meet him on a certain path at a certain time and he was going to give us some information about the insurgents," a soldier told me. "When we showed up, shooting broke out on both sides of us."

If you were looking for clues as to what the insurgents were up to, Sun Tzu's simple instructions in *The Art of War* would provide a hint: "Your battlefield is not to be known, for when it cannot be known, the enemy makes many guard outposts, and since multiple outposts are established, you only have to do battle with small squads."[28]

The deeper the US forces pushed into the Hindu Kush, the smaller their squads became—necessarily. That was just where the "bad guys" wanted us. No one knew this better than the brave young Americans on the ground. For the fighters in the 173rd's Combat Team north of the Khyber Pass, just knowing that they fought in proximity to the masterminds of the 9/11 attacks heightened their own sense of a great divide: a split between what the US forces could and must do in Afghanistan, and the real mystery of what al Qaeda was planning across the border in Pakistan. That said, most of the young fighters who trekked through the mountains were between nineteen and twenty-three years old, many of them still in high school during the 9/11 attacks. They had not joined the military to become aid workers or even intelligence officers. They had been trained to close with and kill the enemy; winning hearts and minds was still not their top priority and—despite their trepidation when alone—when on patrol, they itched for a good firefight.

That night I bunked down with my two traveling companions in an officer's tent. I could hear light shelling going back and forth and the screams of small bands of monkeys, presumably the same genus of monkeys we had seen while fleeing the bombing at Tora Bora in 2001. Early in the morning, close to 2 a.m., I caught up with a patrol on its way into the crisp night air. Tanner Stichter, who had won a Purple Heart for his bravery in the line of fire, spoke to me about insurgent tactics.

"I would say that 95 percent of the time they hit us from the high ground—when our backs are turned," he said. "We have a very difficult time finding these foreign fighters, but they know exactly where we are." Tanner could have starred in a war movie. Handsome, well spoken, and dedicated to his platoon, he also broke down in tears as he spoke of his team's medic, Juan Restrepo, whom he and his mates had tried to keep alive for forty-five minutes after he had been shot in the neck. "He had taught us to do everything we did to try to keep him alive," Tanner said, his lips quivering. "We know he is up there, somewhere, watching over us still."

Reaching out to help the locals when you are getting shot at day in and day out is a recipe for compassion fatigue. A heavy angst had already descended on Stichter's platoon. "You put yourself out there for them," he told me over coffee and a candy bar in the mess hall. "I mean, you are extending your hand, but in return, you are getting nothing. You just give, give, and give. And it takes a toll on you, because then you come back and you think, 'Why am I here?'" The sound of the Russian Dishka punctuated our conversation, as if someone else also wanted to help Stichter make his point.

"Half the time, I don't think they care what we do for them," said one of Stichter's companions, who had seen two of his colleagues killed in the past year. "We stopped taking in food and building supplies two months ago when they attacked us with a roadside bomb. Sometimes, the Afghans play along with us, just long enough to get a little more HA [humanitarian assistance] and then attack again."

In the Korengal, there was a growing sense of frustration that belied the usual air of optimism down at the PRT. Fighters had to make haunting—often fatal—decisions on whether to fire into homes and mosques. Despite the brimming optimism of the commanders down below, where they operated on paved highways patrolled by Apache helicopters overhead, few soldiers at the Korengal outpost saw the daily fighting as a sign of progress. For the US foot soldier, this was a war of attrition that wasn't going away anytime soon. Insurgents were like moles, popping up here and there and then burrowing underground, only to rise to attend their next ambush.

I would return to the region a year later, but from what I had seen on this trip, the Korengal effort was a road and a mission too far for the 173rd Airborne. Despite the new approach to counter-insurgency, which banked less on killing the enemy than on winning over his population base, some things had not changed since we embarked upon this war in September 2001. I was taken aback at how little the US military's mid-level officers still knew about the enemy they were fighting. It was rare—almost never—that US forces could count the dead and find out precisely who was attacking them. "I interact on a daily basis with an enemy that has both local and for-eign elements," an army captain told me. He said he was sure they were foreigners because he could hear Arabic spoken in the radio communications he intercepted. "But just what the foreign element is bringing to the fight, I don't exactly know." There was little men-tion of al Qaeda or Osama bin Laden, but the terror network's shadow loomed large.

Insurgents shadowed the steps of US foot patrols like ghosts. "When we are in a village, we always know that al Qaeda and the Tal-iban will soon be back to try to undercut us and try to one-up us," said Sergeant Mark Patterson, whose platoon in the Korengal Valley had been in some of the heaviest fighting anywhere in Afghanistan. His troops faced a higher concentration of al Qaeda–backed insurgents than those in most regions of Afghanistan. Patterson told me he believed that every attack on his men was being filmed by some jihadist outfit, likely linked to al Qaeda central in neighboring Pakistan.

While most of the locals were indigenous Korengali tribesmen, a thin layer of al Qaeda loyalists had spread itself out in what Chairman Mao once dubbed the "sea of the people" to oversee oper-ations and win over local loyalties. These were the age-old tactics of guerrilla war. Despite the relative successes of the nation-building efforts in the valleys, Kunar Province remained the US military's most violent front in 2007, 2008, and 2009. The firefights were often more intense in tiny Kunar (and just to the north in Nuristan along the Pakistani border) than even in Southern Kandahar and Helmand, where the Canadian and British forces often faced full-on frontal assaults from small bands of Taliban fighters. An attack that killed ten French special forces members (from the famed Chamonix school of mountain warfare) in August 2008 took place in nearby Kapisa Province, a region accessible only through the "rat lines" leading into the province over Kunar's rugged moonscape.

A few weeks after my return to Washington, and as I was planning a trip to Pakistan, the small outpost of Wanat, north of the Korengal, was attacked by some one hundred well-armed insurgents in July 2008. The fight that took place left nine US soldiers dead and was described by injured fighters from the 173rd Airborne Brigade's Combat Team as the most intense firefight that the US forces had experienced in Afghanistan to date. It was just the kind of insurgent attack you would expect as US forces continued to fan out of larger bases and set up small outposts.

The 173rd's commander, Col. Charles Preysler, another Michigan man, whose forces had spearheaded the 2002 Anaconda operations against al Qaeda insurgents south of Tora Bora, and whom I interviewed at length for my book *Al Qaeda's Great Escape*, was incensed at the audacity of the attack on his forces at Wanat, but he insisted these forces had been doing no more than so many other platoon-sized units in his force had been doing.[29] Indeed, they were protecting the extension of the same road that Lieutenant Commander Moore had checked on while building a school a few weeks earlier. It was a road—a key piece in the development puzzle—that would connect the new Afghan provincial capital in Nuristan to larger roads in Kunar.

"The soldiers were there on a reconnaissance mission to establish a presence and find a good location to connect with the local government, populace, and Afghan National Police," Preysler told my friend Herschel Smith, the editor of *Captain's Journal*, a leading military blog.[30] But Preysler was angered by reporting in the *New York Times*, in the immediate aftermath of the battle, suggesting that US forces had subsequently "abandoned" the forward operating base

(FOB), which he claimed was not an FOB at all since it was a "mobile" base. Herschel Smith, however, openly questioned what he called the "propriety of this engagement without the proper force projection, force protection and/or troop presence."[31]

Both Afghan officials and US officials agreed on one thing after the battle: the insurgents had been aided and abetted by local Afghan civilians, an eventuality that was made more likely after several errant US bombing raids occurred in the province, raids that had killed dozens of civilians in the month prior to the battle. American infantry units, including the one attacked at Wanat, had called in the strikes.

The insurgent attack came on July 13, 2008, at 4:30 a.m., as fighters swarmed in and around a US lookout post on a small hill manned by nine American soldiers. Specialist Tyler Stafford, twenty-three, had run to his sandbag post and seized his M-240, only to be blown down the terraced hillside and have his helmet knocked off by a rocket-propelled grenade fired by the insurgents. He watched two colleagues die almost instantaneously before recovering his wits and grabbing a 9 mm handgun, which he fired randomly over the edge of a sandbag. Moments later, he grabbed a dead colleague's M-4, began firing back at the insurgents, and then crawled on his hands and knees toward several injured colleagues in dire need of tourniquets.

The remaining fighters of the 173rd squeezed out rounds so fast that two of their largest guns overheated and jammed, useless. Reinforcements ran to the observation post from the main base below, but fell dead in the crossfire. Along with Matthew Gobble and Sgt. Ryan Pitts, Stafford was the only one left fighting when insurgents tried to trick the soldiers into the open by pummeling them with rocks, hoping that the soldiers would think they were grenades. It was an insurgent tactic that you didn't read about in most fighting manuals. Not until the guerrillas penetrated the sandbag fortifications did Apache helicopters and A-10 Warthogs race to the rescue, laying down strafing runs, but to little avail. Soldiers from lower posts finally made it to the observation tower to help in the fight. One of the soldiers who came to the rescue of his mates, Sgt. Jacob Walker, expressed shock at the force of the enemy attack. "I've never seen the enemy do anything like that," he said. "It's usually three RPGs [rocket-propelled grenades] and some sporadic fire and then they're gone. I don't know where they got all those RPGs. That was crazy."

The attack took place inside Afghanistan, some twenty-five miles from the border with Pakistan, in warm weather, which had aided the mobility of the insurgents. It was the Taliban's and al Qaeda's sanctuary in Pakistan, however, that made such an onslaught possible. You could keep rolling the boulders to the top of the Hindu Kush, but if the realities on the ground on the far side remained the same, those rocks would always come tumbling back down.

That is where I was headed next—the far side.

Chapter 8
OSAMA'S GHOST

In military matters, it is not necessarily beneficial to have more strength, only to avoid acting aggressively; it is enough to consolidate your power, assess opponents and get people, that is all.
—Sun Tzu, *The Art of War*

When I arrived in Peshawar in early 2008 after an absence of seven years, it was much the same as it had been in 2001. "Auntie's" stately guesthouse in University Town was still serving chicken marsala, and the little scuba man with bubbles coming from his mouth was still in the fishbowl in the lobby.[1] A warm, diminutive soul with a bright smile, Auntie wore a purple sari and looked surprised to see me.

Picking up where we left off, Auntie greeted me with a sandwich and some good news. Her husband, a human rights activist who had been for years a "guest" in Gen. Pervez Musharraf's prison system, had been released and was again helping her manage the Continental

Guest House. Like a lot of other democratic-minded Pakistanis, she and her husband were pleased to see that Musharraf's political star was falling off the charts. The trajectory of his fall from grace mirrored that of George W. Bush. Although he still clung to power until late 2008, he could rightly be blamed for many of the country's spectacular woes. His indulgent treatment of extremists as the army's patriotic allies in the fight to keep India at bay had sunk the nation into an abyss of extremism, from which it was not likely to extract itself anytime soon. Fed up with Musharraf—often referred to by common folks in the street as "Busharraf"—most Pakistanis had simply decided that the war on terror was someone else's fight.

This meant we had an ally in high places but not one where we needed one—in the trenches. For Pakistanis, it was America's war, and public opinion polls suggested they didn't give a damn about it. Worse still, as Ahmed Rashid, my former colleague on the *Daily Telegraph*, points out in his 2008 book, *Descent into Chaos*, a general Pakistani hatred of the United States began to take "precedence over hatred of al Qaeda."[2]

That meant that Pakistan's middle class was far less inclined to fight to keep the Northwest Frontier Province (NWFP) from falling into the hands of extremists, who now considered it their private domain. Only when suicide bombers began a series of attacks on Islamabad and Lahore would the broader Pakistani public wake up and demand that an effort should be made to fight back.

I braced myself for one of my biennial tours of Pakistan's tribal badlands, where—despite varying levels of disapproval among the local population—fundamentalists had reaffirmed their control and offered al Qaeda a fast-expanding safe haven.

"Haven't you learned to keep away?" Auntie scolded me when I asked for her help in getting to Chitral, a remote province from which the CIA had recently been expelled by jihadists for hunting too aggressively for Osama bin Laden and his top lieutenants.

Auntie informed me that my former escort through the badlands and her own beloved stepson, Jamal, still drove the same Mitsubishi

Pajero that we had driven to the battle of Tora Bora and was at home giving it a shine. A former orphan and now a well-fed father of five, Jamal's warning in 2001, after the slaughter of four of my colleagues in Afghanistan, still rang in my ears at night: "Kill da infidel, kill da infidel. That mean you, Mr. Philip!"

Before our journey in 2001, Jamal had wisely purchased from a jihadi recruiter a cassette of a musical duet between a mother and son, in which the proud mother admonishes her son to prepare for his own death as a holy warrior. I recalled that just the sound of that music kept armed jihadists from dragging me out of the back seat of Jamal's jeep.

We packed food for a week and we set off in the direction of Abbottabad, headquarters of the Hazara Division in British India and now the last Pakistani government stronghold before jihadi land. The city, founded by one Major Abbott, a Briton, still had the flavor of a military garrison. Male residents appeared to eschew the traditional shalwar kamis, the long pajama-like garments often seen in Pakistan, for Western suits and ties. A number of military preparatory schools dotted the former hill station along with the ubiquitous billboards showing pictures of Mohammed Ali Jinnah, founder of Pakistan, who had famously said, to his later discredit among jihadists, "You may belong to any religion or caste or creed—that has nothing to do with the business of the state." The jihadists, of course, preferred only one creed and wanted that upheld by the state.

Jihadists and government types were in any case fond of working together, for the business of the state in Pakistan *was and is* the military, as is so well documented in Ayesha Siddiqa's 2007 book, *Military Inc.*[3] The country's military-industrial (and nuclear) complex so thoroughly dominates the economy that private entrepreneurs struggle to make small inroads even into fields like tourism and agriculture, which have become the domain of greedy generals and colonels. Young men, often excluded from jobs in the struggling private sector and raised in radical madrassas, grow up aspiring to a life in the military—or, if not that, service as a guerrilla in the name of

Islam. Guns and adventure have lured them in both directions, aided by a government often incapable of distinguishing between a good jihadist and a good soldier.

As we cut through the foothills of the Hindu Kush, Jamal stopped the Pajero on several occasions to cool down the engine. At one point a camel train passed us by, and one of the beasts unleashed an angry shriek. At an elevation of about two miles above sea level, we hit summer glaciers that were silently spreading across the highway, threatening to block traffic altogether. Two young men straddled a six-foot handsaw and yanked it back and forth across the ice to stem the onslaught.

At sunset, we slipped into Chitral. White peaks surged across the horizon, undulating toward their confluence with the mighty Himalayas. This was the land where the rare snow leopard, hunting for easy prey, would slink down through the boulders to snatch a goat or two and then disappear again for weeks on end.

Like Kashmir, Chitral was a special place under the British Raj. To this day it is home to a famous two-mile-above-sea-level polo tournament between rival tribesmen, usually attended by Pakistan's president. The hundreds of jeeps that stream toward the polo ground every summer and spread out among tents lined with kebab grills are the closest thing in Asia to a tailgate party. Despite the fact that this is a Muslim culture, ample amounts of bootleg booze are supplied by a small tribe of about three thousand polytheists, the Kalash people. The polo games are wild and bloody, a kind of institutionalized terror—if you will—that can be compared to a similar equestrian sport across the border in Afghanistan, known as *buzkashi*. The Afghan sport is played on rocky fields using the headless carcass of a goat or calf. The goal is to grab the carcass and thrust it into a large circle. Blood, guts, and a very good time are had by all.

Despite their mountainous charm and fun-loving people, Chitral and its towering snow-capped peaks are also home to an explosive religious mix. Mike Scheuer, the operative who headed the CIA's special bin Laden division until just before 9/11, contends that Saudi nongovernmental organizations and missionary organizations working on both sides of the border have made the Chitral area "thoroughly Salafist-oriented."[4] By that he means "entirely fundamentalist." Indeed, the Al-Khidimat Foundation, an offshoot of bin Laden's original Peshawar welfare and jihadist organization, is a leading actor in Chitral, as evidenced by numerous small clinics that treat wounded guerrillas and then send them back into the fray against US forces.

Radical madrassas have mushroomed across Chitral, even since 9/11—years after Pakistani authorities promised their US allies to try to curtail their growth.

After we had spent an evening in a dingy tourist hotel populated by Punjabi tourists, Jagir Jahangir, the head of the local press association, escorted Jamal and me to meet with Chitral's police chief, who asked us to be seated as an assistant brought in a silver tray laden with cups of green tea. I had heard rumors that the CIA was in hot pursuit of bin Laden in Chitral—or, at least, had been until recently.

The police chief, a young Pashtun from Peshawar, who had spent a summer in Pennsylvania in training on a State Department program, had dealt with the CIA directly. "The Americans are convinced that bin Laden is hiding up here in Pakistan, but we think that is just an excuse for their failure to catch him in nearby Nuristan," he said. "I mean, how much of your taxpayers' money have they already spent hunting this guy?"[5]

"Beats me," I replied.

He explained that it had been no boon to local tourism when an anxious US "consular officer" arrived in May 2006 to open what was supposed to be a secret bin Laden monitoring post. The officer was eventually forced to flee Chitral under Pakistani police escort, after radical religious groups rallied in anger. "The officer told me that he had been on a special mission to set up a guesthouse," chuckled the police chief. "He refused to accept a police security detail, and when his guesthouse was surrounded with angry religious leaders, he had no choice but to ask for our assistance. We made sure he escaped with his life."

As counterterrorism experts on the region have pointed out, it is virtually impossible for Westerners to try to blend into communities in Pakistan's NWFP—even if they are fluent in the local languages. Each valley and each clan displays linguistic and cultural nuances that are unfathomable to an outsider. Unless you study the culture and linguistic traits of every valley, you are unlikely to fit in. Even if you manage to blend in, you will be found out because everyone will know that you are no one's relative. In the end, undercover operations in the NWFP work about as well as sending an NYPD undercover officer to investigate the moonshine business in West Virginia.

As the police chief began to explain the various tribes and cultures sprinkled across Chitral, he mentioned in passing the Kalash people, who are of great interest to anthropologists and ethnographers.

As I would soon discover, the Kalash people and their struggles served as a barometer of the changes and the hardships faced by indigenous people caught between Washington's war on terror and bin Laden's global jihad. Formerly known as Kafirs, or unbelievers, they represented the last vestige of a polytheist culture that once extended across the Hindu Kush. Members of the same ethnic group on the Afghan side of the border were forcibly converted to Islam at the end of the nineteenth century. (This forced mass conversion is cited by historian Bernard Lewis as a classic example of an "offensive jihad," as opposed to the more common "defensive jihad," in which Muslims defend their own faith and culture from outsiders.)[6]

As the police chief told me stories, a young leader of the Kalash people came to talk to him as well. She had come to ask for additional female police officers in her own community, which had a strong matriarchal tradition.

In short order, I was introduced to this leader, Lekshan Bibi, Pakistan Airlines' first female pilot. Lekshan was unveiled and wore an elaborate headdress with a band of cowry shells in front and beads and cowries running down her back. She looked like a photograph in the *National Geographic*, even more striking against the dull background of puritanical Islam in Chitral. I noted that if Osama bin Laden was in the area, he probably would not find a wife among her people.

I sat patiently as Lekshan finished her chat with the police chief and then invited us to follow her to her village along the border with Afghanistan. The road ran on the edge of a cliff for several miles, and we trundled along at about ten miles an hour to keep from slipping into the thundering waters of the river below. Beneath us, men in woolen berets harvested bundles of wheat from the lush brown soil that lined the rushing waters.

We were on the border, just opposite Kunar Province, and although I had expected to find myself close to one of al Qaeda's jungle training camps, I found that the reality was very different. In the first Kalash village we visited, women in long embroidered dresses squatted alongside a rushing river with their laundry, and children scrambled up mulberry trees to collect fruit. We rested at a guesthouse, where a yellow oriole flitted above the head of a little girl. The village was preparing for a three-day feast to mark the death of a teenage boy who had fallen into the river as he was felling trees for firewood to be floated downstream. In the distance, men and women solemnly greeted each other by gently lifting the backs of one another's hands and kissing them. Across a swinging suspension bridge, elders bathed the boy's body in wine.

On an island in the river, hatchets were being used to slaughter several cows, the blood and entrails leaching into the rushing waters as women cried out in dirges for the departed. While ethnographers dispute the claims of the Kalash to blood ties to Alexander the Great's conquering armies, their quirky rituals and skilled wine-making habits suggest that they had picked up a great deal from Hellenistic culture. Most of their history was kept alive by Homeric-style bards—one of whom I was soon introduced to—who sang of the tribe's rich and fascinating history.

We were invited for a glass of wine on Lekshan's porch. Her boyfriend, as she called him, was a retired Pakistani Army major. She wasn't shy about explaining her people's plight. She had been invited only recently to represent Pakistan's indigenous populations at a UN conference on the subject. Her brother sat silently alongside his big sister as she sipped wine and spoke with us. She said he had become a Muslim, forsaking the religion of his elders and breaking his father's heart. "A lot in our religion are leaving for Islamic schools because of what they are being offered," explained Lekshan, who ran a private organization that fought to maintain the Kalash traditions. "The young generation feels they are getting something from the madrassas. They get help for schooling and medicine when they are sick. We cannot offer the same, due to our own limited resources. They also get brainwashed and learn how to hate."[7]

It was the ideological indoctrination that concerned her the most. The days of the multiethnic and multireligious state of Chitral, once a province in the British Raj in which the Kalash practiced their faith virtually free from oppression, were long over. (Of course, this doesn't mean that the Raj wasn't patronizing and driven by economic motives, just that the Kalash weren't surrounded by a threatening culture of zealots.)

"We live in a hub of Islamization and so we are being crushed," Lekshan added. Her credentials for talking on the subject were strong, as she had recently been kidnapped for ransom by Islamic radicals and released only with the help of her retired Pakistani major. Like the Christian students I had met in Solo, Indonesia, she was also concerned that US foreign policy was stirring the jihadist nests and increasing local animosity. "The Taliban are motivated by George Bush's war on terror. The boys go through a form of military training. And if they have to kill, it will be a source of pride at the cost of our own blood."

There were also gender considerations, particularly for the unveiled and often outspoken Kalash women, who loved to put on elaborate dance performances for visiting Punjabi tourists. The new religious schools were pumping out fire and brimstone messages aimed at the alleged wine drinking and debauchery of these women. Unlike their veiled sisters, whose husbands were chosen for them,

Kalash women were still permitted to openly court various males. This made them the object of ridicule from members of the more conservative culture.

The next morning, I was given a Kalash guide, Asmat, a son of the owner of the guesthouse where we were staying. The eight-hour trek up to the Afghan border, through the Shawal Pass, would provide a stunning view across glaciers into Kunar and Nuristan provinces. Jamal remained behind to eat, drink, and fiddle with the engine of his car.

As we set off for the mountain after coffee, I noticed that several dozen Pakistani frontier policemen were still sleeping off a night of drinking by a stream that ran beside our guesthouse. Although Islamabad pledged to preserve the fragile culture of the Kalash, these outside authorities spent most of their time flirting with the Kalash women and drinking their wine. The fiery hate messages about the "debauchery of the polytheists" coming from the Salafist- and Wahhabi-funded religious schools did not seem to be their concern.

Our trek began as a casual stroll, but the path became more treacherous as we passed above the tree line and onto several glaciers above rushing streams. On a grassy bend, two men who had just returned from Afghanistan, exhausted and unkempt, accosted us.

"What are they saying?" I asked.

"That we cannot go there," said my guide, Asmat. "I have tried to explain to them that we are tourists, but they don't believe me."

We marched on defiantly as they sneered at us. After several hours of hiking and at some two miles above sea level, we ran into an old Kalash tribesman with his flock of sheep. Three burly dogs were chained to the rocks outside his small wooden hut, and he told us that he unleashed them at night to stave off a notorious snow leopard. He added that the jihadists, who referred to themselves as mujahedeen—like the two we had earlier run into—usually said little but often asked to buy any guns he might have.

We moved higher, into the snow line, where the winds whipped like a winter storm. At the top of the Shawal Pass, we found an abandoned way station, the redoubt of wayfaring insurgents. We did not stay long, as the sun was setting. A cousin of Asmat, who walked along with us for several hundred meters, said the shelter was a launching pad for cross-border raids into Afghanistan.

During our journey back, we passed by what my guide said was known as the "village of the converted," Kalash people whose menfolk had taken up Islam and whose wives had taken the veil. As we passed, I noticed the women and daughters, bound by the Islamic tradition of purdah, running for cover so as not to be seen by a foreigner. Even as we averted our eyes, two young Muslim teenagers emerged from behind a rocky fence and descended on my guide, Asmat. They threatened to stone him to death for daring to bring an "infidel" into their domain. I sensed they were bluffing, but my heart began to race. They pushed him and teased him and only ended the harassment when I interceded and screamed at them.

Even with their peculiar ethnic nuances, Chitral's borderlands provided bin Laden—or at least his specter, which lurked everywhere in these parts—an ideal stamping ground for his jihad. With cross-pollination from the fighting in Afghanistan and the infusion of born-again Islamic zealotry, Chitral was not so different from the rest of the frontier regions, which run north to south. In the three Kalash valleys, there were now sixteen new madrassas. In 1947, there were only 137 madrassas in all of Pakistan, but they doubled in number every ten years until the 1980s, when they began to triple and quadruple.

As we left the Kalash people and wound our way back up the mountain pass along the cliff face, I had the wistful sense that this tribe was a little like the Pueblo or Navajo of New Mexico, about to be subdued by outside armies.

✳✳✳

Jamal and I left the Kalash valleys and dropped back down through the Himalayas, passing women with bundles on their backs, twice their size. It was a little hard to imagine that monks with begging bowls had once walked these Himalayan foothills, as evidenced by a giant red-brick stupa built to house a single hair of the Buddha. A young boy on horseback pranced by the towering megalith, which cast a long shadow across the parched earth. Archeologists knew the Swat Valley, which we now entered, as a center for Gandaran art, a fascinating West-meets-East mélange of Greek and Buddhist sculpture. As we trekked through the former bastion of the wali (prince) of Swat, who greeted Queen Elizabeth here in 1961, we passed by "Winston Churchill's Picket," a ruined military outpost set on the heights where an ambitious British writer had witnessed the colonial armies' attempts to hunt down "outlaw" tribal leaders who had risen up against the Raj in 1898.[8]

Although capturing your foe in this rugged terrain was no easier back then, at least the British did not have to contend with the full-blown jihad on the Internet and DVD that had now come into being in Swat to inspire the masses to rise against their own government and its Western allies. With the global jihad in full swing after 9/11, even moderate tribal elders had long since been driven out. That rendered the notion of most USAID or military-led nation-building schemes utterly absurd. (Truth be told, there were few, if any, legitimate partners for peace to be found here.)

The frontier provinces were a good place to examine a number of different jihadi groups, however, most of which had great sympathy for al Qaeda leader Osama bin Laden. Indeed, their love for bin Laden and hatred for the United States bound them as firmly as their own religious convictions. In essence, bin Laden supplied the spiritual umbrella under which other groups gathered.

In Swat, the most widespread radical movement was the TNSM, or Movement for the Enforcement of Islamic Laws. The group had come into its own in the 1970s and 1980s, when it led local uprisings and seized control of government institutions.[9] In 2001, the TNSM's leader, Sufi Mohammed, sent thousands of young men into Afghanistan to help defend the Taliban from the US invasion. Few of them had combat experience. In the ensuing fighting, hundreds of young Pakistanis were killed, and hundreds were taken captive. The US-led invasion had also helped to harden a new young generation of TNSM fighters, however. I had seen prisons packed with them in eastern Afghanistan in 2001. Many had died in custody, but most, for lack of a better plan, had been released and returned home. One of the great ironies of the early days of the US war in Afghanistan was that far more Pakistani members of the Taliban were permitted to return home than their Afghan counterparts, who were assumed to be close to al Qaeda and were shipped by the hundreds to Guantanamo Bay. In fact, there was little difference between the two groups, but one major factor in the screening had been the interests of our ally at the time, President Musharraf.

Pakistan's Musharraf had put Sufi Mohammed in prison for fomenting trouble, but his young minions had taken charge back in the frontier provinces. Indeed, by this time, Pakistan's tribal regions were so radicalized that picking off individual leaders made no real difference to the production of more fighters for the fray. It would be as though a huge riot had broken out in a big American city and the police had moved in with a SWAT team to arrest a senior leader. The riot wasn't going to end any faster with the jihad raging in the hearts and minds of so many young men in northwestern Pakistan.

Jamal and I caught a taste of the assembly-line production of young jihadists when we visited a madrassa run by the TNSM. Through an old connection in Peshawar, I had managed to hire a young man who represented the BBC's Pashtun service in the region. As good fortune would have it, my new cover as a British journalist was just right for the occasion.

We drove through the heart of Mingora, Swat's capital city, and along a winding, muddy stream, bumping along a dusty road and climbing up an embankment. A young boy waved us into a courtyard, where Jamal brought the jeep to a halt. Within moments, grizzled and lively Fazul Haq, the headmaster of a madrassa, hobbled up to our jeep. Haq had seen better days as a revolutionary when in the

1970s he helped seize control of the local airport. His demands for Islamic law had earned him a prison stay, but now he had been rewarded with a new school and hundreds of young underlings, whom we noticed crowded in a circle bobbing their heads, unable to tear themselves away from a Koranic chant. These were the same innocent faces I had seen only days earlier in a jihadist recruitment video, which unabashedly displayed five-year-olds in military fatigues trying to run across the floor while weighed down by Kalashnikov machine guns.

Many of these young boys were from the poorest families in Pakistan. Severed from their kin, they were for all purposes orphans whose minds were blank slates ready for the infusion of militant ideals. These youngsters, like Mohammed's early Muslim converts, were drawn mostly from the poor, orphaned, and socially marginal masses. They were being exploited, however, by jihadists with an international agenda.

What came first, the act or the idea? One wonders. George Washington University Professor Jerrold Post has said that "Terrorism at heart is a *vicious species of psychological warfare*; it is violence as communication."[10] The idea begs the question, however, as to where that violence first raises its ugly head—in the mind or on the battlefield?

In response to my questions about the war in Afghanistan, Haq sat us down and launched into a rant about the need to lop off the head of "American spies." I was filming Haq with a video camera and his words flustered me, particularly when Jamal's jaw dropped. "We have informed the government in writing that if we see American spies in Swat, whatever happens to them, we are not responsible." Of course, we were not spies, but I had said I was British, and if anyone checked my identity they would find that I was an American, which would surely be a ticket to the chopping block. "They want us to rescind our order to cut off heads, but we refuse," he continued.

I actually told him he was right to stand his ground, hoping to divert him from any interest he might have in me. Several of Fazul

Haq's local madrassa students nodded like zombies as he spoke. I asked one of them if he had seen any of the myriad jihadi DVDs available in the local market, some of which showed "live" beheadings of American soldiers in Iraq. He nodded with a smile. "I am happy to see non-Muslims beheaded." He was so gleeful that it made me wonder over and over again how he squared this sentiment with his faith.

It became clear over the next few hours, however, that this seemingly boring concrete mass of pillars and classrooms—with its scores of boys and teenagers—was a rear base for the Taliban. Fazul Haq told us that Pakistanis who had fought in Afghanistan against NATO regularly dropped in to talk with his students.

"We don't have to lecture anyone about the call to jihad," he insisted with a raspy smoker's chuckle. "Instead of us lecturing them, the *talibs* [religious students] lecture us. They go to Afghanistan and fight and come back and deliver wonderful lectures about the virtues of Osama bin Laden and his fight there."

I noticed that Haq had brought up bin Laden without any prompting on my part. His casual invocation of the Saudi sheikh's name did not, however, surprise me. The schoolmaster described a network of religious schools that served as centers of rest, relaxation, and religious study for the fighters in Afghanistan. He was proud to tell us that many of the suicide bombers facing the US and NATO forces in Afghanistan were Pakistanis, and his claim was confirmed by the US military.

And did he know where Osama bin Laden is hiding these days, I asked.

"It might be better to ask the [Pakistani] Inter-Services Intelligence [ISI] agencies where bin Laden and Zawahiri are," he said. "They are living in a refuge run by the ISI. The intelligence agencies just keep the tigers to themselves and will wait until the situation changes to release them or hand them over to the US. For now, they still need Osama."

Many Western counterterrorism analysts have long suspected

that bin Laden is viewed as a cash cow in Pakistan, which has been the grateful recipient of billions of dollars in US military assistance for its "help" in the war on terror. Analysts believe that Pakistani officials, privy to the machinations of their own nation's extremist groups, must certainly know bin Laden's whereabouts. If they were to give up his GPS coordinates, the unconventional logic goes, Pakistan would certainly lose standing as a prized ally. Ironically, when Hillary Clinton questioned Pakistan's commitment to catching bin Laden while she was on a trip to the region in October 2009, Western commentators were quick to suggest she had crossed some sacred diplomatic line.[11]

Although Pakistan is a nuclear power that the US government can't ignore, the idea of bin Laden as their ace in the hole is a theory—conspiracy or not—that carries as much weight in the NWFP as it does in certain counterterrorism circles in the West. It is quite possibly a pie-in-the-sky idea, but it helps stoke the legend of bin Laden. Seven years after our futile efforts at Tora Bora, bin Laden was still on the tip of people's tongues in these badlands. That was not good for anyone.

The knowledge that he was out there somewhere, however, gave local jihadists a sense of a hidden hierarchy. It also provided bin Laden with the brand of uninstitutionalized Islam that he favored— one in which an individual's spiritual outlook takes precedence over mediation and ritual. In this type of thinking, each individual fighter is asked not to bow down to a local authority but rather to submit to the greater cause of jihad. In practice, this means a direct relationship with Allah, through both prayer and deeds. It favors an internationalist (even heavenly) view of authority over adherence to more local leadership.

More important than bin Laden's enigmatic "presence" within jihadist circles, however, was the sense that spiritual leaders like Fazul Haq were deferring to him as their own *great leader*. De facto, Haq was part of a spiritual hierarchy—the Ummah—that transcends the various clans and tribes that make up Pakistan's wild, wild

West. Bin Laden's focus on a global jihad with a common enemy has "reinvigorated Islam's original status as a literal, everyman's religion," without ordination or sacraments of any kind.[12] Although bin Laden and his right-hand man, al-Zawahiri, often submit to the authority of religious scholars on questions of faith, they still deliver many of their own edicts, or fatwas.

Pashtuns, as a nation, are a classically infighting ethnic group whose cohesion can slip quickly into clan warfare, as documented by Winston Churchill at the end of the nineteenth century. Bin Laden's brand of extremism has provided a cohesion that allows many tribesmen to put aside their differences and focus on a common enemy—the modern "infidel." Madrassas, scattered like hundreds of military prep schools across the NWFP, solidify that bond. That the schools are stoked with militancy is no longer debatable. They provide a community of believers that is also a nation at arms, a notion that dovetails with an Islamic view of religion as a spiritual force that wields both political and military power.

Pashtuns are not a primitive race of people, but they remain locked into tribal traditions that provide an ideal context for the incubation and growth of militant Islam. Bin Laden and his followers understand these factors and that is why—despite the fact that their American enemy knows right where they are regrouping—they have defied what we might consider common sense and chosen Pakistan's tribal areas as their global base.

Dial back to the seventh century in the Arabian peninsula and you find that the Prophet Mohammed grew his religion in a similar kind of environment. His newfound militancy and no-holds-barred form of warfare transformed Arab militias and clan-based marauders from a collection of families and tribes into a kind of national army loyal to the Ummah, a newly founded spiritual body that superseded the usual ties that bind. Units within the army operated under a unified command structure, according to which all subordinate commanders were expected to carry out the missions assigned to them.

Arab armies in Mohammed's day had been loosely knit raiding parties. They had not been bound by military discipline. According to Richard Gabriel, "Unlike the old clan warriors, Muslim warriors were not primarily motivated by clan rivalries or the desire to loot, although both surely played a role. Muhammad's objective was to destroy the old Arab social order based on clan and kin and replace it with the new type of society, the Ummah."[13]

Once you have the core of a military structure in place, you can begin to change the rules of war, which was essential to achieving the kind of revolutionary goals that Mohammed had set for himself. Crucially, Mohammed, in his day, as al Qaeda has done in its own day, made death something to be sought and not feared. With regard to another tactical matter, just as Mohammed was one of the first great Arab leaders to understand the importance of not putting himself on the front lines, al Qaeda's leaders saw no reason in places like the NWFP to engage directly in guerrilla warfare. They had their dedicated proxies and have relied on them more and more.

Here in Swat, a rugged land of mountains, fields of clay, and mud castles for every clan, Sufi Mohammed's minions were drawn to the charismatic militancy of his nephew, Fazlullah, a young firebrand who had commandeered the local radio airwaves about a year before my return to the region. One of his major propaganda coups against the Americans in 2006 and 2007 was his insistence that a UNICEF polio-prevention campaign was a US-led birth control effort designed to limit the number of new Muslim babies. Bizarrely, locals didn't take much convincing. United Nations vaccination teams came under attack and fled the region entirely as a result of the false accusation.

Although I was a little nervous about meeting Fazlullah, Jamal, a fellow Pashtun, thought nothing of it. I was under his protection. (Jamal would travel anywhere with the exception of Afghanistan, from which he had fled for the last time during the battle of Tora Bora.) The drive took an hour from the capital of Swat. We had to cross a bridge and double back along the bank of the Swat River, due north toward the snow-capped peaks of the Himalayas. The soil along the river was hard and dusty. The grimy-faced, turbaned men and veiled women working it blended like clay figurines into its hue and texture.

We turned into a walled compound where the young firebrand's "clandestine" radio station broadcast its spiteful messages. I noticed that several dozen of Fazlullah's men wore their hair quite long and sported woolen berets, or *pakols*, similar to those worn by jihadists in Waziristan, where several of the largest rear bases for Taliban fighters were situated. They did not smile. The river was wide in this place, and several men had taken a fattened calf down to the bank to be slaughtered. It kicked and bellowed, but they caught it against the rocks and severed its head, a tide of burgundy blood rushing into the stream.

I took several snaps with the camera in my cell phone and managed to capture a jihadist as he strolled by the window of our jeep. I had thought that I was being discreet, but he caught me off guard. He leapt toward the window and grabbed my phone, even as I remained seated in the jeep. Jamal had to bargain with him, and I had to erase the photo in order to get the phone back. It had to do, he explained to me, with the Taliban's strict adherence to the Islamic rule forbidding human images, including those seen on television. It was a rule that was very confusing to me, however, since some jihadist groups had managed to seize control of the Internet for their own purposes, posting image after image, even images of al Qaeda's leaders. There were definite contradictions; providing considerable opportunities for disagreement among the ideological factions.

Fazlullah was finishing prayer and would meet with us shortly. We were permitted to set up our camera on the river bank and film across the water toward the setting sun—"but no people, please." My heart raced a bit as the young cleric strolled out to a small mud-brick hut along the river, where we would sit and talk. We were offered tea, and it wasn't long before a huge metal bowl full of freshly grilled veal turned up. It soon became a carnivorous conversation.[14]

On the surface, the young man's achievements in the realm of jihad were still limited. The thirty-two-year-old mullah had spent a year and a half in a Pakistani jail after fighting US troops in Afghanistan in 2001, so his biography matched that of thousands of Pakistani brethren ordered into the fray by Fazlullah's father-in-law. Associates of Fazlullah had been picked up in early 2007 after a massive suicide attack on a nearby Pakistani army sports field in which a lone bomber killed forty-two and injured thirty-nine recruits at the army's Punjab Regiment Center. Within months of my own chat with the firebrand, Pakistani government forces would be deployed in a full-scale offensive against Mullah Fazlullah and his army of jihadists. Although the government claimed victory as displaced families streamed out of Swat and then back in, Fazlullah remained on the run, and suicide bombing intensified, reaching deeper into urban centers like Peshawar and Islamabad well into 2010. In a positive sign, however, the military and the public now appeared united and committed to fighting "the enemy within Pakistan" despite the earlier public blame for the problem that had been placed on Washington's war on terror.

As we spoke, Fazlullah did not mince his words. "When Muslims are under attack in Iraq and Afghanistan, we have a duty to fight back against the American crusaders and their allies," he said. He was careful, however, not to attack Pakistan's government—at least not yet. He was gracious and kind, even jovial, although his refusal to have his picture taken suggested that he was a true Taliban member. I noted that two weeks later, a Pakistani cameraman convinced him to allow a video camera to record the silhouette of his shadow on the mud-brick wall as a reflection in the candlelight. I guessed that was one way to get around the image problem.

Fazlullah's fight was very much a part of a global jihad, not merely a struggle against American forces in Afghanistan. "America has waged war against Muslims across the globe," he said. That was the message he delivered every day, ceaselessly in his radio talks. The mullah, who would later roam the nearby mountains fighting both Pakistan's government and American forces, was running a religious institution, building a new mosque, and also managing a jihad. Although his radio rants were the purest form of propaganda, aimed directly at the heart of the regime in Pakistan, there was—at least until its military offensive in Swat—a curious reluctance on the part of the government to counter that message.

Fazlullah's words were relayed into a virtual world long since steeped in anti-American hatred. Pakistan's government, even in its tepid support for the United States' counterterrorism efforts, was viewed by Fazlullah and his followers as an accomplice in US crimes against Muslims. Seven years after the Americans had scored an early battlefield victory in Afghanistan and managed to chase Fazlullah and his ilk back (along with bin Laden and his gang) into Pakistan, the long war of attrition had defeated any claims that the Taliban was a spent force. Fazlullah's own militant uprising, weeks after our talk, would make this point in the Swat Valley, just as it had earlier been made in Quetta and in Waziristan. Even when the Pakistani government appeared to have the upper hand militarily and in terms of national public opinion, the survival of the madrassa culture along the border made this multiheaded medusa impossible to eradicate.

One only had to reflect on the idea that that the world's greatest army had now been fighting for years in the world's most impoverished nation, Afghanistan, and that the number of casualties on the US and NATO side had begun to double and triple in number every month. That alone gave jihadist propaganda efforts a boost.

Swat had both the jihad and the propaganda to accompany it like a chamber orchestra. While the age of high technology moves inexorably across Western culture—we've had computers for decades and it is hard for some of us to remember the last time we played a video cassette rather than a DVD—the actual fight in South Asia can sometimes look like the fight portrayed in nineteenth-century lithographs of Afghans fighting the British Raj. The clothes of the defenders of Islam are the same, even though the weapons are new.

The technological advances in propaganda are, however, far greater than those in the weaponry that is used. I recalled the first time I reported on hard-core jihadist activities in 1995 and 1996 in Bosnia. In the town of Zenica, there had been a video store selling short documentaries of jihads from around the world, including those in Chechnya and Afghanistan. Since then, the digital age had revolutionized the spread of such materials like an Internet virus. Al Qaeda's own gristmill of propaganda—which produces a myriad of products, including videos, documentaries, and Internet Q & As with Dr. Ayman al-Zawahiri—now works 24/7. It is parasitic, feeding for its own survival off bloody events taking place elsewhere in the world, often in Afghanistan. Although local struggles are of great interest, there is nothing more dramatic than a taped fight with the American "Rambos."

The battle of images just keeps expanding. As Craig Whitlock observed in a front-page *Washington Post* story in June 2008, "The war against terrorism has evolved into a war of ideas and propaganda, a struggle for hearts and minds fought on television and on the Internet. On those fronts al Qaeda's voice has grown much more powerful in recent years."[15]

In Pakistan, entire communities have gone from having no television a decade ago to having a television in most houses and a DVD player to go with it. That amounts to a revolution in home jihad viewing. For about fifty cents, down at the local DVD shop, which often specializes in religious affairs, Pakistanis can buy DVDs and CDs of the latest fighting just across the border in Afghanistan. Whether or not you are a jihadist, this material still holds dramatic interest and thus commands an expanding audience.

On my trip in Swat, I could find the usual Hollywood and Bollywood thrillers for sale, but the most popular shows in town concerned the international jihad against the American "aggressors." Muslims in league with the Americans were summarily executed— live and in color—whether on a computer screen in one of the myriad Internet cafés or before an open-air audience in a small village. All this represented a major technological leap forward from the cassette music stands Jamal and I had discovered in the same town in 2001.

In the very first DVD shop we entered in Swat on my second visit, I purchased a dozen DVDs and CDs that each included between five and ten fighting scenes. The shop owner, who specialized in religious material, told us that these were his most popular items. They were not just casual depictions of fighting from a distance, of the kind you might see on the news back home about the war in Iraq or Afghanistan. They were close-ups of beheadings. In many of the scenes, the cameraman appeared to have been very much part of the military operation, strategically placed on a corner to see a US jeep being blown to smithereens or an unwitting "spy" having his head pinned to the ground and severed with a long knife. In the videos from Iraq, which were by far the most popular, I saw young men in tennis shoes, looking quite Western, forcing men into the trunks of cars and slamming the trunks shut. When the men refused to comply, they were simply shot in the head as the cameraman carefully recorded their terror. As I watched all this, I was witnessing human fears—just before the moment of death—that spoke volumes about the real nature of war. These "snuff scenes" were as real as they get; far too graphic for the evening news and in many ways far more dramatic.

The footage from Afghanistan was not light fare either. In many scenes, the videographer appeared to be stationed above the action—usually on a mountain watching a US vehicle being blown up and also—surprising to me because of the risk to the videographer—sometimes staying on to watch the rescue choppers arrive. In other cases, a group of Taliban on motorcycles could be seen revving up their engines before speeding off to raid some village. Other shots looked like movie footage of nineteenth-century scenes: turbaned fighters running through an almond grove or diving into a ditch for cover, robes flying helter-skelter.

Probably the most gruesome video that I saw of the Taliban in action in Afghanistan involved the sentencing and beheading of a group of five prisoners. The men in the picture were clearly uneducated peasants, not even senior government functionaries in a village. They would have been killed for the same reason that thousands of Afghans have been slaughtered in the last three decades—being caught in the wrong place at the wrong time. Nevertheless, the method of execution was still gut-wrenching. The men were hog-tied and then held down as their throats were slit and the blood drained in an oddly professional manner, in the way that a trained butcher would take the life of a sheep or goat.

Now, the reader might be asking, how can a reporter sit through hours of this stuff, and what purpose does it serve? My answer is that I'm probably just as sensitive as anyone else, maybe more so since I've seen so much of it "live" and on the battlefield. I admit that I'm still haunted by it all. Sometimes bloodied faces, deep purple with death, distorted with hate and fear, return to me in the twilight. In my most fitful hours of sleep, my well-cultivated correspondent's emotional detachment can't protect me from the vision of a mother and her children slaughtered at close range as they fled through a bramble patch. Each child had been executed almost point-blank.

To understand war, you must examine the actions of men, and to do that—in my view—you must not shy away from their atrocities. On another level, any American who is calling for the United States to abandon Afghanistan outright might want to take the time to watch one of these videos in order to understand the hard, cold, unadulterated truth of the foe we face. I do not recommend that you do it, but it might alter your view of the matter. It is harder to justify not standing with the victims after you have witnessed this kind of killing.

***

The use of the phrase "war on terror" is strange, not only because all war involves some element of terrorism, but also because terror is not particular to any religion or epoch. Large numbers of generals, colonels, majors, cadets, cops, and guerrilla leaders with "good" but undeserved reputations have used terror—whether effectively or ineffectively—throughout history.

Each era brings new atrocities and new terror tactics. In the seventh century CE, Mohammed himself introduced what might be considered terror tactics. They were new to the Arab tribesmen among whom he was working. The slaughter that ensued is perhaps best thought of as a form of psychological operation meant to intensify both zeal and loyalty. It was also intended to weaken the will of his enemies. Over the years, as the Prophet stepped up his raids on caravans in and around Medina, certain atrocities became commonplace.

The battle of Badr, which took place between the cities of Mecca and Medina, was a small fight by any modern measure. Mohammed's new rules of warfare came into sharp focus there. While ancient Arab traditions usually dictated that prisoners were kept alive and held for ransom, history tells us that this was not the case at Badr. Ibn Ishaq wrote: "They hewed them to pieces with their swords until they were dead."[16] Meccan leaders who fell into the hands of Mohammed and his followers were not spared. When the Prophet asked that one Abu Jahal be brought forth, a soldier is reported to have said, "I threw the head before the Apostle and gave thanks to God."[17] When Mohammed heard that one of the few surviving prisoners, al-Nadr, who had ridiculed him in the streets of Mecca, was still living, he ordered the man to be brought before him and beheaded on the spot. Although the sacred Hadiths make it clear that treating prisoners well is "Allah's will" and that the killing of women and children is strictly forbidden, terror, as it would be defined today, was clearly not out of the question in a wartime situation.

I discuss the battle of Badr not to make the point that Mohammed was a "terrorist," as some might suggest I've done, but simply to explain that Mohammed's sanctioning of these actions made them acceptable to his followers as a tactic. Along the same lines, I might have referred to the Continental Army's tarring and feathering of Loyalists in the American Revolution in order to show

how that helped make similar atrocities more acceptable during the course of the Revolution. In all these cases, the actions were taken to instill fear.

Terror (as torture) is sometimes a useful (or utilitarian) tactic, but it becomes effective only when its use and practice are effectively communicated to the world. That is where effective propaganda comes into play. In the videos and DVDs that I obtained along the border, there was an effort to show the war from the jihadist perspective. Religious verse was added to the mix along with "Allahu Akhbars" and machine-gun bursts. I also saw footage taken by Afghan and foreign fighters engaged in fights with the 173rd Airborne Brigade, the group with whom I had spent time in eastern Afghanistan. This did not surprise me because, when I was making the rounds with troops from this brigade, soldiers had referred to the footage.

What was clear to me after the hours and days back in Virginia that I spent reviewing the footage and translating it into English was that the video production abilities of the jihadists in South Asia had improved considerably since 2002 and 2003. Former British diplomat Rory Stewart told me in Kabul: "It is very clear that they are learning from the kind of insurgency that operates in Iraq. They are learning from the success of al Qaeda. They can cut videos and move pictures of the Twin Towers through to black and white stills of the British in the nineteenth century in order to give a generic sense of what they are fighting for."[18]

The real masters of the message in this war were not those who invented the technology but those who managed to use it better than the competition. In a few short years, Islamic militants in South Asia had learned to create their own context, content, and high drama. But one also had to ask where the talent was coming from. It is one thing to chat with a firebrand like Fazlullah and recognize his condemnations of the UN polio vaccinations for what they were, but another thing entirely to take full measure of the sophistication going into the documentation of the war efforts in Afghanistan.

My own right-hand man, Lutfullah Mashal, to whom I owe an

immense debt of gratitude for working with me selflessly in Afghanistan for the better part of two years at the beginning of the conflict, had been paying particularly close attention to this phenomenon. Late in 2001, Mashal penetrated several al Qaeda cells and was taken captive by the Taliban before being reunited with me at the battle of Tora Bora, where he helped me meticulously document bin Laden's getaway. By 2008–2009, he was the governor of Laghman Province in eastern Afghanistan, enduring constant assaults from the Taliban as a public servant.

Fluent in Arabic, Farsi, Pashto, and English, Mashal had earlier served as chief translator for the US ambassador to Afghanistan before going on to receive a master's degree in communications from the University of Kent in the United Kingdom. Upon Mashal's return to Afghanistan, President Karzai had appointed him as director of strategic communications in the nation's National Security Council. With a staff of some two dozen Afghans and working in close coordination with Western embassies, Mashal monitored the communications output of the Taliban and al Qaeda. He wanted to devise ways to counter this propaganda.

He told me in his offices, as we watched several recent jihadist productions, that "Dr. Ayman Zawahiri understands the effectiveness of media and he knows how to use it. It was al Qaeda who instructed the Taliban that everything should be taped, including all attacks on US forces." As-Sahab, al Qaeda's production house, had, in effect, gone into partnership with the Taliban's video production team. The cooperation was seamless and also disturbing for anyone who understands al Qaeda's long-term interests.

"Taliban," like "al Qaeda," is a name broadly applied to a number of like-minded bodies, all with intersecting interests. These interests may meet only on the battlefield, but they may also come together in cyberspace.

One of the more interesting propaganda operations that Mashal and I had come across in recent years was the Tora Bora Military Front (TBMF), which was headed by an Afghan from Jalalabad (fluent in Arabic) whom we had come to know personally at the infamous battle of the same name. The TBMF was headed by Mujahid, the oldest son of Maulvi Younis Khalis, one of the best-known commanders in the Afghan jihad against the Soviet Union. The red-bearded Khalis had been a prominent player at the battle of Tora Bora (he finally died of old age in an "underground location" in 2006), and his son, Mujahid, had been intimately involved with the escape plans made by Osama bin Laden in 2001. During the battle of Tora Bora, the wispy-bearded intellectual had stood with Osama bin Laden in the city of Jalalabad as bin Laden discussed with him his options to fight or flee from the town. A decision had been taken that mid–November 2001 evening to leave and take the fight into the Spin Ghar (White Mountains), where bin Laden had already prepared the terrain for his showdown with the Americans. Mujahid, an Arabic scholar in his own right who would finally make the US military's "wanted list" in Afghanistan nine months after the invasion, had been the manager of the Islamic Studies Institute where bin Laden had held his "last supper" with local supporters in Jalalabad a few days before his departure. Mujahid, loyal to al Qaeda but hoping to see his own city spared a Mogadishu-type battle, had helped to convince bin Laden that his best chance to fight (or flee as it turned out) was to retreat into Tora Bora.[19]

By the summer of 2007, after the death of his father, Mujahid was back in action at the head of the Tora Bora Military Front, a Taliban outfit with foreign fighters that still had intimate and obvious ties to some of the most notorious al Qaeda operatives in the region. The Tora Bora Web site (toorabora.com) featured an exclusive interview with Abu Yahya al-Libi, a senior al Qaeda operative who made a daring and still unexplained escape from the US military's Bagram Detention Center in 2005.[20] Al-Libi had since become a veritable star in the al Qaeda video productions that were distributed around the world. He was on display as a military trainer and as an ideologue. Not surprisingly, Mashal and his fellow intelligence officials now cited al-Libi as a chief propagandist for both al Qaeda and its Taliban affiliates. On the Tora Bora Web site and in dozens of other outlets for his propaganda, al-Libi was alive and well in cyberspace through early 2010. Many believed he was in line to become al Qaeda's number two, should his services be needed. Certainly, anyone who could escape from America's airtight Bagram prison was worth his weight in gold to the terror network—one in which escapes from the world's most powerful military force were held in very high esteem.

For anyone who had followed the war of ideas for the last two decades in South Asia, however, it had become abundantly clear that the major power behind the scenes on the propaganda front was now none other than al Qaeda's senior leader, Dr. Ayman al-Zawahiri, forever the media-savvy chief lieutenant of Osama bin Laden himself. (How much contact al-Zawahiri and bin Laden had on a daily basis was still unclear, but there could be no doubt how much the Egyptian doctor meant to the Saudi chief.) However, unlike the polished and charismatic bin Laden, who speaks in the Arabic equivalent of iambic pentameter, al-Zawahiri is a relentless sophist who both lashes out at his enemies in angry tirades and wraps up terror in a shiny package and a red bow for the Muslim masses. He is to bin Laden what the poet Hassan ibn Thabit was to Mohammed. Hired by the Prophet to spread news of Islam's conquests and Mohammed's own exploits, Ibn Thabit is reported to have stuck his tongue out and commented: "There is no armor which I cannot pierce with this weapon!"[21] Mohammed, like his predecessors, understood publicity. He hired poets and propagandists with sharp tongues to sing his praises and destroy the reputations of his enemies. Similarly, the Taliban had (and has) its own traveling minstrels, a throwback to an earlier age when propaganda was spread by word of mouth. Some of their epic-style poetry even made it into cyberspace—and reached many more eyes and ears—thanks to www.toorabora.com.

In 2008 and 2009, every few days on average, a new video or audio from one of al Qaeda's commanders was being released online by as-Sahab, the terrorist network's production arm. In June 2008, the *Wash-*

ington Post reported that "US and European intelligence officials attribute the al Qaeda propaganda boom in part to the network's ability to establish a secure base in the ungoverned tribal areas of western Pakistan."[22] Furthermore, the report stated that US officials "acknowledge that they missed early opportunities to disrupt al Qaeda's communications operations, whose internal security has since been upgraded to the point where analysts say it is nearly bulletproof."[23]

Meanwhile, Washington was sending out mixed messages on what the propaganda war really meant. If you simply read the dispatches from Washington, you might be tempted to think we were winning the ground war but losing the propaganda war. Unfortunately, the two theaters are so intimately intertwined that they cannot and should not be viewed separately.

As early as 2001, the Bush administration began to insist in public that it was winning the war on terror—this despite CIA insistence that almost every senior al Qaeda figure captured was replaced within weeks. Recruitment for the long war of attrition was always the key to al Qaeda's overall operations and success in the Islamic world. Its own communications efforts were the key to the success of that recruitment—from the bottom to the top of the organization. Even when there was a lull in battlefield attacks, the propaganda machine maintained a steady din or grew even louder in compensation.

Despite all this, most Americans have been left with misleading and confusing impressions of the extent of our progress in combating al Qaeda and its affiliates, particularly the Taliban in Afghanistan and Pakistan. One month we are "winning," according to the "experts," and the next month we are "losing." Take for example a *Washington Post* headline in May 2008: "CIA Cites Big Gains against al Qaeda," quoting CIA Director Michael Hayden, a man who should certainly be able to gauge how well the United States is doing in the war on terror.[24] Hayden, intent upon promoting his agency's success despite the arguable need for a more modest, quiet approach to spycraft, portrayed the terrorist movement as reeling in Iraq and Saudi Arabia and on the defensive in much of the rest of the world—

including the Afghanistan-Pakistan border. A few weeks later the *Post* published what might appear to the unsuspecting US reader to be a strong refutation of Hayden's boasts, headlined, "Al Qaeda's Growing Online Offensive."[25] The article catalogued al Qaeda's amazing, fast-multiplying video and audio releases and the long arm of the organization's propaganda machine.

It is a Western—maybe even peculiarly American—characteristic to want to think of our struggle against al Qaeda as winnable. Nevertheless, an asymmetrical war can't be usefully conflated with American football. If you are a news junkie, you'll also notice that US terrorism analysts (full disclosure: I also appear as such an analyst on occasion and have been caught in the same spin cycle or in the search for telltale signs of success and failure) seem to be looking for a silver lining every time one of the al Qaeda or Taliban releases gets cranked out of the gristmill in Pakistan.

One of the best examples of this type of thinking came in 2002, after the disastrous failure to catch Osama bin Laden at Tora Bora. CIA and Pentagon analysts noticed that bin Laden was seen holding a microphone with his left hand and speculated that he might well have been seriously wounded. In fact, subsequent videotapes suggest, he had no more than a sore shoulder. Nevertheless, such analysis is a metaphor for the deeply held desire to get this war over with—even as it expands its global reach. Much of the analysis—particularly coming from "experts" in the field—is an exercise in intellectual denial and futility.

When Dr. Ayman al-Zawahiri managed to offer himself up for a Q & A session that was spread on the Internet to Islamic followers around the world in late 2007 and well into 2008, West Point's new Combating Terrorism Center (CTC) announced that al-Zawahiri's answers revealed al Qaeda's major institutional shortcomings. Dr. al-Zawahiri's comments were surreptitiously released by the Egyptian doctor's propagandists on the Internet. This suggested that no Western intelligence official knew where in the world this material was being uploaded, subsequently digested by tens of thousands of would-be jihadists around the globe, and then systematically *redistributed* over the same US-built Internet like so many chain letters. According to West Point's CTC, Dr. al-Zawahiri's Q & A revealed (1) Zawahiri's own deep concern "about rising discontent within the Jihadist community"; and (2) new and convincing evidence to suggest that al Qaeda was inventing fictional guerrilla leaders throughout the Muslim world and publicizing them on the Internet (these "leaders" included the so-called emir of al Qaeda in Iraq, whom the CTC deemed to be a fake).[26]

Almost completely lost in the West Point critique and most other news analyses of the al-Zawahiri Q & A, however, was Defense Secretary Robert M. Gates's concern, cogently stated in a November 2007 speech, that "it is just plain embarrassing that al Qaeda is better at communicating its message on the Internet than America."[27] Gates quoted a diplomat (not an American) as asking rhetorically: "How has one man in a cave managed to out communicate the world's greatest communication society?"[28]

The answer to that, of course, has to do with another question: "How has the world's most powerful military failed to capture one man on foot in the mountains in Pakistan?" This question was only partially answered in a report released in late 2009 by the Senate Foreign Relations Committee, which said that "Removing the al Qaeda leader from the battlefield eight years ago would not have eliminated the worldwide extremist threat" but also that "decisions that opened the door for his escape to Pakistan allowed bin Laden to emerge as a potent symbolic figure who continues to attract a steady flow of money and inspire fanatics worldwide."[29]

✸✸✸

As Jamal swerved back and forth through the mountain passes and back down into the desolate and impoverished lowlands, it occurred to me that Pakistan did not appear, on the surface, to have changed a great deal since the fiery, angry days just after 9/11. We were headed back to dearest Auntie and her guesthouse in Peshawar, and Jamal breathed a sigh of relief at every bend in the road. We drove along the banks of a canal and through the heart of Peshawar. I watched a group of boys diving off a tree branch, swinging outward and splashing into the river. Several women in light blue burqas crossed a rickety wooden bridge, and a child bobbed its head in the water as a mother washed her laundry.

Peshawar is an ancient city that sits at the foot of the Hindu Kush near the confluence of three rivers along the ancient Silk Road. For centuries, it has been a place of caravans and military adventures, a place for tribesmen and rebels to exchange tales over cups of green tea. As we passed through the center of the city, we came to the Qisa Khawani Bazaar (the Bazaar of the Storytellers), and I noticed that a group of Pashtun tribesmen had gathered together to discuss the day's news. One of them held up a newspaper headline and beat it with his hand. The themes of their discussions were informed by the renewed fighting in the hinterlands and an unexplained air strike, reportedly from a US drone, on a Taliban position. Several weeks later, fighting would spill over into Islamabad. But in Qisa Khawani the realities would be respun into a narrative as elaborate as an Afghan carpet—a tale of how the jihadists were growing ever stronger despite the high-tech assaults from America. I was reminded that every culture has its own pride and prejudice. George Washington was a mere rebel leader before he ever won a substantial victory against the greatest military force of his day. It was the legend, the embellished stories of his amazing feats, that propelled him along in the bleakest of times.

I was also reminded of the Taliban's singing bards out there in the foothills of the Himalayas, reciting the legends of their own leaders and the exploits of al Qaeda. But their stories did not depend on the caravan routes, lumbering at a camel's pace from one bazaar to the next. It was about time, I thought, to recognize that al Qaeda and its affiliates had raised the art of guerrilla communications to a level never before seen by any insurgent organization in the history of world affairs. That is what has made them so dangerous and difficult to destroy. Maybe, if we were as serious about responding and taking the initiative as I hoped, we could still come out on top.

Chapter 9
AFGHANISTAN'S THIN GRAY LINE

I t was April 2009, and our Chinook landed with two Apache escorts, kicking up a tornado of dust and pebbles. We sprinted down a ramp, leapt into a jeep, and sped up the hill through a row of ten-foot, sand-filled walls. A sign on the inside of the compound read Welcome to Margha Outpost: Duck and Run. A few nights before my arrival in this southeastern province in Afghanistan, Taliban fighters, moving from a staging post inside the ruins of a US-built school, which they had had blown up six months earlier, crept up the blind side of the ridge on which we had just landed to assault the base. On their backs were thin silver "space blankets," which shrouded their body heat and helped them avoid detection by US thermal-imaging cameras. The insurgents crawled to within two hundred meters of the base, darting between the boulders, firing rockets, and diving for cover before slipping away under cover of darkness.[1]

The American fighters, though they had recently lost two colleagues in a rocket attack on the helicopter pad outside the base, displayed surprisingly little fear of their foe. A blond, blue-eyed fighter from Washington State, who would accidentally shoot himself in the face with a grenade launcher a few days later, insisted that Fortress Margha was "Taliban proof." I just nodded. There was enough firepower to destroy the village beneath us. The fortress's three watchtowers housed Mark-19 grenade launchers and 50-caliber machine guns tucked away behind sandbags and had three-inch-thick bullet-proof windows. Indeed, as the soldier walked me through the ten-foot walls and under the heavy wooden beams inside the sand-bagged bunkers, I felt comfortable, protected within a bubble created by the best defenses the world had to offer. The fortress constituted a self-contained world of its own, resupplied by food and fuel slings dropped by Chinooks, each escorted by two Apaches to guard against rocket attacks.

What went on inside the base had little to do with anything on the outside. On one of the nights I was there, the platoon, which had been based in Ft. Richardson, Alaska, watched an old comedy with John Wayne romancing a French beauty and whooping it up during the Alaskan gold rush. On other evenings, the privates and young non-commissioned soldiers polished their electronic guerrilla war–fighting skills in zero-sum games on a flat-screen monitor. In one of these games, the most popular among the American soldiers, a Russian sniper working the ruins of Stalingrad sets out to kill Nazis in a well-defined battle between good and evil, far less murky and confused than the war going on down the hill. I imagined it wouldn't be long before the other side had a jihadist version of the same game.

I was on a three-month tour, in the spring of 2009, of some of the most far-flung outposts in Afghanistan, to spend time with US army officers—colonels, majors, captains, and lieutenants—all of them with a common institutional link: West Point. I had chosen the US Military Academy, which I had visited prior to my arrival in Afghanistan, as a prism through which to view the US military's attempts to turn the tide of history and war in Afghanistan. Since President Barack Obama's designation of Afghanistan and Pakistan as the most crucial front in America's efforts to help pacify the Islamic world and contain the threat from radical Islam, Afghanistan had become the test for a new generation of West Pointers. It was Obama's twenty-first-century war in Asia, the United States' first major war in Asia since its failure in the Vietnam War. I had covered the present war from its outset, and, nearly eight years on, signs of success were hard to find. At the outset, a zero-sum strategy of trying to capture or kill the enemy had produced few positive results in Afghanistan apart from the notable escapes of senior al Qaeda leaders into Pakistan. The American military had spent most of the eight years of the war merely occupying the country but not securing it.

By 2003, any chance of a quick victory or of any semblance of stability in Afghanistan's war of necessity had been sacrificed to the demands of an unrelated war of choice in Iraq. Since 2004, the Taliban had crept back into Afghanistan like a fierce viral infection, infesting the country's forty thousand villages and inflicting more pain and suffering on an already war-weary nation.

I began my journey in March in the northeastern provinces of Nuristan and Kunar, along the undefined thirteen-hundred-mile-long Durand Line, which straddles the Afghanistan-Pakistan border. By May, I had landed in the southeastern province of Paktika in a district, Bermel, which is technically part of Waziristan, a Pashtun tribal area that spans both sides of the border. As elsewhere along the embattled border, in Paktika I gained insight into the Taliban's successful intimidation tactics. The insurgents appeared to be gaining strength in the face of an overly cautious US military posture along the mile-high, dusty no-man's-land not far from the redoubt where bin Laden had declared war on America in 1998.

Paktika Province was bad and getting worse. I suited up in body armor for several foot patrols with 1st Lt. Chip Heidt, who had finished West Point with the class of 2007. Heidt, who hailed from an old newspaper family in Cincinnati, Ohio, was one of America's brightest young officers on the front. He had studied engineering at

West Point but had still embraced sections of the army's *Counter-insurgency Manual* as guideposts for his work in the field.

The twenty-four-year-old was noticeably nervous as we stepped out into the medieval world of Waziri *qalats* (or fortress-like-homes), with their twenty-foot walls and watchtowers intended as gun emplacements. Heidt already knew a bit about the tribe he was dealing with: the Waziris were representatives of the *nang* Pashtun, a fiercely independent tribal group that embraced austerity and egalitarianism. We wound our way on foot toward the town of Bermel, which was spread out along a parched river valley dotted with mud dikes and a maze of adobe homes. It was midday when we passed a pack of stray dogs that had recently attacked one of Heidt's men.

We approached a group of men in dark, baggy clothing and woolen berets standing against a wall. One of them was a former Afghan police officer who had fled Taliban threats and beatings in the town of Margha several weeks earlier. "What will the sign between us be when the Taliban attacks us here?" he asked the young American platoon leader. His tone was pleading, but Heidt did not reply.

He was disturbed at what he heard next. The former policeman said that a friend had gone missing and that his body had been discovered, his head severed, on a nearby mountaintop. When an American soldier questioned whether the story was correct, an interpreter with the patrol sounded insulted. He shot back that the incident was "well known" to Afghans in the area. We soon learned about a spate of recent murders carried out by Taliban fighters, operating within eyesight of Fort Richardson's 509 Geronimo Brigade based in the Bermel district. The most recent killing had involved a close friend of two radio announcers who had worked for the US military–funded Radio Bermel. A seventeen-year-old music salesman, Fareedullah Niazman, who had sent poems and music recordings to the US-financed radio station, had been gunned down only a stone's throw from where we were walking. In the young man's last letter, which was never read on the air, he foreshadowed his own death in a poem written to his erstwhile lover.

"My lover, you were not like this before: These days you have the army of my enemies with you," he wrote, adding in the next line, "As I am separated from you now, the townspeople will not let me stay." I wondered if this wasn't a Shakespearean drama obscured by cultural differences.

The Afghan announcers said that Taliban fighters had pulled Fareedullah aside in late March, two weeks before his death, and warned him to stop selling music. They slapped him across the face, stamped on his disks, and cursed him as "an American lackey." Two weeks later, Taliban soldiers went to the young man's house and pulled him from the arms of his mother before executing him.

Such violence looked calculated to make the local population sever all ties to the US and NATO forces. A senior NATO intelligence officer in the area subsequently confided in me that Afghans "are slaughtered every day for working with us and their government, even if they are only related to someone who is simply trying to feed [his] family." He said he had personally known Afghans whom the Taliban had murdered. The intelligence officer asked that he remain anonymous because of the secret nature of his contacts with Afghan civilians. "They are unprotected and slowly slaughtered for even the mere presumption of US support," he added, bemoaning the increasing loss of large swaths of the countryside to insurgent aggression.

Evidence that the Taliban had the upper hand in Paktika Province was stark and plentiful. On patrol near the market where Fareedullah had sold his music disks, members of our patrol spoke with a forty-five-year-old Afghan midwife, who had been abducted by the Taliban for helping Afghan soldiers. Although after she had been punished she had returned to her home, she now asked the US soldiers with whom I was on patrol not to come around her clinic again. She ran a finger across her throat, indicating what would be her fate if the Taliban got wind of any American assistance to her clinic. "Please help me," she said. "But don't bring me anything yourself—send it at night through someone else." She said that the

Taliban had arrested her and forced her to march for two weeks in the mountains as punishment for providing a bandage to a wounded Afghan soldier. A member of our patrol who was a qualified brain surgeon from Los Angeles, California, emptied his pockets and backpack, as our escorts crouched in an alleyway and mortars rang out in the distance. We marched on foot, slinking like cats on the prowl down a back alley to our protected base.[2]

Lieutenant Heidt, with whom I had several long chats, was dismayed at the problems his unit was facing in Bermel. He told me that he felt like a stranger to the Afghans he met. "We operate under heavy force protection restrictions," he said. "That is just one of our conundrums." In his pants pocket, he kept two white flash cards containing US Centcom Commander General Petraeus's "paradoxes of counterinsurgency." The first read: "Sometimes, the more you protect your force, the less secure you may be." Heidt said this made sense to him because when an army becomes overly defensive it cedes the initiative to the opponent.

The second paradox was more problematic: "The more successful the counterinsurgency is, the less force can be used and the more risk must be accepted." In other words, the assumption of greater risk and the use of less firepower is a necessity if a campaign with Afghan security partners is to win the trust of the local population. If an army is too quick to shoot and is overly cautious about spilling its own blood, the future may inadvertently be mortgaged to pay for the present. You might shrug off an enemy propaganda victory over more dead Americans, but you will lose the long-term positive impact of having US forces and their Afghan counterparts on the move together, making friends.

Heidt was troubled for a good reason. The main base at Bermel and several smaller bases, like Margha to the north, where I had landed, appeared to dominate the nearby terrain. In truth and for all intents and purposes, the bases were fortresses defending no one except the American soldiers living inside them. By almost any measure of General David Petraeus's doctrine that "ultimate success in counterinsurgency is gained by protecting the populace, not the counterinsurgency force," these outposts were inadequate outcroppings in the heart of Taliban country. They assumed the risk that the doctrine requires, but they did not protect the local population.

✴✴✴

As any good soldier knows, book learning does not always translate well to the battlefield.

On the "Plain" at West Point, where I had gone earlier to study the military's new thinking, cadets gathered before lunch each day at the foot of an imposing statue of George Washington—America's great rebel leader, on horseback, his right arm extended toward the Hudson River. The United States, born of an uprising against the world's greatest military power, has cultivated an officer corps capable of fighting a conventional war almost anywhere on the planet. Its best warriors are typified by the stalwart generals who have defeated foreign armies with overwhelming firepower and dogged determination. A bronze statue of Gen. George S. Patton, holding binoculars and in his full "battle rattle," stands as a monument to victory on the lawn at West Point. The general's observation that "war is very simple, direct, and ruthless" and that "it takes a simple, direct, and ruthless man to wage war," still resonates within the austere hallways of an institution that opened its doors in 1807.

Nevertheless, when I arrived on the grounds of the US Military Academy in early 2008, at the dawn of a new era, the cold science of making war was already ceding ground to the arguably more creative science of making peace. When I sat in on a series of classes, I was impressed at the nimbleness of the minds at West Point, once known best for turning out expert warriors and engineers. To win the war or the peace, I was told by cadets and instructors, the United States. would not only have to outmaneuver its foe, but it would also have to outsmart him. Leading the charge was Major Rebecca Patterson, an army mom bent on shaking up the US military's proud image of itself. Patterson, who regularly takes her students to the hard-scrabble inner cities of America in order for them to experience different cultures firsthand, is an instructor in the best Aristotelian sense. I caught her in her small office entertaining a pair of students with a rhetorical question: "What is the incentive to prepare for this new kind of war?" She was talking about breaking out of a conventional view of war and taking up the prospect of US soldiers becoming peacemakers. It was a nuanced idea and upsetting to quite a few at the academy.

Nevertheless, West Point, known for turning out great warriors, is now focused, thanks to Patterson and a slew of forward-looking young officers, on striking a balance between the warrior and the diplomat. Although there is still a great deal of outright patriotism and idealism within the hallowed halls of West Point, cadets are also learning to turn a critical eye on American chauvinism, as a conversation with two of the major's protégés revealed.

"When you look at the US Army from an historical point of view, we often do not fare as well as we should in terms of fostering democracy and openness," said Kyle Wolfley, an Ohioan in his senior year.[3] "Look at Vietnam and Iraq in particular. I think we need to learn more from our mistakes."

Both Wolfley, who told me that "the right approach is not entirely [diplomacy] and not entirely military," and another of Patterson's students, New Jersey Cadet Kelly Ashton, understood that the new wars America would face required a delicate mix of force and communication. Ashton told me she had been impressed by a discussion she had had with fellow students about a US military video of an Apache helicopter firing Hellfire missiles into a mud-brick village. "I think the Afghans must think we are cheating at war by using this crazy technology," she commented. Even before she entered the war zone, she was thinking about the appropriate application of force. Wolfley agreed, stating, "I think that under the new administration of President Obama, we'll see more elements of soft power. We have to start walking a lot more softly with our big stick."

Patterson told me that she thought of her course, "Winning the Peace," as a course in the nonshooting aspects of war and as a study in "strategic nonviolence." (I wondered if President Barack Obama would dare repeat that phrase given the hawkish reply it would likely provoke from congressional Republicans.) Patterson believed her teaching was having an impact, acknowledging that "You still hear in policy circles that the army does not like to do some of these things, but this is not the narrative that has developed here at West Point."

Over a period of two weeks, I sat in on several classes at West Point. I listened to a debate on how to win the battle of ideas against al Qaeda's propaganda machine, and I sat in on a know-your-foe discussion that examined why insurgents and terrorists target the United States. If there was a major gap in the new emphasis on counterinsurgency, however, it involved the cultural and historical nuances of the Afghan conflict, a war that had been neglected in favor of the fight in Iraq. Military arts and sciences at the academy included such mundane concepts as "targets, techniques, and procedure" but little instruction on how to deal with a warring culture or such arcane but necessary information as the strange *pakhtunwali* customs of the Pashtun tribesmen who live along the border between Afghanistan and Pakistan.

Instruction at West Point was still grounded, as is the long-standing tradition, in lessons taught by officers returning from battlefronts. Major Chris Danbeck, who teaches a class in Middle Eastern politics, told me that far more needs to be done to break through the "old-school" warrior mentality at West Point and stress the delicate diplomacy required in the field. By his own admission, the army still had not devised an adequate way to reward soldiers who accomplished great humanitarian deeds, but one of the greatest lessons of the last seven years had been in restraint. Danbeck, an Iraq war veteran, added that "guys who put their game face on will not do well in the Afghan context: You will still have the 'ugly American.'" The young officer, who would continue his work as an academic, served as a reminder that the US military—like the nation at large—still has plenty of innovative and critical thinkers in its midst.

The struggle in Afghanistan, however, required more than new training. It also required the US military to give up its favorite weapons, as it had never managed to do in Vietnam. Senior American commanders in Afghanistan, whom I would speak to at length, told me that they were aware of a disconnect—the overabundance of big bases and the overreliance on air power. Like cigarette smokers who deny the addictive quality of nicotine, however, they said they could quit anytime but did not want to.

With regard to the overreliance on air power, Afghanistan, particularly during the Bush years, was like Vietnam in several respects. Prescient observations about that war—while unheeded in the end—came early. On June 6, 1962, President John F. Kennedy descended on the manicured lawn at West Point to warn a new class of West Point cadets that they would have to embrace a "new and different kind of military training." His speech was about Southeast Asia, but he might just as well have been describing South Asia in the twenty-first century. He warned cadets that the fight would be "new in its intensity, ancient in its origin." It would be war "by ambush instead of by combat, by infiltration instead of by aggression, seeking victory by eroding and exhausting the enemy instead of engaging him."[4] Kennedy foresaw a new kind of American soldier: a warrior, a diplomat, and a nation builder. For several years, West Point's Commandant General Richard Stilwell encouraged the new approach. Generals wrote academic papers and pontificated on the subject in the halls of power. Yet as Rick Atkinson documented in *The Long Gray Line*, a tale of the West Point class of 1966, the US military never made the transition. It suffered from institutional inertia. Try as it might, it could not reinvent itself. By the end of the 1960s, the US Army's scorched-earth effort to dominate the jungles of Southeast Asia with overwhelming firepower had left even its best soldiers and nation builders downhearted.[5]

Not coincidentally, Gen. David Petraeus, West Point class of

1974, was an avid student of the Vietnam War. He wrote a doctoral thesis at Princeton on the Vietnam War and its influence on the US military's thinking about the use of force. The thesis was Petraeus's first effort to understand the inherent dilemmas involved in fighting guerrillas with a conventional army. He quoted one officer as saying: "I submit that the US Army does not have the mind-set for combat operations where the key terrain is the mind, not the high ground."[6]

In Afghanistan, the US forces were still struggling to develop this mind-set, but—as I found out before my journey to the heart of the matter—there were influential players at West Point who still believed strongly that the world's most powerful military shouldn't even bother delving into the terrain of the mind. I had a sobering conversation with an old friend from the Afghan battlefields, Col. Bryan Hilferty, director of communications at West Point. He put it this way: "Nation building and all that kind of thing is the work of the State Department and other agencies. That is not our fight. We are supposed to kill people." That sounded antiquated, but the view—coming from the institution's chief spokesperson—was not to be taken lightly. If that was the case, it dawned on me, then our new commander in chief was working at cross purposes because he had hired the best-known practitioners of counterinsurgency in the army to turn the tables on the Taliban.

What Major Patterson and Major Danbeck, among others, were asking for was essentially a melding of the Peace Corps with the Marine Corps. Many in the US military—macho types who abhorred the idea of a schizophrenic personality—didn't think the two were compatible. Counterinsurgency carried out with the right mix of diplomacy and force is a hard sell, particularly on the battlefield when bullets start to fly. For victory against an insurgency, however, it is essential. The default strategy, using overwhelming firepower and large bases, is a proven nonstarter. It had not worked in Vietnam and would not work in Afghanistan.

✳✳✳

Since its failure to capture Osama bin Laden at Tora Bora in November and December 2001, the US military has built a gargantuan base in eastern Afghanistan at Jalalabad airfield, on the spot where bin Laden landed with family members and aides on his return from Sudan in 1996. In one sense, the base is a less-than-subtle monument to our risk-averse, high-tech-centric approach to the fight. Housed and lubricated at "J-bad" are technological advances that define the US Army's superior firepower and mobility. Apaches dart through the sky, and smaller Kiowas buzz along a ridge of snow-capped peaks on their way back from the Hindu Kush. Aerial drones, with coned noses but no cockpits, on their way to and from Pakistan's tribal areas, circle, land, and take off at the flick of the wrist of a "pilot" in Nevada. All parties to the conflict are making adjustments. Al Qaeda's tried-and-true tactics of improvised explosives and suicide bombings have migrated en masse from Iraq to Afghanistan, and the US military has heightened its own force protection by deploying thousands of MRAPs, or mine-resistant armored personnel carriers: 18-ton beige bubbles of bullet-proof glass and steel with portholes and an explosives-detecting tube that resembles a periscope. One reason why US combat casualties in Afghanistan remain low in comparison to the casualties in the early years of the war in Iraq is that most US soldiers are enveloped behind sand and steel on large bases where they eat lobster tails or Alaskan crab legs in the mess or order Burger King Whoppers and gourmet drinks from the Green Bean. The US military occupies a twenty-first-century bubble in Afghanistan, a country still subsisting in the nineteenth century. American soldiers do not interact with Afghan civilians nearly as often as one would expect them to. In many areas of the country, on most days, even at some of the remotest and most embattled bases, there is no obvious conflict going on outside the wire, apart from the circulation of the Taliban's standard leaflets warning the population not to cooperate with the Americans, punctuated by the occasional beheading to make good on these threats.

Nevertheless, despite a continued overreliance on heavy airpower, a new US counterinsurgency strategy began to be introduced in early 2009 and was expanded in the summer of the same year. It is the brainchild of a West Pointer, General David Petraeus. His implementer in chief as Obama came on board was another classmate, General Stanley McChrystal, a "black operations" expert with extensive experience in Iraq. When it was begun, the new strategy put young US platoon leaders, often also West Pointers, on patrol in the remotest corners of the country. Later, in several regions where the strategy did not produce the desired results, many of these small bases would be shut down.

When I arrived at Lt. Jake Kerr's fortress in Dangam, a tattered Afghan flag fluttered over stone walls, supported by two broken branches lashed together with twine. In the cold dawn, a brown and black, striped sheepdog emerged from a hole in the mud wall of a six-man Afghan police barracks to forage for her pups. The soldiers of "Combat Platoon" curled up, snored, but did not awaken, wrapped in their gray sleeping bags. In the distance were barely visible footprints in a snowy saddle on the tree line, where a column of insurgents, their guns carefully hidden in long robes, had been photographed entering Afghanistan from Pakistan a week earlier. As the sun lit the terraced fields below, an Afghan girl in a green headscarf and flowing purple trousers ventured up the hill with a black lamb on a leash. Further below her, near a stream formed by melting snow, two dozen Afghan men, their small sons by their sides, had already finished their morning tea and begun cracking rocks with sledgehammers. They were being paid a good wage by Lieutenant Kerr to build a road to the new outpost.

Stirring beneath a stone wall, on the rocky hill five hundred feet above the distant streambed, was Kerr, West Point class of 2007. He was leading what Colonel Philip Torrence of the army's Center for Lessons Learned, in Kansas, described to me as the "pilot project" of the 10th Mountain Division's 1-32 Brigade: a mobile platoon, embedded with Afghans, aimed at building a firewall against al

Qaeda and the Taliban. The former cadet rose and rubbed the sleep from his eyes. Tattooed across his bulky right forearm was his family's crest, set against a backdrop of a red mountain range.[7]

For Kerr, from Lake Placid, New York, his choice of a soldier's life was "a personal thing." Every man in his family has served in the armed forces, "as far back as we can remember," he told me. His family members served in the American forces in World War II and before that with the Scottish Highlanders' Black Watch Regiment battling the Mahdi's army in Sudan. As his soldiers rolled out of bed, downed their coffee, and headed back to filling sandbags and cleaning their M-16s, Kerr took me on a tour of his strategic perch in the Dangam District of Kunar Province, north of the Khyber Pass. His rustic fort sat at the crossroads of insurgent transit lines into Afghanistan. In the summer of 2008, nearly two hundred insurgents had stormed the district center below the fort and breached the barbed wire surrounding the district center by tossing woolen blankets over the top and leaping over. The attackers had been driven off, but not before taking a dreadful toll. Combat Platoon's fortress also sat opposite Pakistan's Bajaur District, where a US military air strike had just missed al Qaeda's number two, Dr. Ayman al-Zawahiri, in January 2006. Since then a plethora of insurgent groupings in Pakistan and Afghanistan had grown bolder and stronger, finding their own funding in the Gulf states but also relying on the patronage of al Qaeda's top leadership. Kerr's mission, as his superiors explained it to him, was to engage in counterinsurgency, and with the help of the Afghan security forces with whom he lived, win over the population and block the so-called rat lines that were feeding an expanding insurgency inside Afghanistan.

For several weeks, I followed Kerr as he built his castle and engaged with Afghans. On at least two occasions while we were on patrol, Kerr made kind and random gestures—delivering a pair of crutches to an Afghan war victim and ordering an artificial larynx through his brigade headquarters for a tribal elder who was unable to speak. While he often had to show a stern determination to the men in his platoon, the twenty-four-year-old was chivalrous and charming. He constantly apologized for not being able to do more—even when he was doing a lot.

Kerr would sit cross-legged on a mat with two dozen wizened Afghan elders and introduce small-scale road and irrigation projects. The old men complained that money from past projects had been siphoned off by government officials, but Kerr reassured them that things would be different this time. He gave the projects directly to individual tribal leaders to implement.

I asked him what he thought victory meant for Americans within the Afghan context. "Victory," he repeated. "That is victory for them, which is in a sense victory for us. The people will drive your mission, they will give you the intelligence you need, and they will help you fight. You know, 'the enemy's enemy is my friend' type of deal." Kerr was staring into a thirty-year abyss of war and, like the American optimist he was, discovering something good. You wanted to believe he was on to something, but the enemy—as even US commanders always said—"also had a vote."

Kerr told me he had "majored in counterinsurgency" at West Point. What this really meant was that he had been forced to craft his own set of studies out of the courses offered as part of the academy's military arts and sciences major. In his last two years, he said, all his instructors had been "ex–special forces, infantry, and rangers. That is when it became fun." Kerr had hardly slept. He read up on Vietnam, on Malaya. He made extensive charts detailing the web of relationships between the Taliban, Jalaluddin Haqqani, Gulbuddin Hekmatyar, and known al Qaeda henchmen.

The young lieutenant was all about the army's new counter-insurgency, but his Combat Platoon, was, nevertheless still a hard-core infantry unit in an army that is still a social beast, one in which peer pressure and the passions of youth exert excessive influence at all levels. Many in Kerr's platoon itched for a fight and didn't mind saying so.

I wondered if Kerr understood the push and pull within his own personality. On the one hand, his superiors wanted him to be an expert warrior, but on the other, Afghanistan demanded restraint and nuance. The young lieutenant had been molded in an American institution that has for two centuries been obsessed with turning out warriors, not soldier-diplomats. On the ground in Afghanistan, the message was the same. Flitting from outpost to outpost along the Durand Line while I was there, the US Army's favorite country singer, Toby Keith, on his own combat tour, compliments of our superior airpower, serenaded the US soldiers with lines from a song entitled "The Angry American." The message was direct and to the point: Invade my country and the wrath of America will come down upon you, crashing down on you with a "rocket's red glare." I stood with a crowd of several thousand soldiers, high only on tobacco juice and adrenaline, as they sang along.[8]

This was only a fragment of the broader mind-set. Indeed, the essence of what it means to be an American soldier for a West Point officer is molded not by Toby Keith but rather by heroic images, baptized by fire and reading Washington, MacArthur, and Patton.

These images of victors in a world of good and evil present a dilemma for a counterinsurgency strategy that relies as much on soft power and persuasion as it does on armed coercion. Soldiering is still very much about fighting wars. In an intelligence briefing just before an air assault on a village that straddled the border—one that Kerr and his commanders had planned and replanned for weeks—Kerr stood before his superiors (both of them fellow West Pointers) and said he expected an all-out fight when he descended on the village of Loya Gorigah. "The enemy will be a caged dog, and a caged dog will always fight you first," he told them, as a planning officer flipped through a presentation in a wooden hut. In the two weeks that preceded the air operation, the young lieutenant had built it up in his own mind as a sure-fire trap for the enemy. It would be the payoff for the long hours of work in foot patrolling and tea drinking that he and his soldiers had put into the district.

The evening before the assault, the soldiers in Kerr's platoon were glued to a showing of *Black Hawk Down*, a splendid war movie but one with a searing message: kill or be killed.

In the wee hours of the morning, I was on board as army Chinook helicopters whipped up a fury on a desolate peak in Kunar Province. The American soldiers, in war paint and with camouflage netting over their helmets, scrambled down the rear ramp in the predawn light. Kerr and his men, with me tagging along for the story, plunged into the scrub on a mission "to uncover hidden weapons and arrest members of a bomb-making team" and other insurgents who had been terrorizing local villages. Two platoons from Combat Company of the 10th Mountain Division's 1-32 Brigade, with a platoon of Afghan soldiers, crawled through the matted grass to take up their positions above a string of Afghan hamlets lying beneath a snow-capped peak in the foothills of the Hindu Kush. It was a spectacular scene, but the firepower and expenditure were far in excess of what was actually needed. Kerr was devastated that the assault, planned for the hours of darkness, had gone ahead in the morning light, making it abundantly clear that the US military was on its way. "The Afghans saw us coming down the mountain from the second we were here," Kerr told me as we descended the hill. "Anyone who was going to run would have run and hidden themselves before we knew it."

The multimillion-dollar attack, which also included Apaches and a female bomber in an F-15 with a lilting voice reassuring her boys below, soon turned into a cordial tea-sipping session with Afghan elders.

Despite his initial dismay, the circus of the air assault, a show of overwhelming American air and fire superiority, put Kerr's best qualities on display. He made a calculated last-minute decision not to root through Afghan homes because the Afghan elders he met had overwhelmed him with bear hugs and Pashtun hospitality, or *pakhtunwali*. As the assault unfolded, he told me, "I understand their [the villagers'] predicament. They get the Taliban coming over the border and threatening and shooting at them." William McGinnis, a combat historian with the Center for Military History, who interviewed Kerr in the wake of the assault, was impressed with his restraint: "The US infantry mind-set is to go out and attack the enemy," he said. "Well, you can't do that here. Kerr thinks outside the box in terms of community development."[9]

Unfortunately, peacemaking and economic development did not win the day. The US Army had not been prepared for the contingency of hospitality, and Kerr's commander informed him that he could not offer even a small-scale irrigation project. The valley was too remote and no one could ever oversee the project, he was told. In truth, a hastily planned attack featuring excessive firepower had overshadowed good diplomacy.[10]

***

Kerr's own first test under fire came on a bright morning when Kunar Province's terraced wheatfields rippled gently in the wind under crisp azure skies. Smiling villagers rushed out to watch a column of three dozen Afghan and American soldiers in big boots negotiating their hand-packed mud irrigation dikes. Major Andy Knight, class of 1999, was leading our patrol straight up a known rat line along the "Dry River," a valley that twisted and turned through Kunar Province in the direction of the Korengal Valley, a notorious insurgent redoubt. Although the patrol had been billed as a "key leader engagement" (KLE), Kerr confided to me the night before that he expected trouble. A KLE is a part of the new counterinsurgency strategy in that it targets influential village elders who hold sway in the community and tries to persuade them that development and peacemaking are the focus on the US mission in Afghanistan. But the more I spoke with Kerr and Knight about the impending engagement, the more it sounded like a classic search-and-destroy mission. For the sake of secrecy, Knight didn't send in Afghan allies to map the terrain or talk to villagers in advance.[11]

Afghan villagers waved to our party, and Knight said hello in the Pashtun language. Knight and Sam Meyer, a civilian member of the

Pentagon's anthropological-minded Human Terrain Team, cradled M-16s and crossed their right hands over their armor—an Afghan gesture meant to acknowledge the respected elders on whose paths they walked. Five hours before our arrival in the valley, Kerr (under Knight's orders since the valley was outside his own area of operations) had clandestinely scaled the rocky cliffs above us to the south. At the top of the cliff, Kerr had his fighters carefully mark the GPS coordinates of several dug-in insurgent positions littered with food wrappers.

As we set out to walk the dikes, Kerr's men arrived at designated overwatch positions on a ridge with two M-240 medium machine guns. His soldiers on the main Kunar river valley road turned on a US military scanner to listen to insurgent voice communications, but Kerr's translators did not need the electronic gear to pick up the shouts of men in the smaller valley where we were walking. They yelled, an oral tag team, from man to man: "The Americans are coming! The Americans are coming!" They were locked and loaded.

Within minutes, three men, one in a white shalwar kamis, another in a black one, and a third in a brown shawl and gray pants, sprinted toward us down the valley, machine guns in hand. Kerr ordered his gunners to open fire. Two of the Afghans were hit. All of them dived for cover amid the boulders in the streambed, scrambling on the rocks below. Meanwhile, Afghan soldiers in our party accidentally opened up on Kerr's overwatch team. Confused by the US mission's operational secrecy, the Afghans falsely believed they were under attack from above. The near-fatal error spoke volumes about a twenty-first-century army's inability to trust a local force, despite its official role as a mentor.

I dived behind an interpreter into a hedgerow as the chatter of guns echoed across the valley floor. Meyer, the human terrain expert, splashed past us. He halted, stooped, and spoke to no one in particular: "I think I can conclude these people don't like us very much." A soldier rallied the troops: "Ready to go blast these mother fuckers?"

Kerr had dialed in the Apaches within thirty seconds of the first shot. He fired tracer bullets at the man in a brown shawl, who was still shooting back. A middle-aged man, a baby cradled in his arms, strolled up the valley toward the gunfire, and an Afghan woman in a green shawl emerged from a house to launch a tirade at Knight as we passed. This embarrassed the Afghans at our side. An Afghan soldier sneered and pointed his weapon at her, shooing her back inside. We sheltered behind a wooden shack as an Apache crested a ridge, firing Hellfire missiles into the streambed, "shh-thraap, shh-thraap," and hurling debris helter-skelter. The insurgents, now just beyond Kerr's vantage point, disappeared.

Knight rested against a boulder to direct the operation, asking his lieutenant if there was a map of the villages in the valley. "No, sir," came the reply. "For all intents and purposes, they do not exist." Knight chuckled at the overearnest reply. A group of some twenty women and children shuffled out onto a roof across the valley, where they now squatted, forced there at gunpoint by an Afghan search team.

Enemy radio chatter, passed through Kerr, indicated that the helicopter strikes were hitting the ground just in front of a house in a village set on a ridge. "This is a game of hot and cold, and we are getting hotter," said Kerr over the radio. "We can own this valley, sir!" he shouted to his commander. Knight ordered two Humvees with a 50-caliber machine gun and a Mark-19 grenade launcher to advance toward us to provide more cover. Kiowas and Apaches whirled above in figure eights and peeled off to refuel.

In the riverbed, a platoon-sized search party set out on foot to investigate the village. Within fifteen minutes, a radio call from a young American came crackling through to Knight: "This is a virtual ghost town, sir!"

Two Afghan boys carrying burlap bags approached us across the rocks we had crossed earlier. "Have they seen any bad men in the valley—any strangers?" asked Knight through an interpreter. One of the boys shrugged. "Our parents told us to bring onion seeds so we have done so," said the other, reaching into his bag, smiling and offering an onion sprout.

But the game of hide and seek had not yet ended. We turned to march back out of the valley. Kerr was still getting mixed signals. Intercepts indicated that the insurgents were counting his squad of twelve men. They vowed to hit his men when they broke patrol and regrouped, becoming a more concentrated target for rockets. Kerr's platoon hiked down the ridge toward the dirt road, which snaked in switchbacks above the torrential Kunar River. Expecting to be hit, the soldiers dispersed. Finally back at their jeeps, they dared to reach for a drink of water.

An insurgent commander ordered; "Shoot, shoot!" The radio intercept gave Kerr and his men about ten seconds to lurch for cover. Heavy machine-gun fire and grenades hammered the ground above the river. One of Kerr's fighters fell to the ground, a bullet slicing through his groin. Another cringed in a ditch in a fetal position, still managing to fire back. Kerr slipped behind an armored jeep, grabbed his machine gun, and then realized he had the coup de grâce in his shirt pocket. As more rockets slammed into the road, he ripped out the GPS coordinates of the insurgent positions that his men had scribbled down that morning. From six miles away at their base in Asmar, the members of a 10th Mountain artillery team unleashed a torrent from their 105 mm howitzers. The pine forest exploded. Rocks rained down the mountainside. Kerr's men were exhausted; the battle was over.

✳✳✳

Had it not been for the radio intercepts, Kerr's first fight might well have ended differently. Instead, the Combat Platoon soldiers chalked up their first win and commendations for valor. It was a victory for the warriors but a loss for the diplomats. Afterward, Kerr's major said wryly that the three men running out with AK-47s were "not in a good posture to meet us." Touché. The Afghans in the valley probably thought it odd to see so many modern gladiators approaching them in full metal jackets, weapons in hand, just for an informal chat, of which they had heard nothing in advance.

As David Kilcullen points out in his analytical look at America's foe, *The Accidental Guerrilla*, "People fight us not because they hate the West and seek our overthrow but because we have invaded their space to deal with a small extremist element that has manipulated and exploited local grievances to gain power."[12] Knight had informed me that he was winning in his area of operations because "an enemy leader who hides in caves and can't show his face becomes irrelevant." Nevertheless, while the phantom-like insurgents in the Dry River that day had not lingered long on the battlefield, they had certainly proven themselves relevant. The insurgents had—for hours—remained formless, hidden, observing the world's greatest military toss thunderbolts into the impregnable Afghan rock.

How did the Taliban disappear and reappear with such apparent ease? The Taliban, which consists of half a dozen insurgent groups fighting a common "infidel" enemy, is not a foreign army in Afghanistan. Whereas in 1996, the Taliban fighters rose to power amid the chaos of Afghanistan's long-running civil war by providing security amid chaos, today the group seeks to undermine the Afghan government, sow chaos, and dodge attacks. After regrouping alongside al Qaeda elements in Pakistan between 2001 and 2004, the Taliban fighters organized hit-and-run attacks out of Afghan villages and recruited more local fighters to bolster their ranks. Rather than seizing the government offices in district centers, which would have become easy targets for US assault teams, they have simply embedded themselves further with the local Pashtun population.

Although it was sometimes hard for the Western mind to detect, the Taliban remained engaged from village to village, building alliances with the help of embedded al Qaeda military and media trainers. In this way, insurgents dispersed cells, rallied believers, and eliminated the opposition. With US and NATO forces firmly in control of the skies—with unmanned drones that can read the colored threads of a turban—the Taliban had pragmatically seized the local population as their shield. (This is technically a war crime, but the mullahs guiding the movement do not concern themselves with the incomprehensible ideas found in the Geneva Conventions.) Nevertheless, when US and NATO forces unintentionally inflicted civilian casualties or rounded up the wrong suspects, the insurgents seized the opportunity to enhance their own recruiting pool.

Although no civilians had been killed on Kerr's foray into the Dry River, the residents were angry and dismayed. Although the Americans had come with all their firepower in search of an enemy, Afghans believed, from all the visible signs, that Major Knight and Lieutenant Kerr had come spoiling for a fight. Despite the stated US intention to engage with their leaders, in this case the residents had heard no talk of development or offers of security. Some had joined the insurgents; others would now weigh the possibility.

✳✳✳

Calling in the Apaches every time an insurgent pops his head up achieves little. If we object to insurgents running around in mud-walled compounds, mingling with civilians, the Afghans in these same villages object—with good reason—to our overreliance on air power. In effect, it's comparable to an exterminator employing grenades to deal with a plague of rats. Afghanistan is in Asia, and in Asia perceptions often take precedence over everything else. At the now infamous battle of Tora Bora, I was approached by a young man who mocked me because he knew I was an American. "You Americans want to fly around in your baby suits and drop bombs from ten thousand feet!" he shouted, as B-52s hammered the mountaintops. As it was in 2001 and still was in 2009, fighting from the skies has been the epitome of fighting a twenty-first-century war in a country that still subsists in the nineteenth century. It is bad public relations.

In order to oust the Taliban from their village redoubts in Afghanistan, the US military will have to adjust its sights. A proper counterinsurgency campaign will be a long, problematic affair, characterized by developmental outreach, astute diplomacy, and mobile infantry units remaining for extended periods of time in villages. Given the state of affairs in Afghanistan today as well as the Taliban's major advances since 2004, a successful campaign will take far longer than the twelve to eighteen months that Afghanistan's top general Stanley McChrystal outlined in 2009 for a "turnaround."

Indeed, although the public remains uninformed about what is needed to win the peace in Afghanistan, there will need to be more troops applied to the task at hand and more risk to the lives of these American fighting men and women. From my experience with young American platoon leaders fresh out of West Point, this assumption is clearly understood, albeit not always put into practice due to institutional barriers.

In my effort to understand the changes taking place at West Point and on the ground in Afghanistan, I interviewed senior American commanders in Afghanistan. These men were graduates from an era in which the Cold War was at its height and Vietnam was a subject that instructors spoke of incessantly to their young cadets. "We believed that the way to defeat the enemy was to defeat the enemy," said Gen. James C. McConville, whose home town of Quincy is not far from Cambridge, Massachusetts, where he studied as a Harvard Security Fellow before taking the job as the general in charge of supplies for all US forces in eastern Afghanistan. "Most of our instructors in the late seventies and early eighties had some experience in that war, but, unfortunately, our curriculum had nothing to do with counterinsurgency. It was focused on engineering and the technical side of war."

All that changed, however, when General Buster Hagenbeck, who commanded the 10th Mountain Division during the 2001 invasion of Afghanistan, took over at West Point. Now captains and lieutenants in Afghanistan were regularly engaged in video conferences with cadets back in their New York classrooms above the Hudson, General McConville told me. Cadets were learning fast through such exchanges that, whereas once 95 percent of a warrior's time was taken up with sitting and waiting for war, this same 95 percent of a soldier's time was now required for planning and carrying out the nonviolent aspects of winning the peace in Afghanistan.

McConville told me his biggest challenge was making his superiors in Washington understand that platoon leaders in the field should not have to wait for developmental projects in their respective areas of operations. "You would not want to wait a month for ammunition, so you should not have to wait a month for the 'soft weapons'—like development projects—either," he said, speaking to me in his office inside Bagram Air Base. Like most of the senior commanders in Afghanistan, McConville understood that perceptions were paramount. He mentioned Abu Ghraib in passing, noting that "we are still paying for that," and stressed that every US platoon leader in the field is under intense scrutiny.

But the real problem for the war going forward in Afghanistan has less to do with the abusive policies implemented during the Bush administration and far more to do with our military's own willingness to put more American lives on the line to help pacify Afghanistan. The real toll of the Afghan conflict, more than eight years on, is still minimal compared to that of twentieth-century wars. The actual numbers of military deaths on the US side in Afghanistan to date have been about 20 percent of those in Iraq, even though the Afghan war has lasted significantly longer. Indeed, the hard cost in lives of the Afghan war as of late 2009—five hundred combat-related US deaths—is amazingly low in comparison to that of most long wars, particularly the one with which it is often compared, Vietnam. That war counted 47,359 Americans killed by hostile acts and 58,148 US fatalities from all causes. American deaths should not be held, in any case, as a gold standard of success or failure.[13] There are signs that some senior US commanders now understand that. "One of the mistakes we have made for years here in Afghanistan was to measure the violence in terms of attacks on NATO and US forces," said Maj.-Gen. Michael Tucker, fifty-five, a

Charlotte, North Carolina, native, who is NATO's chief of operations. "When you drive down the road with guns stuck out like porcupine quills, you are going to get shot at. But our measurements are changing now, and we've just begun to try to gauge the levels of violence and intimidation against Afghans."

In order to further clarify the US strategy moving forward, however, I visited Jalalabad airfield again, this time with the intention of talking to the commander of the US ground forces north of the White Mountains. I sat down with Col. John Spiszer, West Point class of 1981, a cordial Californian with a growling, circumspect delivery. What he said was most revealing about the perspective of the up-and-coming generation of new senior leaders in the US military. I asked Spiszer if he thought that the US military had truly embraced its own counterinsurgency strategy. His answer was an unequivocal "Yes." Without prompting, he brought up the Vietnam War as an example of "lessons learned" in counterinsurgency, insisting that many in his own class at West Point had been informed by the failures of the Vietnam War.

So what were these failures that his generation took away from Vietnam?

Spiszer had grown up with the war on television and had taken two elective seminars in his senior year at West Point on the history of the war, one of them a review of Stanley Karnow's brilliant PBS series. "Both of us—the US and the Vietnamese—did very poor jobs of winning over the people," he said. "There was too much Agent Orange, there was too much bombing, too much harsh treatment, and a lot of that." In other words, force had been applied heavily and with little precision.

Was the answer, then, a more diplomatic approach with less force? Spiszer's answer to that was "Yes," as well. That was the standard line one heard from US commanders in the Afghan theater.

But this did not address the real conundrum for the current generation of American commanders in Afghanistan. If you want to take the struggle to Afghanistan's forty thousand villages, you are inevitably going to have to put more American lives on the line. Spiszer believed, however, like most of his peers in the same generation at West Point, that the US public's view, influenced by the media, played an immense role in the final outcome of the Vietnam War. "If you want to talk about a big commitment, like on [the] scale of the [US] bombing campaign here in 2001, I would compare that to about 1965 when the First Infantry Division went to Vietnam," he said. "And in '68 you had the Tet offensive and public opinion crumbled and then—well, it was just a matter of time."

He reminded me, as an aide put his head around the door to remark on an ongoing firefight, that US forces had been in Afghanistan for well over seven years already. Spiszer insisted that he would never have enough young lieutenants to go to all of Afghanistan's villages, adding that "I don't think we are dummies. I think we understand that there is a certain level of treasure in our sons and daughters. I don't think we can throw that away. If you give him [the insurgent] the opportunity, he is going to kill a lot of people." It was hard to disagree about the value of American lives, and, to be fair, it is not easy to order men to their possible deaths, or even to assume greater risk.

But US commanders are wrong if they believe that keeping American casualties to a minimum in Afghanistan will make the public support the war. I respected Spiszer's point of view. Still, I had to wonder if the default strategy of not risking more infantry fighters in the field wasn't just the old-school approach of heavy force protection and overwhelming firepower. The Taliban's gains had urged us toward a new and radical change in approach, but as far as I could see, few in the US military were seizing the moment.

If and when US service members push out on more foot patrols from mobile bases, the Taliban will attack from behind boulders and atop ridges, before attempting to melt back into what Chairman Mao once referred to as the "sea of the people." If America's intentions are to oversee development and provide security for Afghans, US soldiers, working with Afghan colleagues, will be perceived on balance as protectors, not as invaders and mere occupiers. Generals and colonels will not find it easy to order more US soldiers to take on more risk of death. But this is a war, and US service members, who still have firm public backing, signed up to fight it.

✷✷✷

The clock is ticking in Afghanistan, and the conflict awaits a concerted strategy and a commander in chief who seizes the bully pulpit to promote it. Despite an infusion of twenty-one thousand more US troops into the fray in 2009, and another thirty-five thousand on their way in 2010, the Taliban and their al Qaeda advisers are still swarming over the mountains, valleys, and deserts around US military bases, which are strung out from Nuristan in the north to Kandahar in the south. The army's policy of maintaining gargantuan bases, commandeering air support for each and every infantry patrol, and generally building a bubble around its own soldiers means—in practice—that we have essentially surrendered the countryside to the Taliban. The American bases in Afghanistan, surrounded as they are with dozens of surveillance cameras, thermal-imaging detectors, and massive walls, serve—oddly enough —as bastions against "foreign invaders" in a land we claim to be actively pacifying. For now, the US military—while in love with its own detailed counterinsurgency strategy—is assuming far too little risk and still using far too much airpower.

I've been reporting from Afghanistan for nearly a decade. The level of appreciation I've seen from Afghans for the American presence never ceases to amaze me. I was reminded of this on a day out in the field with Lieutenant Kerr's platoon. One day, the platoon left its mountaintop redoubt and headed closer to the border to expand cooperation with a ragged and underarmed unit of the Afghan Border Police. Building up the ability and confidence of the Afghan forces, particularly those along the border with Pakistan, is considered a key to any US exit strategy. Four jeeps drove for an hour along the banks of a rushing stream and into a valley hard against the Durand Line, an arbitrary invention of the British Raj, which divides Afghanistan from Pakistan but is not recognized by ethnic Pashtuns, who live on both sides of the line. Atop the allied fortress, in a thick-walled mud hovel, Kerr sat down cross-legged with a pair of wizened Afghan deputy station chiefs.

The uniquely Afghan litany of worries rose up on about the third cup of tea. "Because of our position beneath the pass, if the enemy fires rockets at us, we can't shoot back at them, because they hide in the rocks on the high ground," said Abdullah, a proud former mujahedeen, cheery despite his concerns and stroking his beard, dyed red with henna. Kerr was in his element for the next three hours as he bantered with Abdullah and tried to reassure him that the US military's strategy, with Afghan help, would prevail. "If we put money into the pockets of the people here, they will stop accepting it from the Taliban," he said.

As in most of the border provinces along the Durand Line, however, the Taliban owned the night. Kerr was new to the game, and Abdullah knew better. "They come for attacks at night into villages, and those guys in the villages don't have any weapons to fend for themselves," he said. "We have mortars but they don't work well."

"Well," said Kerr, smiling, "we do have mortars and ours do work well." The gauntlet had been thrown down, and so the friendly dual of mortars began. For the next hour, Kerr's men watched in astonishment. Afghan border policemen, high on hashish, wheeled out rusted Russian mortars, dropped rounds into the tubes, only to be embarrassed when they did not fire. They kicked the bottom of the tubes to get them to fire anyway. As a grand finale, with the sun receding behind us, crowning the snow-capped Hindu Kush in the distance, Abdullah, his aging frame nearly crushed by the weight of a 73 mm SP-9 recoilless rifle, crouched on the roof of a bunker, knees bent slightly. He fired his best shot. As he tumbled backward, a fireball rolled through the air behind him and an immense roar went up among the stoned Afghans and the amused soldiers of Combat Platoon.[14]

Afghans haven't given up on the United States, and US soldiers haven't given up on Afghans either. Embedded with the army for three months during the spring and summer of 2009, I spent time with a new generation of officers out of West Point more willing than their colonels and generals to accept shared risk with the local population. They felt that many of the "force protection" regulations they were required to adhere to were inappropriate, even cowardly. Many of them longed, like Kerr, to do the hard, gritty work of counterinsurgency, and despite a lack of expertise, they were anxious to learn.

One enthusiastic southerner, Maj. Tommy Cardone, told me he had boiled it down to a slogan: "It's the people, stupid!" Cardone, on his second tour, said the best way to disrupt the Taliban's plans is "to sneak into a village at night and have a cup of tea with the local elders." Apache escorts are not required. The young major from Alabama, who had written his own book on the subject, was not being wistful or flippant when he said this to me.[15] He meant that walking into an Afghan village with goodwill and courage—without a whirlwind of firepower overhead—would win this war for us in the end.

Only a short helicopter hop away, I met another dedicated West Pointer, Captain Will Waddell, thirty-three, a PhD candidate in modern military history at Ohio State. Waddell was doing all he could to push more American platoon-sized units outside the wire with their Afghan National Army counterparts. He was dismayed, however, that some four hundred fifty Afghan soldiers were holed up with US forces inside his base in Paktika Province, commenting to me that the Afghans were in essence mimicking the US presence behind massive sand-filled walls. "Right now they follow our paradigm, which is to build large bases, to sustain large bases, to operate out of large bases now and again," he said. "We have to be thinking about how the Taliban works. He [the insurgent] wants us to go inside large, impervious bases because that leaves the majority of the country open to him."

Afghan and NATO mobile patrols that offer opportunities of

development to the local population, on the other hand, pose a direct threat to the Taliban and its ability to conduct its brand of warfare behind a human shield of Afghans.

Still, the risks are high. As Captain Waddell reminded me, if you go down that road, "at times it is going to look ugly." The world's most powerful military can still try to fudge counterinsurgency, but the dangers of doing counterinsurgency poorly can outweigh the rewards of doing it correctly. It is clear, however, that despite the talk of a new approach to Afghanistan, a fear that the US public is going to cut and run—a product of our catastrophic engagement in Vietnam—still helps compel our military to continue with its risk-averse behavior.

On my last visit to West Point, I walked for a time on the Plain. Beneath the bronze statue of George Washington, a few cadets hurried across the grass for a ceremony or a photograph. In their cutaway coats with brass buttons, helmets bedecked with scarlet feathers, sabers in hand, I wondered if they were prepared to fight America's wars. I thought about Major Patterson's question to her students: "What is the incentive to prepare for this new kind of war?" I thought about how the US Army had roundly disregarded JFK's admonitions about the nature of our foe. It occurred to me that this time around, we might consider that we owe to it our friends and even to our enemies, many of whom might one day be persuaded by our tenacity to stand against tyranny and on the side of our Afghan brothers and sisters.

Chapter 10
THE CHALLENGE

And what rough beast, its hour come round at last,
Slouches toward Bethlehem to be born?
—W. B. Yeats, "The Second Coming"

This book began with a discussion of the worldview that considers America to be a superpower whose national security is forever at risk from religiously inspired violence aimed at the civilization that we hold so dear. According to this view, we must defend ourselves—at all costs—against the onslaught of an enemy that wants to destroy our way of life. We are warned that the wolves are not only at the gates but that they are already among us—often shrouded in sheep's clothing and protected by witting and unwitting allies.

Shortly after the Fort Hood shootings in the autumn of 2009, Oliver North reported live to Sean Hannity from a bar in Branson, Missouri, that all good and patriotic veterans were outraged at the attacks. He said they were mad at a president who would not dare call the assault on America what it really was. Recalling his encounters with patriotic veterans on his Web page, North added: "It is clear these veterans—normally reticent, rarely outspoken, invariably polite—are, in their terms, 'fed up' with our national leadership."[1] North quoted an outraged vet as saying, "A few months ago they were telling us that our biggest threat was disgruntled veterans and right-wing extremists.... That's not who's killing Americans."

So it was that innocent Americans were dying as servants of the public as liberal weenies winced at the use of the word "terrorist" in public. In the immediate aftermath of the Fort Hood killings—while most of us patiently waited for the facts of the case—critics of the administration raced to lay the blame on liberals and say "I told you so," and to lash out at what they called the "liberal" media for not calling a spade a spade.

"Why is this?" they asked. Political correctness had run amok under a liberal regime. Charles Krauthammer, the esteemed *Washington Post* columnist, who also happens to have a degree in psychiatry, couldn't believe his ears when he heard one analyst's suggestion that Major Nidal Malik Hasan might have had secondary post-traumatic stress disorder, calling it "a handy invention to allow one to ignore the obvious." He accused the media of taking a sympathetic tone toward the killer. "Medicalizing mass murder not only exonerates," he wrote, "it turns the murderer into a victim, indeed a sympathetic one."[2]

Was it so impossible for Krauthammer to imagine that the son of two Palestinian parents might have been religiously inspired but also pushed to the brink—been made crazy, as it were—under the pressure of the wars that he daily bore witness to? The major was no doubt a very conflicted character. Krauthammer, North, and their political allies, in their public urgings that we should blame "Islamic terrorism" for the Fort Hood killings, appeared to be denying the need for the kind of even-handed circumspection that is the sacrosanct duty of any journalist or good leader.

We will probably never fully understand the factors that pushed

Major Hasan over the edge to commit the Fort Hood killings. It is a safe bet, however, that Hasan was influenced by his perception or misperception of events in the Islamic realm. He saw what he believed to be injustices toward his own people and so imagined himself as a holy warrior in their defense. He may have had a few loose wires as well.

Nor should it be such a shock to us that there are terrorists living among us. The background on Hasan, who carried out the attacks at Fort Hood—the worst and most heinous attacks on US soil since 9/11—and who grew up a few miles down the road from me in Virginia, fits well with Dr. Marc Sageman's basic profile of a budding terrorist.[3] He had a sense of moral outrage, he justified his anger toward the United States as a reaction to a perceived "war on Islam," and—as Sageman suggests such people invariably do—he made an effort to reach out to a network of like-minded extremists. Hasan does not appear to have taken any direct commands from the radical imam Anwar al-Awlaki, who moved from Falls Church, Virginia, to Yemen just after 9/11, but it is a safe bet that al-Awlaki's writings and speeches were part of a framework and comfort zone that Hasan relied on when he carried out his crimes against humanity. Hasan performed his acts with the knowledge that others would approve, particularly those in the small group of Muslim extremists who preach the merits of such violence.

Robert Wright, the author of *The Evolution of God*, wrote an interesting column in the *New York Times* several weeks after the Fort Hood attacks, suggesting that "the American Right and Left reacted to 9/11 differently. Their respective responses were, to oversimplify a bit: 'kill the terrorists' and 'kill the terrorism meme.' Conservatives backed war in Iraq, and they're now backing an escalation of the war in Afghanistan. Liberals (at least, dovish liberals) have warned in both cases that killing terrorists is counterproductive if in the process you create even more terrorists; the object of the game isn't to wipe out every last Islamist radical but rather to contain the virus of Islamist radicalism."[4] Wright warns us that the expert ability of jihadist groups to spread images of Americans killing Muslims abroad calls into question "the deployment of whole armies to uproot the organization and to finally harpoon America's white whale, Osama bin Laden."[5]

But is it really that simple? America has gone to war and now we are under attack. In fact, those who attacked us on 9/11 had their motives well established decades ago—long before we went to war in either Afghanistan or Iraq. And, as I recall, there was very little Republican-Democrat bickering over the need to invade Afghanistan or—for that matter—the need to continue the seemingly endless hunt for Osama bin Laden.

It was 9/11 that, as Fareed Zakaria points out in *The Post-American World*, "broke the domestic constraints on American foreign policy," adding that "after that terrible attack, Bush had a united country and a largely sympathetic world. The Afghan War heightened the aura of American omnipotence, emboldening the most hard-line elements in the administration, who used the success as an argument for going to war with Iraq quickly."[6] It is worth recalling that it was the so-called liberal media that provided the cheerleading for the Afghan "victory" (an odd victory, indeed, since the "whale" had escaped) and the subsequent failed attempt—starting in Baghdad—to remake the Middle East in our own image.

America today stands at a crossroads in a troubled world in which its military might is diminished, not by a lack of weaponry but by the actual nature of the conflict. Compared to the work of holding the line against the encroachment of Communism, the new role of the world's sole superpower is far more daunting.

I was reminded of the resilience, however, of the old militaristic mind-set at the groundbreaking ceremony for the new US Institute of Peace in Washington in the summer of 2008. George P. Shultz, secretary of state under President Ronald Reagan, lauded then President George W. Bush as a man who would be recalled fondly—he believed—as an innovator, for promoting the idea that wars must sometimes be initiated to address growing threats in advance. It was a little awkward on the surface of things. Shultz had chosen the inauguration of a peace institute to thank Bush for reminding America that war can sometimes promote peace. Addressing the outgoing president, the well-meaning octogenarian told the assembled doves and hawks that "in your time, I think this is one important idea that has real legs and staying power."[7]

In truth, George W. Bush's conception of preemptive war had less to do with a new idea or new approach to a multipolar world than it had to do with a much older concept of projecting power through war in order to create a compliant empire. It was the German strategist Carl von Clausewitz who articulated the idea of "war as an act of violence intended to compel our opponent to fulfill our will."[8] War, in this view, is held in high regard as an instrument of national policy. Indeed, those who oppose war are denigrated and chastised for their lack of courage and bravery. From this Clausewitzian perspective, war is seen as a means to affirm national interests. But the Prussian soldier and writer also had in mind a clear objective in going to war, stating that "war is the means and the means must always include the object in our conception: victory."[9] That included the overthrowing and disarming of one's opponent.[10]

To this day, Clausewitz is viewed in political circles as a controversial thinker, one whose ideas, his critics claim, led German leaders to marry their long-term policies to an ultranationalist use of military power. This, in turn, led to the demise of a nation.

This might be crediting the renowned Western strategist with more than he deserves. While it is probably inappropriate to call the fight in which America is engaged across the Islamic world a war, it is a struggle, nonetheless, whose goal should be the disarming of persons who intend harm to others. In order to accomplish this, however, it will be far more useful to view our most useful tools for success not as weapons but rather as ideas. This is a fight that requires two parts diplomacy and development, two parts intelligence gathering, and one part force.

In most modern strategic circles, the power of persuasion is generally seen as preferable to the use of force. The use of so-called soft power is often incorrectly seen, just as preemptive war is seen by others, as a modern invention. Actually, soft power is as old as the hills. In a conundrum well expressed in *The Art of War*, Sun Tzu states, "Those who win every battle are not really skillful. Those who render other's armies helpless without fighting are the best of all."[11] In another jujitsu-esque pronouncement on the same theme, the East's most famous military strategist explains that "the victories of good warriors are not noted for cleverness or bravery.... their victories in battle are not flukes because they position themselves where they will surely win, prevailing over those who have already lost."[12]

Certainly our opponents, al Qaeda in particular, believe they are clever and have the upper hand. But do they really? Haven't they really already lost? The answer is "Yes" only if we review our own current approach to the Islamic world. Steve Coll, the seasoned author of *The bin Ladens* and director of the New America Foundation, says our chief foe, Osama bin Laden, is "like a Barbary pirate with a marketing degree" who emphasizes the "importance of dragging the enemy forces into a protracted, exhausting, close combat, making the most of camouflaged positions."[13]

But bin Laden and his associates have sought to galvanize more than a band of brothers in arms. Their struggle is one that is filled with powerful metaphors and prosecuted by a loosely connected vanguard of like-minded political thinkers.[14] This leaderless and open-ended strategy allows al Qaeda and allied Islamic militants to pursue their ends while remaining well hidden in the broader population, carrying on their work in the manner of what is known in military parlance as "a force multiplier."

Their approach also conforms to a far more Eastern than Western attitude to warfare. Sun Tzu advises his students to keep even their battlegrounds hidden so that the foe wastes his resources in a desperate attempt to defend himself from the unknown. "Therefore when you induce others to construct a formation while you yourself are formless, [then] you are concentrated while the oppo-

nent is divided," he advises.[15] Nor should al Qaeda be underesti-
mated, as it has already been, in terms of its ability to adapt to the
long struggle ahead. Al Qaeda's avoidance of confrontation in favor
of regrouping and striking at a chosen time and on its own terms is
not a sign of weakness. It is a tactic that it has already put on display
to our detriment. Therefore, it would be foolish to underestimate al
Qaeda's regenerative qualities.

It is, however, America's greatest challenge to prevent al Qaeda
from succeeding. We must not allow our foe to divide us or deprive
us of our values and principles. These are the weapons—in this cold,
calculating war of ideas—that will be most useful in the long
struggle ahead. As surely as bin Laden succeeded in drawing us into
a protracted fight and leading us to eschew—for a time—even our
own nation's ban on torture, the enemy now seeks to portray us as a
ruthless, militarized superpower with no sympathy for the underdog.
The enemy would prefer that we ran secret prisons and made use of
cruel and unusual punishments, even executions. This may be one
reason why Khalid Sheikh Mohammed, al Qaeda's senior planner of
the 9/11 attacks, originally asked to be put on trial by a military tri-
bunal and executed.

But we should know by now that if we drop the ideals that set us
apart at the time of the founding of our nation—namely, the defense
of human rights and the right to a fair trial—we will have fulfilled
our enemy's hopes of drawing us into a tooth-and-nail, no-winners
fight for "civilization."

The real dilemma that the Fort Hood killings—and others like it
across the globe—present to the US government is more akin to the
dilemma that the Indonesian authorities face in their own country,
with young Muslims who are drawn to the firebrand, anti-American
rants of preachers like Abu Bakar al-Ba'asyir. Muslims, like Christians and Jews, are not—by nature—violent extremists, and it must
be our goal to help keep all of them from falling prey to the false
promises of militants. As in the example presented in chapter 5, it is
often militants with a global agenda who seek to disrupt local poli-

tics to serve their own violent, long-term interests. Negative outside influences can cause young Muslims to turn against the government and against peaceful approaches to conflict resolution. Given the chance of achieving reconciliation and reviewing the causes of bloodshed, however, local communities are capable of recognizing errors and calming tensions from within. That is why it is imperative to attack the motivations for violence and allow everyone to get on with the business of living a life in an open and just—hopefully democratic—world.

I've sought to show in this book that America's tendency to go abroad "in search of monsters" is a fool's errand. As discussed, however, it is not just American militarization that has contributed to the radicalization of young Muslims who would otherwise have preferred to see the United States as an open, just, and democratic society.

Patrick Tyler, in *A World of Trouble: The White House and the Middle East—from the Cold War to the War on Terror*, states that "America's destiny in international relations is to play the role of a just, magnanimous, and stabilizing power."[16] Yet his book is a cautionary tale, a look at the political pitfalls that Washington invariably blunders into whenever addressing the problems of the Middle East.

The Middle East is an unforgiving corner of the globe, a place where saying one thing and doing another has become a way of life—even of survival. America, it is no surprise, is not skilled in this unusual game. Just as Americans are not good neocolonial rulers capable of bestowing democracy on the masses, US diplomats are not good at playing a double game and talking out of both sides of their mouths.

Americans are most admired, in my experience, abroad for their directness—even when it comes off as slightly naïve or lacking politesse. Being candid can bruise egos, but, in the end, it doesn't do nearly as much damage as does talking up democracy on the one hand and feeding authoritarian rule or starting preemptive wars on the other. Nor should we expect any American peace broker to be able to promote a so-called two-state peace deal when the highest hills in the cherished land that would be the future Palestine are given out to zealots and settlers who have no intention of allowing the majority of the residents of the land to rule themselves. Average Palestinians—particularly the young people I spoke to in my research for this book—see the inherent contradiction in talking about peace and still losing land as the conversation continues ad nauseam. They also believe that the status quo cannot hold and that something far worse is in the making.

It is worth remembering that even up until 1973 there were still no substantial Israeli settlements to act as a spanner in the works of legitimate peace efforts.[17] Since then, the facts created on the ground by settlers and their supporters, who are viewed as outside the mainstream by many Jewish American groups pushing for peace, have made a final deal less and less feasible. In the past three decades, new settlements have sprung up like mushrooms across the West Bank and in East Jerusalem. Ironically, or maybe by design, they are now part of the "bargain" in a peace process that they severely undermine.

One might easily conclude that there is just too little space and too much religious fervor involved for the United States to weigh in and change the course of history in the Middle East. That view, however, is a dangerous and flimsy excuse for inaction. It ignores the role of the West in helping to set up Israel as a homeland for a Jewish people who had been slaughtered and disenfranchised. One means of resolving the current impasse is to reassure Israel that our guarantee of its sovereignty and right to exist is sacrosanct but does not extend to its continued occupation of the West Bank. This is not such a complicated proposition, after all. The Obama administration has taken limited steps in this direction but has hesitated in the face of continued Israeli intransigence. As Israel's main military backer and aid donor, however, Washington continues to wield substantial influence over its closest ally in the region. Stagnation and inaction are not an option. Just as surely as the Holy Land is the crucible for peace and tolerance between the world's great religions, the violence and stubbornness that surround the struggle there—as I have tried to demonstrate—influence events and minds across the greater Islamic realm.

Peace in the Middle East will not eliminate the feeling in the Islamic realm that the United States is at odds with Islam, but it will go a long way toward turning the prevailing paradigm on its head. The globalization of a mentality of fighting back against perceived injustices, from Palestine and Afghanistan to Bosnia and Iraq, has left the West wavering about how to deal with such an amorphous threat. Our actions have inadvertently fed propagandists and conspiracy theorists across the region. At times, we have been our own worst enemy. In the minds of many otherwise apolitical Muslim young people, an Apache helicopter or an F-16 that is attacking a village represents the same symbolic humiliation whether it has an Israeli or an American pilot in the cockpit. One violent image morphs into another—and together they leave an indelible scar.

In Palestine, Afghanistan, Bosnia, and Iraq, specific American policies—or a lack of them—have served to strengthen the jihad directed against the United States and its allies. Just as it would be a gross oversimplification to say that America's policies are to blame for militancy across the Islamic world, it is just as simplistic to deny that a more even-handed and direct approach in the Middle East from Washington will have a pacifying effect. The choice of stubbornly continuing to fight without attempting to see through the eyes of our brothers and our enemies is a dead end. Worse, it could also exacerbate a deep-seated problem and engender untold devastation.

The United States—despite the existence of a caring and often generous citizenry—can still do better in its promotion of democracy and tolerance. We are not a shining city on a hill; we are, rather—as always—a work in progress.[18] Citizens complain that American politics are corrupted by special interests and greed. Some of the more tolerant communities in the United States are home to radicals of varied faiths who openly espouse hatred and violence. Yet our shared ideals, particularly those defined in the Bill of Rights, shine through, providing a firm basis for others to admire our efforts to remain open and true to our beliefs.

Islam, Christianity, Judaism, Buddhism, Hinduism, and all other religions provide no cultural assurances that we can live together. Yet all religions play positive roles in varied corners of the globe. As we have seen in the case of the lives of impoverished villagers in the Sahel, Islam remains—for the most part—a force for positive change and tolerance. The myriad choices for development and economic progress that Washington will make in this area must surely be aligned with the cultural and religious lives these people lead, which are mostly defined by varied interpretations of a religion about which most Americans still know little. A defensive and militarized approach is bound to backfire and, inevitably, create more resistance to progress.

In South Asia, which now looks like America's most daunting challenge, the goals should be the same, even though the choices are not as clear. There is evidence that al Qaeda and its affiliates are just as much engaged in a war of ideas across the region as are the United States and its allied governments, or even more so. For al Qaeda and its affiliates, the battle is focused on the minds of what should be our own target audience—young Muslims.

Past policies of neglect, combined with a zero-sum game of attempting to stamp out terror cells (played to little avail), have put Washington—yet again—in dire straits in Afghanistan and Pakistan. That does not mean it is time to surrender to extremists and end our renewed efforts to stabilize the region with economic and security assistance. Ironically, one of the silver linings in a security environment that appears to deteriorate from year to year is still found in the US military men and women who favor a new course toward peacemaking and development. It may be ironic that to win the peace we'll have to turn our swords into plowshares even as we assume more risk, standing alongside our embattled Afghani and Pakistani brother and sisters. Nevertheless, it remains unclear at the time of writing whether the US military machine, in its nascent stages of change, can adjust to the long-term challenges it faces in South Asia.

It may appear riskier in the short run to stand by our ideals and fight for what we believe in, but the rewards for actively making peace and preventing war are far greater than those for retrenching and simply trying to hold the line. America still has the upper hand against its clever but nihilistic foe. We will prevail if we understand our enemy and assist our brothers. We must take the high road and win with our own ideas, not stoop to the enemy's level at the expense of principle. War is the enemy's calling, and peace is our reward. As is well stated in the *Tao Te Ching*, "Weapons [of war] are inauspicious instruments, not the tools of the enlightened."

ENDNOTES

FOREWORD

1. Bob Woodwdard, *State of Denial* (New York: Simon & Schuster, 2006), p. 408.

2. Barack Obama, "Text: Obama's Speech in Cairo," *New York Times*, June 4, 2009.

3. Nasser al-Bahri, interview with Paul Wood in Sana'a, Yemen, February 2010.

4. Ibid.

5. Obama, "Text: Obama's Speech in Cairo."

6. Barack Obama, remarks to State Department employees, January 22, 2009. Available online at "President Obama Delivers Remarks to State Department Employees," *Washington Post*, January 22, 2009, http://www.washingtonpost.com/wp-dyn/content/article/2009/01/22/AR2009012202550.html (accessed March 30, 2010).

CHAPTER 1: MARK OF THE BEAST

1. "Hannity vs. Moore on 'Capitalism: A Love Story,'" televised interview, Fox News, October 7, 2009, http://www.foxnews.com/story/0,2933,561680,00.html.

2. ABC News Poll, "Americans Skeptical of Islam and Arabs," March 8, 2006, http://abcnews.go.com/images/International/Islam_views.pdf. This ABC News/*Washington Post* poll was conducted by telephone March 2–5, 2006, among a random national sample of one thousand adults. The results have a three-point error margin. Sampling, data collection, and tabulation by TNS of Horsham, PA. Other extensive polling data suggest the same.

3. See Samuel Huntington, "The Clash of Civilizations," *Foreign Affairs*, November/December 1993. Professor Huntington provoked great debate with this extremely influential, often-cited article.

4. Walid Phares, *The War of Ideas* (New York: Palgrave MacMillan, 2008), p. 13.

5. Ibid.

6. *Obsession: Radical Islam's War against the West*, directed by Wayne Kopping and produced by Raphael Shore, Peace Arch Home Entertainment LLC, 2007.

7. "Kyra Philips Interviews Raphael Shore on CNN," December 14, 2006, video available on YouTube, "'Obsession' on CNN Newsroom: Radical Islam & Nazism," http://www.youtube.com/watch?v=ZvpKQTjAb2U (accessed April 1, 2010). Also cited in promotion materials for the movie.

8. *Obsession*, dir. Kopping, 2007.

9. Itamar Eichmer, "Moroccan King Nominated for Righteous among Nations Title," *YNETNEWS*, July 20, 2007, http://www.ynet.co.il/english/articles/0,7340,L-3427804,00.html.

10. Karen Gray Ruelle, *The Grand Mosque of Paris: A Story of How Muslims Rescued Jews during the Holocaust* (New York: Holiday House, 2008). This is a children's book based upon factual materials gathered by both Jewish and Muslim groups.

11. *Obsession*, dir. Kopping, 2007.

12. Steven Emerson, "Call the Terrorists What They Are," *Daily Beast*, May 21, 2009, http://www.steveemerson.com/5617/call-the-terrorists-what-they-are.

13. Caroline Glick, interview by *National Review*, "Political Messiah in the Holy Land," *National Review*, July 25, 2008, http://article.national review.com/364638/political-messiah-in-the-holy-land/interview.

14. Brigitte Gabriel, *Because They Hate* (New York: St. Martin's Press, 2006).

15. Deborah Solomon, "The Crusader," *New York Times Magazine*, August 17, 2008.

16. Steve Schifferes, "The Iraq War: Counting the Cost," BBC News, March 19, 2008, http://news.bbc.co.uk/2/hi/7304300.stm. Although some estimates of the total cost specify three trillion dollars, the BBC story estimates that by the end of 2009, the total cost of the Iraq conflict will have reached one trillion dollars.

17. Neil MacFarquhar, *The Media Relations Department of Hizbollah Wishes You a Happy Birthday* (New York: Public Affairs, 2009), p. 344.

18. Phares, *War of Ideas*, p. 9.

19. See 2:191 and 2:256 (Qur'an, trans. M. A. S. Abdel Haleem [London: Oxford University Press, 2008]).

20. David Levering Lewis, *God's Crucible: Islam and the Making of Europe, 570–1215* (New York: W. W. Norton, 2008), p. 47.

21. Ibid., p. 35.

22. Ibid., p. 114.

23. Ibid., p. 203.

24. Ibid., p. 204.

25. Ibid., p. 326.

26. Bernard Lewis, *The Crisis of Islam: Holy War and Unholy Terror* (New York: Random House, 2003), p. 5.

27. Ibid, p. 11.

28. Ibid, p. 33.

29. John Quincy Adams, "Address on US Foreign Policy," July 4, 1821, text available at http://www.presidentialrhetoric.com/historicspeeches/adams_jq/foreignpolicy.html.

30. Joby Warrick, "To Combat Obama, al Qaeda Hurls Insults," *Washington Post*, January 25, 2009.

31. Ibid.

32. Quoted in Lewis, *Crisis of Islam*, p. xxv.

33. Samantha Power, "The Democrats and National Security," *New York Review of Books*, August 14, 2008. Power notes the work of Peter Bergen

of the New America Foundation, which assembled large amounts of data on the incidence of terrorist attacks.

34. David Kilcullen, *The Accidental Guerrilla* (New York: Oxford University Press, 2009), p. 24.

35. Emerson, "Call the Terrorists What They Are."

36. Juan Cole, *Engaging the Muslim World* (New York: Palgrave Macmillan, 2009, p. 245.

37. Richard Clarke, *Against All Enemies* (New York: Free Press, 2004), p. 244.

38. "Al Qaeda Message Blames Obama, Egypt for Gaza Violence," CNN, January 6, 2009, http://edition.cnn.com/2009/WORLD/meast/01/06/gaza.alqaeda/index.html.

39. Michael Scheuer, *Marching toward Hell* (New York: Free Press, 2008).

40. Ibid., p. 57.

41. Akiva Eldar, interview with the author, November 2008.

42. US Department of State, "Background Note: Egypt," US Department of State, http://www.state.gov/r/pa/ei/bgn/5309.htm (accessed March 30, 2010).

43. Ahmed Rashid, *Descent into Chaos* (New York: Viking, 2009), p. 2.

44. Ibid., p. 227.

45. Adams, "Address on US Foreign Policy."

46. Luke 6:35, text available at http:www.bible.cc/luke/6-35.htm.

CHAPTER 2: THIS LAND IS MY LAND

1. Hilary Leila Krieger, "Exit Polls: 78% of Jews Voted for Obama," *Jerusalem Post*, November 5, 2008.

2. Barack Obama, "Text: Obama's Speech in Cairo," *New York Times*, June 4, 2009.

3. Idith Zertel and Akiva Eldar, *The Lords of the Land: The War over Israel's Settlements in the Occupied Territories, 1967–2007* (New York: Nation Books, 2007).

4. Ibid., p. 278.

5. Ibid.

6. Ibid., p. 281.

7. Ibid., p. 285.

8. Ibid., p. 404.

9. Ibid., p. 408.

10. Ibid., p. 386.

12. Ibid., p. 320.

12. Ibid., p. 433.

13. Ibid., p. 244.

14. Ibid., p. 260.

15. Quoted in Ari Berman, "Obama: Palestinians Matter, Too," *The Nation*, April 14, 2007.

16. Obama, "Text: Obama's Speech in Cairo."

17. Ibid.

18. Statistics/Fatalities, B'tselem Web site, http: www.btselem.org/English/Statistics/Casualties.asp. B'tselem is the Israeli Information Center for Human Rights in the Occupied Territories.

19. Breaking the Silence, "Israeli Soldiers Talk about the Occupied Territories," July 15, 2009, http://www.shovrimshtika.org/news_item_e.asp?id=30.

20. Paul Wood, "Breaking Silence on Gaza Abuses," BBC News, July 15, 2009, http://news.bbc.co.uk/2/hi/middle_east/8151336.stm (accessed March 30, 2010). Quotations taken from Wood's questioning of Majdi Abed Rabbo.

21. Ibid.

22. Ibid.

23. Paul Wood, "Just Married and Determined to Die," BBC News, October 13, 2008, http://news.bbc.co.uk/2/hi/7667031.stm (accessed March 18, 2010).

24. "Hamas TV Pictures Promote Female Suicide Bombers Squad," *CBS News*, posted by CBS News Investigates, January 14, 2009, http://www.cbsnews.com/blogs/2009/01/14/monitor/entry4722620.shtml.

25. "UN Finds Evidence of War Crimes in Gaza Fighting," *News Hour*, PBS, September 15, 2009. Both Goldstone and Oren are interviewed. See http://www.pbs.org/newshour/bb/middle_east/july-dec09/gaza_09-15.html.

26. For United Nations statistics cited here, see, for example, "Palestinian Refugee," *Wikipedia*, http://en.wikipedia.org/wiki/Palestinian_refugee.

27. John Ging, "Hope amid Tragedy: John Ging Assesses the Latest Developments in Gaza," talk given at the NewAmerica Foundation, October 13, 2009. The present author was in attendance.

28. Philip Smucker, "Once High, Arab Hopes for Bush Fall," *Christian Science Monitor*, February 19, 2003.

29. Bernard Lewis, *The Crisis of Islam: Holy War and Unholy Terror* (New York: Random House, 2003), p. 20.

30. See "Hamas," Backgrounder, Council on Foreign Relations, August 27, 2009, http://www.cfr.org/publication/8968.

31. Khalid Meshal, interview with the author, November 2008.

32. "Hamas," Backgrounder, 2009.

33. Howard Schneider and Glenn Kessler, "Ex–US Diplomat Talks with Hamas," *Washington Post*, July 16, 2009.

34. President Barack Obama's words spoken to Prime Minister Netanyahu, as reiterated publicly on the *White House Blog: Foreign Policy*, "Images of Abbas," May 28, 2009, http://www.whitehouse.gov/blog/issues/Foreign-Policy (accessed March 30, 2010).

35. Ibid.

36. Josef Federman, "Israeli Official: US Should Honor Past Deals," Associated Press, July 21, 2009.

37. Akiva Eldar, interview with the author, November 2008.

38. Ibid.

39. Daniel Kurtzer, "The Settlements Facts," *Washington Post*, June 14, 2009.

40. Ibid.

41. Ibid.

42. Charles Krauthammer, "The Settlements Myth," *Washington Post*, June 5, 2009.

43. Kurtzer, "Settlement Facts."

44. "Arab Anger as Hillary Clinton Backs Israel on Settlements," *Guardian*, November 2, 2009, http://www.guardian.co.uk/world/2009/nov/02/arab-anger-clinton-backs-israel.

45. Laura Rosen Foreign Policy Blog, "Netanyahu: What the Hell Do They Want from Me?" May 28, 2009, http://thecable.foreignpolicy.com/posts/2009/05/28/netanyahu_what_the_hell_do_they_want_with_me.

46. Schneider and Kessler, "Ex–US Diplomat Talks with Hamas."

47. Neil MacFarquhar, *The Media Relations Department of Hizbollah Wishes You a Happy Birthday* (New York: Public Affairs, 2009), p. 351.

48. Eldar, interview.

49. George Washington, "Washington's Farewell Address, 1796," http://avalon.law.yale.edu/18th_century/washing.asp. Originally published in David Claypoole's *American Daily Advertiser* on September 19, 1796, under the title "The Address of General Washington to the People of the United States on His Declining of the Presidency of the United States."

50. Ibid.

51. Eldar, interview.

52. Obama, "Text: Obama's Speech in Cairo."

CHAPTER 3: WHAT BECOMES A TERRORIST MOST

1. Marc Sageman, *Leaderless Jihad: Terror Networks in the 21st Century* (Philadelphia: University of Pennsylvania Press, 2008).

2. Juan Cole, *Engaging the Muslim World* (New York: Palgrave Macmillan, 2009), p. 75.

3. "Confidence in Obama Lifts US Image around the World: 25-Nation Pew Global Attitudes Survey," July 23, 2009, Pew Research Center, Global Attitudes Project, http://pewglobal.org/reports/display.php?ReportID=264.

4. Rudyard Kipling, "The Ballad of East and West," in *A Victorian Anthology, 1837–1895*, ed. Edmund Clarence Stedman (Cambridge: Riverside Press, 1895), line 1.

5. Cole, *Engaging the Muslim World*, p. 68.

6. Philip Smucker, "Children of Bosnia Trying to Heal," *Toronto Globe & Mail*, March 29, 1996; *Washington Times*, March 29, 1996.

7. Philip Smucker, "Bosnia Terrorized by Foreign Soldiers Who Aided Muslims," *Washington Times*, August 8, 1996.

8. Ibid.

9. Philip Smucker, "Iran's Arms Give Muscle to Bosnians," *Washington Times*, April 6, 1996.

10. Philip Smucker, "US 'Meddling' Grating on Bosnia: Deputy Defense Minister Seen Tied to Iran," *Washington Times*, November 3, 1996.

11. Philip Smucker, "Yemenis Defy President and Keep Chewing," *Daily Telegraph*, February 11, 2001.

12. Philip Smucker, "Where Holy Warriors Learn the Fundamentals," *Christian Science Monitor*, February 6, 2001.

13. Faris Sanabani, interview with the author, January 2001.

14. Ibid.

15. Stephen Day, interview with the author, January 2001.

16. Mohammed Ali Sauti, interview with the author, October 2001.

17. Philip Smucker, "To Many Pashtuns, bin Laden Is a Muslim Brother," *Christian Science Monitor*, October 15, 2001.

18. Ibid.

19. Ibid.

20. Philip Smucker, "Reporters on the Job," *Christian Science Monitor*, February 6, 2002.

21. Ibid.

22. Ibid.

23. Philip Smucker, "McDonalds Drops 'I Hate Israel' Singer from Adverts," *Daily Telegraph*, July 12, 2001.

24. Philip Smucker, "Egyptian Movie Stirs Intifada Sympathies," *Christian Science Monitor*, September 4, 2001.

25. Ibid.

26. Ibid.

27. Ibid.

28. Ibid.

29. Philip Smucker, "Israel Suffered Its Biggest Military Loss of the Current Intifada Tuesday, as Powell Met with Egypt's President," *Christian Science Monitor*, April 10, 2002.

30. Philip Smucker, "Powell Faces Changed Arab World," *Christian Science Monitor*, April 20, 2002.

31. Philip Smucker, "Egypt Praises Suicide Bombers," *Daily Telegraph*, April 9, 2002, http://www.telegraph.co.uk/news/worldnews/middleeast/israel/1390300/Egypt-praises-suicide-bombers.html.

32. Nabil Osman, interview with the author, April 2001.

33. Mahmoud Ashour, interview by the author, April 2001.

34. Ibid.

35. Ibid.

36. Hala Mustafa, interview with the author, April 2002.

37. Neil MacFarquhar, *The Media Relations Department of Hizbollah Wishes You a Happy Birthday* (New York: Public Affairs, 2009), pp. 149–79.

This chapter, "Talking about Jihad," contains an extended discussion of Islamic interpretations of jihad.

38. Ibid.

39. Qur'an, trans. M. A. S. Abdel Haleem (London: Oxford University Press, 2008).

40. Richard A. Gabriel, *Muhammed: Islam's First Great General* (Norman: University of Oklahoma Press, 2007), pp. 22–52. Gabriel, a military historian, writes in detail about how the Prophet melded Bedouin tribes into an Arab army and unified them under a single religious banner.

41. Ibid., p. 77.

42. Sun Tzu, *The Art of War*, trans. Thomas Cleary (London: Shambhala, 2003).

43. Philip Smucker, "Arab Elite Warms to Al Qaeda Leaders," *Christian Science Monitor*, July 30, 2002.

44. Ibid.

45. Ibid.

46. Ayman al-Zawahiri, *Knights under the Prophet's Banner*, December 2001, in Laura Mansfield, *His Own Words: Translation and Analysis of the Writings of Dr. Ayman al-Zawahiri* (Raleigh, NC: Lulu.com, 2006).

47. Smucker, "Arab Elite Warms to Al Qaeda Leaders."

48. Ibid.

49. Philip Smucker, "How bin Laden Got Away," *Christian Science Monitor*, March 4, 2002.

50. Sun Tzu, *Art of War*.

51. "Bin Laden: Goal to Bankrupt the US," CNN, November 1, 2004, http://www.cnn.com/2004/WORLD/meast/11/01/binladen.tape/index.html.

52. Dexter Filkins, *The Forever War* (New York: Alfred A. Knopf, 2008).

53. Ibid.

54. Ibid.

55. Ibid., p. 164.

56. Abu Farras, interview with the author, December 2003 and January 2004.

57. Ibid.

58. Ibid.

59. Ibid.

60. Anthony Shadid, "Iraqi Town Bears Scars of War," *Washington Post*, January 13, 2009.

61. Farras, interview.

62. Romesh Ratnesar with Philip Smucker, "The Rise of the Jihadists," *Time*, January 26, 2004, http://www.time.com/time/magazine/article/0,9171,993164,00.html.

63. Gilles Kepel, *Muslim Extremism in Egypt: The Prophet and Pharaoh* (Berkeley: University of California, 2003).

64. Ratnesar with Smucker, "Rise of the Jihadists."

65. Joe Klein, "Why the War President Is under Fire," *Time*, February 15, 2004.

66. Quoted in Peter Dale Scott, *The Road to 9/11* (Berkeley: University of California Press, 2007), p. 139.

67. Abu Ali, interview with the author, January–February 2004.

68. Ibid.

69. Filkins, *Forever War*, p. 160.

70. Ali, interview.

71. Kevin Peraino, "Destination Martyrdom," *Newsweek*, April 28, 2008.

72. Ibid.

CHAPTER 4: ISLAM IN THE SHADOW OF DEMOCRACY

1. Theodore Friend, *Indonesian Destinies* (Cambridge, MA: Harvard University Press, 2003), pp. 89, 117, 603. Dr. Friend's book is a sweeping, in-depth look at modern Indonesian history, as seen through the eyes of a roving anthropologist.

2. Jane Perlez, "Islamic Party Confronts Critics in UK," *New York Times*, August 7, 2007.

3. Muhamad Ali, "Islamic Caliphate Revival, Unnecessary, Unrealistic," *Jakarta Post*, August 10, 2007.

4. Pew Global Attitudes Project, "Confidence in Obama Lifts US Image around the World," July 23, 2009. See further Pew polling data on the Islamic world at http: www.pewglobal.org.

5. Steven Kull, interview with the author, April 2007.

6. Friend, *Indonesian Destinies*.

7. Tigor Dalimunthe, interview with the author, summer 2007.

8. Ibid.

9. Ibid.

10. Friend, *Indonesian Destinies*, p. 39.

11. Ibid., p. 69.

12. Theodore Friend, interview by the author, October 2009.

13. Hissan Sobar, interview with the author, summer 2007.

14. Ibid.

15. Sadanand Dhume, *My Friend the Fanatic* (New York: Skyhorse, 2009), p. 18.

16. Friend, *Indonesian Destinies*, p. 93.

17. Mardi Widayat, interview with the author, summer 2007.

18. Vita Manaan, interview with the author, summer 2007.

19. Mark Woodward, e-mail to the author, October 17, 2009.

20. Mohammed Farisy, interview with the author, summer 2007.

21. Woodward, e-mail.

22. Dhume, *My Friend the Fanatic*, p. 265.

23. Friend, *Indonesian Destinies*, p. 20.

24. Ibid., pp. 116–22.

25. Dhume, *My Friend the Fanatic*, p. 25.

26. Ibid., p. 65.

27. Friend, *Indonesian Destinies*, p. 121.

28. Ibid., p. 91.

29. Joko Pitoyo, interview with the author, summer 2007.

30. Ibid.

31. Ibid.

32. Dhume, *My Friend the Fanatic*, p. 105.

33. Zachary Abuza, "Jemaah Islamiya and the Inverse Triangle," paper given at Simmons College, November 15, 2006, p. 1. Also see a version of this paper at http://www.meforum.org/2044/jemaah-islamiyah-adopts-the-hezbollah-model.

34. Ibid., pp. 1–21.

35. Farisy, interview.

36. Ibid.

37. Ibid.

38. Zulkieflimansyah, "Understanding PKS as a Living Entity," *Jakarta Post*, August 10, 2007.

39. Thomas Hwi, videotaped interview with the author, September 2007.

40. Ibid.

41. Ibid.

42. Imdadur Rahmat, interview with the author, August 2007.

43. Ibid.

44. Amnesty International Reports, "Briefing to the UN Committee against Torture," April 2008, section titled "Torture and Other Ill-Treatment during Detention" and "2009 Annual Report for Indonesia," August 3, 2009. According to a survey cited by the first Amnesty report, "over 81 percent of persons arrested between January 2003 and April 2005" in three major detention centers in Jakarta were "tortured or ill-treated. About 64 percent were tortured or ill-treated during interrogation, 43 percent during arrest and 25 percent during subsequent detention." In the second Amnesty report, the UN committee expresses deep concern about "routine and widespread use of torture and ill-treatment of suspects in police custody."

45. Samuel Huntington, "The Clash of Civilizations," *Foreign Affairs*, November/December 1993.

46. Khalid Saifullah, interview with the author, August 2007.

47. Dhume, *My Friend the Fanatic*, pp. 206–11.

48. Saifullah, interview.

49. Ibid.

50. International Crisis Group (ICG), "Jemaah Islamiyah in Southeast Asia: Damaged but Still Dangerous," August 26, 2003, http://www.crisis group.org/home/index.cfm?l=1&id=1452. The ICG reports are detailed and definitive, but for further research and insight into al Qaeda's ties to Jemaah Islamiya, the work of Zachary Abuza is recommended.

51. Yasir Kandai, interviews by the author, July 2007, and "The Role of Kinship in Indonesia's Jemaah Islamiya," *Terrorism Monitor* 4, no. 11 (June 2, 2006) The information provided on pp. 160–61 regarding Yasir and his family is derived from the author's interviews of Yasir.

52. Philip Smucker, "The Voice of the Bali Blasts Speaks, Abu Bakar Ba'asyir," *Asia Times Online*, October 25, 2007, http://www.atimes.com/ atimes/Southeast_Asia/IJ25Ae03.html. The information about and quotes from al-Ba'asyir are derived from the author's interview with al-Ba'asyir.

53. Interviews with personnel in the US embassy, Jakarta. Senior American diplomats concerned with monitoring terrorism across Southeast Asia say that Indonesian authorities, while appearing to be lax, are often polished investigators.

54. Natasha Robinson, "Beat Up Infidel Tourists, Says Radical Cleric," March 24, 2008, *News.com.au*; also quoted in the London *Daily Telegraph*, March 24, 2008.

55. Richard Shears, "Holiday Britons Threatened in Bali," *Daily Mail* (London), March 24, 2008, as quoted from an Australian student who captured the al-Ba'asyir sermon on his video camera. Also available from Natasha Robinson, "Bashir Urges Attacks on 'Infidel' Australians," *Australian*, March 24, 2009, http://www.theaustrailian.com.au/news/bashir-urges-attacks-on-infidel-australians/story-e6frg6t6-1111115870183 (accessed March 30, 2010).

CHAPTER 5: SPICE ISLAND JIHAD

1. Giles Milton, *Nathaniel's Nutmeg* (New York: Farrar, Straus, and Giroux, 1999). This book contains a splendid account of the Dutch and British rivalries over the Spice Islands.

2. Theodore Friend, *Indonesian Destinies* (Cambridge, MA: Harvard University Press, 2003), p. 482.

3. Dieter Bartels, "When God Has No Answer, Search for Ancestral Wisdom: Revival of Traditional and Colonial Institutions in Conflict Resolutions between Muslims and Christians in the Central Moluccas, Indonesia," pp. 1–36. See Nunusaku Ethnofilm Productions & Consultancy Web site, for all of Bartels's writings since 1974, when he began his extensive research on the island chain (http://www.nunusaku.com/).

4. Dieter Bartels, telephone interviews with the author, September–October 2009. Bartels also read a draft of this chapter, "Spice Island Jihad," and provided more details of his frightening experience.

5. Bartels, "When God Has No Answer," p. 9.

6. Bartels, interviews.

7. David Liklikwatil, interview by the author, August 2007.

8. The death of Haris Fadillah, aka Abu Dzar, was reported on Saparua Island in October 2000; see International Regional Security Agency, http://www.irs-agency.us/ji_2.htm; and APSN: Asia Pacific Solidarity Network, http://www.asia-pacific-solidarity.net/southeastasia/indonesia/reports/ igc _howjemaahislamiyahoperates_111202.htm. Abu Dzar was a leading *preman* or gangster from West Java, who had assisted in the movement of JI

members earlier and became the top Laskar Mujahideen leader in the Moluccan Islands at the time of the heavy fighting.

9. Damien Corsetti, taped interview with the author in the Washington Hilton Hotel (Dupont Circle), Washington, DC, December 2007. Corsetti discussed his trial on charges of causing the deaths by beating of two prisoners. The government first altered the charges against him and then dropped them.

10. Yasir Kandai, interviews by the author, July 2007.

11. International Crisis Group, "Jemaah Islamiyah in Southeast Asia: Damaged but Still Dangerous," August 26, 2003. Also see extensive ICG reporting on recruitment activities also available through the group's Web site, http://www.crisisgroup.org/home/index.cfm?l=1&id=1452.

12. Zachary Abuza, *Militant Islam in Southeast Asia: Crucible of Terror* (London: Lynne Rienner Publishers, 2003), p. 148.

13. Dieter Bartels, "Your God Is No Longer Mine," Nunusaku Ethnofilm Productions & Consultancy Web site, http://nunusaku.com/03_publications/articles/yourgod.html. Bartels discusses at length the factors that created the tensions that led to the explosion of violence. He traces threads back hundreds of years.

14. Ibid., pp. 7–10. These pages contain a lengthy discussion of the ancient traditions that bound Christians and Muslims.

15. Bartels, "When God Has No Answer," pp. 18–19.

16. International Crisis Group, "How the Jemaah Islamiyah Terrorist Network Operates," December 11, 2002, http://www.crisisgroup.org/home/index.cfm?id=1397&l=1.

17. Frans Yusak, interview with the author, September 2007. Yusak was a special investigator and was able to speak both on and off the record to me about the work the police are doing in Ambon and beyond.

18. Kirsten Schulze, "Laskar Jihad and the Conflict in Ambon," Spring 2002, http://www.watsoninstitute.org/bjwa/archive/9.1/Indonesia/Schulze.pdf.

19. For earlier examples of cooperation between Islamic militants and the Indonesian military, see Friend, *Indonesian Destinies*. Friend discusses the ties between Islamic militant groups and the military in the early years of the nation's independence as well as the involvement of some jihadist groupings in the killings that followed Suharto's seizure of power.

20. International Crisis Group, "Jemaah Islamiyah in Southeast Asia," p. 4.

21. George Washington, letter to John Bannister, *The Quotable George Washington: The Wisdom of an American Patriot*, compiled by Stephen E. Lucas (Madison, WI: Madison House Publishers), p. 29.

22. Dan Murphy, "Indonesian Cleric Fights for a Muslim State," *Christian Science Monitor*, May 2, 2002.

23. Ibid.

24. Zachary Abuza, "Jemaah Islamiya and the Inverse Triangle," paper given at Simmons College, November 15, 2006, pp. 2–3.

25. Ibid.

26. Zachary Abuza, interview with the author, December 2007.

27. Ibid.

28. Abuza, "Jemaah Islamiya and the Inverse Triangle," pp. 2–3.

29. Ibid.

30. Ibid, p. 14.

31. "UN Cancels Aid Contract over Bashir Links," ABC News (Australia), June 15, 2006, http://www.abc.net.au/news/stories/2006/06/15/1664180.htm.

32. Conversation with UN official in Washington, DC, July 2009.

33. Dhume, *My Friend the Fanatic*, pp. 30–36.

34. John McBeth, "What Made Jakarta Suicide Bombers Tick," *Asia Times Online*, July 27, 2009, http://www.atimes/printN.html.

35. Ibid.

36. Ibid.

37. Norimitsu Onishi, "Extremists' Ideas Survive Crackdown in Indonesia," *New York Times*, July 23, 2009.

38. Ibid.

39. Ibid.

40. Seth Mydans, "A Terrorist Mastermind Whose Luck Ran Out," *New York Times*, September 18, 2009.

41. Bartels, interviews.

42. Barack Obama, *Dreams from My Father: A Story of Race and Inheritance* (New York: Three Rivers Press, 1995). Obama makes fond references to the years he lived in Indonesia when his mother was married to an Indonesian national.

43. Theodore Friend, telephone interview with the author, October 2009.

44. Ibid.

CHAPTER 6: GOOD SHEIKH HUNTING

1. Ross Dunn, *The Adventures of Ibn Battuta* (Berkeley: University of California Press, 2004). This is an excellent, detailed account of Battuta's impressions of Africa and beyond. The quotations within this paragraph are derived from this source.

2. Leo Africanus, "Description of Timbuktu," edited by Paul Brians et al., the Department of English, Washington State University, http://www.fordham.edu/halsall/med/leo_afri.html. Africanus was born in Grenada in 1485. The following quotations within this paragraph are derived from this source.

3. Abdel Kader Haidara, interview with the author, late 2004.

4. Ibid.

5. Interviews with Dr. Hamidou Magassa and others used in this chapter were conducted by the author across Mali from Bamako to the northern deserts, November 2004.

6. Philip Smucker, "As Locusts Hit Niger Delta, Mali Fears Famine," *New York Times/International Herald Tribune*, August 10, 2004.

7. Philip Smucker, "Sahara Town Booms with People-Smuggling," *New York Times/International Herald Tribune*, September 9, 2009.

8. Ibid.

9. Gen. Charles Wald, telephone interview with the author, arranged through Eucom Public Affairs, October 2004.

10. Ben Soares, *Islam and the Prayer Economy* (Ann Arbor: University of Michigan Press, 2005), p. 54. Soares's book came out after our conversation, but it contains many of the ideas that we discussed. Soares is one of the most insightful scholars on the region. It is notable that Robert Pringle, former US ambassador to Mali, praises Soares's work as well. Conversations with Pringle also provided useful background and information that have informed my discussion.

11. Soares, *Islam and the Prayer Economy*.

12. Ibid., p. 56.

13. "Al Qaeda in the Islamic Maghreb," Backgrounder, Council on Foreign Relations, http://www.cfr.org/publication/12717/.

14. Mike McGovern, interviews with the author, 2004–2005. McGovern is now a professor at Yale University.

15. Ibid.

16. US Constitution, amend. 1. For more information on the First Amendment, see *Wikipedia*, http://en.wikipedia.org/wiki//First_Amendment_to _the_United_States_Constitution.

17. Frank Kryza, The *Race for Timbuktu: In Search of Africa's City of Gold* (New York: Harper Perennial, 2006). Kryza's lively and well-researched account of the city's history and the explorers who mapped the Niger's course is an excellent source of anecdotal information on the city.

18. McGovern, interview.

19. Ibid.

20. Philip Smucker, "Discovering a Heritage in Timbuktu: Lost Texts Find New Life," *New York Times/International Herald Tribune*, September 8, 2009, http://www.nytimes.com/2004/11/29/news/29iht-timbuktu_ed3_ .html.

21. Stephanie Diakite, interview with the author, November 2004.

22. Ibid.

23. Ismael Diadie Haidara, interview with the author, November 2004.

CHAPTER 7: ALONG THE WATCHTOWER

1. Interviews with Sgt. Wayne Amos and others in Kunar Province, 2008. Thanks to PRT Commander Larry LeGree, over the course of several weeks, I was provided with inside access to the provincial reconstruction team's efforts to stabilize Kunar Province.

2. Philip Smucker, "Afghanistan's Eastern Front," *U.S. News & World Report*, January 4, 2007, http://www.usnews.com/usnews/news/articles/ 070401/9afghan .htm.

3. Michael Prawdin, *The Mongol Empire* (New York: Transaction Publishers, 2005), pp. 480–83.

4. Sanjar Qiam, interview with the author, June 2007. Sanjar was an up-and-coming radio host based in Kabul, where I met him.

5. Ibid.

6. Philip Smucker, *Al Qaeda's Great Escape* (Washington, DC: Potomac Books, 2005), pp. 36–135.

7. Conversations with Captain Coughenour and Commander LeGree, January–February 2008.

8. Ibid.

9. The UN helped fund this communal problem-solving exercise. Several UN officials in Jalalabad provided added insight into these activities.

10. Mohammed Shahid, interview with the author, February 2008.

11. Ibid.

12. Ibid.

13. The Campaign for Innocent Victims in Conflict, director Sarah Holewinski, has done the most extensive work on this subject. The organization's founder, Marla Ruzicka, a friend, was killed in April 2005 by a suicide bomber in Baghdad, but the group has continued to make amazing inroads into the halls of power in both Congress and the Pentagon. The group's incisive field reports are available at http://www.warvictims.org. Although the US military has recognized the need to compensate those killed or maimed in the crossfire, particularly those injured by US fire, the coordination of the effort leaves much to be desired. Often it comes down to a US commander putting a price on an Afghan life—often far below what is reasonable for an innocent victim.

14. After the first year of occupation, ambitious, young Western aid workers began streaming into Kabul, taking up work with the UN, work with nongovernmental organizations, or high-paid consultancies, often with the government but paid for by Western donor nations. Thousands of twenty-five- to forty-year-olds called Kabul their home and transformed the city—even arranging for nude bathing and wild dance parties, which made both the Afghan police and Taliban sympathizers uncomfortable.

15. Sayed Fazlullah Wahidi, interview with the author, February 2008.

16. Ibid.

17. Ibid.

18. I came across these T-shirts in the Bagram airbase PX.

19. For a detailed account of the excesses of the early years of the Afghan conflict, see the documentary *Taxi Ride to the Dark Side*, directed by Alex Gibney, 2008. Damien Corsetti, who was one of the leading characters in Gibney's film, spoke to me on videotape for several hours in the Washington Hilton Hotel. Corsetti detailed for me what he witnessed inside the secret Bagram detention center, including beatings, hanging of prisoners from chains, and water torture. He said that "federal authorities" had regularly required him to watch while they interrogated prisoners, including several leading al Qaeda figures. Corsetti also said that the top US com-

mander at the time at Bagram Airfield, Gen. Dan McNeil, was well aware of the torture and took regular tours of the prison facility at the height of the abuses. At the same time, Corsetti had been under orders from the US military to unshackle prisoners when representatives from the International Committee for the Red Cross toured Bagram in 2002 and 2003.

20. Donald Rumsfeld, "Donald Rumsfeld's War-on-Terror Memo," *USA Today*, October 16, 2003, http://www.usatoday.com/news/washington/executive/rumsfeld-memo.html.

21. Philip Smucker, "Looking for the Good Guys in Afghanistan's Badlands," *U.S. News & World Report*, February 14, 2008. For some details on Ikhlas, see http://www.usnews.com/articles/news/world/2008/02/14/looking-for-the-good-guys-in-afghanistans-badland.html.

22. Smucker, *Al Qaeda's Great Escape*, pp. 10–210. I later befriended the CIA's top operative at Tora Bora, Gary Berntsen, who argued to me that the CIA was better informed than the US military on al Qaeda's activities in eastern Afghanistan. In 2007 and 2008, senior US military commanders on the provincial level were not being fully briefed on al Qaeda activities within their province.

23. Video footage provided by Camp Wright soldiers.

24. Hajji Mohammed, interview with the author, February 2008.

25. See Gregg Mortenson and David Relin, *Three Cups of Tea* (New York: Penguin, 2007). Montana native Mortenson's experiences building schools in South Asia have made him a well-known name in military circles, where commanders are trying to adjust their own sights and work more closely with local communities. Indeed, Mortenson provided advice to the PRT in Kunar on several projects.

26. See Rory Stewart, *Places in Between* (New York: Harvest Books, 2006). Stewart runs a successful charity in Kabul and is considered a leading Western expert on Afghan development. I met with him inside an ancient fortress home in Kabul where he provides woodworking and calligraphy training for locals through his charity, the Turquoise Mountain Foundation.

27. See Dan Marston and Carter Malkasian, *Counterinsurgency in Modern Warfare* (Oxford: Osprey Publishing, 2006). Malkasian, a graduate of the University of California, Berkeley, and an expert in the field, has spent time observing US operations in Iraq and Afghanistan. He offered special insights into the actions of LeGree and his fellow soldiers.

28. Sun Tzu, *The Art of War*, trans. Thomas Clearly (London: Shambhala, 2003), p. 112.

29. Smucker, *Al Qaeda's Great Escape*, pp. 178–80

30. Herschel Smith, "Analysis of the Battle of Wanat," *Captain's Journal,* archive for 2008–2009, http://www.captainsjournal.com/category/battle-of-wanat/page/2/. Smith's analysis generally stresses the need to provide adequate troops and reinforcements in order to secure remote regions of Afghanistan. Along with a handful of other analysts, Smith pushed early for a major surge of US forces in Afghanistan in order to achieve success in the counterinsurgency mission that the Pentagon said it was attempting. Smith has also catalogued the various reports on Wanat since the battle—even as several similar, successful insurgent attacks have been launched in the area against undermanned and highly vulnerable US outposts.

31. Ibid.

CHAPTER 8: OSAMA'S GHOST

1. For "Auntie" in 2001, see Philip Smucker, *Al Qaeda's Great Escape* (Washington, DC: Potomac Books, 2005), pp. 1–32, chapter 1, "Been Loadin' for bin Laden."

2. Ahmed Rashid, *Descent into Chaos* (New York: Viking, 2009), pp. 265–300. Rashid is an acknowledged expert on South Asia. Throughout the Bush years, he was critical of the US government's approach to Afghanistan. But he is particularly astute in his analysis of the long relationship between the US military and the Pakistani military, which has often held out its hand and rarely done Washington's bidding.

3. Ayesha Siddiqa, *Military Inc.: Inside Pakistan's Military Economy* (London: Oxford University Press, 2007), pp. 106–108.

4. Michael Scheuer, *Marching toward Hell* (New York: Viking, 2009), pp. 112–15.

5. See Philip Smucker, "Chitral Now on the Jihadi Radar Screen," *Asia Times,* June 28, 2007, http://www.atimes.com/atimes/South_Asia/IF28Df02.html.

6. Bernard Lewis, *A Brief History of the Last 2000 Years* (New York: Scribner, 1996), p. 237.

7. See Philip Smucker, "A View from the Roof of the World," *New York Times*, June 28, 2007, http://www.nytimes.com/2007/06/28/opinion/28iht-edsmucker.1.6383239.html.

8. See Winston Churchill, *The Story of the Malakand Field Force* (London: Longmans, Green, 1898). The specific picket referred to here is designated as such even today, a reminder of the imperialist past in the heart of what is now a jihadist stronghold. Oddly, the historical marker has not come under attack from vandals—or "miscreants" as Churchill might have called such troublemakers.

9. Fazul Marwat, *Talibanization of Pakistan* (Peshawar, Pakistan: University of Peshawar Press, 2005).

10. Jerrold M. Post, *Leaders and Their Followers in a Dangerous World* (Ithaca, NY: Cornell University Press, 2006), p. 9.

11. *New York Daily News*, "Hillary Clinton to Pakistanis: Can't You Get Osama bin Laden?" October 30, 2009.

12. Scheuer, *Marching toward Hell.*

13. Richard A. Gabriel, *Muhammed: Islam's First Great General* (Norman: University of Oklahoma Press, 2007), p. 27.

14. Philip Smucker, "Where Radicals Call the Shots," *U.S. News & World Report*, September 8, 2007. This includes parts of the exclusive interview with Fazlullah.

15. Craig Whitlock, "Al Qaeda's Growing Online Offensive," *Washington Post*, June 24, 2008.

16. Quoted in Gabriel, *Muhammed*, p. 101.

17. Ibid.

18. Rory Stewart, interview with the author, Kabul, July 2007.

19. Smucker, *Al Qaeda's Great Escape*, pp. 55–58. This short section details the role of Mujahid, Khalis's son, in bin Laden's retreat into Tora Bora. He was on the road with bin Laden as the Saudi chief left in a convoy for what was to be his "last stand" or "great getaway."

20. Philip Smucker, "Al Qaeda Plays Key Role on Both Sides of the Pakistan-Afghan Border," McClatchy Newspapers, June 8, 2009. Also see *The News* (Islamabad and Karachi), February 26, 2007, for Rahimullah Yusufzai's report ("New Taliban Group Named after Tora Bora") from Peshawar on the new Tora Bora Front, its leadership, and its background.

21. Gabriel, *Muhammed*, p. 104.

22. Whitlock, "Al Qaeda's Growing Online Offensive."

23. Ibid.

24. Joby Warrick, "US Cites Big Gains against al Qaeda," *Washington Post*, May 30, 2008.

25. Whitlock, "Al Qaeda's Growing Online Offensive."

26. "The Power of Truth," Combating Terrorism Center, US Military Academy, West Point, April 21, 2008.

27. Ann Scott Tyson, "Gates Urges Increased Funding for Diplomacy," *Washington Post*, November 27, 2007.

28. Ibid.

29. Scott Shane, "Senate Report Explores 2001 Escape by bin Laden from Afghan Mountains," *New York Times*, November 29, 2009.

CHAPTER 9: AFGHANISTAN'S THIN GRAY LINE

1. Philip Smucker, "US Soldier's Options Limited to Protect Afghans from Taliban," McClatchy Newspapers, May 25, 2005.

2. Philip Smucker, "US Soldiers Search for Midwife in Warzone," McClatchy Newspapers, May 12, 2009.

3. My visit to West Point was facilitated by Frank deMarco and by Col. Bryan Hilferty, an old friend from the days that came after Tora Bora in Afghanistan. My visit included interviews with instructors, students, and Brian Fishman, who is with the academy's prestigious Combating Terrorism Center.

4. Quoted in Rick Atkinson, *The Long Gray Line* (New York: Henry Holt, 1989), pp. 22–23.

5. See Atkinson, *Long Gray Line*.

6. *Washington Post*, "Petraeus on Vietnam's Legacy," July 14, 2007. Also posted on a military Web site, http://www.military-quotes.com/forum/petraeus-vietnams-legacy-t31666.html.

7. Philip Smucker, "Killing Season Opens in the Afghan Hills," *Asia Times Online*, March 27, 2009, http://www.atimes.com/atimes/South_Asia/KC27Df01.html; *Afghanistan's Gray Line: The Education of "Combat Platoon,"* documentary film produced and narrated by Philip Smucker, AfPak Channel of *Foreign Policy* magazine, November 19, 2009, http://afpak.foreignpolicy.com/posts/2009/11/18/afghanistans_gray_line.

SELECT BIBLIOGRAPHY

Abuza, Zachary. *Militant Islam in Southeast Asia: Crucible of Terror.* London: Lynne Rienner Publishers, 2003.

Africanus, Leo. "Description of Timbuktu." Edited by Department of English, Washington State University. http://www.fordham.edu/halsall/med/leo_afri.html.

Atkinson, Rick. *The Long Gray Line.* New York: Henry Holt, 1989.

Bartels, Dieter. "When God Has No Answer, Search for Ancestral Wisdom: Revival of Traditional and Colonial Institutions in Conflict Resolutions between Muslims and Christians in the Central Moluccas, Indonesia." Nunusaku Ethnofilm Productions & Consultancy Web site. http://www.nunusaku.com/. To be published 2011.

———. "Your God Is No Longer Mine." Nunusaku Ethnofilm Productions & Consultancy Web site. http://nunusaku.com/03_publications/articles/yourgod.html.

Bergen, Peter. *The Osama bin Laden I Know.* New York: Free Press, 2006.

Bradley, John. *Inside Egypt: The Land of Pharaohs on the Brink of a Revolution.* New York: Palgrave Macmillan, 2008.

Churchill, Winston, *The Story of the Malakand Field Force.* London: Longmans, Green, 1898.

Clarke, Richard, *Against All Enemies.* New York: Free Press, 2004.

361

Clausewitz, Carl von. *On War.* New York: Penguin Classics, 1982; first published 1832.

Cole, Juan. *Engaging the Muslim World.* New York: Palgrave Macmillan, 2009.

Coll, Steve. *The bin Ladens: An Arabian Family in the American Century.* New York: Penguin Press, 2008.

Dhume, Sadanand. *My Friend the Fanatic.* New York: Skyhorse, 2009.

Dunn, Ross. *The Adventures of Ibn Battuta.* Berkeley: University of California Press, 2004.

El-Nawany, Mohammed, and Iskandar Adel. *Al Jazeera: The Story of the Network That Is Rattling Governments and Redefining Modern Journalism.* Cambridge: Perseus Books, 2003.

Filkins, Dexter. *The Forever War.* New York: Alfred A. Knopf, 2008.

Friend, Theodore. *Indonesian Destinies.* Cambridge, MA: Harvard University Press, 2003.

Gabriel, Brigitte. *Because They Hate.* New York: St. Martin's Press, 2006.

Gabriel, Richard A. *Muhammed: Islam's First Great General.* Norman: University of Oklahoma Press, 2007.

Huntington, Samuel. "The Clash of Civilizations." *Foreign Affairs,* November/December 1993.

International Crisis Group. "How the Jemaah Islamiyah Terrorist Network Operates." December 11, 2002. http://www.crisisgroup.org/home/index.cfm?id=1397&l=1.

―――. "Jemaah Islamiyah in Southeast Asia: Damaged but Still Dangerous." August 26, 2003. http://www.crisisgroup.org/home/index.cfm?l=1&id=1452.

Jerecki, Eugene. *The American Way of War.* New York: Free Press, 2008.

Jones, Seth. *In the Graveyard of Empires.* New York: W. W. Norton, 2009.

Kilcullen, David. *The Accidental Guerrilla.* New York: Oxford University Press, 2009.

Kinzer, Stephen. *Overthrow: America's Century of Regime Change from Hawaii to Iraq.* New York: Henry Holt, 2006.

Kryza, Frank. *The Race for Timbuktu: In Search of Africa's City of Gold.* New York: Harper Perennial, 2006.

Lewis, Bernard. *A Brief History of the Last 2000 Years.* New York: Scribner, 1996.

―――. *The Crisis of Islam: Holy War and Unholy Terror.* New York: Random House, 2003.

Lewis, David Levering. *God's Crucible: Islam and the Making of Europe, 570–1215.* New York: W. W. Norton, 2008.

MacFarquhar, Neil. *The Media Relations Department of Hizbollah Wishes You a Happy Birthday.* New York: Public Affairs, 2009.

Marston, Dan, and Carter Malkasian. *Counterinsurgency in Modern Warfare.* Oxford: Osprey Publishing, 2006.

Marwat, Fazul. *Talibanization of Pakistan.* Peshawar: University of Peshawar Press, 2005.

Milton, Giles. *Nathaniel's Nutmeg.* New York: Farrar, Straus, and Giroux, 1999.

Mortenson, Gregg, and David Relin. *Three Cups of Tea.* New York: Penguin, 2007.

Obama, Barack. *Dreams from My Father: A Story of Race and Inheritance.* New York: Three Rivers Press, 1995.

———. "Text: Obama's Speech in Cairo." *New York Times,* June 4, 2009.

Phares, Walid. *The War of Ideas.* New York: Palgrave Macmillan, 2008.

Post, Jerrold M. *Leaders and Their Followers in a Dangerous World.* Ithaca, NY: Cornell University Press, 2006.

Prawdin, Michael. *The Mongol Empire.* New York: Transaction Publishers, 2005.

Rashid, Ahmed. *Descent into Chaos.* New York: Viking, 2008.

Ruelle, Karen Gray. *The Grand Mosque of Paris: A Story of How Muslims Rescued Jews During the Holocaust.* New York: Holiday House, 2008.

Sageman, Marc. *Leaderless Jihad: Terror Networks in the 21st Century.* Philadelphia: University of Pennsylvania Press, 2008.

Sanger, David. *The Inheritance.* New York: Harmony Books, 2009.

Scheuer, Michael. *Marching toward Hell.* New York: Free Press, 2008.

Scott, Peter Dale. *The Road to 9/11.* Berkeley: University of California Press, 2007.

Siddiqa, Ayesha. *Military Inc.: Inside Pakistan's Military Economy.* London: Oxford University Press, 2007.

Smucker, Philip. *Al Qaeda's Great Escape.* Washington, DC: Potomac Books, 2005.

Soares, Ben. *Islam and the Prayer Economy.* Ann Arbor: University of Michigan Press, 2005.

Stewart, Rory. *Places in Between.* New York: Harvest Books, 2006.

Tyler, Patrick. *A World of Trouble: The White House and the Middle East—From the Cold War to the War on Terror.* New York: Farrar, Straus, and Giroux, 2008.

Tzu, Sun. *The Art of War.* Translated by Thomas Cleary. London: Shambhala, 2003.

Widmer, Ted. *Ark of the Liberties.* New York: Hill and Wang, 2008.

Wright, Lawrence. *The Looming Tower.* New York: Vintage Books, 2006.

Wright, Robin. *Dreams and Shadows.* New York: Penguin Press, 2008.

Zakaria, Fareed. *The Post-American World.* New York: W. W. Norton, 2008.

Zawahiri, Ayman al-. *Knights under the Prophet's Banner.* Translated by Laura Mansfield. Raleigh, NC: Lulu.com, 2006. http://www.lulu.com/content/paperback-book/his-own-words-translation Lulu-and-analysis-of-the-writings-of-dr-ayman-al-zawahiri/366458.

Zertel, Idith, and Akiva Eldar. *The Lords of the Land: The War over Israel's Settlements in the Occupied Territories, 1967–2007.* New York: Nation Books, 2007.

INDEX